BROADCAST
JOURNALISM

SECOND EDITION

BROADCAST JOURNALISM

A Guide for the Presentation
of Radio and Television News

David Keith Cohler

Prentice Hall, Englewood Cliffs, New Jersey 07632

Library of Congress Cataloging-in-Publication Data

Cohler, David Keith.
    Broadcast journalism : a guide for the presentation of radio and
television news / by David Keith Cohler. —2nd ed.
      p. cm.
    Includes index.
    ISBN 0–13–088659–9
    1. Broadcast journalism. I. Title.
PN4784.B75C63 1994
070.1′9—dc20

93-17586
CIP

Acquisitions editor: Steve Dalphin
Editorial assistant: Caffie Risher
Editorial/production supervision: P. M. Gordon Associates
Cover design: Rich Dombrowski
Production coordinator: Kelly Behr

Printed in the United States of America
10 9 8 7 6 5 4 3 2 1

ISBN 0-13-088659-9

Prentice-Hall International (UK) Limited, *London*
Prentice-Hall of Australia Pty. Limited, *Sydney*
Prentice-Hall Canada Inc., *Toronto*
Prentice-Hall Hispanoamericana, S.A., *Mexico*
Prentice-Hall of India Private Limited, *New Delhi*
Prentice-Hall of Japan, Inc., *Tokyo*
Simon & Schuster Asia Pte. Ltd., *Singapore*
Editora Prentice-Hall do Brasil, Ltda., *Rio de Janeiro*

This book is dedicated to the memory of my parents,
Charles and Esther Cohler,
and to the memory of NBC News correspondent Welles Hangen,
who was killed on assignment in Cambodia in May, 1970.

Contents

10   Audiotape I: Actualities   131

11   Audiotape II: Reports   150

12   Audiotape III: Interviewing, Editing, Field Reporting   169

13 Radio Newscasting   185

PART 3   TELEVISION NEWS

20   Reporting III: Basic Story Coverage

279

21   Performing

297

Preface to the Second Edition

To say that much in broadcast journalism has changed since publication of this book's First Edition is to indulge in flagrant understatement.

The decade saw the once invincible ABC, NBC, and CBS, their audiences eroded by the rise of cable, cede news leadership to CNN. A fourth network, Fox, successfully competed in entertainment programming and announced plans to build a news organization. So-called "reality-based" shows, including tabloid lookalikes bearing the form (if not the content) of newscasts, became a programming staple everywhere. Thanks to access to visuals from CNN and other suppliers, local independent stations mounted the first successful challenges to the news dominance of network affiliates. And, with a few notable exceptions, radio news faded into a clutter of commercials and six-second sound bites.

The technology that drove these and other changes has advanced so far that what once seemed extraordinary, even fantastic, now seems commonplace. The American tourist watching CNN or the "CBS Evening News" in Paris, like the French tourist watching FR-3's "Journal Télévisé" in Los Angeles, no longer marvels at the communications wizardry that makes such electronic cross-fertilization possible. The long-awaited "global village" is now our home town, our once distant "neighbors" now just the click of a remote button away.

By the very nature of their field, broadcast journalists have always been at the cutting edge of new technologies. Nowadays, many of them no longer call themselves "broadcast" journalists, preferring the term "electronic" because it covers both news delivered the old-fashioned way, over the air (hence "broadly"), and the newer way, by satellite and cable ("*narrow*casting").

Whatever they may call themselves, their task, like the world itself, has grown ever more complex. There are constantly more electronic buttons to push and more ways in which to push them. Now more than ever, it is easy to lose the message in the packaging, to lose sight of the forest for the trees.

And yet, at its core, the task of most broadcast-news programming remains unchanged: to inform and enlighten. The delivery systems may be different, but what is delivered remains—or *ought* to remain—an integrated, coherent combination of sights and sounds aimed at informing and enlightening.

Most of the sounds are still *words*. Therefore, while this book has been revised to reflect the "media marketplace" of the 1990s (including the ever-growing status of women in the field), its task remains essentially unchanged. We shall continue to concentrate on the words—specifically on writing the news simply, clearly, and directly.

As we said in our Preface to the First Edition, the ability to arrange live and recorded words and pictures in a coherent manner is a function of human brain power, not electronic circuitry, one of protoplasm, not silicon. This book's focus, therefore, shall remain on promoting the development of brain power among students who wish to join the ranks of those who gather, write, and present the news to a public more than ever in need of information and enlightenment.

Acknowledgments

Like its predecessor, the Second Edition of *Broadcast Journalism* contains proprietary material from dozens of professional sources. Most of the new material comes from organizations that are at the forefront of broadcast news gathering and presentation at both the network and local levels.

My special thanks go to Alyssa Levy, Director of Publicity at CNN, Atlanta; Colleen Ragan, Administrative Assistant to the News Director at KCAL-TV, Los Angeles; and Ed Dorsey, Director of Operations at KFWB-AM, Los Angeles, for facilitating the photographs and/or sample scripts reproduced in the text. I would also like to thank the reviewers: Claudia Clark of the University of Alaska–Fairbanks and John Dillon of Murray State University.

I am also grateful to the Associated Press and United Press International for permission to use much new material; to the Society of Professional Journalists for allowing me to reprint its revised *Code of Ethics;* and to Arbitron for providing updated research on market composition.

It is in the nature of broadcasting for many of the people cited or pictured in these pages to move on to new assignments. Wherever they go, I wish them well.

David Keith Cohler
Los Angeles, 1993

Introduction to Broadcast Style 1

BROADCAST JOURNALISM: CRAFT OR PROFESSION?

To make a career in broadcast news, it helps to look and sound like Peter Jennings or Diane Sawyer. But it's not necessary. Most people in broadcast journalism have "average" looks and voices.

It helps to have a famous parent or marry the boss's son or daughter. But patronage and nepotism are no more prevalent in broadcasting than in other fields.

It helps to be able to write as well as Charles Kuralt or Meredith Veiera (both of CBS News). No "buts" about it. Despite 75 years of sweeping technological changes in radio and television news, writing ability and a "nose for news" are *still* the basic requirements for a successful career in the field. In sum, substantive skills in journalism far outweigh cosmetic appearances.

Often, what you see and hear on your local news broadcasts, particularly in anchor positions, seems to contradict this. But it is important to remember that by and large, local news anchors are chosen mainly for their perceived ability to attract the largest possible audiences. Like newspapers and magazines, radio and television stations are business enterprises. Their aim is to make money for their owners and investors. The larger their audiences, the more money they can charge advertisers, hence the greater their profitability.

Apart from public-supported radio and television (NPR and PBS), the profit motive indirectly affects the nature of virtually all news broadcasting in the United States. It imposes a distinct style on news presentation. A newscast in a commercial system must strive to catch and hold the audience's attention. Newscasts must be unflaggingly *interesting*.

You might argue that news events are inherently interesting—and most working journalists would agree with you. But they would also caution that the news does not "tell itself." No matter how intrinsically interesting, a news story requires a trained journalist, an effective writer and communicator, to preserve and impart that interest to a general audience.

Fortunately, many (perhaps most) U.S. broadcasters recognize that the news is a vital service for an informed and democratic citizenry. For every "pretty face," they hire dozens of talented, trained, hard-working writers, reporters, producers, researchers, tape editors, camera crews, graphic designers, and so forth—the kind of people who elevate broadcast journalism from a mere craft to a full-blown profession.

THE IMPORTANCE OF WRITING ABILITY

Essentially, there are two sides to the broadcast news profession: the editorial side, which includes all nontechnical personnel; and the production/engineering side, which includes the technicians who operate the electronic machinery. In large cities and at networks, the distinctions between these two sides tend to be fixed. For example, a camera operator (sometimes dubbed a "photojournalist") shoots videotape but never writes a news script, while a reporter writes the script but never operates the camera.

However, at the lower levels where newcomers begin their careers, such distinctions barely exist. News staffers are often expected to do it *all:* shoot and edit tape, report, write, anchor—and possibly sweep the studio before turning out the lights. But broadcast news executives say the single most important talent they look for in newcomers is the ability to write well in broadcast style. They point out that almost anybody can learn to run a camera in a few days; it takes training to write well under pressure—training which they themselves have neither the time nor the inclination to provide. And they will not accept an applicant's word that he or she knows how to write; they will require the applicant to pass an audition *proving* it.

Thus, this book's first seven chapters are devoted to this most basic of broadcast journalism's skills.

WRITING FOR THE EAR

The first "words" human beings ever spoke were undoubtedly no more than inflected grunts, perhaps reactions to stepping on a sharp rock or biting into an especially tasty hunk of raw meat. The point is, the first words were *spoken,* not chiseled in stone at Hunter/Gatherer U. Chiseling—writing, that is—came much later in our cultural development.

In a way, broadcast newswriting is a reversion to the original method of communication, by voice. Yes, the words are written, but they are written expressly to be spoken aloud. The structure of the written sentences follows the cadences of human speech—short, simple, direct.

Broadcast style is often described as "writing for the ear" rather than for the eye. The reader's eye can skip back and forth, and pause while the intellect ponders words and meanings. The listener's ear has no such luxury. A listener or viewer of broadcast news gets only one brief chance to comprehend. If a word, phrase, or sentence is not immediately clear on first hearing, the audience may become lost and unable to follow the rest of the story.

In short, broadcast newswriting is a form of oral storytelling in which the words committed to paper or computer file have no reality until given a human voice.

Some of you may have been trained to write in newspaper style. If so, you were taught to make your lead sentence a capsule version of the entire story. You were taught to cram the most significant story elements (Who, What, When, Where, Why, How) into that sentence and perhaps a follow-up sentence, then to add details in descending order of importance. This gave your story an "inverted pyramid" structure which enabled an editor to trim from the end to fit the story into the available space. This approach to newswriting gives the published story an artificial, convoluted structure that is inherently distant from human speech.

Thus, if newspaper style were imposed on, say, the story of Little Red Riding Hood, the lead might go something like this:

> THE WOODS, OCT. 31—An eight-
> year-old girl narrowly missed serious injury
> Friday when she was rescued in a remote
> cabin by a woodsman who snatched her

from the claws of a transvestite wolf which
had just devoured her grandmother, according to accounts by forest rangers.

That sort of writing is known as "journalese." It rearranges a chronological series of events into a formalized structure aimed at the intellect via the eye. Although frequently clumsy, it is very useful if your job is putting out a newspaper.

But it has virtually nothing to do with broadcast news. Just try reading that paragraph aloud and you'll hear why.

(Go ahead, try it. Reading aloud is a habit you should form early in broadcast news.)

Chances are you ran out of breath before reaching the comma. Obviously, no one *talks* that way. Furthermore, no one *listens* that way.

Now let's try a radical departure from newspaper style. Suppose we lead the Red Riding Hood story by saying,

```
A remarkable rescue in the Woods today...
```

Grammatical purists might complain that this is not a complete sentence. They're right, it's only a fragment. And, journalistically speaking, it tells What, Where, and When in only the most rudimentary fashion. But have we piqued people's interest? Do we have their attention? You bet. Very simply, we have begun to *tell a story*. We have picked a starting point, and now, step by step, we are going to reveal further details in a way that allows the audience to stay with us. No journalese, no jargon, no verbal overload. The essence of broadcast style lies in its *simplicity*.

News stories, of course, are rarely as simple as fairy tales. Nor do they seek to teach moral lessons. They are often about a reality that is ugly or complex. You can't start a broadcast story by saying, "Once upon a time there was a brutal murder." But you *can* start by saying,

```
A drive—by shooting on the West Side today...
```

That is a legitimate and effective way to catch people's attention.

There are many other, less abrupt ways, and in coming chapters we shall examine them. But for the moment, let's try to think of broadcast style as old-fashioned, sit-around-the-campfire storytelling—with a dynamic beginning.

A word of caution: While broadcast style is supposed to be conversational and follow the cadences of normal speech, it should also follow the rules of grammar and syntax. That makes it a kind of hybrid. In casual conversation, people make mistakes. They confuse the facts, garble their syntax, and use words incorrectly (saying "lay down" when they mean "lie down," confusing "infer" and "imply," "flaunt" and "flout," and so on).

So let's put it this way: Broadcast style is writing the way people talk when they use language correctly and get the facts straight.

BROADCAST NEWS VOCABULARY

In addition to conversational language, broadcast journalists use a limited vocabulary. Compared to books, literary magazines, and scholarly writings, the vocabulary of print journalism is small, somewhere around 10,000 words. The vocabulary of broadcast journalism is even smaller.

Adjectives are deliberately kept short and simple: A "spherical" object is *round* or *shaped like a ball;* a "lanky" or "wiry" person is *thin;* a person with "flaxen" hair is *blond;* "coniferous" trees are *evergreens* and "deciduous" trees are *leafy;* and so on.

Verbs are short and active: To "regard" something is to *watch* it; "purchase" becomes *buy;* to "participate" becomes to *take part;* to "extinguish" a fire is to *put* it *out;* "hasten" becomes *hurry;*

"inculcate" becomes *teach;* "make a determination" becomes *decide.* And, perhaps most importantly, verbs used to report what people *say* are simplified greatly. Thus, "assert," "aver," "avow," "declare," "recount," "relate," "opine," "expound," "explicate," "elucidate," and the like, all become *say, tell, explain,* or, in rare cases, *state.*

Nouns, too, are kept as simple as possible: A "residence" or "domicile" is a *house, home,* or *apartment;* a "purchaser" is a *buyer;* an "octogenarian" is an *80-year-old;* "mnemonics" is *memory improvement;* and so forth.

Some critics of broadcast news allege that its limited vocabulary leads to the impoverishment of language and, in effect, promotes functional illiteracy. Such charges might be tenable if the aim of broadcast newswriting were to be literary. But that is manifestly not its purpose. Its aim is to make the news clear to a mass audience—immediately and without verbal obstacles.*

WYSWYS (WHAT YOU SEE IS WHAT YOU SAY)

People using computer word-processing software are familiar with the acronym WYSWYG, which stands for "What You See is What You Get." It means that the screen displays a written text exactly as it will appear in the eventual printout (that is, without funny-looking formatting symbols). We've modified the acronym to WYSWYS—What You See Is What You Say—to describe another characteristic of broadcast style: the frequent need to *add* words, phrases, and/or punctuation marks that are not required in print style.

For example, if the U.S. trade deficit in a given month is "$15.3 billion," that figure looks fine on the printed page. But the text of a broadcast news script, including the "$," must be read aloud. Thus, in broadcast style, the figure should be written as *15-point-3 billion dollars.* Similarly, the figure "7.5%" should be written as *seven-point-five percent,* or better, rounded off to a conversational *seven-and-a-half percent.* (Notice the hyphens linking the parts of each figure. As we shall see in coming chapters, hyphens are handy tools for broadcast newswriters.)

A related concern arises in quoting people's words, especially if the remarks constitute an opinion or moral judgment. In print style, a direct quote is indicated by quotation marks:

> "President Smith is a horse's ass," Senator Jones said.

Clear enough. But what happens when we read that aloud? No one can *see* the quotation marks. Thus, broadcast writers often choose to paraphrase or reinforce the attribution of a direct quote to make clear who said what. Examples:

```
Senator Jones called President Smith "a horse's ass."

Senator Jones said President Smith is -- in the senator's

words -- "a horse's ass."
```

The foregoing illustrates yet another aspect of broadcast style: placement of the attribution. In print, the attribution (the name of the speaker or the source of the information) is generally placed at the end of the sentence, preceded by a comma:

```
WASHINGTON (AP)--Higher postage rates, including a 29-cent
charge for first-class mail, will begin April 3, the Postal
Service announced Tuesday.
```

*Since the 1970s, studies have consistently shown that most Americans list television as their primary source of news. Other recent studies indicate that for an ever-growing number of Americans, television is the *only* source of news. If the studies are true, talk of mass illiteracy is almost beside the point. News broadcasters are obligated to use language the broad mass of people understand.

Now read that aloud. Notice how placing the attribution at the end deviates from the cadences of everyday speech? In conversation, we are more likely to speak the sentence the other way around. Thus, in broadcast style we most often place the attribution at the *start* of the sentence:

```
The Postal Service is raising rates once again.  It says a

first class stamp will cost 29 cents starting April Third.
```

Yet another major concern for broadcast writers is pronunciation. Suppose a story includes the name of Lech Walesa, the former leader of Solidarity and president of Poland. Print writers need concern themselves only with the proper spelling of Walesa's name. But broadcast news anchors and reporters must *speak* the name *aloud*. Therefore they should be able to pronounce it correctly. Since the proper pronunciation can often catch news anchors unawares, broadcast writers script a parenthesized phonetic rendering immediately after the actual spelling:

```
Polish President Lech Walesa (Lek Va-WEN-sah)...
```

This and the other quirks of broadcast style discussed so far require relatively minor adjustments for most students; they soon become second nature.

However, certain major adjustments are necessary because of the very nature of radio and TV news, which exists not in space, but in *time*. Broadcasters are ruled by the clock, and the clock can be a very cruel master.

THE BURDEN OF BREVITY

Newspaper and magazine editors may shorten or lengthen stories to fit the available space. They often have great latitude. Sometimes entire pages may be added if the load of news is especially heavy.

Radio and television producers ("producer" is the customary broadcasting term for "editor") have no such flexibility. Although top executives may order entertainment programming preempted for extended news coverage of a major story, there are still only 24 hours in a day and 60 minutes in an hour. Come flood, fire, or earthquake, that's all the time there is—period.

To demonstrate the effect of time's tyranny on broadcast journalists, let's pick an actual story sent by the Associated Press news agency:

```
     NEW YORK (AP)--A jetliner aborted takeoff, veered off a
runway and caught fire Thursday at John F. Kennedy
International Airport, authorities said. All 292 people aboard
were evacuated safely, but at least 51 suffered minor
injuries.
     Trans World Airlines Flight 843, a three-engine Lockheed
1011 headed from New York to San Francisco, was engulfed in
flames from the wings to the tail. The plane's fuselage was
cracked near the tail and its belly was on the ground. The
fire was extinguished after about 50 minutes.
     A fire may have started in an engine, though it wasn't
immediately known why the pilot aborted the takeoff, a federal
official said.
     "People were gasping," said passenger Marianne Levine of
San Francisco. She said she thought:" I hope we're not going
to die. Oh, my God, I don't think he'll be able to come to a
stop."
     Passengers slid down inflated emergency chutes to flee the
plane.
     "Everything was calm, as calm as it can be when you know
you've got to get out of there because you can see flames and
```

smell smoke," said Tim Scheld, a reporter for WCBS-AM in New York, who was aboard the plane.

The jet carried 280 passengers and 12 crew members, said Don Fleming, a TWA spokesman.

Charles DeGaetano, an Emergency Medical Service Spokesman, said 51 passengers suffered minor injuries such as bruises, abrasions and neck and back pain. A dozen rescue workers also were treated for minor injuries.

As the plane was attempting to take off," there was a slight bang" and "we came back down on the ground in a violent fashion," Scheld said.

"We were hurtling down the runway. Then at some point, the plane veered right softly into the soft sand-grass portion to the right of the Tarmac.

"We were all bracing each other, bracing ourselves against the seats in front of us, hoping that pieces of the plane would not come free, and they did not. The plane stayed intact on the inside," Scheld said.

Passenger Deena Anderson said she heard an explosion. "It was a big ball of flame and noise, and I looked back to the tail of the plane and all I saw was fire," said Anderson, 48, of Sacramento, Calif.

Julia Elhauge, 31, of Berkeley, Calif., said two exits with chutes were opened, but "then the stewardess opened the rear exit . . . and a ball of flame came into the cabin."

Scheld said: "There was a little pushing and shoving but not that much." Once everyone was out, Scheld said, "it was just a real surreal scene--200-plus passengers and crew standing out on the Tarmac looking at this plane that we were just sitting in go up in flames."

The plane was departing runway 13 Right. "The pilot for reasons we do not yet know elected not to take off, and he put on the brakes and in the process veered off the runway," said Duncan Pardue, a spokesman for the Federal Aviation Administration. He said the plane never was airborne.

The plane burst into flames, ending up about 100 feet off the runway, Pardue said.

"It appears to be destroyed from the wings back, leading officials to suspect that the fire may have started in an engine," Pardue said. Two of the engines are mounted on the wings; the third is atop the fuselage in the rear.

An FAA official who spoke on condition his name not be used said the agency was investigating a report that the pilot aborted the takeoff after he was told about smoke or fire in an engine.

The fire was reported at 5:42 p.m. EDT. The airport was closed for several hours.

That story contains about 750 words—an average length by modern newspaper standards. Most people can read it in a minute or two.

But as we've noted, broadcast news is designed to be read aloud—and by that measure it would take more than *five minutes* to read the story!

Some radio and television stations, mainly in New York (where this was obviously a major local story), would indeed spend that amount of time, or much longer, reporting the near-disaster of TWA Flight 843. However, the overwhelming majority of U.S. stations would follow the basic rule of *brevity*. They would give this story anywhere from 10 to 45 seconds on radio and anywhere from 15 seconds to about two minutes (2:00) on television. Thus they would only have time to report a small fraction of the story's details. This is a fact of life in U.S. commercial broadcasting, even on all-news outlets. The standard practice is to tell stories many times in many different ways, but each time *briefly,* instead of just one or two times at length.

There's no *regulation* stating broadcast stories must be so brief. Rather, it is a matter of long-standing practice based on the assumption, supported by market research, that mass-audience attention spans are extremely short. To run stories longer, it is argued, is to risk losing a big part of the audience, and thus deprive advertisers of the "target" they are paying to reach.

This is a source of constant frustration to many, many broadcast journalists, who often feel themselves precluded from reporting enough important details for a story to make much sense. For this reason, some decide to go into public radio and television, which are not apt to be swayed by arguments about the audience's presumed short attention span.

In any event, the policy regarding story length is determined by top management; it is fundamentally a business decision, not a journalistic one. Thus, for now and for the foreseeable future, extreme brevity will remain the rule in commercially sponsored broadcast news.

As you were reading the TWA jetliner story, you may have noticed a few of the matters we mentioned regarding the transformation into broadcast style: the need to write shorter sentences, the need to spell out certain figures (for example, "L1011" should become *"L-Ten-Eleven"* or *"L-10-11"*), the need to attribute at the start of sentences, the need to clearly identify direct quotes, the need to add pronunciation help ("Charles Dee-Guy-TAH-no," "Julia El-HOJ," and so forth.)

But those are trifles compared to the main task, which is: How do you reduce a 750-word (5-minute) story to 10, 20, 30, or 45 seconds without losing its essence (its key details)? How do you decide which facts to include and which to leave out? How do you decide the order in which to present them?

That, of course, is what broadcast journalism is really all about, and in this book we shall be laying out the tools with which to fashion your own answers to the above questions. Yes, your *own* answers. Journalism, you see, is more art than science. There are rules, but they sometimes overlap or bend. In the end, the way you use the tools, the editorial decisions you make, the "news judgment" you acquire, will determine your eventual success in broadcast journalism.

Meanwhile, here are some broad guidelines for the overall approach to broadcast style:

1. Assume at the outset that people interested in a story's wealth of details will read newspapers, because they know radio and TV will usually not take the time to include them. Let's not kid ourselves: Any radio or TV newscast that promises to deliver "all" the news is grossly misrepresenting itself.

2. Reduce a story to its journalistic bare bones: Who, What, When, Where, and if there's time, Why or How.

3. Eliminate historical background except for those few facts which make the latest development significant or understandable.

4. Try to eliminate direct quotes. You'll find it is almost always shorter to paraphrase. (This applies to *written* copy only. Direct quotes in broadcast news are typically presented on tape, in the speaker's own voice—a matter we shall take up in great detail after first covering the basics of writing.)

WRITING TO TIME

Because broadcast writers and reporters fill time instead of space, they learn to approach news stories from a sharply different viewpoint than print writers.

Not knowing in advance how much newspaper space their stories will eventually fill, print writers automatically adopt the inverted-pyramid structure. But broadcast writers almost always know *in advance* how much time they will have for each story. An editor or producer will tell them. For example, a producer will say, "Give me story X in 20 seconds," or "You have 35 seconds for story Y." Once they know the alloted amount of air time, practiced broadcast writers know what approach to take, what overall structure to give each story. They know a story time of 20 seconds allows for only the barest of bones, a story time of 35 seconds allows for adding a little flesh to those bones, and a story time of 2 minutes allows for laying on some muscle tissue. In broadcast news, there is *never* any time for fat.

The broadcaster's approach is called "writing to time." It is a basic talent required of broadcast writers, especially in television. Developing the know-how to write a story based on its alloted air time requires patience, practice, and knowledgeable supervision.

So let's get started.

EXERCISES

1. To give yourself and your instructor an idea of your raw talent, use the foregoing TWA jetliner story as source material for a 20-second version written in broadcast style. Slug it JUMBO JET. (Do not concern yourself for now with the rules of style and copy appearance that appear in Chapter 2. Just try to tell the story simply, and use short sentences.)

2. Now write a second version, slugged JET MISHAP, this one running 30 seconds. Make this version *different* from the 20-second version. Do *not* use the same lead, wording, or sentence structure.

Training, Reference Materials, and Copy Appearance

2

Since the mid-1960s, the so-called "media explosion" (created by new technologies derived from the space and defense programs) has yielded a concurrent explosion in news and news-related programming on television. The latest of these technologies—cable TV and worldwide satellite transmission—have had major effects on viewing patterns. Cable TV, while drawing news and entertainment audiences away from the traditional networks and network-affiliated local stations, has increased the total number of news and news-related jobs in the industry.

In addition to two all-news cable network outlets (CNN and CNN Headline News), there are now numerous regional all-news cable services, as well as cable networks for sports news (ESPN), financial news (FNN, CNBC), entertainment news (E!), medical news (Lifetime), trial coverage (COURT TV), and others. All of them employ people who were initially trained in broadcast journalism.

However, anyone who has looked for employment recently can testify that the larger pool of jobs has *not* made it easier to find work. Quite the contrary. The field has continued to attract an overflow of applicants, mainly young people in search of entry-level positions. Intense competition makes getting that first job a daunting prospect.

Why are so many people attracted to careers in broadcast news? More than a few, no doubt, are motivated by the traditional role of journalism as eyewitness to history. Others feel a societal duty to dig for the truth in order to expose wrongdoing. Others see "the media" as an elite fraternity/sorority offering the chance to meet people and go places that are generally off-limits to nonjournalists. Still others perceive broadcast news as a field offering relatively high pay (a perception true only of on-air personnel and top management in the biggest cities and at networks). And others view broadcast news as a glamorous field in which their high visibility will make them "stars." Broadcasting is a huge industry, and there's enough variety of opportunity to satisfy (or disappoint) any of these motives.

But it is not our purpose to assess motives. Rather, our purpose is to examine those qualities and talents which best prepare newcomers for long, fruitful, and satisfying careers.

Although many journalists specialize in particular "beats" as their careers progress, most begin and remain as *generalists*. That is, they are expected to know a little about a lot of things. They must be versatile and able to assimilate new information quickly. They seldom know, upon arriving for work, what subjects will be occupying their energies on that day. Yet they will be expected to tackle those subjects efficiently and explain their importance to their fellow citizens. Thus they require a boundless curiosity about the world and its people. Successful journalists must *yearn* to know Who, What, When, Where, Why, and How.

READING HABITS

First and foremost, journalists must be avid *readers*. They must be in the *daily* habit of reading at least one newspaper, but preferably two—either two local papers or a combination of one local paper and one national "newspaper of record" such as *The New York Times, The Washington Post,* The *Los Angeles Times,* or *The Wall Street Journal.** They must read weekly magazines of fact (*Time, Newsweek, U.S. News & World Report,* for example) and opinion (*The New Republic, National Review, The Nation, The New Yorker,* to name just a few), as well as monthly magazines treating issues in depth (*Harper's, Atlantic Monthly, Commentary, Texas Monthly,* and the like). And they must read nonfiction books on subjects that tend to recur in the news: the economy, politics, race relations, crime, popular culture, the space program, foreign relations, and so forth.

The point of all this reading is not to become an "instant expert" (although that is sometimes required in the news business), but rather to build up, over time, a solid foundation of knowledge on which to draw in assessing and writing the news.

VIEWING AND LISTENING HABITS

Broadcast journalists have the added responsibility of knowing what's on radio and television. They should be in the habit of waking up to radio news in the morning and watching TV news in the evening—on not just one but on several competing stations. They should compare the ways different stations handle (present) the same stories, always asking themselves, "How would *I* handle those stories? What is truly new or important about them? What does the audience want or need to know?"

Whenever possible, they should also watch and listen to daily programs that treat issues in greater depth than most commercial-station newscasts (for example, "The MacNeil/Lehrer NewsHour" on PBS, "Nightline" on ABC, and "Morning Edition" and "All Things Considered" on NPR). They should watch weekly news programs, too—those appearing across the entire spectrum of broad- and cablecasting: news/interview shows (such as "Meet the Press" on NBC, "Face the Nation" on CBS, "This Week with David Brinkley" on ABC, and "Newsmaker Saturday" and "Newsmaker Sunday" on CNN); journalist/panel shows (such as "Washington Week in Review" on PBS and "Journalists' Roundtable" on C-SPAN); programs featuring debate, analysis, and commentary (such as "Firing Line" on PBS, and "Crossfire" and "The Capital Gang" on CNN); "magazine" shows (such as "60 Minutes" on CBS and "Prime Time Live" on ABC); and, last but not least, the only remaining regularly scheduled long-form documentary program on network television, "Frontline" on PBS.

Sure, that's an awful lot of viewing. Perhaps no one can be expected to watch all of it. But professional journalists must undoubtedly spend more time watching these shows, not to mention reading and studying, than does the general public. Because journalists' work consists of selecting which facts and assertions to include in news stories, it should be evident that their foundation of knowledge must be greater than the average reader's or viewer's. A newscast is supposed to be "authoritative," a test which can only be met if it is prepared by knowledgeable professionals.

PROFESSIONAL GOALS AND RESPONSIBILITIES

Although Chapter 1 stressed the differences between print and broadcast styles, we must pay attention to matters that unite journalists in the different media.

Most broadcast writing is either original, as in the case of reporters covering events and/or interviews, or is based on writing meant for print, as from news agency copy, government or industry

*A "newspaper of record" is one with a large roster of experienced staff reporters based across the nation and around the world, as well as in its home town. Such a newspaper constantly strives to report local, world, and national news more accurately and in greater depth than other newspapers. Its pages are used as source material by historians, economists, political scientists, educators, diplomats—and by other journalists.

handouts, and so on. As we've said, a basic job of the broadcast writer is to transform this eye-oriented copy into ear-oriented copy. However, the *content* of the news copy, as opposed to its form, must meet the same *journalistic* criteria as in print:

- It should be *accurate*. Insofar as time allows, no effort should be spared to check the facts of a story. When in doubt about a story's accuracy, do not use it!
- It should be *fair*. Journalists strive for objectivity, but they are only human and thus view the world through subjective prisms. Although complete objectivity thus remains an elusive goal, *fairness* is readily attainable. This means reporting *all sides* of a story.

Because broadcast news is highly competitive, newsroom executives love scoops (exclusive stories), and they love *to be first*. Broadcast deadlines occur far more frequently than print deadlines. In the case of all-news radio and TV, deadlines occur literally by the minute. Staffers are expected to work very quickly. Indeed, it is extremely satisfying, professionally speaking, to broadcast a story ahead of the competition. Unfortunately, the temptation is strong to sacrifice accuracy in the name of speed.

However, all broadcast news executives agree: In the last analysis, it is far more important to be right than to be first.

READY-REFERENCE SOURCES

Broadcast newsrooms usually provide essential reference materials—dictionaries, atlases, telephone books, government directories, street maps, ward and precinct diagrams, and so on. Lamentably, many of these materials are often nowhere to be found when you need them in a hurry. (Staffers tend to borrow them and then neglect to return them to their proper place.) Therefore, many career journalists prefer to assemble their own ready-reference works on a nearby shelf or in their desks.

Most such resources serve equally well for print or broadcast use. However, broadcasters require certain "extras."

Dictionaries

Because his or her words will be spoken aloud, a broadcast writer's dictionary should include easy-to-read pronunciations. This can be a two-edged sword, because some dictionaries list more than one pronunciation for the same word (look up the word "controversial" to see what we mean). Some grammarians insist the first of the listed pronunciations is the "preferred" and therefore correct one. Others contend that alternative pronunciations carry equal weight. Whatever the case, the total number of disputed pronunciations is very small, and the important thing is that your dictionary contain pronunciations for each word, along with its definition, so that you don't have to flip to some other part of the book for guidance.

Ever since its publication in 1961, Merriam-Webster's *Third New International Dictionary* (unabridged) has been the standard reference dictionary in most U.S. newsrooms. However, in 1987 it got a worthy competitor in the *Random House Dictionary of the English Language* (unabridged, 2nd edition), which has quickly been adopted in many newsrooms. Both are excellent . . . but far too big, heavy, and expensive for personal use. For everyday, quick-reference use, you can choose from a number of inexpensive paperback abridged dictionaries, including the *Scribner-Bantam* and the *Oxford American*. (But do *not* throw money away on the type of cheap, big-print pocket dictionaries sold at some supermarket checkout counters; such dictionaries are for elementary schoolchildren.) Whatever dictionary you use, it should

- be up-to-date, containing words having entered common use in the preceding decade;
- contain clear pronunciations (as already noted);
- contain alphabetized historical names and places;
- contain brief usage guidelines, also alphabetized

(For help in pronouncing tricky words, as well as foreign names and places frequently in the news, the *NBC Handbook of Pronunciation* [HarperCollins, 4th revised edition, 1991] is a trustworthy addition to your personal or professional bookshelf.)

Grammar and Usage Guides

When may you split an infinitive? Does "presently" mean "soon" or "now"? Does one "flout" the law or "flaunt" it? Should you write "The man *who* was going" or "The man *that* was going"? A good writer needs to find the answers to those questions, and the answers are not always in dictionaries. That's where grammar and usage guides come in handy.

Until recently, the standard reference was H. W. Fowler's *A Dictionary of Modern English Usage* (revised 1983 by Sir Ernest Gowers, Oxford University Press), usually known just as "Fowler" for short. Although Fowler remains the standard in many parts of the English-speaking world, its advice, apart from being somewhat long-winded, is keyed to British standards, not American. All of which is fine if you are writing for the BBC. American audiences, however, prefer Americanisms because that's the way they speak. (It's been said that Britain and America are "two countries divided by a common language." For example, the statement "I'm mad about my flat" means in America, "I'm angry about my flat tire," whereas in Britain it means, "I just love my apartment.")

There are two American-oriented language guides in widespread use: Wilson Follett's *Modern American Usage* (paperback, Warner Books, 1966) and Theodore Bernstein's *The Careful Writer* (paperback, Atheneum, 1965). Both list things alphabetically (as other guides do not), enabling the broadcast writer to resolve language problems quickly. Of the two, Bernstein is the more complete and more entertaining.

Serious writers and students of language will, over time, refine their skills by reading works by authors such as William Safire, Edwin Newman, Richard Mitchell, and John Simon, to name but a few. They will also follow magazine columns such as William Safire's "On Language" in the Sunday *New York Times Magazine*.

Atlases and Almanacs

Where is Maracaibo? What is the capital of Angola? Who won the heavyweight boxing crown in 1947? What movie won the Oscar for Best Picture in 1933? What does the U.S. Constitution say about the private ownership of firearms? Is a train from Prague to Budapest going east or west? Who was Speaker of the House before the present one?

These are the kinds of questions, ranging from the important to the trivial, that pop up every day in the news business. If you're like most of us, your first impulse will be to shout around the newsroom in hopes that someone will know the answer. The answer you usually get is, "The train would be going east—*I think.*" So you end up looking up the information anyway, which is what you should have done in the first place. For some reason, that short trip across the newsroom to the reference shelf seems like a major undertaking.

Save yourself the trip by buying a world almanac. There are several published each year. The publishers change frequently; past almanacs have been issued by CBS News, *The New York Times, The Washington Post,* and the Associated Press, among others. They all provide the same basic facts and figures. Just be sure the one you buy includes world maps of sufficient detail to enable you to tell listeners which way that train was going.

Research by Computer

Computers are now an integral part of the newsroom landscape. Although some newsrooms are not entirely "computerized" (that is, with workstations and specialized software for newscast production), their number is dwindling rapidly. In any event, you are likely to find at least one computer workstation nearby with a modem enabling you to do research via a commercial database (such as Nexis, CompuServe, or Prodigy, to name just a few). Obviously, you must know how to access and navigate the system. Therefore, if computers are still a mystery to you, you must strive to become "computer literate" as soon as possible, or you will be at a disadvantage in today's professional marketplace.

When in Doubt, Ask!

Despite the presence of your personal or shared reference materials, the nature of the news business is such that sooner or later (probably sooner) you'll come upon a story which you've been asked to rewrite in broadcast style but which you simply don't understand. Don't let this throw you. Remember that no journalist, no matter how wide his or her experience, can be expected to understand all the complex information flooding into the newsroom.

Remember, too, that the newsroom, like the classroom, is a shared experience. Rely on teamwork. Don't hesitate to ask a fellow student or an instructor for help. It is not stupid not to know something. It *is* stupid not to seek help.

And, above all, *do not attempt to write a story you do not understand!* If *you* don't understand it, chances are your *audience* won't understand it either. It is far, far better to make the audience wait than to risk passing along false information.

COPY PREPARATION

Before digging into the meat and potatoes of broadcast style, we must spend a few moments setting the dinner table. Just as your dinner guests would expect to find their forks on the left and their knives and spoons on the right, so does broadcast usage mandate a specific appearance for your written news copy.

Fortunately, the form is fairly standard throughout the industry. (Given the mind-boggling variety of electronic equipment in use these days, this is a small favor for which we can be grateful.) In some places you will type your stories directly onto 8½″ by 11″ copy paper, in other places into a computer file for eventual printout. Either way, the settings for spacing, margins, and fonts (typefaces) are virtually identical.

Basic Rules

1. Use a 70-space line for radio, a 35-space (or 37-space) line for television. Set radio script left margin at 10, right margin at 80. Set TV script left margin at 43 (or 45), right margin at 80.
2. *Double-space.* (You may have to adjust this somewhat depending on your typewriter or electronic printer. The idea is to leave lots of space between lines for the addition of minor typed or handwritten corrections.)
3. Use a 10-pica font (10 characters per inch). Anything smaller (such as elite type) is too difficult to sight-read during a broadcast. On a computer, set the printout for letter quality (LQ) or near letter quality (NLQ). (Draft quality is not sharp enough for sight-reading.)
4. Set the top margin at 1½ inches (15 picas). This allows room for your name, the date, and the air time of the newscast (all of which go in the extreme upper left of the page), the slug (a one- or two-word identification of the story), and the running time (length in minutes and seconds) of the story.
5. Type only *one story per page.* On a computer, *save* each story separately, calling up a *new page* for each successive story.
6. Type in *upper/lower-case.* This allows maximum flexibility in providing eye-oriented punctuation, phonetic pronunciations, and cueing instructions. (Some on-air personnel prefer all caps since they are larger and thus easier to sight-read.)
7. Make sure the computer is set for *wordwrap* and for *eliminating widows and orphans* (partial sentences at the top and bottom of pages). If you are using a typewriter without wordwrap, make sure:

—*not* to split or hyphenate words between lines. (Split words are difficult for the anchor's eyes to follow, causing announcing errors);

—*not* to split sentences or paragraphs between pages (which cause the same sight-reading problems).

8. *Time* the story by *reading it aloud* against a stopwatch. (Professional newsroom computers are set to time copy automatically, as it is being written.) Another (less satisfactory) way to time copy is by *counting lines:* Two lines of radio copy = :05 (five seconds); four lines of TV copy = :05.

Round off the timing to the nearest :05 (:31 and :32 become :30; :33 and :34 become :35; and so on), enter the figure at the *upper right* of the page, and *circle* it. (On a multi-page story, enter the story's total running time on the *first page only*.)

Your completed typewritten script should resemble the following model:

Bard, 9/15, 6p   HURRICANE

    A powerful hurricane slammed into parts of Hawaii this evening.

    The full force of Hurricane Iniki's (Ee-NEE-kee's) 130-mile-an-hour

winds struck the island of Kauai (Kuh-WAH-ee), causing heavy damage and

cutting off all power and telephone service. So far, there are no

reports of serious injuries among tourists or the island's 50-thousand

residents.

    On the nearby island of Oahu (Oh-AH-hoo), 20-foot waves lashed

coastal highways and the tourist Mecca of Waikiki (WY-kee-kee) Beach.

Civil Defense authorities said the hurricane blew the roofs off several

houses. But there, too, no one is reported hurt so far.

    Iniki is Hawaii's worst storm of this century, with winds gusting up

to 160 miles an hour. Tourists and residents had received several hours'

warning -- and most were able to seek shelter on higher ground, away from

the coasts.

A computer-generated printout looks virtually identical, except for a template across the top* containing the identifying and timing information:

```
PG____   SLUG___HURRICANE_____   CT#____   VO_____   SND_____   CUME _:41__
SHOW_6p_  COPY_:41_  WTR_Bard_____   ANC__Jones___  DATE/TM__9-15_____
```

A powerful hurricane slammed into parts of Hawaii this evening.

The full force of Hurricane Iniki's (Ee-NEE-kee's) 130-mile-an-hour winds struck the island of Kauai (Kuh-WAH-ee), causing heavy damage and cutting off all power and telephone service. So far, there are no reports of serious injuries among tourists or the island's 50-thousand residents.

On the nearby island of Oahu (Oh-AH-hoo), 20-foot waves lashed coastal highways and the tourist Mecca of Waikiki (WY-kee-kee) Beach. Civil Defense authorities said the hurricane blew the roofs off several houses. But there, too, no one is reported hurt so far.

Iniki is Hawaii's worst storm of this century, with winds gusting up to 160 miles an hour. Tourists and residents had received several hours' warning -- and most were able to seek shelter on higher ground, away from the coasts.

Amending Scripts

There are some additional rules to observe when altering or correcting news copy after it has been printed out or removed from the typewriter:

1. Do *not* use print copyediting symbols. Correct errors by *striking out* the *entire* erroneous word or words, then retype or carefully print the correction *directly above* the strikeout. Corrections should be *bold* and easy to read. If handwritten, use block lettering, *not* longhand.

---

*The template is a characteristic of a widely used newsroom computer system called BASYS. Another widely used system is called NEWSTAR. Learning either system is akin to learning a powerful word-processing program such as WordPerfect or Miscrosoft Word.

```
No:           The  brown quick  fox  jumped  over  the  lazy  d  o
                                                                  ^ g.


                     quick brown                                      dog
Yes:          The  brown quick  fox  jumped  over  the  lazy  dig.


                              bacon                                     Dg
No:           The  quick  black  fox  jumped  over  the  lazy  cat.


                              brown                                    dog
Yes:          The  quick  black  fox  jumped  over  the  lazy  cat.



or retype entirely:



              The  quick  brown  fox  jumped  over  the  lazy  dog.
              The  brown  quick  fox  jumped  over  the  lazy  dig.
```

2. If a sentence or page contains so many corrections that sight-reading the copy might be difficult, *retype* the *entire* sentence or, if necessary, the *entire* page. (Or call up the computer file, edit the copy on-screen, then print out the corrected substitute page.)

   Corrections can alter a story's timing, so remember to retime your copy and enter the new running time at the top of the page.

3. If a story continues onto another page, indicate "more" by *drawing an arrow* in the lower right corner.

```
to 160 miles an hour.  Tourists and residents had received several hours'

warning -- and most were able to seek shelter on higher ground, away from

the coasts.
```

4. Do *not* clip, staple, or paste script pages together. (To facilitate last-minute changes, the pages must remain freely interchangeable and be of uniform size.)

PUNCTUATION

Overall, the best way to "punctuate" a broadcast news story is to use short sentences. However, even short sentences can profit from punctuation marks to help guide the anchor's eye.

In particular, broadcast writers make liberal use of capital letters, commas (,), hyphens (-), dashes (two hyphens together, --), ellipses (. . .), and colons (:), but *not* semicolons (;). These punctuation marks serve to break up long clusters of words which might throw anchors for a loop.

Here's an example of a 10-second story using only periods and commas as punctuation:

```
        Mayor Tom Smith said today he will not seek re-election to a

   third term.  The mayor, who had been considered a shoo-in, said

   he is, in his words, "growing tired and stale."
```

Now here are two ways to apply broadcast-style punctuation, the first using capital letters, the second using ellipses:

```
        Mayor Tom Smith said today he will NOT seek re-election to a

   third term.  The mayor, who had been considered a SHOO-IN, said

   he is, in HIS words, "growing TIRED AND STALE."

                                 -0-

        Mayor Tom Smith said today...he will not seek re-election to

   a third term.  The mayor...who had been considered a shoo-in...

   said he is...in his words..."growing tired and stale."
```

There is also a way to punctuate a script *after* it has been printed out or removed from the typewriter: by underlining by hand the words you want the anchor to stress:

```
        Mayor Tom Smith said today he will not seek re-election to a

   third term.  The mayor, who had been considered a shoo-in, said

   he is -- in his words -- "growing tired and stale."
```

PARAGRAPH STRUCTURE

In print, the start of a new paragraph usually indicates the start of a new thought or a new story element. But in broadcast news, listeners and viewers can't see or hear the paragraph breaks; all they hear is the anchor's or reporter's voice. Thus, broadcast paragraph structure is important only insofar as it helps oral delivery.

Some broadcast writers neglect paragraph structure altogether. Others begin a new paragraph after each and every sentence. The best writers, however, use paragraphing the same way they use punctuation, to help anchors read stories at a glance. Sometimes, they include one or two paragraphs toward the end of story *in parentheses*. The parentheses tell the anchor that if he or she is running short of time, the parenthesized copy may be omitted entirely.

SPELLING

In the heyday of radio, some broadcast writers were notorious for their bad spelling. After all, what difference did it make, they reasoned, if they wrote "there" instead of "their" or "Jon" instead of "John"? Listeners would never know the difference.

But the television age has put an end to such carefree attitudes. In addition to news copy, TV staffers must write the words viewers *see* in electronic graphics and titles. Any misspellings or mis-identifications (especially of people or places) reflect badly not only on the person who wrote them but also on the entire news department. (Besides, "Jon/John" himself may be watching and may not take kindly to seeing his name misspelled.)

PRONUNCIATION AND PHONETICS

No matter how good your dictionary, it is unlikely to offer much help in pronouncing many of the foreign names and places that appear each day in the news. Fortunately, the news agency broadcast divisions (to which most broadcast news organizations subscribe) provide some relief by transmitting pronunciation guides on a daily or twice-daily basis. Here's part of one from United Press International (UPI):

```
World-Prono-Guide 0597
AL-WAZIR, Khalil (Kah-lihl Ahl-vah-ZEER'), Palestine
Liberation Organization Number Two man assassinated in a
Tunis, Tunisia, suburb; also know as Abu Jihad (AH-BOO'
Zhee-HAHD')
AQUINO, Corazon (KOH'-rah-zohn Ah-KEE'-noh), president of
the Philippines.
ARAFAT, Yasser (YAH'-sehr Ahr-ah-FAHT'), head of the
Palestine Liberation Organization
Chernobyl (Chihr-NAW'-bihl) nuclear power complex in
Ukraine
CUOMO (KWOH'-moh), Mario, New York Democratic governor
Daedalus (DEHD'-ehl-ehs), U-S-designed human-powered
aircraft
DE MITA, Ciriaco (Chee-ree-AH'-koh Day MEE'-tah), new
Italian prime minister
DELVALLE, Eric Arturo (Ahr-TOO'-roh Dehl-VAH'-yeh), ousted
Panamanian president
DEMJANJUK (DEHM'-yahn-yook) John, retired American auto
worker convicted in Israel on charges of committing Nazi war
crimes while a death camp guard
DUKAKIS (Doo-KAH'-kihs), Michael, Massachusetts Democrat
Hezbollah (Hehz-BOH'-lah), Islamic party in Lebanon, also
known as "Party of God"
Hormuz (HOHR'-mooz), Strait of, channel connecting the
Persian Gulf with the Gulf of Oman
Jihad (Zhee-HAHD'), Islamic, a pro-Khomeini terrorist
group
```

```
        Kabul (KAH'-buhl) capital of Afghanistan
        Kharg (Kakrk), Iranian island in Persian Gulf, site of key
oil terminal
        Kuwait (Koo-WAYT'), Persian Gulf oil state
        NIDAL, Abu (Ah-BOO' Nee-DAHL'), leader of Libyan-backed
P-L-O splinter group
        NORIEGA (Nohr-ee-EH'-gah), Manuel Antonio, former
Panamanian military strongman
        Noumea (Noo-MAY'-uh), New Caledonia, French territory east
of Australia
        PERES, Shimon (Shee-MOHN' PEH'-rehs), Israeli foreign
minister
        RABIN, Yitzhak (YIHTS'-hahk Rah-BEEN'), Israeli defense
minister
        SHAMIR, Yitzhak (YIHTS'-hahk Shah-MEER'), former Israeli
prime minister
        Shiite (SHEE'-ight), Moslem sect
        Sikh (Seek), religious sect
        Sunni (SOO'-nee), Moslem sect
        Tbilisi (Tuh-bihl-YEE'-see), capital of Georgia
```

The UPI "Prono-Guide" makes good use of upper/lower-case typing and simple phonetics (without the sort of diacritical marks usually found in dictionaries) to boost newswriters and anchors over many of the hurdles of foreign language pronunciation. But, unavoidably, it is incomplete. What is needed is the sort of comprehensive phonetic table which we include herewith—and which you might care to photocopy and place among your other reference tools:

Phonetic Table

Letter(s)	As in	Phonetic rendering in news copy
a	fat, glad, cap	a
a	late, great, race	ay
a	father, car	ah
a	(unstressed syllable) lull*a*by, *a*ffect	uh
an	*banc, sang, Le Mans* (French)	awnh (nasal)
ao	*Macao, gabao* (Portuguese)	onh (nasal)
au	*braun, kauen* (German)	ow (as "now")
au(x)	*faux, chapeau* (French)	oh
b	boy, build, drub	b
c	cede, citizen	s
c, ch	cord, chemical	k
ch; c,cc	cheap, beach, *citta, bacci* (Italian)	ch
ch	*cher* (French)	sh
ch,gh	loch (Scottish), *Bach* (German), Gogh (Dutch)	kh (guttural)
d	dog, stud	d
e	neck, edge	e
e,ee	cede, seek	ee
é,er	*éclair, passé, diner,* (French)	ay
è	*grève, cèpe* (French)	e (as "get")
eu	*Heute, Kreuz* (German)	oy (as "boy")
eu,ö, ü	*feu* (French), *schön, kühn* (German)	ooh (as "foot")
f,ff	fix, offer	f or ff
g	(hard) get, go	g
g	(soft) gem, ledge	j
gn	*bagno* (Italian), *magnifique* (French)	n'y
gu	*Miguel* (Spanish), *gueppe* (French)	g (as in "go")
h,j	him, how; *joya* (Spanish)	h
h	*hirondelle* (French, unaspirated)	(silent)

continued

Phonetic Table Cont'd.

Letter(s)	As in	Phonetic rendering in news copy
i	bit, miss, sin	i
i,y	bite, sky	y (as vowel)
i	*mineur* (French), *si, mi* (Italian, Spanish)	ee
in	*vin, lapin* (French)	a (as "fat," nasalized)
j	justice, jerk	j
j	*Jahr, jung* (German)	y (consonant)
j	*je, juste* (French)	zh
k	kid, like	k
l,ll	lip, killer	l
ll	*llegar* (Spanish); *oreiller* (French)	y (consonant)
m	man, ember	m
n	not, knot	n
ñ	*niño, piña* (Spanish)	n'y
o	note, toad	oh
o	not, body, closet	ah
o	dog, frog	aw
oo	room, shoot	oo
oi	*moi, trois* (French)	wah
ou	*pour, nous* (French)	oo
oy	boy, buoy	oy
p	pot, slip	p
ph	phone, lymph	f or ff
qu	quick, square	kw
qu	*chequier* (French); *quemar* (Spanish)	k
qu	*quer, Quatsch* (German)	kv
r	rude, rodeo, car	r
r,rr	*trois* (French); *perro* (Spanish)	rr (rolled)
s,ss	sit, risk, assess, kiss	s or ss
sh	shrug, sure, crush	sh
sch	*Schade* (German)	sh
shtch	*tovarishtch* (Russian)	sh'ch
t	ten, wait	t
th	thick, thin (hard) *and* this, the (soft)	th (for both)
u	but, upper	u
u	burn, curse	u
u	usual, sure, butte	yoo
v	vixen, novice	v
v	*Volk, vier* (German)	f
w,wh	wit, what	w
w	*warum, wo* (German)	v
x	extra, sex	x
y	sky, byline	y (vowel)
y	mainly, *Lyon* (French)	ee (vowel)
y	yes, yolk	y (consonant)
z	size, zoo	z
z	azure; *muzik* (Russian)	zh
z,zz	*Zigeuner* (German); *mezzo* (Italian)	ts

The phonetic renderings given in the right-hand column are the spellings to include in broadcast news scripts. Note that *unstressed* syllables should be typed in *lowercase* (except for the first letter of the first syllable of proper nouns) and that *stressed* syllables are typed in *all-caps*. Note also that phonetic renderings are typed *in parentheses, immediately after the actual spelling.*

Here is an example of how to apply the table:

```
(print)        WARSAW (AP)--Parliament on Friday approved centrist
          lawmaker Hanna Suchocka as the first woman to head a Polish
          government, ending the nation's five-week political crisis.
               Hours earlier, the Sejm (lower house) had accepted the
          resignation of Prime Minister Waldemar Pawlak.
               Suchocka, 46, is a constitutional lawyer and member of the
          Democratic Union Party, the largest group in the highly
          fragmented Parliament.
```

```
(b-cast)       Poland has its first-ever woman prime minister. Elected

          today, she is 46-year-old Hanna Suchocka (HAH-nah Soo-KAW-skah),

          a constitutional lawyer and political centrist.  She replaces

          Prime Minister Waldemar Pawlak (VAHL-duh-mar PAHV-lahk).
```

Other examples:

```
          Former Soviet Leader Mikhail Gorbachev (Meek-hah-EEL

GOR-bah-choff)...


                              -0-


          French President François Mitterand (FRAWNH-swah

MEE-ter-awnh)...


                              -0-


...the siege of Sarajevo (SAH-rah-YAY-vo)...


                              -0-


...the tourist industry in Oaxaca (Wah-HAH-kah)...
```

Unfortunately, no phonetic guide for English language writers and speakers can be entirely comprehensive—for the simple reason that Anglo-American speech does not include certain types of spoken sounds (for example, the nasal suffixes of French and Portuguese, the guttural consonants of German or Dutch, the harsh sibilants of Russian and other Slavic tongues, or the click-sounds of some African languages).

Other problems stem from the way some foreign alphabets are transliterated into the English alphabet. Chinese is one example of this. You may see the Chinese capital of Beijing written as "Peking," "Beiping," or "Peiping," depending on the system of transliteration in use at the time of writing. ("Bay-ZHING" is the closest we can come, phonetically, to the correct pronunciation.) In cases like this, newsroom personnel can try to locate a native speaker for guidance by calling the nearest consulate, cultural or trade association, or the appropriate university languages department.

However, it is not always necessary to be strictly accurate to foreign pronunciation. If it were, we might be saying "Pah-REE" instead of "PA-ris." What *is* necessary is to avoid the kind of *mispronunciation* that gives listeners the impression we haven't the foggiest idea what we're talking about.

EXERCISES

1. Using the following news agency story as raw material, write a maximum 30-second radio story slugged COLLAPSE. Use your name, today's date, and make the story for a 7 p.m. newscast. Be careful to make your copy conform to the rules given in this chapter.

```
     BURNABY, British Columbia (AP)--A rooftop parking area
collapsed Saturday during the grand opening of a grocery
store, dropping automobiles and blocks of concrete onto store
displays and injuring 21 people, police said.
     It was not immediately known how many people were in the
Save-on-Foods store when the parking area, holding about 22
autos, collapsed, but Constable Lloyd Wall of the Royal
Canadian Mounted Police in Burnaby said estimates ran as high
as 900. Many were elderly people being given a preview tour.
     Three of the injured were admitted to hospitals, with one
in serious condition.
     Police used cranes to remove huge blocks of concrete and
cars that fell about 40 feet from the parking area to the
floor of the store, in the Metrotown shopping center, Mounted
Police Constable Dave Muir said.
     It took several hours for searchers, who used police dogs,
to get through the rubble. Officials believed everyone was
accounted for, Wall said.
     "We're being optimistic there won't be any deaths," said
Mounted Police Sgt. Gary Schauer. "But we're still going
through the rubble."
     Some cars were piled on each other on the supermarket
floor amid soda and produce displays, while above, other autos
teetered on the edge of a hole about half the size of a
football field.
     "I heard a crack and I looked up and saw the center beam
wobble and saw the floor from the parking garage come down so
I immediately told people to get outside," said one witness,
George Sanderson.
     "As soon as the first crack came (in the beam), they
started getting people out," Heppell said.
     The collapse was preceded by the sound of a buckling beam
and spray from a bursting water pipe, officials said. There
were three warnings over the store's loudspeaker system to
clear the area.
     Clarence Heppell, president of Overwaitea Foods, which
operates the store chain, said a structural failure caused the
cave-in.
     Eight people were taken to a hospital by ambulance, and
others went to emergency wards on their own.
```

Is your copy clean?
Did you time it by reading it aloud against a stopwatch?
Did you make an attempt at "visual punctuation" of any sort?
Did you use any phonetic renderings, and did they resemble the following?

   Burnaby (BURN-uh-bee)
   Gary Bauer (BOW-er)
   Clarence Heppell (HEP-el)

2. Applying the phonetics table, write a 15-second broadcast version of the following story, slugged STOLEN ART. (You may have to consult with an art dealer or art historian to get the proper pronunciations of the artists' names.)

NICE, France (AP)--Four valuable paintings stolen from the villa of a French-Lebanese businessman were found undamaged in a parked car early Tuesday after an anonymous phone tip, investigators said.

The Matisse, Modigliani and two by Degas--with an estimated total value of $50 million--were stolen Friday from a villa in the southern French resort of Cap d'Ail.

The paintings were found in a car in a hotel parking lot near the Nice airport, officials said. They said the art appeared undamaged.

Story Structure, Leads, Language

3

Now that the table is set, we're ready for the meat and potatoes of broadcast style. Instead of an appetizer, we're going to start with the main course.

STORY STRUCTURE

As we noted in Chapter 1, broadcast news exists in time rather than space. This imposes an overall structure, a story *organization* that is far, far different from that used in print.

For example, in print journalism, it is customary to write a "roundup" that groups a number of related developments into a single story. Typically, the first sentence of a print roundup is an umbrella lead mentioning two or more of the developments. Follow-up sentences and succeeding paragraphs then skip back and forth from development to development, adding a few details here and a few there. Readers are not bothered by this hopscotch approach because they can go back, if necessary, and reread the earlier information.

But viewers and listeners do not have this luxury. They hear the story's many facets only once. "Hopscotching the news," skipping back and forth, can be disorienting and confusing. Therefore, broadcast style imposes a *linear* (straight-line) approach toward storytelling. Broadcast newswriters must *tell only one story element at a time,* deal with it completely, and only *then* go on to the next element.

We'll use a print-style story as our working model:

```
        TEL AVIV (AP)--Hundreds more Arab policemen in the
occupied West Bank and Gaza Strip resigned Saturday to protest
Israeli treatment of Palestinians in the territories, while in
Tel Aviv, about 100,000 Israelis rallied on the eve of Prime
Minister Yitzhak Shamir's trip to the United States to urge
him to support the American peace initiative.
        Israel Radio said about 450 of the 800 to 1,000 Arab
police officers in the occupied territories have quit their
```

```
          jobs in the past two days. About 20,000 Palestinians work for
          the government in the territories.
               The resignations began Friday, one day after the
          self-styled Unified National Leadership for the Uprising in
          the Occupied Territories issued a statement reiterating its
          call for the Arab policemen to retire immediately.
               Israeli warplanes, meanwhile, struck five Palestinian
          guerrilla targets east of the port town of Sidon in southern
          Lebanon, the army said. Police said one guerrilla was killed
          and at least eight others were wounded. It was Israel's second
          raid this year in the region.
               A palestinian military leader said on Saturday that Arabs
          will continue to protest in Israeli-occupied territories
          despite the air raids.
               Scattered violence was reported in the West Bank and Gaza
          Strip on Saturday.
               Near Tulkarm, a 50-year-old woman was wounded when prison
          service employees opened fire after their bus was stoned.
               On Friday night, Israeli soldiers shot and seriously
          wounded a Palestinian from Bani Naim, near Hebron, after he
          threw a hand grenade at them, the army command said. The
          grenade did not explode.
               At least 89 Palestinians have been killed since the
          uprising began Dec. 9.
               In the Tel Aviv demonstration, the group Peace Now urged
          Shamir to support a U.S. peace initiative.
               Tzaly Reshef, one of the Peace Now activists who organized
          the demonstration, told the crowd, "One hundred thousand
          people tonight in this square send a clear message to Prime
          Minister Shamir: You can't say no to peace plans in our name."
```

There are a total of four elements (news developments) in that story:

1. More Arab policemen resigned in the West Bank.
2. More Palestinians were wounded in the West Bank and Gaza Strip.
3. Israeli planes attacked suspected guerrilla bases in Lebanon.
4. An estimated 100,000 Israelis staged a peace rally in Tel Aviv.

The print writer has interwoven these four elements, sometimes not referring back to a previously mentioned development until many paragraphs later. For example, the Peace Now rally is mentioned in the lead sentence but is then not mentioned again until the last two paragraphs.

Broadcast writers should *not* do this. They must bear in mind that *time will have elapsed* between first mention of the Peace Now rally and its next mention many paragraphs later—time in which many listeners will have forgotten what is being spoken about. Thus, in addition to shortening the sentences and simplifying the language, they must *reorganize* the entire structure, telling each story element in turn—no jumping forward, no going back:

```
Bard, 11/27, 5p                    ISRAEL                    (:45)



     An estimated 100,000 Israelis rallied in Tel Aviv tonight, in

support of the latest U-S Mideast peace plan.  They urged Prime Minister

Shamir (Shah-MEER) to accept the U-S formula for ending the Palestinian
```

```
uprising in the West Bank and Gaza Strip.  Shamir leaves tomorrow for

talks in Washington.

     The uprising gained momentum today with the resignations of hundreds

more Arab police.  Israeli radio says about 450 Arab police officers have

quit in the past two days.  That's roughly half the entire force.

     Israeli forces shot and wounded at least two more Palestinians

today.  Near Hebron (HEH-brun), soldiers shot one man they said threw a

hand grenade.  At least 89 Palestinians have been killed since the

uprising began last December.

     Also today, Israeli warplanes attacked suspected guerrilla targets

in Southern Lebanon.  Lebanese police said one guerrilla was killed and

eight wounded.
```

Notice how the broadcast writer has told each story element in linear fashion. The foregoing model led with the Tel Aviv rally because it was the latest of the day's events. But notice also that the technique of telling each element separately permits *rearranging* the story to lead with a different element:

```
PG____    SLUG__ISRAEL_____    CT#____    VO_____    SND_____    CUME__:34__
SHOW_6p_   COPY_:34_   WTR__Bard_____    ANC__Jones___   DATE/TM__11-27___
```

```
     Hundreds of Arab police in Israel's occupied territories resigned

today at the request of Palestinian leaders.  According to Israeli radio,

a total of 450 Arab police officers have quit since yesterday in the West

Bank and Gaza Strip.  That's about half the force.

     Israeli forces shot and wounded at least two more Palestinians

today, as the anti-occupation uprising continued.  In one incident,

soldiers shot a man they said threw a hand grenade at them.

     In Tel Aviv tonight, about 100,000 Israelis rallied in support of

the latest U-S peace proposals.  They called on Prime Minister Yitzhak

Shamir (YEE-tsak Shah-MEER) to accept the plan during his upcoming talks

in Washington.
```

Here's another reason why the straight-line approach is so important and useful in broadcast style: A story like the foregoing might appear just once, in a single version, in a single edition of a daily newspaper. But at a radio or TV news department, newscasts occur many times a day. Each time, a *different* version is used. That means a story's elements must be rewritten frequently (perhaps as often as every 30 or 60 minutes in radio). Linear style facilitates frequent rewriting of differing versions.

LEADS

By and large, a print-style lead seeks to impart a wealth of information in a single sentence. The result is a kind of mini-story, told in journalese, which stands on its own.

By and large, a broadcast-style lead seeks to impart only as much information as can be grasped easily. Sometimes a broadcast lead can stand on its own—but just as often it can not.

Although news agencies and many daily newspapers have now adopted a style favoring shorter sentences, the traditional print-style lead is still likely to resemble the following:

> WASHINGTON—Supreme Court nominee Douglas H. Ginsburg issued a statement Thursday admitting that he smoked marijuana on a number of occasions, apparently including the period when he was a member of the Harvard University Law School faculty—an announcement that raises questions about his continued viability as a candidate for the nation's highest court.
>
> "It was a mistake, and I regret it," he said.

(David Lauter and Melissa Healy, © *Los Angeles Times,* reprinted with permission)

Counting the dateline, the lead sentence in that story is 54 words long. If you say it aloud (go ahead, try it!), you will run out of breath long before you reach the period. It is a fine *newspaper* lead; it is comprehensive, contains all five W's, and summarizes the important points of the story as a whole.

But as a *broadcast* lead, it is entirely unacceptable. Not only is saying it fluently a virtual impossibility, but it contains *too much* information for listeners to swallow in one gulp. The sentence is complex in structure and uses long words and locutions ("issued a statement" instead of "said," "occasions" instead of "times," and "continued viability" instead of "chances" or "prospects"). So the first step is to cast it aside in favor of shorter, simpler, more direct sentences.

```
     Supreme Court nominee Douglas Ginsburg admitted today that

he smoked marijuana when he was a law school professor.

     The admission raises serious doubts about his chances for

confirmation.
```

The first sentence in that broadcast version is 18 words long, the second 10 words long, for a total of 28 words—about half the number in the print version's single lead sentence. Both sentences are direct and to the point—no wasted verbiage. Most important, they tell the essence of the story (the bare facts and their significance). They do not get bogged down by long words and unwieldy grammar.

Using the same approach, let's try a few other versions:

```
     A potentially damaging admission today from Supreme Court

nominee Douglas Ginsburg...
```

```
            Ginsburg says he smoked marijuana several times while on the
        faculty of Harvard Law School.

                                      -0-

            Douglas Ginsburg says he smoked marijuana many years ago.
            The admission raises doubt that the president's latest
        Supreme Court nominee can win confirmation.

                                      -0-
```

And, using information from the print version's second sentence:

```
            Calling it a regrettable mistake, Supreme Court nominee
        Douglas Ginsburg admitted today that he has smoked marijuana.
            Ginsburg said it happened a number of times while he was a
        law professor at Harvard.
```

As you can see, using conversational language provides a wide variety of options for broadcast leads. There's no hard and fast rule about the maximum number of words in each sentence. The main concern is to be able comfortably to speak the sentence aloud.

As a guideline, however, if you find yourself consistently writing sentences longer than about 20 to 24 words (about two lines of radio copy or four lines of TV copy), make a deliberate effort to tell *less* in each sentence until you get the hang of writing shorter sentences.

And say goodbye to long, complex sentences. Don't even use them for direct quotes. Instead, *paraphrase,* using short sentences.

Except for the word "tonight," the following lead could serve equally well for print or broadcast:

```
            A bullet-proof vest saved a policeman's life in the Kenmore

        District tonight, stopping a handgun bullet fired by a teenage

        assailant.
```

But the following leads lend themselves only to broadcasting:

```
            There's a lucky cop in the Kenmore District tonight...

                                      -0-

            A Kenmore District patrolman is alive and well tonight,
        thanks to his bullet-proof vest...
```

Such leads, which require follow-up sentences to complete the essential information, serve the double function of piquing the listener's interest while setting up the rest of the story.

Leading with the Latest

Most of the time, a broadcast lead will reflect the most important development of a story. Frequently, however, it will merely reflect the *latest* development.

The lead can be the best place to exploit broadcasting's built-in speed advantage over print:

```
          Democratic nominee Bill Clinton brought his presidential

     hopes to North Carolina tonight after a long day campaigning in

     California.

          In San Diego, Clinton vowed to make universal health care a

     top priority of his administration.  The Arkansas Governor

     criticized the Bush administration's health proposals as "much

     too little, much too late."
```

Clearly, what the candidate said in California was more newsworthy than the mere fact of his having flown to another state. But newscasts airing after the dinner hour must strive to find "now" angles to freshen their stories. In other words, it's okay—in fact it's often desirable—to lead a story with a less newsworthy angle as long as the story as a whole includes the more newsworthy angles.

Leading with a Quote

A pithy, colorful quote can be an especially attention-getting way to lead a story. A quote "leads" the audience to continue listening to find out who said it and why. Here's how the technique might work with the Ginsburg story:

```
          "It was a mistake, and I regret it."

          Those were the words of Supreme Court nominee Douglas

     Ginsburg today as he admitted to having smoked marijuana.

          The admission threw doubt on Ginsburg's prospects for

     confirmation.
```

The effectiveness of leading with a quote depends on *not* doing it too often. And it is vital to follow up a quote *immediately* by identifying the speaker and the context.

Another consideration is the ability of the anchor or reporter to deliver the quote effectively and without appearing foolish. A deadpan, flat delivery is death to a choice quote.

Leading with a Sentence Fragment

As we've noted repeatedly, broadcast style permits loosening the grammatical constraints of written English. An incomplete sentence may be "bad grammar" to some, but to broadcast lead writers it's a standard technique:

```
     Trouble for the Ginsburg nomination...

     Supreme Court nominee Douglas Ginsburg admitted today he
```

```
                smoked pot while a professor at Harvard Law School.

                     The admission raised doubts... (etc.)
```

Of all the possible ways to lead broadcast news stories, chances are the sentence fragment is the one you'll hear most often.

The Chronological Lead

It can sometimes be very effective to *reverse* the normal newswriting process and tell a story chronologically, delaying the payoff:

```
                After years of calling them nuisances, beat cops last month

            finally began wearing those new-model bullet-proof vests.

                     Well, tonight one of those "nuisances" saved a cop's

            life....
```

The chronological lead begins with old information (background) in order to set the stage for the latest or most important information (the news):

```
                Last week, Douglas Ginsburg looked like a shoo-in for

            confirmation to the Supreme Court.

                     But the nomination is now in trouble.  Ginsburg admitted

            today he smoked marijuana while on the faculty at Harvard Law

            School....
```

Like leading with a direct quote, it's best to use chronological leads sparingly.

The "What's Next" Lead

Sometimes what is *going* to happen is more interesting or newsworthy than what has already happened.

For example, newscasts airing after the dinner hour contain a preponderance of past-tense stories telling what happened that day. But by that time, many in the audience will have heard much of the day's news and will be more interested in later developments. That's when we can use the "what's next" lead.

We already saw a type of story to which this approach can be applied:

```
               WASHINGTON (AP)--Higher postage rates, including a 29-cent
          charge for first-class mail, will begin April 3, the Postal
          Service announced Tuesday.
               The postcard rate will increase to 19 cents.
               First-class mail will cost 14.7% more under the new rates,
          compared with increases of 18.1% for newspapers and magazines
          and 24.9% for advertising materials.
```

The news agency ran that story two weeks *before* the new rates were scheduled to take effect. Thus, while announcement of the increases was "today's" news, the effective date was in the *future*— enabling broadcasters to say:

> `Starting next month, you'll be paying 29 cents to mail a`
>
> `letter....`

or

> `You'll soon be paying more to mail a letter....`

This is also known as leading with a *next-day angle* and can be applied to many types of stories.

Let's say your station has spent the entire day reporting closing arguments in a murder trial; the jury has now retired for the night and will resume its deliberations in the morning. Although what transpired in court will continue to form the substance of your evening and nighttime stories, you might *lead* them this way:

> `A verdict could come as early as tomorrow in the murder`
>
> `trial of...`

or

> `A jury may deliver its verdict tomorrow in the trial`
>
> `of...`

The flexibility of lead-writing in broadcast style requires some adjustments for writers whose previous training has been in print journalism. Their tendency is to write a comprehensive, self-contained lead for each and every story. But that is a poor practice in radio and television.

Remember the context: Broadcast news stories are presented in a series, a framework, formally known as a *newscast*. If each story in a newscast has the same kind of lead as the one before and the one after, the result is a lack of variety and pacing. In other words, it sounds dull. And you can bet your paycheck that your boss does not want you boring the audience!

So learn to think of broadcast leads in non-newspaper terms. In broadcast news, a lead is nothing more than a *beginning,* a way of getting into a story. A lead may indeed be a capsule version of the story as a whole. But more likely its main purpose is to command attention—like saying, "Stay tuned, folks! Wait till you hear this!"

LANGUAGE

In a way, writing broadcast news is like translating a foreign language—that is, you translate the language of a newsmaker or the print-style language of written copy into a conversational language your audience can easily understand.

English is one of the world's richest languages. It long ago supplanted French as the language of diplomacy and German as the language of science. English has become so international that people all over the world must study it as a second language if they ever wish to communicate with anyone across a national border.

But despite (or because of) its richness, English lends itself to imprecision, whether in the form of the ungrammatical coarseness of the undereducated, the color and verbal shorthand of slang, or the dense and sometimes deliberate obfuscation of bureaucratic jargon. Broadcast journalists encounter such linguistic deviations every working day and must "translate" them into plain English.

Jargon

If you ask a politician, "Well, Senator, have you decided to run for re-election?" and get the reply, "I am studying the position with a view toward making a determination on the eventuality of a viable candidacy," you have just looked jargon squarely in the eye. You may well smile as you write, "Senator Jones says he hasn't made up his mind whether to run for re-election." Changing the senator's bafflegab into simple English is what we mean by translating jargon into broadcast style.

But not all jargon is baffling or impenetrable. Some is colorful. In fact, most of us speak jargon in one context or another, usually related to the office or to our peer groups. For example, when police officers announce "the apprehension of a perpetrator," they know everyone on the force will understand it as "the arrest of a suspect." This sort of jargon is easy to translate into simple English. (We broadcasters are no exception to jargon-mongering. When we speak of "sound bites" or "talking heads," we know those terms will be understood by other broadcasters.)

On the other hand, some jargon is so dense as to be mind-numbing. To spend a few hours reading the *Congressional Record,* corporate stockholder reports, or transcripts of speeches at academic conferences or at the U.N. Trusteeship Council is to risk such an overdose of bloated, jargon-filled prose that our eyes glaze over. And yet, that is often the raw material from which news reports must be written. To repeat the newsmakers' jargon in a broadcast news story is virtually guaranteed to confuse the audience—and that is completely unacceptable.

To list all forms of unacceptable jargon is well beyond the scope of this book. In general, however, you will readily recognize it when you see or hear it. The words or their meaning will not be immediately clear to you. And if they are not clear to *you,* they will almost certainly not be clear to your audience. Therefore, always ask yourself, "If I write something *this* way, will it be clear to people I know—friends, family, fellow students, and so forth?" If the answer is *no,* rewrite it in words they *will* understand. When in doubt, ask for help.

Here are some types of jargon to watch out for:

1. Avoid redundancy.

    Politician: "I want the American people to realize their *hopes and aspirations.*" (Strike "aspirations." It means "hopes" and is three syllables longer.)

    Designer: "This skirt is *very unique.*" (Strike "very." Something is either unique or it isn't. There's no middle ground. "Unique" means "one of a kind.")

    Witness: "The truck *narrowly missed hitting* the car." (Strike "hitting," or say "almost hit.")

    Sales Clerk: "This model has many *new innovations.*" (Strike "new." An innovation *is* something new.)

2. Avoid foreign words and expressions for which there is a clear English equivalent. Translate them colloquially.

    Book Critic: "This novel's sole *raison d'être* is to make money." ("This novel's only purpose (or aim) is to make money.")

    Professor: "The Soviet Communist *Weltanschauung* resulted inexorably in paranoia." ("The Soviet Communist world view resulted in paranoia.")

    [*Note:* Some foreign words entered the broadcast news vocabulary long ago and may be used without losing the audience; examples are *coup* (short for the French *coup d'état,* meaning the overthrow of a government) and *junta* (from the Spanish for "military regime.") Occasionally, there are newcomers; an example is *glasnost,* Russian for "openness," and meaning the liberalization of the former Soviet system.]

3. Avoid bookish, "highbrow" words where simpler words will do.

    Restaurant Critic: "The chef's *gustatory* instincts were *awry.*" ("The cook's taste buds were flat.")

    Art Critic: "Heaven knows where the gallery acquired its predilection for antediluvian tableaux!" ("I don't know where the gallery got its taste for primitive art.")

4. Avoid clichés, even though they may be all around you.

Guest Speaker: "I'm *pleased as punch* to address this assemblage of *movers and shakers.* ("I'm very happy to address this important group.")

Football Coach: "We're gonna *get up* for this one and really *sock it to 'em* and *come up smellin' like a rose.* ("We're going to win big next Saturday.")

5. Avoid mixed metaphors.

Politician: I'm *throwing* the tax bill for *a long pass* and hoping someone *crosses home plate* with it (mixing football and baseball).

Historian: Roosevelt was a *colossus,* taking the world of economic troubles *onto his back* (confusing the Colossus of Rhodes with the Atlas of Greek myth).

6. Avoid trendy, overworked expressions that become clichés.

Reporter 1: The *bottom line* was he had to start all over again. (Make it "result" instead of "bottom line.")

Reporter 2: The administration hopes to get its foreign policy back *on track* by next year. (Make it "straighten out" or "reorganize" or "adjust.")

Remember, the foregoing list of "don'ts" applies to the language *you* use to write the news in broadcast style. Whenever you quote someone directly, you must obviously report the speaker's exact words, jargon and all.

Slang

Just as jargon and pretentious language must be "translated down," so must substandard or unsuitable language be "translated up." Solecisms such as "ain't got" and "can't hardly" are taboo if they're *your* words. If they're someone else's words, someone you wish to quote, then the matter must be decided on a case-by-case basis. That's because some slangy words or expressions lend color to a story. So let's make this distinction:

Slang is permissible when it is *both* (1) widely understood and (2) spoken by a news*maker,* not a news*caster.* Put another way, you may quote people in the news who use slang, but you yourself may not use it. Examples:

yes: The senator called the president's remarks "dopey" and "tomfoolish."

(It's clear that the senator used those words.)

or: The senator called the president's remarks stupid.

(paraphrase)

but not: The senator says the president's remarks are dopey and tomfoolish.

(Sounds like the newscaster is using those words.)

–0–

```
yes:        In farmer Smith's words, "You can't hardly get them kind of
        ducks no more."
```

(Substandard English quoted for colorful effect.)

```
or:         Farmer Smith said that breed of duck is a rare bird indeed.
```

(Paraphrasing to retain semblance of colorful effect.)

```
but not:        Farmer Smith said you can't hardly find them kind of ducks
        no more.
```

(Substandard writer and newscaster.)

Again, space does not permit an exhaustive listing of slangy examples. Your dictionary and language guide will indicate if a word or expression is considered slang. Suffice it here to warn you to keep your ears open to the way you and your friends talk.

Each of us spends most of his or her time in a limited setting among people of the same general group, whether at home, at school, or at the office. We converse so often with these people that we no longer question certain words and expressions, without realizing that people on the next block or on the other side of town may not know what those expressions mean, or may think they mean something entirely different.

For example, a student newscaster wrote,

```
        After his lecture, Professor Carmichael attended a beer and
        munchies...
```

On her university campus, the term "beer and munchies" was a well-known way to describe a get-together where food and beverages were served. The food was not necessarily snacks, and the beverage was not necessarily beer. The expression had thus taken on a generic meaning quite apart from its component words. Although virtually everyone on campus understood it, the radio station served several communities well outside the campus. The station was known to have many, many listeners in those areas who were not or had never been students; they simply liked the programming. For them, the term "beer and munchies," especially used as a noun, was either confusing or meaningless. The student newscaster, aware she was addressing an audience not just of students, should have written,

```
        After his lecture, Professor Carmichael joined students for
        refreshments.
```

A mistake like this isn't the end of the world, but it's the kind of thing a broadcast newswriter has to watch for.

The same watchful eye should be kept on idiomatic expressions and colloquialisms. Because such language is often colorful, it can and should be used in broadcast newswriting, but *judiciously*. It must truly lend color, be widely understood, and should be grammatically accurate as well.

```
no:        The mayor, looking like Uncle Ned's whiskers, attacked the

      city council for what he called "laziness."
```

(Was the mayor angry? Red-faced? Disheveled? This kind of idiomatic expression should not be used; few people understand it.)

IMPACT OF WORDS

Broadcast journalists have a special responsibility to mind their tongues. That's because spoken words drive more deeply into the psyche than do written ones. This becomes apparent even in childhood. Somehow, the words, "Fe, Fi, Fo, Fum, I smell the blood of an Englishman," just don't seem to strike as much terror on the page of a book as they do from the mouth of a parent. And at the very next words, uttered in Dad's best Ugly Giant voice—"Be he live or be he dead, I'll grind his bones to make me bread!"—some youngsters retreat under the covers.

In the broadcast news business, we don't want to send listeners retreating under their figurative covers. We recognize that, even for adults, words invested with the dimension and fullness of the human voice contain a special power to move people emotionally, to grab at their guts, and sometimes to make them act rashly or foolishly.

Above all, broadcasters must remain calm in their words and tone of voice. We've come a long way since a radio program—Orson Welles' *Mercury Theater* production of "War of the Worlds" in 1938—was able to make thousands of Americans believe that Martians had landed. But we should never come so far as to drain spoken words of their emotional impact. Here are a few cases in point.

The word "violence" is tricky and troublesome. It carries more impact spoken than written. If we say,

```
      Violent clashes marred an antinuclear demonstration today in

   West Germany...
```

we lead listeners to expect some awfully bloody details. But if it turns out that the "violent clashes" amounted to half a dozen people slightly injured in a series of shoving matches, we have grossly overstated the case and robbed the words of their true meaning.

There is a way to avoid this: *Be specific* as to what happened, *without* characterizing it as "violence" or "violent." Let the facts speak for themselves.

A distinction should be made, too, between "wounds" and "injuries." They are *not* synonyms. If we say,

```
      The bomb wounded six people...
```

the meaning is that the bomb was *deliberately* detonated. If we say,

```
      The bomb injured six people...
```

the meaning is that it went off *accidentally*. In newsroom parlance, injuries happen in accidents, wounds in deliberate violence such as war or terrorism.

Race and Religion

Even more caution is required for stories involving race or religion. As a first step, you must decide if a story really does involve either of them. If we say,

```
        A group of Southern congressmen, including two blacks,

        called today for reform of the income tax laws...
```

we are mentioning race unnecessarily. The race of the congressmen has nothing to do with the issue they are espousing, and should therefore not be mentioned.
    And if we say,

```
            In a rash of anti-Semitism in France, vandals today painted

        swastikas on two Paris synagogues...
```

we are overstating wildly and irresponsibly. "Paris" does not equal "France," and "two synagogues" defaced do not constitute a "rash of anti-Semitism." The facts of the story are vivid enough and speak for themselves. They do not need "dramatization" through the addition of inaccurate, inappropriate, or irresponsible language.
    On the other hand, some stories do require racial specification:

```
        JOHANNESBURG, South Africa (AP)--A special Easter weekend
    passenger train jumped the tracks near Pretoria on Friday, and
    at least 16 black passengers were killed, authorities said.
        Three locomotives and five passenger cars derailed at
    10:45 a.m. about six miles north of Pretoria, the railway
    police department said in a statement. The police said the
    cause of the accident is unknown.
        Fourteen people were reported dead at the scene. A
    spokeswoman for the South African Transport Services said two
    more people died later in a hospital. She said 30 people were
    injured.
        The train, packed with black travelers from the
    Johannesburg and Pretoria areas, was heading to Pietersburg in
    the northern Transvaal.
        Both Friday and Monday are holidays in South Africa, and
    hundreds of thousands of blacks travel from urban centers to
    their traditional homes in rural areas.
```

Because South Africa is still a racially segregated society, and because its racial policies, though evolving toward black empowerment, are protested by most of the world, the race of the victims is an important part of the story. Thus, a broadcast version might go this way:

```
        An Easter holiday train carrying black workers to their

        traditional homelands derailed near Pretoria, South Africa,

        today. Authorities said at least 16 passengers were killed and 30

        injured.
```

To sum up the impact of broadcast language on the audience: Do *not* include details of race, religion, national origin, cruelty, or violence *unless* such details are germane to the point of the story. In fact, it might be a good idea to mutter to yourself, "Fe, Fi, Fo, Fum!" whenever you come across a story involving

· race	· cruelty	· bodily functions
· religion	· bodily injury (blood and gore)	· sexual conduct

Measure the impact of your language on the audience. You are writing and speaking to fellow human beings.

OBSCENITY

Obscenity is in the eye of the beholder. One person's "art" is another person's "pornography." The U.S. Supreme Court has held that obscenity shall be determined by community standards. What may be held to be obscene in Roanoke may not necessarily be held to be obscene in Milwaukee; the people in those two communities may have different standards.

That said, broadcast standards, in actual practice, are far more strict than print standards. Reading is a deliberate act. Listening or viewing can happen by accident. A 3-year-old will not read words that he or she may accidentally hear. All of which is not to say that broadcasters are prudes. It's just that broadcasting, by its very nature, reaches a wider audience than print. And since broadcasters are forever trying to reach an even wider audience, it stands to reason that they do not want to risk offending people.

And make no mistake about it: People *are* easily offended. Although standards in entertainment programming have been relaxed over the years (not long ago it was forbidden to say "hell," "damn," "bastard," or "son-of-a-bitch," even in the context of dramatic dialogue), standards remain strict in news programming. Specifically, it is taboo to use the name of the Lord in a profane way or to use the popular words for excrement, genitalia, or sexual activities.*

The vast majority of newsmakers understand this and consequently watch their language in public, especially when cameras and microphones are present. But sometimes they forget themselves and let slip an occasional "Shit!" or "God damn it!" Such language is almost always edited out during preparation for broadcast.

But standards are changing. Some words and expressions once considered obscene are now considered acceptable, depending on context and the hour of the newscast. A newsmaker may talk about being "pissed off" or call someone a "son-of-a-bitch," and such remarks may occasionally be aired—repeat, *occasionally*—because they accurately reflect the speaker's strong feelings, and because such remarks have become publicly acceptable; they have lost their former shock value.

Pornography

Even under today's relatively relaxed standards, it remains a matter of news judgment how far broadcasters should go in reporting *about* alleged obscenity. News agencies almost always warn their subscribers that a story contains potentially offensive material by preceding it with the advisory "note nature." An example:

```
bc-obscene 2ndld-writethru 6-27 0668
MetroWire
editors: note nature
(complete writethru--quotes, details of verdict, background)
     LOS ANGELES (UPI)--A man was convicted Monday of
distributing short stories and a video depicting the sexual
torture and murder of children, becoming the first person to
be found guilty under a new state obscenity law.
     Police said the materials, including "Die Kiddie Die,"
"Kiddie Killer" and "Human Bedpan," plus a recording, are the
most obscene ever uncovered in the city.
     City Attorney James Hahn called Gary Jerome Levinson's
obscenity conviction, the first by a Los Angeles jury in 10
years, the "dawn of a new era in obscenity prosecutions."
```

---

*In 1990, The Federal Communications Commission (FCC) voted to uphold a 24-hour-a-day ban on "indecent" programming. The Commission reserved to itself the right to decide what is indecent and to determine the punishments (warnings, fines, loss of license, etc.) for breaking the rule. However, inasmuch as "indecency" is open to interpretation, and inasmuch as FCC commissioners are political appointees, it is a good idea to keep abreast of the inevitable shifts of FCC policy.

Hahn said the case also represents the first California
prosecution stemming from materials that depict sexual torture
and murder and the first conviction in city history involving
obscene videos.
Levinson, 38, of Hollywood, is scheduled to be sentenced
July 6, when he could be sent to County Jail for up to 3 1/2
years and be fined $7,000. He additionally faces a pending
trial in U.S. District Court on federal obscenity charges.
Following the verdict, a bitter-sounding Levinson said his
conviction represents "a total encroachment of the freedoms
we're supposed to enjoy under the First Amendment."
"But I realize that it's stacked against you in court," he
said. " You're there to get buried. If you win, it's a fluke."
Defense lawyer William Grayson said he would appeal the
conviction on grounds the law is unconstitutional.
A Municipal Court jury of seven women and five men
convicted Levinson of five counts of distributing obscene
material and one count each of possession of obscene material
with the intent to distribute and advertising obscene
materials.
Those charges stem from the distribution of one video, one
tape recording, four short stories and a catalog advertising
many of the materials, said Deputy City Attorney Michael
Guarino.
The jury, which deliberated for three days, acquitted
Levinson of one count stemming from the distribution of a
video entitled "Little Boy Snuffed."
The jury deadlocked on two other counts stemming from the
distribution of two other videos, including one showing adults
having sex with animals, Guarino said.
City Attorney James Hahn said the materials, which
Levinson distributed through his Hollywood mail-order company,
Fischer Publications, was the "most vile type of obscenity
that could appeal only to the darkest side of human
imagination."
Hahn said Levinson, who produced, performed in and
distributed the videos, was the first person in California to
be convicted under a new, strengthened state obscenity law.
The law, which became effective Jan. 1, 1987, incorporated
the redefinition of obscene material contained in the 1973
U.S. Supreme Court decision, Miller vs. California.
Under the new law, a prosecutor only has to prove that no
reasonable person would find the material to have significant
value, Hahn said.
"Under the old definition, a prosecutor had to prove that
material, regardless of how repugnant it might be, was without
any value whatsoever, which was very difficult to do," Hahn
said.
Grayson had argued that the materials do not violate the
law, that the youngest actor featured in the videos is 21 and
that Levinson's right to distribute them to consenting adults
is protected by the Constitution.
Levinson said he no longer is involved in pornographic
videos and recently helped produce the R-rated, low-budget
movie, "Hollywood Chain Saw Hookers," and acted in another
low-budget film, "Surf Nazis Must Die."
----
upi 07:25 ped

Although that story is obviously of more interest in California than in other states, which have
their own laws regarding obscenity, it does have some national interest by virtue of California's
reputation as the country's "trend-setting" state: If a child pornographer can be convicted in California, he or she can probably be convicted anywhere in the United States.

The question is, how far can news broadcasters go in telling the story without themselves risking
an appeal to prurience? Specifically, should broadcast versions include the titles of the pornographic
materials and describe their subject matter?

The handling of the story's details, just like the matter of obscenity itself, will depend on local
standards. Stations in some cities and towns will not air the story at all; stations in other cities and

towns will report only the conviction and its significance; and some stations, mostly in big cities where obscenity has long been an issue and where pornography is a thriving business, will report the details without fear of offending the vast majority of the audience. Thus, in cities where public life is conditioned by reserve in the discussion of sex and pornography, a broadcast version might be circumspect:

> A Los Angeles jury today delivered the first guilty verdict
> under a new state obscenity law. The jury convicted a
> 38-year-old man of distributing material depicting child
> pornography.
>
> Under the new California law, prosecutors must prove only
> that such material has no significant value to reasonable people.
> Previously, they had to prove such material has no value
> whatsoever.
>
> The convicted man faces a jail term of up to
> three-and-a-half years...and a fine of up to seven thousand
> dollars.

That version is sedate. It does not risk offending impressionable or prudish listeners. It is, for lack of a better word, "safe."

However, in big cities, it is not competitive. By that we mean that big-city audiences are used to seeing and hearing about a much wider range of human activities than less urbanized audiences. For better or worse, urban audiences are used to assaults on their sensibilities, and many people will wonder, What could this guy have done that was so bad he'll probably go to jail for it? Big-city stations are likely to tell them:

> A Los Angeles jury today convicted a man for distributing
> "kiddie porn" -- child pornography. It was the first conviction
> under a new California law making it easier to prosecute
> pornographers.
>
> Thirty-eight-year-old Gary Jerome Levinson was found guilty
> of distributing printed and videotaped material depicting the
> sexual torture and murder of children. Police called it the most
> obscene child pornography ever uncovered in Los Angeles.
>
> Levinson faces three-and-a-half years in jail and a fine of
> up to 7,000 dollars. His lawyer plans an appeal based on the
> Free Speech clause of the U-S Constitution.

Note that not even that example includes the titles of the pornographic materials. Some stations, however, would name them, knowing full well the disgust they might raise among listeners and viewers. In short, the issue of handling stories about obscenity and pornography is, like so much in the news business, a matter of judgment.

TONGUE-TWISTERS

"Rubber buggy bumpers" is hard to say. So is "Thirteen thieves of Thebes thinned three thickets of thistles." And no newscaster should ever be forced to attempt either one during a broadcast.

We all like "bloopers," those instances of entertainers tripping over their tongues on the air. Such boners are rarely heard these days, since virtually all entertainment programming is recorded on film or tape and the bloopers edited out. Sports is just about the only entertainment still broadcast live.

News, on the other hand, is almost always delivered live. Even in those instances where the East Coast edition of the network news is taped for later replay in the Pacific and Mountain time zones, the content is "protected"; that is, news staffs on the West Coast update and change the newscast as necessary, right up to and during the rebroadcast. Even the 24-hour all-news radio and TV outlets are programmed live.

Live programming inevitably results in occasional mistakes and miscues, both human and electronic. The goal is to keep such miscues to a minimum. There is no need to manufacture them by using the wrong language, the language of tongue-twisters. For example, there is no good reason to write,

> Federal narcotics agents have thwarted a cocaine smuggling ring.

when it's just as easy to write,

> Federal narcotics agents have **broken up** a cocaine smuggling ring.

"Thwart" is hard to say. "Break up" is not. In this context they mean the same thing, but "break up" is better in broadcasting.

The same is true of "furor," which is spoken better as "stir" or "outburst," and "cause a furor" is better put as "cause a scene." Sometimes the problem pops up not in single words but in word combinations:

> Governor **S**huster **s**igned the legi**s**lation at **s**even thi**s** morning.

That sentence contains an overabundance of sibilants ("s"-sounds), guaranteed to leave many a newscaster hissing or spitting. We can fix the problem by choosing slightly different wording.

> Governor Shuster signed the bill this morning . . .

(By the way, the words "bill" and "law" are far preferable to more formal words such as "legislation," "ordinance," or "statute." In everyday speech, people are more likely to say "drunk driving *law*" than "drunk driving *statute*.")

Another sound to watch out for is the plosive letter "p":

> **P**olice a**pp**rehended a dozen **p**icketing gra**p**e-**p**ickers . . .

might be better rendered as

> Police arrested a dozen picketing farm workers . . .

("Apprehend" is also a no-no. "Arrest" will do just fine.)

There's no room in this book to list every hard-to-pronounce word or word combination that comes to mind. The point is to sensitize you to the problem. For a career in broadcast news, you must train yourself to recognize potential tongue-twisters and to change your wording when necessary. The best way to do this is to read your copy aloud—always.

EXERCISES

1. The following news agency roundup illustrates the problems inherent in translating print-oriented copy into broadcast style. Slug it DISASTERS and write a 40-second version for the 6 P.M. News, taking care to reorganize the story as discussed in this chapter.

```
AM--Disasters Rdp, 2d Ld--Writethru, 0872
Search Continues For Last Body In Wake Of Three Disasters
By The Associated Press
     Tangled wreckage hampered the search for a worker still
missing Saturday in the wake of an explosion and fire at a
Louisiana oil refinery, while fire officials said California's
tallest building would remain closed indefinitely following a
deadly fire.
     An official of a rocket fuel company whose plant exploded
on the edge of a Nevada town said a replacement plant would be
built at a more remote location.
     Six bodies had been recovered at the refinery. Two people
died in the Nevada blast, and the California disaster killed
one person.
     Two crews worked through a maze of wrecked equipment
Saturday at the refinery at Norco, La., skirting small fires
in the search for the missing man.
     Shell Oil Co. spokesman Bill Gibson said company engineers
and safety and environmental experts were trying to find out
what caused the explosion.
     "They've gotten out right into the area, as close as they
safely could," he said Saturday.
     The causes of the three conflagrations, all of which began
during a 14-hour period Wednesday and Thursday, have not been
determined.
     In Los Angeles, fire officials were joined by state
legislators and local politicians in calling for a tough new
law requiring sprinklers in hundreds of older high-rises in
the wake of the fire late Wednesday and early Thursday that
destroyed 4-12 floors of the 62-story First Interstate Bank
tower.
     The building was built in 1973, one year before a law was
passed requiring sprinklers in all new buildings over 75 feet
tall.
     The building was ordered closed indefinitely Friday, said
Russell E. Lane, the city's chief building inspector. He said
repair work cannot begin until the steel superstructure is
extensively tested.
     In advance of that testing, "We had the original
architects and engineers go in and they were very pleased with
the shape of the building," said bank vice president Simon
Barker-Benfield. He said a few people had been allowed into
the building "to begin the process of salvaging files and that
kind of thing."
     Operators of the demolished Pacific Engineering
Production Co. rocket fuel plant at Henderson, Nev., were
fined four times in the last five years for safety violations,
but state officials defended the plant Friday as having a
"good, moderate record" overall.
     Keith Rooker, counsel for the company, said locations in
more remote regions of Nevada, Texas and Utah were being
considered for a replacement for the plant destroyed
Wednesday.
     The plant had been given 10 citations from 11 state
inspections since 1983 but the problems were "mostly minor,"
said Jim Barnes, state industrial relations director.
     The company produced ammonium perchlorate, a component of
the solid rocket fuel used in some military missiles and the
space shuttle's booster rockets.
     Kerr-McGee Corp. makes the same chemical in a plant about
a mile closer to most of Henderson's residential area. That
```

plant was shut down voluntarily Thursday, and some worried
residents want to keep it closed.
The blast damaged homes and businesses in Henderson and
326 people were treated for injuries.
The explosion at a Shell Oil Co. refinery at Norco, La.,
shattered hundreds of windows in homes and stores in the area
and shook buildings in New Orleans, 30 miles to the east.
"The area is very much in disarray," plant manager Fred
Foster said Friday. "There are large pieces of equipment off
of foundations and down around the cat cracker."
The catalytic cracker is used to break crude oil into
usable products.
"We still have a few small flames burning and so we have
not gotten into the unit," company spokeswoman Wendy Jacobs
said Saturday.
The body of one Shell employee was found shortly after the
blast and five others were found Friday. One person was
missing.
The cause of the Los Angeles high-rise fire may never be
known because of the extreme heat of the blaze, said Fire
Department Battalion Chief Gary R. Bowie.
The chief spokesman for First Interstate Bancorp
discounted arson speculation prompted by news that the
company's capital markets group, which employs 100 people on
the floor where the fire apparently broke out, was sold in a
deal that closed Wednesday night.
"I firmly believe that at this stage it's random chance,"
said spokesman John Popovich. "If the idea is that there is a
disgruntled employee, that would have been six months ago,"
when the decision to sell was announced.
A sprinkler system was being installed in the building but
was not yet complete. Los Angeles City Councilman Nate Holden
introduced a motion Friday to require owners of all high-rises
to install sprinkler systems.
About 200 members of the California Fire Chiefs
Association, attending an annual convention, urged that
sprinklers be required in all buildings more than 75 feet
tall.
State Sen. Art Torres said Friday he will introduce a bill
in the state Legislature this week to require sprinklers in
all commercial high-rise structures in California.
AP-NY-1757EDT--

2. Slug the following story AIR FARES and write three (3) leads, each in a different style—including a sentence fragment (plus a follow-up sentence) and a "what's next" lead:

CHICAGO (AP)--The nation's major airlines said they will
raise fares Saturday between $10 and $15, after previous
attempts to boost prices failed because of stiff competition
in the ailing industry.
American Airlines, Delta Air Lines, United Airlines, Trans
World Airlines, Continental Airlines, USAir and America West
Airlines said Thursday that they planned to go ahead with
scheduled increases--delayed as recently as last week.
"This is a return to what we think are sensible levels for
both the industry and the public," said Tim Smith, a spokesman
for American, the nation's largest carrier, adding that "in
the long run, no industry can continue to price its product at
below cost."
The new fares will be based on miles traveled rather than
the popularity of a particular run between two cities. The
increases were expected to mark the end of a summer that saw
big fare cuts and packed planes but also huge losses for the
nation's air carriers.
While most fares will rise between $10 and $40, some
longer runs will go up $50 or more, and some markets won't see
any increase in fares.

3. The following story contains factual material that some people might find objectionable, offensive, or revolting. Slug it ROSTOV RIPPER and write a 35-second broadcast version suited to the standards of your own local audience.

ROSTOV-ON-DON, Russia (AP/UPI)--A man dubbed the "Rostov Ripper" after an orgy of killings was found guilty Wednesday of 52 murders in southern Russia.

Andrei Chikatilo, 56, his head shaven and eyes bulging, sat in a special white metal cage in the courtroom as the judge began reading a 330-page verdict.

Judge Leonid Akubzshanov ruled that Chikatilo, who had raped and killed boys, girls and young women and escaped police detection for 12 years, was sane. Chikatilo seemed likely to face the death penalty when sentenced.

Chikatilo killed 21 boys between ages 8 and 16, 14 girls aged 9 to 17, and 17 women. He buried most in woodlands.

"He tortured his victims while they were alive by biting out their tongues, tearing away their sexual organs, and cutting their bellies open," the judge said.

The emotional scenes that marked the trial earlier in the year when Chikatilo sometimes baited victims' relatives from his cage--once waving a pornographic magazine through the bars--were repeated in the courtroom.

"I can't breathe the same air as him! I can't live on the same Earth with him!" a woman in a black mourning dress, clearly the relative of a victim, screamed from the public gallery. "Execution by firing squad is not enough for him. Let me tear him apart with my own hands!"

She was calmed with the help of a nurse who was busy taking care of many relatives who had to stand, according to court rules, listening to the verdict detailing each murder.

The former teacher, Communist Party member and "perfect husband turned monster" terrorized southern Russia, Ukraine and Uzbekistan. He was arrested after a 12-year hunt.

During the pursuit--named "Operation Forest Strip"--police made dramatic mistakes.

They arrested three men on suspicion of committing some of the crimes. One of the three suspects committed suicide, another tried to kill himself, and the third was executed for the first of Chikatilo's murders.

Under Russian law, the death penalty would be carried out by a single bullet to the back of the head.

"Who" and "What"

4

So much for the main course. We turn now to the entrées and side dishes on the broadcast-style menu. In this chapter we'll look at how broadcasters handle the first two of journalism's Five W's, Who and What. Specifically, we'll consider how to identify and describe people, organizations, and numbers (figures and statistics).

IDENTIFYING PEOPLE IN THE NEWS

Print's customary way of identifying people is to include their full names, titles, and ages in the same sentence. We broadcasters proceed less inclusively. Here's how:

1. *First mention.* The first time we identify someone, we give the person's *title, first name, and last name:*

```
      Los Angeles Mayor Tom Bradley (or Mayor Tom Bradley of Los

Angeles)...
```

-0-

```
      Senator Edward Kennedy of Massachusetts...
```
(*not* "Ted" or "Teddy." Do *not* use nicknames. That's *too* informal.)

-0-

```
      Former U-N Secretary-General Javier Perez de Cuellar

(HAH-vee-air PEH-rez dah KWAY-ahr)...
```

Broadcasters do *not* give a person's middle name or middle initial *unless* it is part of his or her *customary* identification:

```
       Economist John Kenneth Galbraith...

                        -0-

       Actor Michael J. Fox...
```

2. *Second mention*. On second and all subsequent mentions, we give a person's *last name only:*

```
       Bradley also said...

                        -0-

       Later, Kennedy visited...

                        -0-

       Returning to U-N Headquarters, Perez de Cuellar...
```

(Note that the phonetic rendering is *not* repeated after the first mention.)

In many U.S. newsrooms, there are four *exceptions* to those two main rules:

1. The President of the United States is shown respect by being reidentified as "Mr." or "President" on *every* mention. (The same degree of respect does *not* normally apply to foreign leaders.)
2. Members of the *clergy* are usually reidentified by ecclesiastical title on *every* mention:

```
       Archbishop John Mahoney (first mention); Archbishop (or
   Cardinal) Mahoney (thereafter)...

                        -0-

       Rabbi Arnold Gold (first); Rabbi Gold (thereafter)...

                        -0-

       (The) Reverend Jerry Falwell (first); Reverend Falwell
   (thereafter)...
```

3. A few news organizations continue to insist that *women* be identified on second mention as "Miss," "Mrs.," or "Ms."

```
       Former British Prime Minister Margaret Thatcher (first);
   Mrs. Thatcher (thereafter)...

                        -0-
```

```
      Actress Michelle Pfeiffer (first); Miss Pfeiffer

(thereafter)...
```

(However, most newsrooms now give them equal treatment by reidentifying them simply as "Thatcher" and "Pfeiffer.")

4. In *obituaries,* the deceased is often identified by full name on *both first and last mention:*

```
      Earl Tupper (first mention), the man who made his name a

household word by marketing plastic containerware, died today in

Costa Rica.  Tupper (subsequent mention) developed his

"Tupperware" line after World War Two, became wealthy, and

retired a decade ago.  Earl Tupper (last mention) was 76.
```

THE TITLE OR THE NAME?

As you may have noticed in the foregoing Javier Perez de Cuellar example, fully identifying a newsmaker can sometimes require a mouthful of words. In such cases, it is often preferable *not* to fully identify on first mention. Instead, use a *partial ID on first mention,* and *complete the ID on second mention:*

```
      The former head of the United Nations (first mention) is

calling for...Former Secretary-General Javier Perez de Cuellar

(HAH-vee-air PEH-rez dah KWAY-ahr) (second mention)

says...Perez de Cuellar (thereafter) also wants...

                              -0-

      Senator Alan Simpson today proposed a sweeping revision of

U-S trade policy with Japan.  The Wyoming Republican said...
```

(Instead of "Wyoming Republican Senator Alan Simpson" or "Republican Senator Alan Simpson of Wyoming")

Frequently, the title or role of a newsmaker is more vital to the audience's immediate understanding of the story than the newsmaker's name. If this is the case, *start* by giving the title, then give the name in a follow-up sentence:

```
print:     FAIRWAY, Kan. (UPI)--"Doonesbury" creator Garry Trudeau
      will take a leave of absence early next year and temporarily
      cease production of his Pulitzer Prize-winning comic strip in
      more than 700 newspapers, Universal Press Syndicate officials
      said Wednesday.
           "I need a breather," Trudeau, 34, told Universal Press
      Syndicate officials in a telephone conversation from his home
      in New York City.
```

b'cast: Doonesbury is going on extended vacation -- or, more

exactly, his creator is. Garry Trudeau, whose "Doonesbury" comic

strip appears in some 700 newspapers, says he needs a rest...

or

The creator of "Doonesbury" says he'll take a leave of

absence next year--and take his comic strip along with him.

Cartoonist Garry Trudeau says...

Sometimes it is preferable in broadcasting to omit names altogether if they are obscure and not relevant to understanding the story:

print: SINGAPORE (UPI)--Garlic, known to scare away vampires and
members of the opposite sex, may soon do the same to
mosquitoes, two Indian scientists say.
      The pungent herb has been found to be an effective
pesticide, New Delhi scientists A. Banerji and S. Amonkarby
said in an article in the Singapore Scientist Tuesday.

b'cast: Two Indian scientists have come up with what they say is a

new and effective way to chase mosquitoes: squirt them with

garlic. The scientists report...

or

Bothered by mosquitoes? Two Indian scientists say they've

found a product that'll drive mosquitoes away. The product is

garlic. Of course, it may drive your friends away, too...

(This last version is an example of a "kicker," a light item often used at the end of a radio or TV newscast. More about kickers in Chapter 7.)

AGES

In print journalism, a person's age is given after his or her name, set off by commas.

      ST. LOUIS (UPI)--A couple said to be members of a white
supremacist group were ordered held without bail Tuesday on
charges they conspired to assassinate the Rev. Jesse Jackson.

```
     Londell Williams, 30, and his wife, Tammy J. Williams, 27,
of Washington, Mo., appeared Tuesday before U.S. Magistrate
Carol Jackson. She determined that there was enough of a
threat to the Democratic presidential candidate to hold the
couple without bail pending grand jury action.
     The pair are charged with conspiring to kill Jackson and
with possession of illegal weapons. They were arrested Friday
in Franklin County, Mo., about 50 miles west of St. Louis.
```

In broadcast journalism, a person's age *precedes* his or her name. "Year-old" is spelled out and hyphenated along with the age:

```
     A Missouri couple accused of plotting to kill Democratic

     presidential candidate Jesse Jackson has been ordered held

     without bail.

          Thirty-year-old Londell Williams and his 27-year-old wife,

     Tammy, were arrested last week about 50 miles west of St. Louis.

     They are said to be members of a white supremacist group.
```

Unlike print journalists, broadcasters do not automatically include people's ages in their stories. There's no hard-and-fast rule about when to include ages and when not—except that ages should be included whenever they are essential to the nature of a story. For example:

```
     A grandmother won today's seven-mile run in Chesterton.

     Forty-four-year-old Elise Harvey was met at the finish line by

     her daughter, 22-year-old Cornelia, and her granddaughter,

     18-month-old Elaine.
```

Sometimes an age may be given and a name omitted entirely, depending on the nature of the story and its distance from the immediate audience.

```
print:     NAPLES, Italy (UPI)--Two young muggers stripped their
           victim of his trousers Tuesday when he refused to hand over
           $4,100 in his pockets, police said. Enrico Barcella, 48,
           appeared at police headquarters in his underwear to report the
           robbery in Piazza Bovio in the center of Naples.
```

```
b'cast:    In Naples, Italy, a pair of muggers took more than a man's

           money today.  They also took his pants.

           Police say the muggers forced the 48-year-old man to strip

           when he refused to hand over the 41-hundred dollars stashed in

           his pockets.
```

NUMBERS

Many news stories deal in some fashion with numbers, not just in telling people's ages and amounts of money, but also in the form of statistics issued by companies, government agencies, researchers, international organizations, and so on. Journalists come upon an endless stream of statistics to measure everything from the economy to law enforcement.

Broadcast news organizations (which themselves rely on statistics to measure audiences: the ratings) treat numbers very differently from their colleagues in print—chiefly by reporting *fewer* of them. On paper, numbers can be reread at leisure. On radio and TV, numbers are heard or seen only once. Thus, a steady barrage of them can overwhelm the audience in a hurry.

Here's a comparatively short example of the statistics-laden copy streaming into newsrooms:

```
          WASHINGTON (AP)--Black family incomes grew during the
1980s, but they still fell well below Americans in general,
1990 Census figures released Friday show.
          A set of minority economic profiles released by the Census
Bureau show that black households had a median income of
$19,758 at the time of the 1990 census, up 84% from 1980.
During that period, white median household incomes climbed
68%, but at $31,435 were still ahead of blacks and Latinos.
          Median incomes of all Latino households climbed 77% during
the decade to $24,156 in 1990, the report showed.
          And the median income figure for all households was
$30,056, a 75% rise over 10 years. Median income means half of
all households brought in more than that amount and half less.
          The report concentrating on minorities also showed that
Asian households had the top overall incomes at $36,784. The
figure for American Indian households was $20,025. Comparable
figures for 1980 were not available.
          The profiles also addressed educational attainment and the
share of Americans in poverty. The findings included:
          Some 29.5% of blacks were below the poverty level in 1990
compared to 13.1% of Americans in general. Poverty rates were
9.8% for whites, 30.9% among American Indians, 14.1% for
Asians and 25.3% of Latinos.
          The age group with the highest poverty rate among blacks
was children under age 5, with 44% living in poverty. There
was a 33.4% poverty rate for Latino children under 5, and the
rate for that age group was 17.5% for Asians, 44.4% for
American Indians, 13.8% for whites and 10.1% for Americans
overall.
          The 1990 Census found that among blacks aged 25 and over,
63.1% had finished high school and 11.4% had completed
college. Comparable figures were 77.9% finishing high school
and 21.5% completing college among whites.
          Among American Indians, 65.5% had finished high school and
9.3% college, Asians had a 77.5% high school and 36.6% college
rate, while among Latinos 49.8% had completed high school and
9.2% college.
```

The news agency staffer who wrote that story probably spent a great deal of time combing through the raw data, as well as the Census Bureau's news release, before deciding which figures to include and in what order. The resulting story is in print style, aimed chiefly at newspapers. But no broadcast writer could hope to include more than a fraction of the information on radio or television. How, then, do we transform this material into broadcast style, both in terms of retaining its essential content and of making it highly "tellable" (readable) as a news script?

Before answering that question as specifically as we can, let's take a look at what we're striving for:

```
          Despite recent gains by blacks, the disparity between annual

black and white family income in this country remains high.

          Figures just released by the Census Bureau show the average

black family's income nearly doubled from 1980 to 1990.  But that
```

```
family's income remained less than two-thirds the average white

family's -- under 20-thousand-dollars as compared to over

30-thousand.
```

$$(:20)$$

No doubt about it: That is a *radical* transformation. (By now this should no longer surprise you.)

In fairness, we might have stretched this story to 30 seconds in order to include figures on Hispanic-Americans, Asian-Americans, and American Indians. Or, the story might form the basis for a much longer report on television; a TV reporter might be handed the news agency copy and assigned to bring back a completed "package"—a report combining visual elements, interviews, and narration—*showing* the results of the disparity in incomes. We'll examine how to do this later in this book. For now it's important to remember that *most* broadcast use of this story, if it is used *at all,* would be limited to versions running between 20 and 30 seconds.

So we return to our question: What are the specifics of transforming statistical information into broadcast style? Here they are:

1. Choose only a *few* numbers—the ones you deem the most important.
2. Never report a statistic without telling its *significance.*
3. *Round off* numbers whenever possible.
4. *Spell out* the numbers *one through nine.* Use *figures* for all other numbers—*except* when the number occurs as the *first word of a sentence;* in that case, spell it out.
   (note previous example: "**Thirty**-year-old Londell Williams . . .")
5. *Spell out* any numbers *subject to error in pronunciation.* The year "2010," for example. Should the anchor say "Twenty-ten" or "Two-thousand-ten"? The writer must decide, then script it that way.

   Street addresses are another example. Addresses are expressed differently in different localities, according to local custom. The address "3049 E. Main St." may be expressed as "three-oh-four-nine East Main Street" in one locality but "thirty forty-nine East Main" in another. It's important to follow local usage.
6. *Hyphenate* connected numbers.
7. *Avoid long numbers.* A number scripted as "4,372,612" is destined to cause sight-reading trouble. If it is vital to give the exact number, script it as "four million, 372-thousand, six-hundred-12." Otherwise, round it off ("nearly four-and-a-half million").
8. *Spell out all signs, fractions, and decimals.* "$600" becomes "six hundred dollars" or "600 dollars." "18¼" becomes "eighteen and a quarter." "20.7 million" becomes "20-point-7 million."
9. Do *not* use Roman numerals, mathematical symbols, or print-style abbreviations for weights and measures.
   Super Bowl XXXV should be written as "Super Bowl 35" or "Super Bowl Thirty-five."
   Pope John Paul II is "Pope John Paul the Second," and Shakespeare's *Henry V* is "Henry the Fifth."
   Einstein's formula "e = mc^2" becomes "E equals M-C squared."
   Always spell out "plus," "minus," "times," "divided by," and so on.
   If a college wide-receiver stands 6′3″ and weighs 220 lb., a broadcast-style description should say he "stands six-three and weighs two-twenty."
10. Whenever possible, *personalize* numbers for your audience. Example:

```
print:      BIGTOWN (CNS)--The City Council voted on Thursday to raise
            $2.4 billion through a 1% retail sales surtax, effective next
            Monday, to finance construction of a crosstown expressway.
```

```
b'cast:      The City Council passed a surtax today that'll add a penny

             to each dollar you spend at the store.

                  The retail surtax of one percent goes into effect next

             Monday.  It's designed to raise nearly two-and-a-half billion

             dollars for a new crosstown expressway.
```

The foregoing is a very effective way to relate numbers to a viewing and listening audience. It tells the effect of numbers on *them*. In other words, it puts the audience in the story.

11. Remember that the foregoing rules apply only to news copy voiced by the anchor. *Text appearing in electronic graphics and titles reverts to print style.*

ABBREVIATIONS AND ACRONYMS

By now you are sufficiently aware of the need to spell things out in broadcast news copy. So let's formalize it.

Rule:
Do not use abbreviations.

That said, let's note a few exceptions. "Mr.," "Mrs.," and "Dr." are okay, as are military rank designations such as "Gen.," "Sgt.," "Lt.," etc. Among clergical titles, "Rev." is clear enough, but *not* "Msgr.," which should be written out ("Monsignor").

Among political designations, "Sen." and "Rep." are okay, but *not* "Cong." Why? Because an anchor seeing "Cong. Pat Schroeder" might say "Congress*man*," realizing too late that it should have been "Congress*woman*." The same applies to all titles where English makes a distinction as to gender: Chairman(woman), Spokesman(woman), etc.*

What about all those government agencies—FCC, FAA, FHA, SEC, and so on? They should be *hyphenated* in broadcast copy: F-C-C, F-A-A, S-E-C. However, if the agency is relatively obscure (that is, if most listeners wouldn't recognize it by its initials), then it should be *named* on first mention and its letters used only on subsequent mention:

```
            The Securities and Exchange Commission filed suit against

       two Wall Street firms today for alleged stock manipulation.  The

       S-E-C suit charges that the two firms...
```

Once again, the practice is to write things the way they are to be said. Thus,

```
            N-double-A-C-P leader Benjamin Hooks says...(not "NAACP" or

       "N-A-A-C-P")
```

---

*The subject of gender in language has become rather touchy in recent years, largely because of the feminist movement and the major advances of women in the professions, including broadcast journalism (where women now number roughly half of the people entering the field). Unfortunately, the battle against "sexism" in language has led to certain excesses. Sometimes you will hear newly coined titles like "Chairperson" and "Spokesperson." Most broadcast news departments reject such designations as being uncolloquial.

In the effort to avoid "sexist" language, some writers lapse into grammatical errors, such as "The consumer gets *their* money's worth." Proper English requires the masculine pronoun (he, him, his) when the gender of the singular antecedent is unspecified. To be grammatically correct, the sentence should read "The consumer gets *his* money's worth."

Because broadcast newswriting should follow the rules of grammar, and because using nonsexist language is a good idea, the solution is to put such constructions in the *plural*: "Consumers get *their* money's worth."

As for acronyms (initial letters pronounced as a word), the practice is to begin with a capital letter and put all remaining letters in lowercase. Thus,

```
        Nato commanders met in Brussels today...

                        -0-

        Senator Murphy said Nasa's budget should be increased

    drastically...

                        -0-

        In Vienna, the Opec ministers ended their meeting without a

    decision on oil prices...
```

Some initials and acronyms are so obscure as to require virtual translation to be comprehensible. For example, CINCPAC, which is pronounced "Sinkpak" and which is the Pentagon abbreviation for "Commander-in-Chief, Pacific," should be rendered as "The U.S. Pacific Command" or "U-S Naval headquarters in the Pacific." In other words, whenever you come upon an abbreviation or an acronym for an agency whose function you do not know, find out what that agency does and include that information, if pertinent, in your story:

```
        The Government Accounting Office -- that's the agency that

    oversees federal spending -- says the Commerce Department is

    overspending its budget.  The G-A-O says the Commerce Department

    spends 40 million dollars a year just for paper...
```

LISTS

Like long series of numbers and long titles, long lists can bog down newscasters and listeners alike. An example of a "list story":

```
        WARSAW--Crowds of Poles jammed stores throughout the
    country Tuesday to buy milk, eggs, bread, salt, sugar, frozen
    meat, canned goods, and other food products affected by
    drastic government austerity moves that will raise prices by
    as much as 50 percent by Thursday.
```

If you tried to say all that on the air, you'd risk losing listeners well short of the checkout counter. For broadcast use, the shopping list must be shortened radically:

```
        Poles rushed today to stock up on basic foodstuffs to beat

    huge price increases set for later this week.  The Polish

    government has decreed price hikes of as much as 50 percent on

    bread, sugar, and other foods.
```

Another type of list story is an account of a newsmaker's spoken or written remarks beginning with "I would like to make four points. First . . ." or "The panel makes the following recommendations: 1 . . ." followed by a point-by-point list. Print journalists can retain the newsmaker's structure ("The President also made these points:"). But that won't work on radio or TV because of time constraints; it would simply eat up too much time to respect the newsmaker's organization. Therefore, broadcast newswriting requires the rejection of the "list of points" structure and the substitution of straightforward wording:

```
      ...The President also said he has asked the Commerce

Secretary to work up a new trade policy with Eastern Europe.

On still another matter, the President said he will ask Congress

to increase the budget of the Drug Enforcement Agency.
```

Getting rid of the list structure enables you to pick and choose among the points, according to your news judgment, and to keep your sentences short.

LABELS

People can be touchy about what you call them. They usually don't like to be labeled. Nevertheless, the news media, always on the lookout for verbal shorthand, routinely label people whether they like it or not.

During the 1992 presidential campaign, for example, businessman H. Ross Perot of Texas was routinely identified as "Texas billionaire Ross Perot." Other labels pinned on him were "Dallas computer-systems tycoon Ross Perot" and "Unannounced presidential candidate Ross Perot." Perot himself said he disliked all such labels but understood journalists' need for them.

Broadcast style tends to emulate print style in labeling newsmakers—with the important exception, as noted earlier, of splitting long identifications over two or more sentences. Such labels consist mainly of nouns used as adjectives in front of a person's name (and known in broadcast news jargon as "multiple preceding adjectives"). The language is neutral; that is, it carries no hint of the newswriter's personal beliefs or values. "Homeless advocates," for example, is neutral shorthand for "people championing the rights of the homeless."

However, some cases are not so simple:

```
      MILWAUKEE (AP)--More than 500 abortion protesters jammed
sidewalks outside a women's clinic, waved photos of
dismembered fetuses, sang hymns and shouted Bible verses
Saturday. Seventy-seven people were arrested.
      More than 500 abortion-rights advocates surrounded the
clinic's entrance and escorted 16 women with appointments
inside, while the more than 500 anti-abortion activists
protested.
      Some of the protesters gathered in groups to pray. Others
wept as women entered the Summit Women's Health Organization
clinic.
      "It's anti-God," said Jim Minnema, 46, an electrician who
lives 60 miles north of Milwaukee." As Christians, we must
rescue those going to the slaughter, or we will have to answer
for it."
      Some protesters ran across the street in front of the
clinic, dropped to the sidewalk and tried to crawl through the
legs of police officers guarding entrances.
      Police Lt. Vincent Flores said 77 abortion protesters,
including 15 children, were arrested, most on disorderly
conduct charges.
      Outside the Summit clinic, abortion rights advocates
chanted "Milwaukee has spoken, the clinics will stay open!"
```

Perhaps no issue in American life has been as controversial as abortion. People on all sides tend to become emotional about it—to the point where they angrily reject some of the labels ascribed to them by the news media. For example, people favoring a woman's legal right to an abortion prefer to be called "pro-choice" rather than "pro-abortion." Those opposing the legal right to abortion, while content with the label "anti-abortion," prefer to be called "pro-life." It is hard, sometimes impossible, for journalists to please everyone. Nevertheless, broadcast rewriters should make a stab at it:

```
     In Milwaukee today, a face-off between demonstrators on both

sides of the abortion issue...

     About 500 anti-abortion protestors gathered at an abortion

clinic...which had been surrounded by an equal number of

pro-choice advocates.

     A total of 77 abortion opponents were arrested when they

tried to break through police lines.
```

(:15)

Many news departments have formal policies on the wording to use in controversial cases. Frequently, the policy comes in the form of a memo from the news director or executive producer. It is a staff journalist's obligation to know company policy—and to follow it.

EXERCISES

1. The following is a statistics-laden news-agency story. Write a 30-second broadcast version slugged WORKING WOMEN.

```
     WASHINGTON (AP)--The problem of women having to dress the
kids, wash the clothes, cook the meals, make the beds and take
out the garbage--all before they go to work to earn less than
men--is a worldwide inequity, according to an International
Labor Organization report released Friday.
     Nearly everywhere in the world, women work harder and earn
less than men, and the gap in many countries is widening, the
report by the U.N. agency said.
     Women work more hours a week, including housework, than
men in every part of the world except North America and
Australia, the report estimates.
     They work the hardest in Africa. The report estimates that
African women work 67 hours a week, compared to 53 for men. In
Asia, women work 62 hours a week while men average 48 hours a
week.
     In North America and Australia, men work 49 hours a week,
while women work 47.5, the report said.
     In Western Europe, women average 48 hours, men 43; Japan's
women work 56 hours and men 54; in Latin America, women work
60 hours to 54 for men.
     Australian women are at the top of the pay equality scale,
with salaries increasing from 86% of men's in 1980 to nearly
88% in 1990, the most recent year for which figures were
available.
     U.S. women's salaries increased from 60% of men's to 65%
over about the same period, and Canadian women increased their
salaries by nearly the same percentages.
     Women lost ground in Japan, with earnings falling from
53.8% in 1980 to 50.7% in 1990. A seniority wage system in
Japan favors men, and women are concentrated in lower-paid
jobs, the report said.
```

2. Slug the following story SPACE LAUNCH and write a 25-second broadcast version, taking care to express names, ages, and pronunciation in broadcast style:

> MOSCOW (AP)--The Soyuz TM-15 spacecraft with two Russians and a French researcher on board blasted off Monday on a mission to the Mir space station that is to include the removal of the defunct hammer-and-sickle flag.
>
> Live television showed a perfect liftoff at 10:09 a.m. Moscow time from the steppes of Kazakhstan, home to much of the once-mighty Soviet space program.
>
> The spacecraft that blasted off from the Baikonur cosmodrome was scheduled to link up with the Mir station, which is badly in need of new equipment, on Wednesday.
>
> Russian cosmonauts Anatoly Solovyov, a 44-year-old space veteran, and Sergei Avdeyev, 36, will deploy new equipment to help keep the station aloft. They are to remain aboard until January.
>
> Frenchman Michel Tognini, 42, will return to Earth next month after completing experiments.
>
> The astronauts are scheduled to remove the old Soviet hammer-and-sickle flag from one of the space station's masts-- a final, symbolic blow to what was once a proud Soviet space program.

3. Slug the following story PERKINS OBIT, and write a 20-second broadcast version.

> LOS ANGELES (AP)--Anthony Perkins, who played the murderous motel keeper Norman Bates in the classic Hitchcock thriller "Psycho," died Saturday of AIDS complications. He was 60.
>
> Perkins died in the bedroom of his Hollywood home at 4:06 p.m. with his wife and sons at his side, said his publicist, Leslee Dart.
>
> Earlier in the week, Perkins made a statement about his condition, Dart said. "There are many who believe that this disease is God's vengeance," Perkins's statement said, "but I believe it was sent to teach people how to love and understand and have compassion for each other."
>
> Other stars who have died of AIDS include Rock Hudson, Brad Davis, Amanda Blake, Robert Reed, Liberace, and rock star Freddy Mercury.
>
> Perkins, the son of stage and film actor Osgood Perkins, gained fame playing awkward, often neurotic young men. Later, his name became synonymous with horror films.
>
> He broke into movies in 1953, appearing in "The Actress" with Spencer Tracy and Jean Simmons. He won an Oscar nomination for best supporting actor playing Gary Cooper's son in "Friendly Persuasion" in 1956, and portrayed baseball player Jimmy Piersall in the 1957 film "Fear Strikes Out."
>
> But it was "Psycho," director Alfred Hitchcock's classic 1960 horror film, that made Perkins--and his character Norman Bates--film legends.
>
> In 1973, he married photographer Berry Berenson, sister of actress Marisa Berenson.
>
> Besides his wife, Perkins is survived by sons Osgood Perkins, 18, and Elvis Perkins, 16.

"When" and "Where"

5

Now let's tackle two more of journalism's Five W's, beginning with "When."

You will have noticed by now that in our broadcast-style copy we have been saying "today" instead of naming the day of the week. This is not by accident.

IMMEDIACY

Broadcast journalism's key advantage over print journalism is the speed of its delivery. Because a morning newspaper must be run through the presses, baled, distributed, and delivered to homes, offices, newsstands, and vending machines, it must usually be "put to bed" before midnight. Any new developments occurring after deadline must await the next edition—which may be as long 24 hours away.

Radio and television, on the other hand, can deliver the news immediately. The only delays are until the next scheduled newscast, usually no more than minutes (or at most a few hours) away. And all-news radio and TV abide no delays whatsoever; they report new developments almost instantaneously.

This built-in speed advantage is called *immediacy,* and broadcasters exploit it relentlessly. In fact, modern broadcasters are reluctant to use the word "today" when they can specify "this morning," "tonight," or "at this very moment." The expression "This just in . . ." has become part of the national vocabulary.

Thus, if we can make any absolute rule about stating the When element in broadcast style, it is this:

> *Rule:*
> *Always use wording that shows immediacy.*

Here's a list of "When" words and locutions broadcasters commonly use to exploit the immediacy of radio and TV news:

- today
- tonight
- this morning
- this afternoon
- this evening
- yesterday
- tomorrow
- last night
- the day before yesterday
- the day after tomorrow
- last week
- next week

- in a few days
- a few days ago
- next Sunday (Thursday, Friday, etc.)
- a week from Thursday (Sunday, Friday, etc.)
- by next week
- this (last, next) month
- "This just in . . ."
- moments ago
- at this hour
- within the hour
- a short time ago

We may have missed some, but you get the idea. In broadcast news, the "When" element is expressed in relation to *now*, the moment the story is on the air.

We don't want listeners and viewers to lose the thread of the story by having to recalculate the When element in their heads. If the date is April 14 and tax returns are due on April 15, we do not want to go on the air and say "The tax filing deadline is April 15th . . ." because people might pause to think, "Well, let's see, today is April 14th, and tax returns are due April—Hey, that's *tomorrow!*" We do the calculating for them. On the air we say, "The tax filing deadline is tomorrow."

Exploiting broadcasting's immediacy requires far more than just throwing in a "today" or a "moments ago." It requires keeping on top of the news in order to be able to air the latest angles of stories and to be prepared for what happens next. Depending on which fresh story elements are available at air time, the wording broadcasters use at 6 P.M. is different from the wording at 3 P.M.; it changes again at 10 P.M., again after midnight, again in mid-morning, again at noon, and again in mid-afternoon.

Proper use of the When element in broadcast newswriting also depends on understanding the heart of the broadcast-style sentence—the verb and its attendant voice, person, and tense.

VERBS

Broadcast verbs should be short and active. "Short" is easy enough to understand: *buy* instead of "purchase," *say* instead of "declare," and so on. But "active" gives newcomers (and some veterans) a lot of trouble. So let's take a few minutes to revisit English 101.

Voice

The "voice" of a verb is either active or passive. When a verb shows the subject of a sentence to be doing the action,

He sees the ball

the verb is in the *active* voice. When the verb shows that the subject is being acted upon,

The ball is seen by him

the verb is in the *passive* voice.

So when we say broadcast verbs should be active, we mean they should be written in the active voice; the subject of the sentence should be acting upon the object of the sentence. Whenever possible, a print-style news agency story written in the passive voice should be rewritten in the active voice.

Before this gets to sound too much like grammatical jargon, let's cite a typical example:

```
      TAMPA, Fla. (AP)--More than four tons of cocaine were
discovered in hollowed-out Brazilian lumber bound for U.S.
cities, federal authorities announced Wednesday.
```

The verb in that sentence—"were discovered"—is in the passive voice. And "discover" is a long word compared to "find." So putting the verb in broadcast style requires both a change of word and a change of voice. To do that, you must rearrange the sentence:

```
Federal agents have found more than four tons of cocaine

hidden in Brazilian lumber bound for U-S cities.
```

By now your eyes should be growing accustomed to the form of broadcast-style sentences. But in case they are not, please read both the print and broadcast versions aloud. Perhaps your ears will tell you what your eyes may have missed—namely, that the broadcast version is easier to say and easier for the listener to follow. And see what a change of voice does for the following:

```
The Supreme Court today handed down a ruling on civil

rights...
```

(instead of: "A ruling on civil rights was handed down today by the Supreme Court . . .")

–0–

```
Governor Clements has announced his stand on the proposed

highway tax...
```

(instead of: "A stand on the highway tax was announced today by Governor Clements . . .")

–0–

```
Observers saw the action as a thinly veiled response to...
```

(instead of: "The action was seen by observers as a thinly veiled response to . . .")

Why the active voice? Because most of the time it is

1. Clearer
2. More concise
3. More natural to the rhythms of spoken English

That said, using the active voice is not an ironclad rule. There are exceptions. Most of the time, it is better to say "Police arrested so-and-so" rather than "So-and-so was arrested by police." However, in the case of a well-known person, a "name in the news," opening the story with the name works as an attention-getter, even though the verb winds up in the passive voice. Thus,

```
Pope John Paul was released from the hospital today...
```

(Instead of "The hospital released Pope John Paul . . .")

–0–

    A New Jersey senator **was indicted** today on charges of...

(Instead of "A grand jury indicted a New Jersey senator today on charges of . . .")

    Please remember that by using conversational language, you can often avoid the active/passive dilemma altogether:

    Pope John Paul the Second went home today. The Pontiff left the hospital less than a week after intestinal surgery to remove a benign tumor...

–0–

    A New Jersey senator is in legal trouble tonight, following his indictment on influence-peddling charges.

Person

    Okay, back to English 101. Grammatically, "person" refers to the relationship between an action (expressed by a verb) and the person being addressed. The distinguishing pronouns are:

- First Person: I, we
- Second Person: you
- Third Person: he, she, it, they

    In broadcast journalism, just as in print journalism, the expression of the verb/person relationship is overwhelmingly in the third person. A reporter may occasionally write a first-person "eyewitness" story saying "I saw this" or "I'm told that," and a writer may have occasion to use a phrase like "As we reported earlier." But as narrative, broadcast storytelling usually assumes the detached viewpoint inherent in the third person.

    Where print and broadcast journalism differ markedly is in the use of the second person—*you*. As we've noted repeatedly, broadcast newswriting favors the informality of everyday speech, and when people converse, they throw in a lot of "yous." Even though the anchor/listener "conversation" is one-sided, the reality of one person talking to another should be exploited. A "you" may refer to viewers and listeners directly, or it may be impersonal, the equivalent of the French *on* or the German *man*. Either way, the effect of "you" is to make broadcast newswriting even more like traditional storytelling.

    We used some examples of the second person earlier:

    If **you** think the world's crowded now, just wait till the year 2000...

–0–

    The City Council passed a surtax today that'll add a penny to each dollar **you** spend at the store...

In broadcast news, there is also a special use of the third person plural "they." "They" may be used like the impersonal "you" as a substitute for "people" or "observers," or, in a limited way, for official sources. For example, people normally say something on the order of "They say it'll rain tomorrow." "They" may refer to an official weather forecast heard on radio or TV, or merely to an idle remark overheard at the supermarket. Broadcasters have the freedom to use "they" informally from time to time—provided that they go on to specify who "they" are:

```
     They came from all over the Southwest -- young people

packing a fair grounds near San Bernardino for what's being

billed as the largest rock music festival since Woodstock...


                              -o-


     They're calling it the largest stock swindle in U-S history.

The Justice Department has charged two Wall Street firms with

bilking thousands of retired people of their life savings...
```

After a while you will begin to recognize the kind of news agency copy that lends itself to "you" and/or "they" rewriting. Typically, it will be a feature story where the action itself (the What element) is more compelling than the specific person(s) who did it (the Who element). For example:

```
          NEW YORK (AP)--The first bales of the nation's best-known
     garbage collection were unloaded, inspected and burned Tuesday
     after being towed 6,000 miles on a barge, rejected by six
     states and three nations, challenged in court and lampooned on
     television.
          "Good riddance," city Sanitation Commissioner Brendan
     Sexton said as he oversaw the work at the Southwest Brooklyn
     Incinerator.
          It was the beginning of the end of the five-month saga of
     the garbage barge. Incineration of the 3,186 tons of trash is
     expected to take about two weeks, and the ashes will be
     trucked away to be buried at a landfill at Islip, on Long
     Island.
          The barge set out on March 22 from a private dock in
     Queens. The barge was turned away from a North Carolina
     landfill for lack of proper permits. That started the 6,000-
     mile trip, on which the cargo met with angry rejections from
     Alabama, Mississippi, Louisiana, Texas, Florida, Mexico,
     Belize and the Bahamas.
```

Some broadcast versions will retain the third person (but will nevertheless put the story in the active voice):

```
          In New York, sanitation workers have at last begun

destroying that bargeload of garbage nobody wanted...
```

However, by using "you" and "they," a broadcast writer can do a more arresting job of storytelling:

```
          You remember that bargeload of garbage nobody wanted?  Well,

today they finally started to burn it.
```

> Sanitation workers destroyed the first bales of the more
> than 3,000 tons of garbage at an incinerator in Brooklyn, New
> York. The trash had gone on a barge ride that covered 6,000
> miles in five months. Six states and three foreign countries
> refused to accept it.
>
> Are **they** happy the odyssey is over? Well, in the words of
> the New York Sanitation Commissioner, "Good riddance."

Viewers and listeners are going to remember a story written that way. It is storytelling as only radio and television can do, relying on the informality and inflections of spoken English.

But a word of caution: The trick to using "you" or "they" effectively is not to overdo it. Most news stories involve serious matters and thus require a serious approach. So save "you" and "they" for stories where they do not detract from the seriousness of the subject matter.

Tenses

We've seen that the When element in broadcast news is expressed according to two factors:

1. The time an event occurs
2. The air time of the newscast

Grammatically, this entails choosing the verb tense that best demonstrates immediacy. Thus, our last stop at English 101 requires a review of verb tenses. We'll use "say," which is by far the most frequently written verb in broadcast news.

· infinitive:	to say
· present participle:	saying
· past participle:	said
· present gerund:	saying
· **present tense:**	**say, says; is (are) saying**
· **past tense:**	**said**
· past imperfect tense:	was (were) saying
· **present perfect tense:**	**has (have) said**
· past (plu)perfect tense:	had said
· **future tense:**	**will say; will be saying**
· future perfect tense:	will have said
· conditional future tense:	would say; would be saying
· conditional future perfect:	would have said

The four boldfaced tenses—present, past, present perfect, and future—are the ones used overwhelmingly in broadcast news copy. Context and shades of meaning may occasionally require use of other tenses, but such cases are rare. Much of the time, you will be changing the verb tenses you see in print-style news copy. Because the present—the here-and-now—is broadcasting's trump card, to be played whenever possible, you will often be changing a print-style past tense into a broadcast-style present tense. And in compound sentences, you will be changing the past/conditional to the present/future.

Now let's translate all this grammar into detailed guidelines and examples:

1. Use the present tense whenever possible, especially for events that are occurring at air time (known as "breaking news").

The school board **is meeting** (**at this hour**) on the teachers'
request for a pay raise...

-0-

A fifth hook—and—ladder company **is on its way** (or **is en
route**) to a three—alarm fire on the South Side...

-0-

Senator Danforth **is** the guest speaker tonight at a downtown
fundraiser...

2. Use the present tense for statements or conditions that, although having occurred earlier, are still true at air time.

Three Ridgewood businessmen **are** under indictment (**this
evening**) for alleged bid rigging at Westwood Mall...

-0-

The District Attorney **is lodging** fraud charges against the
Widget Corporation...

-0-

Building Commissioner Rex Danforth **is announcing** his
retirement...

3. Because statements by newsmakers and allegations from official sources usually require you to write compound sentences, use the broadcast-style present/future or present/past tenses in place of the print-style past/past or past/conditional.

The White House **says** President Jones **will veto** the new trade
bill...(present/future)

-0-

Senator Smith **says** he **will not** (or **won't**) run for a third
term...(present/future)

-0-

Police **say** the suspect **fired** twice before escaping...
(present/past)

-0-

```
            The indictment alleges the businessmen conspired to rig

      construction bids on the Westwood Mall...(present/past)
```

4. Use the simple past tense for one-time events that took place shortly before air time.

```
            Fire destroyed a warehouse this morning on West Eighth

      Street.

                                  -0-

            A bridge over the Lackawanna River collapsed a short

      time ago.  First reports say no one was hurt.
```

5. Switch to the present perfect tense as the time lag widens between event and air time.

```
            Fire has destroyed a warehouse on West Eighth Street.

                                  -0-

            A bridge has collapsed over the Lackawanna River.

                                  -0-

            Three Ridgewood businessmen have been indicted on

      bid-rigging charges.
```

Many fledgling newswriters get confused on the wording of past tense and present perfect tense sentences. Here's a guideline: *include* the specific When element with the simple past tense, and *omit* the specific "when" with the present perfect:

```
            A one-armed man swam the English Channel today, in both

      directions.  (past)

                                  -0-

            A one-armed man has swum the English Channel, in both

      directions.  (present perfect)

                                  -0-

            Peru this morning warned foreign fishermen to stay out of

      its territorial waters.  (past)

                                  -0-

            Peru has warned foreign fishermen to stay out of its

      territorial waters.  (present perfect)
```

or

```
Peru is warning foreign fishermen...(present)
```

Again, consider the flexibility of *spoken* English, allowing broadcasters to break the grammatical constraints of written English:

```
It's never been done before -- a one-armed man swimming

round-trip across the English Channel...

                         -0-

A warning from Peru to foreign fishermen: Stay out!
```

Using the foregoing guidelines, let's take a typical local news story and see how the broadcast-style When element works in practice. Situation: A fire breaks out at a warehouse at 10 A.M. and is put out by 10:30 A.M. Only between 10 and 10:30 may we use the present tense on the air:

```
Firefighters are battling a warehouse fire on West Eighth

Street...
```

or

```
Firefighters at this hour are at the scene of a burning

warehouse on West Eighth Street...
```

By 11 A.M., the fire having been extinguished, we must switch (obviously) to the past tense for the 11 A.M. News and the Noon News. But we can still show immediacy by saying "this morning."

```
Fire destroyed a warehouse on West Eighth Street this

morning.
```

or

```
Fire destroyed a warehouse on West Eighth Street a little

while ago.
```

For the 1 P.M. and 2 P.M. News, we can still say "this morning." After all, it happened only a few hours ago. We will still sound fresh and immediate.

But by 3:00 P.M., we risk sounding stale if we retain "this morning." (In the news business, staleness sets in *very* quickly.) We have two options. We can switch to "today":

```
Fire today destroyed a warehouse on West Eighth Street.
```

or

```
Fire destroyed a warehouse today on West Eighth Street.
```

or we can switch to the *present perfect* tense:

```
Fire has destroyed a warehouse on West Eighth Street.
```

What we have done in each case is to slightly de-emphasize the time lag between the event and our reporting of it. And in so doing, we have preserved our *sound* (or "image") of immediacy.

To show you how far this goes, let's continue with the present example. The word "today" or use of the present perfect tense will carry us through the Evening News (radio or TV). But by the Late News (10:00 P.M. or 11:00 P.M.), not only will the story be stale but it will also be very close to ancient history. (In broadcasting, ancient history is hot on the heels of staleness.) So once again, we must find a way to preserve our immediacy. By Late News time, we want very much to be able to say "tonight." So we must find a legitimate way, both in news gathering and in language, to remain on top of the story.

```
Investigators tonight are ruling out arson in a fire that
    destroyed a warehouse on West Eighth Street.
```

or

```
Fire investigators tonight are probing the cause of the
  blaze that leveled a warehouse on West Eighth Street today.
```

This way, we have not only found a way to get "tonight" into the lead, we have been able to return to the present tense as well.

And to push the example a step farther, let's say it's now the next morning—nearly 24 hours after the event (which, for the record, is fast receding into prehistoric times). If we report the story at all, it must only be in terms of a fresh and immediate angle.

```
Fire investigators are still puzzled this morning over the
  cause of that warehouse fire on West Eighth Street.
```

Okay, that's not all that fresh. The point is, that's the kind of wording and approach you must use if you decide to use the story at all. It emphasizes what is happening *now* and treats what happened yesterday as common knowledge.

Contractions and "Not"

Contractions may be forbidden in most print journalism, but they are very useful in broadcast journalism because they are characteristic of informal speech. We've used lots of examples in our model stories—and you should use them, too.

However, be careful in using *negative* contractions and the word "not." In news stories, "not" is often used to stress something important and out of the ordinary. If you write (for example),

```
          President Jones says he won't visit the Philippines next

     month...
```

the meaning may in fact be clear enough. But if the development was unexpected (that is, if the visit had been on the president's schedule), you should consider avoiding the contraction in order to stress the change in plans:

```
          President Jones says he will not visit the Philippines next

     month...
```

In their scripts, many newswriters and anchors like to underline the word "not," just to make sure the word is not overlooked and the meaning of the story therefore reversed. Another way NOT to lose "not" is to capitalize it.

Still another method of avoiding the pitfalls of "not" is to choose completely alternative wording. For example,

```
          President Jones has cancelled plans to visit the

     Philippines...
```

PLACEMENT OF "WHEN"

A few words about where to put the word "today," "tonight," and so on: Take the sentence "The White House announced President Jones will visit Mexico today." The meaning of such wording is that the *trip* begins today. That's probably not what the writer meant. If the meaning is the *announcement* came today, the sentence should read, "The White House announced today that President Jones will visit Mexico."

That was a rather obvious example. Even so, it illustrates the general rule that in broadcasting, **the "when" should be placed close to the verb it modifies.**

```
     No:       A bomb exploded at the El Al ticket office in Manhattan,

          wounding 12 people this morning.

                              -0-

     Yes:      A bomb exploded this morning at the El Al ticket office in

          Manhattan, wounding 12 people.

                              -0-

     No:       Today a truck collided with a school bus on Interstate-80,

          injuring six children and the bus driver.

                              -0-

     Yes:      A truck collided today with a school bus...
```

or

```
Yes:        A truck ran into a school bus today on Interstate-80,

       injuring...
```

As with so many things concerning writing, there are exceptions, especially when we wish to maintain informality or to achieve stylistic effect:

```
       Last month, President Jones said he did not intend to visit

Mexico in the near future. Today he changed his mind. The White

House announced the president will go to Mexico City and Cancun

next Friday and Saturday...
```

"WHERE" IN BROADCAST STYLE

Newspapers and news magazines often publish a map alongside a news story to help readers pinpoint the location. Readers may pause at any point to study the map, then resume reading.

Television news uses maps also, sometimes showing them full-screen, but more often confining them to the electronic "window" over the anchor's shoulder. Even so, there is no "dateline" to refer back to. Thus, most of the time in television, and *all* of the time in radio, it is necessary to express the Where element in terms the audience can easily understand.

As is our custom, we begin with a print-style model:

```
        PHOENIX (AP)--Hundreds of U.S. and Mexican firefighters on
   Sunday battled fires that burned thousands of acres of brush
   and timber on both sides of the border and raced across an
   Apache Indian reservation, officials said.
        A forest fire that started in Mexico charred 6,000 acres,
   about 3,500 on the U.S. side of the border near Nicksville,
   and damaged two structures in a park picnic area, said U.S.
   Forest Service spokesman Jim Payne in Phoenix.
        Payne called the blaze "a raging monster out of control"
   and said it had threatened ranch homes in the Coronado
   National Monument, about 50 miles south of Tucson, before they
   were saved by crews who started backfires.
        Nearly 200 miles north, a second fire that was sparked by
   lightning Friday on a reservation near Cibecue had burned more
   than 500 acres of timber and brush by early Sunday, Payne
   said.
```

Stylistically, that story offers all sorts of rewriting challenges for broadcast journalists. Especially appealing as a lead is the quote from the forest ranger (who called the forest fire "a raging monster out of control"—words that may be somewhat overdramatic but which certainly do provide a terrific opening). You are also familiar by now with many of the routine changes required to achieve broadcast style: changing "Sunday" to a more immediate "today" or "this morning," switching to the present tense, reorganizing the structure to tell each element separately (there are two fires, hundreds of miles apart), shortening the sentences, keeping the numbers to a minimum, moving attribution to the start of sentences, and so forth. That takes care of Who, What, When, and Why/How. But handling the Where element is somewhat tricky and requires closer examination.

The AP datelined the story "Phoenix" because that is where the agency got its information (from the U.S. Forest Service). But the events themselves were taking place hundreds of miles away. That is often the case in the news business; reporters may be forced to rely on public or private agencies (which have their own internal communications systems) to provide information that might otherwise be inaccessible. So there are really two Where elements to consider:

1. In writing stories for radio and TV, the first priority is telling the location of the events themselves.
2. The second priority is telling the location of the source of information. But if that source is trustworthy, it is permissible to omit its location altogether.

Here, then, are some of the ways broadcasters might rewrite this story:

A forest fire is raging out of control **along the Arizona—Mexico border**. The U—S Forest Service says the fire has destroyed 6,000 acres so far, mostly **on the Arizona side near Nicksville**.

Farther north, a brush fire charred more than 500 acres, including an Apache Indian reservation **near Cibecue**.

There are no reports of injuries in either fire.

—0—

"A raging monster out of control." That's how a U—S Forest Service spokesman describes a forest fire still burning **along the Arizona—Mexico border**. He says the fire has charred 6,000 acres so far, more than half of them **on the U—S side near Nicksville**.

About 200 miles north of that fire, a brush fire triggered by lightning swept across an Apache Indian reservation. There are no reports of injuries.

—0—

Hundreds of U—S and Mexican firefighters are battling a forest fire **along the Arizona—Mexico border**. A U—S Forest Service spokesman **in Phoenix** says the fire has destroyed 6,000 acres so far, mostly **on the Arizona side**. The spokesman calls the fire "a raging monster out of control."

In central Arizona, a brush fire raced across an Apache Indian reservation —— but there are no reports of injuries.

Each of these versions is short, running about 20 seconds. However, despite their brevity, each paints a clear mental image of the *geography* of the story. It is a judgment call whether or not to place the Forest Service spokesman in Phoenix. It is a judgment call whether or not to place the fires near Nicksville and Cibecue; both communities are so small they do not appear on many maps. But since virtually everyone knows where Arizona and Mexico are, it is vital to situate the action in geographical terms that the audience can understand. We can formulate this into a rule:

Rule:
Always state an unfamiliar location
in relation to a more familiar one.

That rule is worth closer consideration, because some news agency stories contain little help with geography (which is why we suggested several chapters ago that you provide yourself with an almanac or world atlas). Here's an example of how consulting a map can help you draw a geographical picture for your audience:

print model: TAYLORSVILLE, Ky--A coal mine collapsed during the early
                   shift Monday morning, killing at least 11 miners and sending
                   at least 14 others to nearby hospitals, authorities said.

broadcast rewrites: A coal mine collapse killed at least 11 miners today in

Taylorsville, Kentucky, about 30 miles southeast of Louisville.

At least 14 miners were injured.

                                        -0-

At least 11 miners died in a coal mine collapse this morning

in the **town of Taylorsville, southeast of Louisville, Kentucky.**

                                        -0-

A coal mine collapse **in Kentucky** today...At least 11 miners

were killed in **Taylorsville, midway between Louisville and**

Frankfort.

                                        -0-

In Taylorsville, Kentucky — that's about 30 miles from

Louisville — a coal mine collapsed this morning, killing 11

miners.

                                        -0-

At least 11 miners are dead in a coal mine collapse

in north central Kentucky. It happened **in Taylorsville, outside**

of Louisville.

However, if you happen to be working at a station in the Louisville-Taylorsville-Frankfort region, where people *already know* the geography, you need only write,

A coal mine collapsed **in Taylorsville** this morning, killing

at least 11 miners...

And if your station is *in* Taylorsville or a nearby community, you can come right out and name the mine and its address:

```
At least 11 coal miners died this morning in the Cardwell

Number Four mine on West Burnham Road.  The mine collapsed just

after nine A.M.
```

You see, just as stating the When elements depends on a combination of time of occurrence and time of broadcast, so stating the Where element depends on a combination of (1) the location of the event and (2) the location of your station.

ADDRESSING THE LOCAL AUDIENCE

It comes as no surprise that most people are more interested in what happens down the block than in what happens halfway around the world. People are more interested in events close to home or in places they have visited, or where they have friends and relatives, than in what to them may be obscure points on a map.

Unless you work at a network, where you must write for a widely scattered audience, you must tailor your copy to suit the needs of your specific local audience. Most of you will begin and end your broadcast news careers at local stations . . . for the simple reason that that's where most of the jobs are. At the same time, however, most of the news agency copy you receive is, like network news, aimed at a nationwide (or worldwide) audience. Part of your job will be to tailor copy like the following for local consumption:

```
     SOUTH CHARLESTON, W.Va. (AP)--A natural gas explosion
destroyed a crowded supermarket Monday, injuring at least 17
people, authorities said.
     All employees and customers were believed accounted for,
said a state police superintendent, but searchers continued to
use shovels to dig for more victims possibly trapped inside.
     "All those who were in the store have now been accounted
for. We no longer expect to find any bodies," said Supt. John
O'Rourke, but he said he could not rule out the possibility
that someone may be in the debris.
     The explosion occurred shortly after an employee lit a
cigarette in the supermarket, said State Trooper A. W.
Robinson, but he said it was not immediately known if the
cigarette caused the explosion.
     Also under suspicion was a major gas line about 40 feet
from the Foodland supermarket that was accidentally ruptured
about noon by construction crews working on an Appalachian
Corridor G highway project, said Bill Reed, district manager
for Colombia Gas of West Virginia. The line was leaking at the
time of the blast, he said.
```

If you were writing for a network or a local station *far away* from the scene, you might make it,

```
At least 17 people have been hurt in a gas explosion at a

supermarket just outside (or near) Charleston, West Virginia....
```

If your station is closer to the scene, say, in the same state or a bordering state, you might make it,

> **In South Charleston, just west of Charleston,** a gas
> explosion today injured at least 17 people at a supermarket...

And if your station is in the immediate area, you might make it,

> At least 17 people are hurt in a gas explosion **at the**
> **Foodland supermarket near the Appalachian Corridor G highway**
> **project...**

Note that in the first example, only the larger, better-known place is named in the lead, and in the third example the exact location is named. As the audience grows more specific, so does the Where element grow more specific.

Do not be disturbed that spelling out the Where element causes you to write extra words and thus eat up precious air time. The extra words are normal and necessary in broadcast writing. Again, the objectives are clarity and immediate understanding.

RESTATING LOCATION

As for reinforcing the Where element, the wording can be much simpler. In fact, a single word will usually suffice, that word being the name of the location used as an adjective: "The *New York* Governor," "The *Taylorsville* mine," "The reaction of the *Roanoke* town council," and so on. In the case of the preceding South Charleston explosion story, "where" reinforcement might go this way:

> A natural gas explosion injured 17 people today at a
> supermarket **near Charleston, West Virginia.** The explosion
> leveled the store, but rescuers who combed the debris say all
> shoppers and employees are now accounted for. The supermarket
> was near a gas line and highway project in the town of **South**
> **Charleston.** **West Virginia** state police speculate the explosion
> was caused when a lighted cigarette touched off leaking gas
> fumes. A gas company official confirms the gas line was leaking
> at the time of the blast.

The desirability of renaming the location in the body of the broadcast story is one major difference with print style. Another major difference is that sometimes you don't have to name the location geographically *at all*. In broadcasting, some "datelines" are superfluous:

> The White House announced today *in Washington*...

–0–

> *In Paris,* the French government said today its soldiers will
>
> stay in Lebanon...

In these examples, naming the city was unnecessary. *Of course* the White House is in Washington and the French government is in Paris! It is only when events occur *outside* their accustomed place that it's necessary to tell where:

> President Smith announced today **at Camp David**...
>
> –0–
>
> Governor Thompson, **on a visit to Rockford,** called today for
>
> a massive highway repair project...

Normally, those two officials would be located, respectively, in Washington and Springfield. Had they made news in those locations, naming the cities would have been superfluous. But since they spoke elsewhere, the specific "where" had to be included.

LOCALIZING THE NEWS

In addition to expressing the Where element in terms relevant to the local audience, broadcast journalists also reshape the *substance* of news stories for the local audience. Whenever it is possible to find a local angle, a local reaction, or a local follow-up to a national or foreign news story, no matter where it occurs, the local elements are given prominence. The process is called *localizing*. It entails the careful, complete reading of news agency material to identify angles of interest to specific local audiences. For example:

> CLEVELAND (AP)––About 4,700 United Rubber Workers members
> struck Firestone Inc. plants in six states Sunday, and another
> 15,000 union members are poised to strike Goodyear Tire
> Rubber Co. at noon Tuesday.
>   The Firestone employees walked out after negotiators in
> Cleveland failed to reach an agreement prior to a 12:01 a.m.
> Sunday deadline.
>   The disabled Firestone facilities are in Akron, Ohio;
> Noblesville, Ind.; Des Moines, Iowa; Decatur, Ill.;
> Russellville, Ark.; and Oklahoma City. The Des Moines,
> Decatur, and Oklahoma City plants make tires, the Noblesville
> plant makes molded rubber products, and the Russellville plant
> makes inner tubes.
>   In Des Moines, about 20 Firestone employees picketed the
> plant's five gates Sunday afternoon, even though no work
> shifts were scheduled until 11 p.m., said Bill Winslow, a
> production worker and picket captain.
>   At Firestone's tire plant in Oklahoma City, about 10
> workers were on a picket line, said Don Adams, vice president
> of Local 998.
>   As the Firestone strike began, a vote Sunday by a local in
> Danville, Va., threatened to produce an even larger nationwide
> strike Tuesday against Goodyear.
>   The Goodyear pact was negotiated as an agreement to serve
> as a pattern for the other rubber companies. But Goodyear's

```
15,000 URW members rejected the tentative contract by a 3-1
ratio two weeks ago.
     Fewer than half of the 1,668 members of Local 831 turned
out for the secret ballot on Sunday on whether to take another
look at the proposal. The vote was 467-339 against
reconsidering, union officials said.
     "If nothing changes, if the union and the company don't
get back together at 12 o'clock Tuesday, high noon, there will
be a strike," said Linwood Saunders, president of the local.
     URW President Milan Stone said Firestone's latest proposal
did not match the pattern settlement.
```

Clearly, that story contains two developments of national (that is, network) interest: a rubber workers' strike against Firestone, and a threatened strike against Goodyear. However, the story names a total of eight cities where the story has immediate *local* interest: Cleveland, where labor negotiations were held; Akron, Noblesville, Des Moines, Decatur, Russellville, and Oklahoma City, the sites of the struck Firestone plants; and Danville, site of a URW Local at Goodyear. In those eight cities—and in all other cities where Goodyear plants are located—local journalists will be giving prominence to developments in their areas. They will reach deep into the news agency copy to "lift up" and stress those angles affecting local listeners and viewers.

Thus, radio and TV stations in Oklahoma City might say:

```
The Firestone rubber plant here in Oklahoma City is one of

half a dozen struck today by the United Rubber Workers.
```

or

```
The rubber workers' union struck Firestone plants across the

country today, including the tire plant here in Oklahoma City.
```

They might also come right out and give the plant's street address. They will also get on the phone to local company and union officials, and they will dispatch reporters and camera crews to the plant and local union headquarters. In short, they will transform the story from a network one into a local one.

Meanwhile, local journalists in the other affected cities will be doing the same in their areas, shifting the emphasis to developments affecting their own local listeners. In Danville, Virginia, local radio and TV might say:

```
Danville Local 8-3-1 of the United Rubber Workers today

rejected a new contract with Goodyear.  The rejection raises the

possibility of a nationwide strike against Goodyear beginning

Tuesday.  The strike would follow a strike that began today

against Firestone.
```

As you can see, the original news agency copy is treated as raw material to be refashioned and rewritten to suit local needs and interests. To put it another way, the most desirable "where" is *here*.

Another example of what to watch for:

> NORFOLK, Va. (AP)--Navy salvage workers found the bodies
> of three missing sailors at their work stations aboard the
> drifting submarine Bonefish on Wednesday, nearly three days
> after explosions and fire forced the evacuation of the vessel.
>   Eighty-nine crew members evacuated the submarine, which
> filled with smoke and toxic fumes from an explosion in a
> forward battery compartment.
>   "Shortly after midnight, the salvage crew went aboard and
> discovered the bodies," said Chief Petty Officer Terry D.
> Borton, a spokesman at Atlantic Fleet headquarters here. "Two
> of the victims were discovered in the control room and the
> other in an administrative compartment."
>   The crewmen were identified as Lt. Ray Everts, 30, of
> Naoma, W.Va.; Petty Officer 1st Class Robert W. Bordelon Jr.,
> 39, of Willis, Tex.; and Petty Officer 3rd Class Marshall T.
> Lindgren, 21, of Pisgah Forest, N.C.

In the three localities named in the last paragraph, the hometowns of the dead sailors, there are people who knew the victims: family, friends, teachers, merchants, and so on. To these people, the victims are far more than cold statistics; they were flesh and blood, and there are strong emotional reactions. So in Naoma, West Virginia; Willis, Texas; and Pisgah Forest, North Carolina, listeners and viewers must be told more than "Salvage workers have found the bodies of three sailors on the derelict submarine Bonefish. . . ." In each town, the story should be localized to mention *in the lead* that a hometowner was involved:

> (In Willis, Texas, and surrounding communities)
>
> The U-S Navy says **Robert Bordelon, Junior, of Willis** was one
>
> of three victims of the Bonefish submarine disaster. Salvage
>
> workers found the 39-year-old Petty Officer First Class...and two
>
> other seamen...dead at their workstations aboard the derelict
>
> sub. They were found three days after explosions and fire forced
>
> the sub's evacuation at sea. Eighty-nine crew members survived.

Meanwhile, in Naoma and Pisgah Forest and their surrounding communities, local broadcasters were giving similar prominence of place to the local victims.

Not every story can be localized; local journalists should not invent local angles where none exist. However, it's a rare story out of Washington or a state capital that doesn't have ramifications, or at least reaction, on the local level. Local journalists should constantly be asking, "What is the effect of this story on people in *my* listening area?"

If the defense budget is cut, do any of the cuts affect local defense contractors and their employees? If the president or the governor proposes a highway reconstruction bill, would local roads and traffic patterns be affected? How do local elected officials feel about it? What are their reactions and counterproposals? If the Supreme Court rules on abortion, what are the reactions of local pro- and anti-abortion groups? And what are their next moves?

The examples are endless. And so must be your efforts to find local angles. You are broadcasting to neighbors and fellow residents who have an immediate interest in such things. You are also competing with newspapers and other local stations. You can bet that the competition won't be sitting back waiting for local angles to drop into their laps. They'll be out digging for them.

"WHERE" AS TRANSITION

In broadcast news, a "transition" refers to the words bridging the gap between two stories. We will examine transitions—also known as "links"—in a later chapter. But since we're in the midst of the Where element, it's worth noting that "where" serves extremely well as a simple transition, especially when you don't know in advance which stories will precede and follow the one you are writing.

If you *start* a story with the Where element, the chances are good that you, an editor, or a producer can place that story almost anywhere in a newscast without later having to rewrite a more specific transition:

```
In Boston, Mayor Richard Roe announced today...

                        -0-

On West 23rd Street, a bus jumped a curb this morning...

                        -0-

In Seoul, South Korea, student demonstrators clashed...
```

Using "where" as a transition to make a clean break from an as yet unknown preceding story is especially useful in small news departments. In large news departments, producers usually have enough staff to assign a single writer a group of stories destined to run together; the writer will thus have time to link the stories with creative transitions. But in smaller news departments, where the workload tends to be heavier on everyone, writers have little time for such niceties; they will find that using "where" as an opening transition comes in very handy.

But, again, a caution: Do not overdo it. You can't start every story with the Where element without the newscast sounding monotonous.

EXERCISES

1. The following story is slugged JUNK FOOD. Write a 30-second version utilizing the second person "you" or the third person "they" in your lead sentence.

```
     LONDON (UPI)--Teen-agers' consumption of junk food and
soft drinks is to blame for the rise in soccer hooliganism,
delinquency and weekend rural rowdiness, two leading
nutritionists said in a report published today.
     "You cannot hope for good behavior on a junk-food diet,
whatever social improvements are made. If only the government,
(soccer) authorities and schools realized this, we could start
to make progress," said Dr. Damian Downing, and Ian Stokes of
the British Society for Nutritional Medicine.
     "Unruly schoolchildren almost always turn into delinquent
teen-agers: and analysis of the diet of (soccer) hooligans
would show a huge amount of nutritional deficiencies," Downing
and Stokes wrote in Healthy Living.
     They want school shops to ban soft drinks, potato chips,
ice cream and chocolate, and instead serve fresh and dried
fruits, sandwiches and pure fruit juice.
     School cafeterias should quit selling french fries,
sausages and baked beans, and offer salads, fresh green
vegetables, meat and fish, they said.
```

2. Write *two* versions of the following story, slugged ADOPTION RULING.

Treat the first version as a 20-second "bulletin" that happened shortly before the 5 P.M. News. Begin it, "This just in . . ."

Make the second version run 30 seconds for the 11 P.M. News, when you need a later angle because many in your audience will already have heard the basic story. (For example, you might lead with the reaction to the ruling instead of with the ruling itself.)

> ORLANDO, Fla. (AP)--A judge Friday ruled in favor of a 12-year-old boy who set a legal precedent by going to court to "divorce" the biological parents he said had mistreated and abandoned him.
>
> Circuit Judge Thomas S. Kirk told Gregory Kingsley he was now formally adopted by his foster parents. "Gregory, you're the son of Mr. and Mrs. Russ at this moment," he said as the courtroom broke into applause.
>
> Kirk said the boy's biological mother had "lied consistently" during the legal battle Gregory initiated to sever his relationship with her.
>
> "I believe by clear and convincing evidence, almost beyond a reasonable doubt in this case, that this child has been abandoned . . . and neglected by Rachel Kingsley and it is certainly in his best interests that her parental rights be terminated immediately."
>
> Gregory's adoptive parents, George and Lizabeth Russ, said they were delighted. "We just hugged," Lizabeth Russ said of Gregory. "It was really exciting. I didn't expect it would happen that fast."
>
> Harry Morall II, a lawyer for Rachel Kingsley, said his client "should have been judged by her lifestyle now, not in the past."
>
> Rachel Kingsley was not in the courtroom for closing arguments and the ruling. Morall told the judge just before he announced his ruling that she had become ill and left the courtroom. She never reappeared.
>
> Later, at Morall's office she said, sobbing, "I just want Gregory to know that I love him very much. He is welcome to come home any time he likes. He will always be my son. All I ever wanted was a chance to be with him."
>
> The case was considered precedent-setting because the lawsuit was pursued by a 12-year-old boy and the ruling gave a minor increased standing in a court of law. Lawyers say they deal with similar custody cases frequently, but the legal action is usually initiated by a foster parent or by the state.
>
> The judge's ruling culminated a day in which Gregory took the witness stand and nervously recalled bouncing from his mother's home to foster homes until he finally "thought she forgot about me."
>
> As his mother wept in the courtroom, Gregory recounted a joyless childhood filled with uncertainty and abandonment.

3. Slug the following story EXPLOSION and write a 15-second story, being careful to give listeners a mental map of the location.

> MOSCOW (UPI)--Dozens of explosions wrecked a warehouse at a rubber factory on Friday, starting fires which injured a number of workers, Tass news agency reported.
>
> Tass said the blasts at the Rezinotekhnika works in Saransk, an industrial town 270 miles southeast of Moscow, were caused by a glowing cigarette ash in a garbage can.
>
> It said "several dozen explosions" sent goods stored in the warehouse flying into the air and shattered the windows of two adjoining workshops.

4. The following story contains statistics relating to every region of the United States. Slug it TOOTH DECAY and write a 30- to 40-second *localized* version for your area.

Half of US School Children Are Free Of Tooth Decay, Study Says

WASHINGTON (AP)--Half of America's 43 million school-age children have never experienced tooth decay, a dental problem that affected almost all of America's youth just a generation ago, according to a federal study released Tuesday.

In a study that included the oral examination of about 40,000 youngsters coast-to-coast, the National Institute of Dental Research found that dental cavities have declined by 36 percent among children ages 5 to 17, and that 49.9 percent of these children had no tooth decay at all.

Officials said the sample population examined was selected to represent the approximately 43 million school-aged children in the nation.

Dr. James P. Carlos, chief of epidemiology at the NIDR, said that dental decay, a problem that has plagued humankind throughout history, has been steadily declining since the use of fluoride became widespread and that the trend probably will continue.

"This disease, which is probably the most chronic disease of childhood, is being decreased very fast," said Carlos, "It is declining 35 to 36 percent every seven years and now half the children in the country have never even experienced dental decay."

Carlos said the decline in tooth decay follows a pattern consistent with the increased use of fluoride in the nation's drinking water, in toothpastes, and in mouth washes.

He said the increased use of dental sealant also has affected the decline in tooth decay. The sealant is a plastic material that dentists paint on the chewing surfaces to protect teeth from decay.

For the survey, specialists counted the amount of decay or fillings noted on each of the 128 surfaces of a typical set of 28 teeth in the school children. A missing tooth was counted as five surfaces. Wisdom teeth were not counted since few school children have them.

The result showed that the statistical mean of tooth surfaces with decay was 3.07 per child. The mean in a survey taken in 1980 was 4.77, reflecting a 36 percent decline in tooth cavities.

In 1980, the survey found that 36.6 percent of the children were free of tooth decay. This compares to almost half, 49.9 percent, found without decay in the recent survey.

Carlos said no similar surveys were taken prior to the 1980 finding, but experts estimate that only 28 percent of the school children in the 1970s were without tooth decay, and that a generation earlier virtually every child experienced some tooth decay between age 5 and 17.

He said in the 1940s, it was estimated that U.S. school children averaged seven teeth each that were decayed, missing or filled.

Now, instead of counting teeth, he said, the survey must count surfaces affected in order to get a meaningful statistic.

Carlos said school children in the Southwest, which includes Texas, New Mexico, Arizona and Colorado, showed the least amount of tooth decay with a mean of 2.4 tooth surfaces affected per child. That region showed a mean of 3.4 in 1980.

The New England states, Maine, New Hampshire, Vermont, Massachusetts, Connecticut and Rhode Island, showed the highest rate, with a mean of 3.6, compared to a mean of 6.1 in 1980.

Other regional findings, with the mean number of tooth surfaces per child affected and the same mean from the 1980 survey in parenthesis, are:

Northeast (New York, Pennsylvania, New Jersey): 3.4 (5.4).

Midwest (Minnesota, Wisconsin, Michigan, Iowa, Missouri, Illinois, Indiana, Ohio): 2.9 (4.7).

Southeast (Maryland, Virginia, Delaware, North Carolina, South Carolina, Georgia, Florida, Alabama, Mississippi, Tennessee, Kentucky, West Virginia, Arkansas, Louisiana): 3.1 (4.6).

Pacific (Alaska, Hawaii, Washington, Oregon and California): 3.4 (5.1).

Northwest (North Dakota, South Dakota, Nebraska, Kansas, Oklahoma, Montana, Idaho, Wyoming, Nevada and Utah): 2.8 (4.4).

Carlos said the reason for the regional difference "has never been satisfactorily explained and is one of the enduring mysteries of dental epidemiology."

At one time, he said, experts thought that the varying amounts of fluoride in the drinking water of the national regions accounted for the differences, but that has now been discounted because fluoride is present in about 60 percent of the water systems in the nation.

Dr. Preston A. Littleton Jr., deputy director of The NIDR, said the decline in childhood dental decay will make it possible for the agency to concentrate more of its research efforts toward dental problems experienced among adults and older Americans.

"The results give us the opportunity to redeploy efforts and attempt to make similar gains among the older population," said Littleton.
AP-NY 1541EDT

Libel, Attribution, Quotation, and Ethics

6

Several chapters ago, we spoke of the professional goals and responsibilities uniting journalists in all media: accuracy, fairness, and speed. Now we must consider how broadcasting's immediacy, its unrelenting demand for speed, can sometimes be a disadvantage in striving for accuracy and fairness. We must also examine how to overcome this disadvantage.

EDITORIAL CONTROL

In the main, newspapers and magazines follow a multi-layered system for safeguarding accuracy and balance: A reporter or copyeditor writes a story to the best of his or her ability, then submits it to an editor (either in person, via computer, or, from the field, by phone, fax, or modem). The editor proceeds to check the story for accuracy, balance, grammar, and clarity. The editor may send it on to the compositor without changing a word. More likely, though, the editor will make corrections, additions, deletions—or, if completely dissatisfied, shoot the copy back to the reporter or copyeditor for a complete rewrite. All this takes time. Only when approaching final deadline does this editorial process gain momentum at the risk of cutting corners.

Broadcast news practice, geared to frequent deadlines, seems almost haphazard by comparison: A writer or reporter submits his or her copy to a producer or assistant producer. The producer may approve it as is, make corrections, or request a complete rewrite. But while the newspaper editor's sole concern is the story's editorial content, the broadcast producer's attention is, to say the least, divided. The producer is usually preoccupied with the overall content and structure of the newscast. He or she must decide which video- or audiotape to use, the order in which to use it, the type and position of any electronic graphics, the availability of camera crews and reporters, the expense of putting personnel on overtime, and so forth. Thus, news copy alone seldom has a producer's full attention. And, in the case of a reporter ad-libbing from the scene during a live broadcast, there is no mechanism for editorial control whatsoever.

Therefore, the responsibility for fairness and accuracy lies more heavily on broadcast writers and reporters than on their print colleagues. Broadcasters *must* be familiar with the rules of attribution—

for if they are not, they risk committing *libel,* the civil penalties for which, in case of conviction, may be extremely severe.

AVOIDING LIBEL

In the broadcast news business, you may be committing libel when you as a writer, reporter, anchor, editor, or producer broadcast false information about someone's activities or character, the effect of which is to harm that person's reputation and/or livelihood. In effect, if *you* convict someone before a court does, the result may be a libel suit against you and your employer; if you lose, you both may be sentenced to pay an enormous sum of money in actual and punitive damages.

In short, libel is to be strenuously avoided. The matter is so serious that many news departments have a policy of clearing potentially libelous stories with a company lawyer before putting them on the air.

However, it is in the nature of broadcast news to work fast, to report breaking developments as quickly as technically possible—indeed, even transmit them live. Thus, in the everyday course of writing and airing newscasts, there will seldom be time to consult a lawyer. Broadcast journalists must understand both the law and the *language* that will protect them.

So let's be precise on how to avoid libel. If you as a journalist go on the air and say

"John Doe robbed a bank today,"

and John Doe did *not* rob a bank, you have committed a libel, and Mr. Doe's lawyer may come after you. But if you say

"**Police say** John Doe robbed a bank today,"

you have not committed a libel—as long as the police did say it. The police may be wrong, and if so, Mr. Doe can sue them for false arrest. Mr. Doe's lawyer may think he can sue you for libel because you broadcast a false charge and possibly harmed his client's reputation—but unless you knew the charge was false and aired it anyway, Mr. Doe's lawyer will not be successful.

What you have done is to follow routine journalistic practice by placing responsibility for the charge with an established authority, also known as an "official source." You have attributed the accusation to an executive agency. You have, in effect, put the charge in someone else's mouth.

Rule 1:
Always attribute. Tell what you know and how you
know it.

But wait. Suppose you had said,

"Bank manager Richard Roe said his bank was robbed today by John Doe."

Matters have suddenly become tricky. Is bank manager Roe right or wrong? Did John Doe do it or didn't he? Roe has made the accusation, but are you as a journalist correct in reporting it?

The answer is *no*—especially if all you have is Roe's accusation. Bank manager Roe is not an official source. His charge against John Doe is not an official one. Only law enforcement agencies (police, prosecutors, grand juries, etc.) can make official charges.

Suppose, however, that you have not only Roe's accusation but also John Doe's denial. May you broadcast both the accusation and the denial? Again the answer is *no*. If Doe is innocent, he may sue both Roe, for raising a false charge, and you, for propagating (spreading) a libel.

Realistically speaking, there will be times when you will be writing news stories containing unofficial charges against private citizens. The stories may be a result of your own investigation, or the result of a tip from a source you cannot name on the air. Either way, you must *not* air the story without giving accused persons the chance to tell their side. And if you were unable to reach such accused persons, you must be prepared to prove that you made diligent, repeated efforts to contact them in person or by phone. Thus:

Rule 2:
You must make every effort to give accused parties a chance to defend themselves.

Although your station's attorney may contend that your repeated efforts to get the other side of the story demonstrate your fairness and good intentions, the safest course is *not* to report Roe's accusation, even with Doe's denial. It is better to wait until the authorities take legal action—in other words, until you have an official source—than to air a potentially libelous story.

Why so much caution? Because John Doe is a private citizen, fully entitled to the presumption of innocence and due legal process. Private citizens have the right to be left just that—private. Only when established public agencies name them, or when news organizations have compiled convincing documentary evidence, may private citizens be named as alleged wrongdoers.

Now suppose the story goes like this:

"Bank manager Richard Roe said today his bank was robbed by Mayor Jones."

May you legally say that on the air even before you get Mayor Jones's reaction? Yes, you may—because Mayor Jones is a *public official,* not a "private citizen." (However, if you *know* Roe's charge to be false, but you broadcast it anyway because of its "human interest" value, you may be opening yourself up to a libel charge.)

You see, current U.S. law makes a distinction between how the news media may treat public officials as opposed to private citizens. The Supreme Court, in the landmark Sullivan decision (*The New York Times Co.* vs. *Sullivan,* 1963), ruled that public officials may not successfully sue for libel even if the reporting is wrong, unless the news media act out of *actual malice,* showing a *reckless disregard* for the truth. In other words, to wage a successful libel suit, a public official must prove that a news organization deliberately printed or aired falsehoods in full knowledge of their falsity, or without taking steps to substantiate the information. The Court held that granting public officials the same absolute protection as private citizens would tend to inhibit and discourage reporting on important public issues.

In subsequent decisions, the Court broadened the definition of public officials to include public *figures,* anyone voluntarily in the public eye—such as performers, professional athletes, etc.

To summarize:

1. The best defense against libel is truth—to report only what is ascertainable or can be clearly attributed to official sources.
2. The next best defense against libel is to report both (or all) sides of an accusation—to diligently seek out an accused party and report his or her reaction to the charge.

This may sound complicated to some of you. Although we've tried to simplify matters, libel is in fact a complicated facet of American jurisprudence. Libel laws are different in each state. Ideally, you should familiarize yourself with the libel laws in each state where you find employment. At the very least, you must adhere to the two rules given in this chapter. In a professional broadcast newsroom, you will be expected to follow them routinely as you write and air the day's news.

There is also a commonsense way to approach these matters once you start working in a radio or TV newsroom. As you gather information on a story, and then as you write it, ask yourself, Am I being fair to all parties mentioned in my story? Have I done everything possible to reach all sides? Have I made every effort to double-check the facts as I know them? What can I do to follow up any loose ends after the broadcast?

And then, just for good measure, put yourself in the shoes of the accused and imagine how they fit. If they pinch your toes, perhaps you better do some more checking.

PROTECTIVE LANGUAGE

Those of you with experience in print journalism probably know most of the words commonly used in connection with potentially libelous stories. Chief among the verbs are

- · say
- · allege
- · charge
- · accuse

and past participles used as adjectives

- · alleged
- · accused
- · reputed

Chief among the nouns are

- · allegations
- · charges
- · accusations

All these words, especially the verb "say" or "said" put in the mouth of police or other official sources, serve to protect the rights of accused persons even as they protect you and your employer against libel charges. They signify "What I'm reporting is an official charge or accusation. I cannot vouch for its ultimate truth, which, in time, will be decided by the proper authorities."

The trouble with such protective words is that, except for "say" or "said," they are seldom used in informal speech and therefore tend to sound stilted on the air. Unfortunately, there is really no adequate solution to the problem. The matter of legal rights and duties is too important to risk avoiding occasional stodginess in favor of everyday speech. So this is one area where the phrasing you must use in broadcast news is very close to the phrasing of newspapers and news agencies.

However, you can often rely heavily on "say" and "said"—provided you mention the source of an allegation in *every sentence*. For example:

```
      Police have arrested a suspect in this morning's First

National Bank robbery.  They identified him as 41-year-old John

Doe.  Police say Doe was caught three blocks from the bank with

the stolen money in a laundry bag slung over his shoulder.  They

say he was identified by bank employees.
```

That sort of language is simple, the storytelling style informal, and the wording nonlibelous (even if it turns out that suspect Doe is innocent and merely picked up the bag dropped by the real culprit; police accounts are often inaccurate and demolished in court by defense attorneys. And the bank employees could be mistaken).

Indictments

Indictments are a bit trickier. An indictment is merely an *accusation* of wrongdoing, not proof. Anyone under indictment has a right to a trial in a courtroom, not in the news media. But since public perception of this elementary legal point is somewhat shaky (to say the least), broadcasters are better advised to use the more stilted wording:

```
      A Nelson County grand jury today indicted two Ridgewood

building contractors in an alleged bid-rigging scheme.

Contractors John Doe and Richard Roe are accused of conspiring to
```

```
drive up the price of county garage-building projects.  The
indictment charges that Doe and Roe overbilled county taxpayers
to the tune of nearly four million dollars.
```

In reporting charges and indictments, you should be aware of nuances in wording that can endanger the legal protection of your story. If you say

"Police are seeking 18-year-old John Doe *for* the kidnapping and murder of (or *for* kidnapping and murdering) an 8-year-old girl..."

you are in effect saying that Doe did it; you have convicted him, when in fact he merely has the status of suspect. If he is innocent, your story is potentially libelous.

However, if you say

"Police are seeking 18-year-old John Doe **in** (or **in connection with**) the kidnapping and murder of..."

you are on safe ground. "In connection with" is a loose term connoting Doe's suspect status; it indicates that police think he *may* have done it. At this point they want to arrest him for questioning, and formal charges may or may not follow. Such wording is nonlibelous.

Safeguarding Nonlibelous Attribution

If you are writing a story based on original reporting—if, for example, you are covering a police beat either on the scene or by phone—it will be up to you to use the proper nonlibelous language; you will have no print model to work from. But much of the time you will be writing a broadcast version of a story you have received from a news agency—perhaps a story like the following:

```
        SAN ANTONIO (AP)--A former Libertarian congressional
candidate was accused Tuesday of trying to hire a "patriot" to
kill Mayor Henry G. Cisneros, authorities said.
        Parker E. Abell, 74, a tax protestor who claims to head a
political extremist group called the American Patriots, was
held without bail in the Bexar County jail on charges of
solicitation of capital murder.
        Abell, who had been under surveillance for about a month,
was arrested after agreeing to pay an undercover officer
$5,000 to kill Cisneros, Dist. Atty. Fred Rodriguez said.
        "He didn't want just anybody. He wanted a patriot to carry
out the execution," Rodriguez said.
        Cisneros, 40, a four-term mayor and former president of
the National League of Cities, said he was not getting
additional protection and joked that he was insulted he was
worth only $5,000.
        Abell, a resident of Natalia, 18 miles east of San
Antonio, mentioned other possible targets, including State
Comptroller Bob Bullock, before deciding on Cisneros, the
prosecutor said.
        Officers arrested Abell at a supermarket pay phone. In his
car were a .22 caliber rifle and "executive warrants" issued
by the "Sovereign Court of the People," police said.
        "The above-named traitor or traitors are to be executed on
sight," the warrants read. "Each accused has given public
proof of guilt beyond reasonable doubt that he or she is a
traitor to the people of the United States and the United
States Constitution."
        Abell was a Libertarian candidate for the 23rd
Congressional District seat in 1982. Gary Johnson, secretary
of the Libertarian Party of Texas, said Abell's affiliation
with the party ended in 1985.
```

As with virtually all news agency copy, the writer and editor were extremely careful to give the specific source of each specific allegation before transmitting that story to newspapers and broadcast news departments. The radio or TV newswriter's job is to transform the story into broadcast style, without compromising its nonlibelous nature. For the broadcaster, the freedom to choose a lead remains. So does the freedom to shorten sentences. So does the freedom to use informal language. But there is *no* freedom to omit the specific source of a specific allegation. Thus, a 20-second version might go this way:

> San Antonio **police** have arrested a man for **allegedly** plotting to kill Mayor Henry Cisneros.
>
> **A prosecutor** identified the man as 74-year-old Parker Abell, a one-time congressional candidate on the Libertarian ticket.
>
> **The prosecutor said** Abell was arrested after offering an undercover cop posing as a hit man 5,000 dollars for Cisneros's murder. Abell is being held without bail.

That is a bare-bones version. Longer versions (30 or 40 seconds) can detail the right-wing extremist background of the detainee, and perhaps mention Cisneros's reaction. But notice how the lead contains the modifier "allegedly" and how every sentence containing an allegation also contains an official source. It was not necessary to identify "District Attorney Fred Rodriguez" by name or title (unless your station is in San Antonio), but it was necessary to specify his official role, that is, prosecutor or prosecuting attorney. No matter what your personal feelings or opinions, you are obliged as a matter of journalistic fairness to "play it straight"—to tell *who* is making an accusation.

ATTRIBUTION (SOURCING)

Naming the source of potentially libelous statements is just one part of the larger matter of attribution. Journalists in all media attribute (give the source of) all events and remarks they have not witnessed personally. Because journalists cannot be everywhere, that means accounts of most events are attributed to other people. The purpose of attribution is to give readers, listeners, and viewers a guide by which to judge the accuracy of the reporting.

To put it another way: What you see with your own eyes is firsthand information and needs no attribution; the attribution is implicitly yourself. What other people tell you is secondhand information and does need attribution because it cannot always be confirmed quickly.

The difference between attributing in print style and attributing in broadcast style is more of form than of substance. Each medium must attribute, but not in the same way. By and large, print journalism requires the writer to attribute in the lead and follow-up sentences. But as we've seen, this can result in longwinded, convoluted language. An illustration:

WASHINGTON—Because of better food distribution and improved health care, the world's population has reached 5 billion—more than triple the level at the turn of the 19th century—and is likely to grow by another billion by the end of this century, **the Population Crisis Committee** reported today.

Growth rates are highest in Third World countries, where more than 75% of the world's population lives and nine out of 10 infants are born, **according to a study by the committee, a Washington-based group that works to slow population growth.** At current rates, *it said,* populations will double in Africa, Latin America, and Asia in 24, 31, and 37 years, respectively.

(Don Irwin, © 1988 *Los Angeles Times,* reprinted with permission)

Broadcasters are faced with their customary task of turning this into conversational language. At the same time, they must specify the source of the information. Part of the technique, as we've seen in earlier chapters, is to attribute at the start of sentences instead of at the end:

> **A research group** predicts world population will reach six billion by the end of this century.
>
> **The Washington—based Population Crisis Committee** says a billion people will be born between now and the year 2000. It says 90 percent of them will be in the less—developed nations in Asia, Africa, and Latin America.

However, in the effort to find an attention-getting lead, broadcasters may *delay* the attribution until a followup sentence:

> World population will reach six billion by the end of the century. That's the prediction from **the Population Crisis Committee, a Washington—based group that favors slow population growth.**
>
> **The group** says one billion people will be born...etc.

> or

> If you think the world's crowded now, just wait until the year 2000. **According to a Washington—based research group,** that's when world population will reach six billion. **The Population Crisis Committee** says a billion people...etc.

Raising Doubt

Another reason for attributing carefully is to raise doubt about the reliability of the information you are reporting. You may well ask, If information isn't reliable, why report it at all? Well, ideally, you wouldn't. But the job of newsgathering and reporting does not operate under ideal conditions. Without the benefit of firsthand observation—in other words, most of the time—journalists are forced to rely on information supplied by others. Most of the time, such secondhand information is accurate and trustworthy. Very often, however, it is not. It ranges from the honest mistake (a wrong date, a wrong time, a wrong name), to the misperception (John Doe didn't knock the man down; he was trying to help him up), to the outright lie ("We are not negotiating a hostage deal with Iran"; "I am not a crook").

Despite repeated efforts to check and verify what they are told, journalists are often at the mercy of their sources of information, and it sometimes happens that mistakes, misconceptions, and lies are reported as fact. As noted, broadcast news is especially susceptible to editorial inaccuracies because of its very speed. In an environment of intense competition and pressure to exploit immediacy, the temptation to broadcast now, this very minute, is almost irresistible. Therefore, the doubt-raising nature of clear attribution is often the only help listeners or viewers may get in deciding whether to believe what they hear.

For example, foreign reporters based in Mainland China are seldom, if ever, permitted to roam freely about the country to gather firsthand information. They are therefore forced to rely on information supplied by China's Communist-controlled government. As a rule, such information is highly unreliable. For a hard-line Communist regime to report information unfavorable to itself is almost unimaginable. Therefore, *naming the source* may be the only tip-off to listeners and viewers that the reported information may be suspect.

As you gain experience in journalism, you will develop a sense for which sources are generally trustworthy and which are not. But as a matter of basic writing technique, you should *always* include an attribution.

GIVING CREDIT

Proper attribution also includes giving credit to other, possibly competing, news organizations when they report exclusive stories.

Every journalist wants a "scoop," an exclusive. Getting a scoop makes an entire news organization feel proud. But scoops are rare. Sometimes they are matter of luck, but mostly they are a journalist's reward for tireless investigative work or personal contact with newsmakers and their staffs. The downside is a feeling of discouragement when a scoop goes to a competitor. Even so, the feeling should not prevent giving credit where credit is due.

Suppose a newspaper—let's call it the *"Daily Blatt"*—reports an exclusive story:

> DALLAS--Amid widespread speculation that his campaign has bogged down, Texas billionaire Ross Perot will shortly announce that he will not be a candidate for President, sources in his campaign said today.

Seeing this report in the *Daily Blatt,* or an account of it in a news agency story, broadcast news executives will be hounding their own campaign reporters to get a confirmation or a denial. Once they do, they'll be able to use it as the basis for their own stories. But until that time, they must swallow their pride and credit their competitor—in broadcast style, of course:

```
          Ross Perot may be about to call it quits.  The Daily

     Blatt reports this morning that the Texas billionaire has decided

     NOT to run for President.


                                    or


          The Daily Blatt reports this morning that Ross Perot is

     about to throw in the towel.

          Quoting sources in the Perot campaign, the paper says the

     Texas billionaire is about to announce he won't run for President

     after all.
```

In the real world of broadcast news competition, there are a few organizations whose top executives might order their staffs to ignore the *Blatt's* exclusive and not to run the story until such time as they have their own angles on it. This is especially true if the competitor is another broadcaster rather than a newspaper.

However, most news organizations follow a modified version of the Golden Rule: "Do unto your competitors as you would have them do unto you."

Unnamed Sources

So far we've looked at how broadcasters rewrite material compiled by other news organizations. But how do they handle their own original material which, for one reason or another, cannot be attributed to an official source?

Unfortunately, there's no simple rule that applies throughout the profession. Some news organizations permit very loose attribution ("Sources say . . ." or "Sources tell W-W-X-X News . . ."). Some require slightly more precise, but still loose attribution ("City Hall sources say . . ." or "W-W-X-X News learned at City Hall this morning . . ."). And some require a still higher degree of precision ("Sources in the Mayor's office say . . ." or "Sources on Mayor Smith's staff tell W-W-X-X News that . . .").

To complicate matters, different news departments have different policies on the sort of "bargain" you may enter into with your sources. Typically, a source will agree to tell you something "off the record" in return for a guarantee of anonymity. However, some news departments forbid the reporting of "off the record" remarks under any circumstances. Others grant staffers wide leeway in using material from unnamed sources.

There is also a legal dilemma facing reporters and editors. There are risks in reporting unsourced information because a judge may order a reporter to reveal the name of his or her sources or be cited for contempt of court, and even go to jail. Although most news organizations fully back the presumed right of reporters and editors to guard the privacy of their news sources, the "right" is not absolute; in the meantime it is the reporter who may go to jail.

In short, this is a very thorny issue abounding with legal and professional traps.

That said, here are some guidelines to serve in most situations:

1. Make sure you thoroughly understand the policy of your news department regarding the gathering, writing, and reporting of information from unnamed sources.
2. Always be as precise as you can. For the sake of credibility, it is important to establish as close a link as possible between the subject matter and its source.
3. Some editors and producers will ask you to divulge the identity of your sources—not for broadcast, but rather as a means of judging your story's credibility. Whether you decide to share the names of your sources with your superiors is up to you, but *in no case* should you reveal the names to other people, not even to your colleagues, family, or friends. You must allow them the legal privilege, in case they are asked, of honestly being able to say, "I don't know."

QUOTATION AND PARAPHRASING

Quoting someone's words is, of course, the most direct form of attribution. Much of the time, broadcast journalists quote people by means of recorded excerpts of their remarks; the excerpts are integrated into the written news stories. Called "actualities" or "voice cuts" in radio and "sound bites" or "talking heads" in television, these recorded excerpts employ writing techniques so specialized that they require lengthy consideration in later chapters. For now, we'll limit ourselves to quotation in broadcast style without the use of audio- or videotape.

As you read the following print-style story, remember that while *you* can see the quotation marks, your eventual viewers and listeners cannot:

```
      WASHINGTON (UPI)--Dick Gregory, a comedian who used
prolonged fasts to draw attention to civil rights and other
issues, came to Capitol Hill on Wednesday to ask Congress to
help Americans who are so overweight that their health is in
danger.
```

```
          Gregory, who appeared at a news conference with several
     patients he is now treating, said: "The crisis of obesity in
     America, which threatens the lives of more than 11 million of
     our citizens who are dangerously overweight, is a public
     nightmare that demands immediate federal attention."
          Referring to a Hempstead, N.Y., man he helped to lose
     about 400 pounds, Gregory said: "Thanks to Walter Hudson and
     the press, thousands of obese folks decided to come out of the
     closet. I got thousands of calls."
          The comedian said he became aware of Hudson's case after
     newspaper reports described how a rescue team had to free him
     when he got stuck in a doorway. Hudson, who had remained in
     his bedroom for 17 years and remains homebound, once weighed
     1,200 pounds.
          Gregory urged Congress to establish a hot line, to set up
     an institute for obesity at the National Institutes of Health,
     and to conduct hearings on the problem.
```

Suppose, in rewriting this story for broadcast, we said,

```
     Comedian Dick Gregory called on Congress today to help end

     "the crisis of obesity in America."  Gregory said "Eleven million

     of our citizens are dangerously overweight" — "a public

     nightmare that demands immediate federal attention."
```

Please read that paragraph *aloud*.

Do you *hear* the effect of listeners not being able to see the quotation marks? In case you retain any doubts, the effect is to give the impression that Gregory's *opinions* are factual. Unless we make crystal clear that a newsmaker is stating opinions rather than facts, we risk giving listeners inaccurate information.

Is there a "crisis of obesity" in the United States? Although Gregory says so, we have only his word for it. Are "Eleven million of our citizens dangerously overweight?" Where did Gregory get that statistic? Is it accurate and reliable? And in what sense is being overweight "dangerous" for 11 million people? The story doesn't say. So again we have only Gregory's word for it. Is the matter of obesity really a "public nightmare"? Does obesity demand "immediate federal attention"? Again, these are Dick Gregory's opinions, not facts. He may be right, but he may also be wrong, in whole or in part. As journalists, it is not up to us to decide if his opinions are right or wrong—but it *is* up to us to write a *clearly labeled* account of them.

In sum, Gregory's words are so laden with value judgments and questionable assertions that we must make clear that the remarks are his alone and that we, the transmitters of his assertions to a wider audience, do not necessarily accept or share them. We do this by using certain verbs and locutions to enable listeners to identify quotes whose punctuation they cannot see. The most commonly used verbs and locutions are:

· call	· terming it
· term	· in his (her, its, their) words
· claim	· as he (she, they) put it
· what he (she, it, they) called	· —and these are his (her, their) words—
· what he (she, it, they) termed	· in the words of
· calling it	· according to

By careful paraphrasing and by using one or more locutions, we can clearly label opinions in broadcast style. (Frequently, the verbs "say" and "said" will suffice to identify an opinion, usually a noncontroversial one. But if that opinion is to be quoted exactly, it is better to use a locution.)

Examples:

> Comedian Dick Gregory urged Congress today to take action on **what he called** the "public nightmare" of obesity in America. **In Gregory's words,** 11 million Americans are "dangerously overweight" and need public assistance.
>
> Gregory called on Congress to set up an "obesity hot line" and an institute for obesity at the National Institutes of Health.

-0-

> In Washington today, a call for help for the overweight and obese: Comedian Dick Gregory urged Congress to set up an obesity hot line...and an obesity section at the National Institutes of Health.
>
> **According to Gregory,** 11 million Americans are "dangerously overweight" -- a situation **he called** "a public nightmare that demands immediate federal attention."

-0-

> **Claiming** that 11 million Americans are "dangerously overweight," the comedian and political activist Dick Gregory called today for aid to the obese.
>
> **As Gregory put it,** obesity is "a public nightmare that demands immediate federal attention." He said Congress should create an obesity hot line...and an obesity division at the National Institutes of Health.

Notice that in each of the above broadcast rewrites, it is possible to delete the quotation marks without misleading the audience. However, the quotation marks are left in as a sort of visual punctuation for the anchor. With or without the quotation marks, the combination of paraphrasing and locutions makes clear to the audience that it is hearing opinions rather than facts.

Paraphrasing can be a delicate matter. After all, many newsmakers choose certain words because they think they're the right ones. For newswriters to reject those words in favor of other ones that lend themselves to broadcast style can be viewed as unfaithful to the real meaning, or even arrogant. Using your words to report someone else's ideas and opinions does indeed hold that risk. However, most of the time a careful newswriter can use clearer words, and *fewer* words, to convey accurately the sense of a newsmaker's remarks.

But there are times when broadcast newswriters must closely adhere to the exact words of a newsmaker, even though the result might sound stilted and unwieldy on the air. A case in point:

WASHINGTON—Ultraconservative Sen. Jesse Helms (R-N.C.) bitterly attacked the late Dr. Martin Luther King, Jr., in a speech Monday on the Senate floor, calling him unworthy of a holiday in his honor and denouncing him as a communist sympathizer.

"Dr. King's action-oriented Marxism . . . is not compatible with the concepts of this country," Helms said as he launched a filibuster to prevent the Senate from voting on a bill to make the third Monday in January a paid federal holiday in honor of the assassinated civil rights leader's Jan. 15 birthday.

"The legacy of Dr. King was really division, not love," Helms said many people in this country believe.

Helms' Senate remarks seemed almost temperate compared with a report prepared by his office and released Monday that accuses King of "hostility to and hatred for America" and speculates:

"King may have had an explicit but clandestine relationship with the Communist Party or its agents to promote, through his own stature, not the civil rights of blacks or social justice and progress, but the totalitarian goals and ideology of communism."

Evidence "strongly suggest(s) that King harbored a strong sympathy for the Communist Party and its goals," said the report, which concluded, nonetheless, that "there is no evidence that King was a member of the Communist Party."

(Ellen Warren, © *Chicago Sun-Times,* reprinted with permission)

The racial and political overtones of that story make it pretty strong stuff: a U.S. senator describing as a crypto-communist a man perceived by millions of Americans as a hero. The senator's words are potentially offensive, and the standard locutions may not suffice, especially if the story runs longer than 20 seconds on the air. So here are the more formal locutions that serve for this kind of story:

- quote
- unquote
- end quote

- quoting him (her, them) directly
- and these are his (her, their) exact words

Thus, broadcasters might render the foregoing story this way:

```
The senator leading the fight against a national holiday for
the late Dr. Martin Luther King Junior today called Dr. King a
communist sympathizer.  In a speech on the Senate floor and in a
report released by his office, Senator Jesse Helms of North
Carolina denounced Dr. King in very strong terms.  Helms said,
and these are his words, "Dr. King's action-oriented Marxism is
not compatible with the concepts of this country."  Helms said
many Americans -- again quoting him directly -- believe "the
legacy of Dr. King was really division, not love."  The report
from Helms' office said there's evidence, quote, "that King
harbored a strong sympathy for the Communist Party and its
goals," end quote.  Helms' remarks came at the start of a
filibuster against a bill to make the third Monday in January a
federal holiday in Dr. King's honor.
```

Yes, that's a mouthful, and yes, it sounds stilted. But this is a case where the nature of the material overrides the customary informality of broadcast newswriting. The material cries out for quotation at length: You can't have a U.S. senator calling someone a communist and let it go at that.

So, in cases where you want to (or must) quote at length, it is fine to use the words "quote . . . end quote" (or "unquote"). But try not to overdo it. Rely whenever possible on the more informal phrasing.

To sum up,

1. If *you* can say something more clearly and directly than the original speaker, then *paraphrase*.
2. If the original speaker's words are clear, colorful, biased, or controversial, then *quote directly*, either formally or informally, as the story dictates.

ETHICS

You are no doubt coming to realize that the techniques of broadcast journalism embrace a wide range of choices—not just of style and presentation, but also of ethics. Just as attorneys argue amongst themselves about courtroom ethics and doctors about medical ethics, so journalists are constantly debating journalistic ethics. The issues of unnamed sources and crediting competitors are relatively minor aspects of this debate, which really centers around the issues of fairness and accuracy.

In coming chapters, we shall encounter numerous broadcast news techniques that involve ethical choices: the right to know versus the right to privacy, TV news "staging," and "teasing" the news versus full disclosure, to name but a few. While a textbook should not dictate those choices to students, it should, at the very least, describe them and indicate their consequences. To that end, we conclude this chapter with the Society of Professional Journalists (Sigma Delta Chi) *Code of Ethics*. The *Code* spells out the aims and responsibilities of all those who wish to make journalism their careers, whether in print or broadcast.

The first amendment to the U.S. Constitution (Article One of the Bill of Rights) guarantees freedom of the press. But just how far to push that freedom is a matter of endless debate. As Fred W. Friendly, a pioneer broadcaster and former president of CBS News, once put it: "Unless we are careful, we may think that because we have the right to do something means that we are right to do it. The two are not necessarily the same."

EXERCISES

1. The following story tests your ability to use nonlibelous language. Slug it INDICTMENT and write a broadcast version running 20 to 25 seconds.

```
        SHREVEPORT, La. (AP)--The father and brother of former
Gov. Buddy Roemer were indicted by a federal grand jury
Thursday on bank fraud charges involving a $9.6-million loan
for a real estate deal.
        The former governor wasn't named in the indictment.
        The indictment of Roemer's father, Charles E. Roemer II;
his brother, Franklin Danny Roemer; and a third man, R. Lee
Harvill, followed an 18-month probe by the FBI and federal
prosecutors, the U.S. attorney's office said.
        The two-count indictment accuses the three of conspiracy
and bank fraud, the U.S. attorney's office said. If convicted
on both counts, each could be imprisoned for five years and
fined $250,000.
        The indictment alleges that the Roemers and Harvill
conspired to defraud Liberty Federal Savings & Loan of
Leesville through a $9.6-million loan for the purchase and
development of a 92-acre tract of land in Shreveport.
```

Society of Professional Journalists

Code of Ethics

SOCIETY of Professional Journalists, believes the duty of journalists is to serve the truth.

We BELIEVE the agencies of mass communication are carriers of public discussion and information, acting on their Constitutional mandate and freedom to learn and report the facts.

We BELIEVE in public enlightenment as the forerunner of justice, and in our Constitutional role to seek the truth as part of the public's right to know the truth.

We BELIEVE those responsibilities carry obligations that require journalists to perform with intelligence, objectivity, accuracy, and fairness.

To these ends, we declare acceptance of the standards of practice here set forth:

I. RESPONSIBILITY:

The public's right to know of events of public importance and interest is the overriding mission of the mass media. The purpose of distributing news and enlightened opinion is to serve the general welfare. Journalists who use their professional status as representatives of the public for selfish or other unworthy motives violate a high trust.

II. FREEDOM OF THE PRESS:

Freedom of the press is to be guarded as an inalienable right of people in a free society. It carries with it the freedom and the responsibility to discuss, question, and challenge actions and utterances of our government and of our public and private institutions. Journalists uphold the right to speak unpopular opinions and the privilege to agree with the majority.

III. ETHICS:

Journalists must be free of obligation to any interest other than the public's right to know the truth.

1. Gifts, favors, free travel, special treatment or privileges can compromise the integrity of journalists and their employers. Nothing of value should be accepted.

2. Secondary employment, political involvement, holding public office, and service in community organizations should be avoided if it compromises the integrity of journalists and their employers. Journalists and their employers should conduct their personal lives in a manner that protects them from conflict of interest, real or apparent. Their responsibilities to the public are paramount. That is the nature of their profession.

3. So-called news communications from private sources should not be published or broadcast without substantiation of their claims to news values.

4. Journalists will seek news that serves the public interest, despite the obstacles. They will make constant efforts to assure that the public's business is conducted in public and that public records are open to public inspection.

5. Journalists acknowledge the newsman's ethic of protecting confidential sources of information.

6. Plagiarism is dishonest and unacceptable.

IV. ACCURACY AND OBJECTIVITY:

Good faith with the public is the foundation of all worthy journalism.

1. Truth is our ultimate goal.

2. Objectivity in reporting the news is another goal that serves as the mark of an experienced professional. It is a standard of performance toward which we strive. We honor those who achieve it.

3. There is no excuse for inaccuracies or lack of thoroughness.

4. Newspaper headlines should be fully warranted by the contents of the articles they accompany. Photographs and telecasts should give an accurate picture of an event and not highlight an incident out of context.

5. Sound practice makes clear distinction between news reports and expressions of opinion. News reports should be free of opinion or bias and represent all sides of an issue.

6. Partisanship in editorial comment that knowingly departs from the truth violates the spirit of American journalism.

7. Journalists recognize their responsibility for offering informed analysis, comment, and editorial opinion on public events and issues. They accept the obligation to present such material by individuals whose competence, experience, and judgment qualify them for it.

8. Special articles or presentations devoted to advocacy or the writer's own conclusions and interpretations should be labeled as such.

V. FAIR PLAY:

Journalists at all times will show respect for the dignity, privacy, rights, and well-being of people encountered in the course of gathering and presenting the news.

1. The news media should not communicate unofficial charges affecting reputation or moral character without giving the accused a chance to reply.

2. The news media must guard against invading a person's right to privacy.

3. The media should not pander to morbid curiosity about details of vice and crime.

4. It is the duty of news media to make prompt and complete correction of their errors.

5. Journalists should be accountable to the public for their reports and the public should be encouraged to voice its grievances against the media. Open dialogue with our readers, viewers, and listeners should be fostered.

VI. MUTUAL TRUST:

Adherence to this code is intended to preserve and strengthen the bond of mutual trust and respect between American journalists and the American people.

The Society shall--by programs of education and other means--encourage individual journalists to adhere to these tenets, and shall encourage journalistic publications and broadcasters to recognize their responsibility to frame codes of ethics in concert with their employees to serve as guidelines in furthering these goals.

CODE OF ETHICS
(Adopted 1926; revised 1973, 1984, 1987)

> Prosecutors described the alleged scheme as a "Land flip" in which the property would be purchased but then the construction funds would be diverted to the defendants' personal use.

2. The following story tests your ability to paraphrase and to quote in broadcast style. Write a 30-second version slugged GINGRICH.

> WASHINGTON (AP)--A daughter of House Republican Whip Newt Gingrich publicly broke with her father Tuesday and urged the GOP to reject the anti-abortion stance it has embraced since 1980.
> "If the Republican Party is to appeal to young people in general, and specifically to women, we must throw off this stranglehold that the anti-choice movement has on the apparatus of the party," said Kathy Gingrich Lubbers.
> Lubbers, 29, a Greensboro, N.C., businesswoman, said her father was "very supportive" of her decision to make public her opposition to the Republican platform that reflects her father's anti-abortion views.
> "He has never, never attempted to silence me, unlike the Republican platform committee," Lubbers said. "Our family is big enough to encompass both sides of this issue, and I would only hope that our party is just as big."
> Gingrich, who was in Georgia awaiting the outcome of a recount that Tuesday confirmed his victory in last week's 6th District GOP primary, said that while he disagreed with his daughter on abortion, "both my family and my party are strong enough to have healthy, spirited debates, even about the most sensitive of topics."

3. The following story tests your ability to attribute accurately in broadcast style. Slug it POSTAL SCAM and write a 40-second story. (Hint: You must credit the Associated Press.)

> WASHINGTON (AP)--A draft congressional report alleges that the former House postmaster inflated mail-handling statistics by as much as 100 million pieces a year to justify more political patronage workers for his operation, sources familiar with the report said.
> The report is being thrashed out by three Democrats and three Republicans on a task force looking into wrongdoing and mismanagement at the House post office.
> The report, already four days overdue, now appears likely to be delayed even longer because of partisan disagreement over what it should include and how to present the findings.
> Both Democrats and Republicans on the task force agree that the institution's internal, independently run mail system was rife with mismanagement and abuse of political patronage, said task force members.
> Former Postmaster Robert V. Rota, who resigned amid the controversy earlier this year, boosted estimates of mail coming through the facility to provide more jobs for influential politicians, the report says, according to sources.
> Rota did not immediately return telephone calls to his home seeking comment.
> The investigation by the six-member bipartisan task force of the House Administration Committee parallels a grand jury probe by U.S. Atty. Jay B. Stephens in Washington.
> The federal investigation has included subpoenas of office expense records for at least three Democratic representatives. Among matters being investigated are whether lawmakers used their office expense accounts to buy stamps, then traded the stamps back for cash for other uses.

Special Segments

7

Local newscasts customarily encompass much more than hard news stories. Typically, they cover sports and the weather, deliver one or more sets of headlines, and often include a brief stock-market report and a "light" item known as a *kicker*.

While stocks and the weather are primarily written "straight," sports and kickers give broadcast newswriters wide latitude in both style and content.

SPORTS

Strictly speaking, amateur and professional sports belong to the realm of entertainment rather than news. The fate of the world does not hinge on the outcome of the Super Bowl or the World Series. A sports story must have transcending interest to be included in a network newscast. But at the local level, sports occupies a large chunk of news time, as news departments try to satisfy the audience's apparently unquenchable thirst for information about local teams, be they high school, college, or pro.

Perhaps the most colorful sportswriting in America appears in the major daily newspapers. Print sportswriting almost *has* to be colorful to command readers' interest. After all, readers already know how the games came out. They heard the final scores reported on radio or TV. In the age of television, print sportswriting must concentrate not on who won, but rather on how the game was played.

Due to time constraints, most broadcast sportswriting is limited to reporting the latest scores. However, in longer newscasts, especially on television, sportswriters and reporters have time to strive for color and originality. Unfortunately, few of them make good use of the opportunity. All too often they merely pile cliché upon cliché in the mistaken notion that they sound clever or original.

One explanation for this shortcoming may be that sportswriting and sports reporting tend to be "orphans" in college journalism departments and not deemed worthy of the seriousness accorded to covering hard news. Another may be that sports journalism attracts a different sort of student, the sort attracted mainly by the field of play rather than by politics, history, or the arts.

Whatever the explanation, you can bank on this: If you go into broadcast journalism, sooner or later you *will* find yourself writing sports copy. It matters not that your eventual goal may be to cover the White House for CBS News; starting out, you'll have to write stories about the president *and* about the local volleyball tournament. *You* may not care much about sports, but a large chunk of your *audience* does care, passionately. So you might as well learn some basics here and now.

Rule One is to follow broadcast style and *avoid clichés*.

In baseball, for example, there is a very simple name for what players use to hit the ball. It's called a *bat*. There is no need whatever to find substitute words—such as "stick," "baton," "lumber," "wood," "war club," and so on, all of which are clichés. Using them does not make sports copy sound more interesting. They do make it sound silly and trite.

Rule Two is to *keep it short*.

The news agency copy you receive will contain far more information than you can possibly hope to include in a broadcast version. If a hometown team is involved, you will be able to write lengthier copy and include more details. Even so, you will usually be limited to the bare bones.

Let's stick with baseball, the professional sport with the longest season (eight months: spring training through the World Series) and a staple of sports reporting. The following is a typical news-agency account of a baseball game:

```
bc-bba-chisox 7-1 0556

     CHICAGO (UPI)--Gary Redus, whose game-winning single in
the ninth inning Friday night lifted the Chicago White Sox to
a 2-1 victory over the New York Yankees, said he was
determined to get a hit because of opportunities he muffed
earlier in the game.
     "My thinking was I've got to do something for the two
mistakes I made earlier," said Redus, who twice flied out
after Ron Karkovice led off with doubles.
     "If I had done my job earlier in the game, it would have
been a different situation. So I kind of feel like I redeemed
myself in that respect."
     Redus's single down the third-base line with one out in
the ninth drove home Fred Manrique and gave the White Sox
their first victory over the Yankees in six attempts this
season.
     Manrique had led off with a single and took second when
Ozzie Guillen's sacrifice was bobbled by reliever Steve
Shields for an error, allowing Guillen to reach first. Dave
Righetti relieved and struck out pinch hitter Darryl Boston.
Cecilio Guante then came on and surrendered Redus's
game-winning hit on the first pitch.
     Bobby Thigpen pitched one inning to improve to 5-5.
Shields fell to 1-3.
     Chicago starter Jack McDowell allowed one run on three
hits in eight innings. He struck out six and walked two before
being relieved by Thigpen in the ninth.
     "He's still got a lot to learn but I thought he just
pitched the best game I ever saw him pitch," Chicago Manager
Jim Fregosi said of his right-handed rookie.
     The White Sox took a 1-0 lead in the third inning on an
RBI single by Harold Baines after Karkovice led off with a
double and moved to third on Steve Lyons' groundout.
     The Yankees, who had been limited by McDowell to one hit
through six innings, tied the score 1-1 in the seventh. Gary
Ward doubled and scored two outs later on a single by Mike
Pagliarulo.
     New York's Ron Guidry, making his first start of the
season after recuperating from shoulder surgery last December,
gave up six hits over 4 2/3 innings. He was lifted with two
outs in the fifth after the White Sox loaded the bases on
Karkovice's second double, an intentional walk to Baines and a
walk to Greg Walker. Shields fanned pinch hitter Dan Pasqua to
end the inning.
     Guidry, who threw 90 pitches, gave up one run, struck out
one and walked two. "I didn't know what to expect," said
Guidry, who was reactivated from the disabled list when the
Yankees placed Richard Dotson on the 15-day DL with a strained
groin muscle. "I'm not happy with the outcome (of the game),
```

```
but personally I was content. I managed to have fairly good
velocity and control, and that's a good sign."
    Yankees Manager Lou Piniella also was pleased with
Guidry's performance.
    "I couldn't be happier," Piniella said. "He threw the ball
well; it was just an excellent outing.
    "We just didn't hit the ball well tonight," he said. "But
you have to give McDowell credit. He held us to three hits.

That's a pretty good performance."
    ------------------
upi 12:34 aed
```

Unless you are writing for a station in Chicago or New York, or for a cable sports outlet, that story will wind up as part of a wrap-up of late scores. As such, it will merit a grand total of two seconds' air time!

```
                    Chicago 2, the Yankees 1.


                                  or


                    Chicago beat the Yankees, 2-1.
```

(Note the use of figures that in regular news copy would be spelled out. Since sports scores are numbers by definition, there is little chance of confusing anchors. Note also that the specific When element is omitted. Scores are automatically assumed to be "today's" or "tonight's" results—unless specified otherwise.)

If the newscast for which you are writing allows a little more time for sports, the story can include a few key details:

```
        Chicago beat the Yankees tonight on a ninth-inning single by

        Gary Redus.  It was the first time the White Sox have beaten New

        York all season.

                                  (:07)
```

On stations in Chicago and New York, where this game is a local story, and in other cities whose stations devote sufficient time to their sports segments, the story will run longer, possibly from 15 to 30 seconds. This is where broadcast sportswriting risks sounding trite instead of colorful. To avoid triteness, newcomers are best advised to "play it straight":

```
        For the first time this season, the Chicago White Sox beat

        the New York Yankees tonight.  The score was 2 to 1.  The

        game-winning hit came on a single by Gary Redus in the bottom of

        the ninth.

        Veteran Yankee lefthander Ron Guidry (GID-ree) made his

        first start of the season following shoulder surgery.  Guidry was

        lifted in the fifth after throwing 90 pitches.
```

> Chicago reliever Bobby Thigpen got the win, Yankee reliever
> Steve Shields the loss.
>
> (:20)

Admittedly, there's nothing very "colorful" about that version. But it is clear, concise, and reports the highlights. Once you have learned to write sports in this fashion, deliberately suppressing the urge to be "colorful," you can begin striving for a zippier style:

> The Chicago White Sox finally overcame the Yankee hex
> tonight, beating New York for the first time in six tries.
> Chicago's Gary Redus singled down the third base line in the
> bottom of the ninth, for a 2-to-1 Sox victory.
>
> Yankee southpaw Ron Guidry, his shoulder repaired by
> surgery, got his first start of the season. Guidry went five
> innings, throwing 90 pitches, and allowing only one run before
> being lifted for Steve Shields.
>
> Shields took the loss, the win going to Chicago reliever
> Bobby Thigpen -- his fifth of the season.
>
> (:30)

Now, that might not be "zippy" enough for some of you. Perhaps you can do better. In fact, we urge you to give it a try—but only *after* mastering the knack of "playing it straight" by writing simply and clearly.

Something else about the foregoing broadcast versions: They are all *radio-style* copy. That is, the anchor can announce them without reference to *pictures*. But *television style* usually requires a very different approach, because the copy must be linked closely with what viewers are *seeing*.

We will be spending a lot of time on writing to visuals later in this book. For now, it is sufficient to note that videotaped highlights look very odd if they are out of sequence and if they do not match what the anchor is saying. In this case, for example, the tape sequence cannot begin with Gary Redus's game-winning hit, which came in the ninth inning, and then show what happened in earlier innings. Instead, the tape must follow a natural order of events. Thus the accompanying *TV news copy must follow the same order as the tape.*

Here's an example of how a TV version might be structured:

> (on/camera) The Yankees
> have been giving the White Sox
> fits all season, beating them
> five out of five. But at
> Comiskey Park tonight, things
> were different.
>
> (voice/over) The Yankees
> started their ace lefthander Ron

Guidry (GID-ree) for the first
time since shoulder surgery.
Despite holding the Sox to one
run, Guidry was lifted in the
fifth after throwing 90 pitches.

Then, in the bottom of
ninth, the score tied one-one,
Chicago's Gary Redus singled off
Cecilio Guante (GWAN-tay) down
the third base line, scoring
Fred Manrique (Man-REE-kay), and
giving the Sox the victory, 2 to
1.

(:30)

Regardless of news medium, if you never master the basics of simplicity and clarity, you might go your merry way, perhaps referring to the White Sox as "the Pale Hose" and the Yankees as "the Pin-Stripers," thinking you invented those terms, while in the audience are legions of sports fans, groaning "Oh, no, not *that* again!"—and possibly switching to another channel.

Professional sportswriters and reporters usually serve a long apprenticeship in broadcasting's minor leagues (small towns, small stations, small paychecks) where they strive to develop an idiosyncratic style that will one day land them in the majors (big cities, big stations, big paychecks). The ones who succeed most quickly are generally the ones who start out writing simply and clearly and *then* develop a personal style.

Sports Statistics

Sports fans love statistics. Newspaper sports pages and radio-TV sportscasts are happy to oblige. But the journalists who assemble this statistical material must know what it's all about. In addition to the names of the players, the rules of the games, and the economics of the sports industry, sports journalists must understand the shorthand of sports statistics. They must know how to reconstruct a sporting event merely from a statistical analysis of it.

For example, the same news agency sports wire that sent the foregoing written account of the Chicago/New York baseball game also sent the following, called a *box score:*

```
pm-bba-alboxes 2ndadd sked 7-2 0561
NEW YORK              ab  r  h  bi   CHICAGO              ab  r  h  bi
Washington cf         4   0  0  0    Redus lf             5   0  2  1
Ward rf               4   1  1  0    Lyons 3b             4   0  1  0
Mattingly 1b          4   0  1  0    Baines dh            3   0  1  1
Clark dh              3   0  0  0    Walker 1b            3   0  0  0
Pagliarul 3b          3   0  1  1    Williams rf          2   0  1  0
Cruz lf               3   0  0  0    Pasqua rf            2   0  1  0
Buhner rf             1   0  0  0    Gallagher cf         4   0  2  0
Santana ss            3   0  0  0    Manrique 2b          3   1  1  0
Skinner c             2   0  0  0    Guillen ss           3   0  0  0
Meacham 2b            1   0  0  0    Karkovice c          3   1  2  0
Winfield ph           1   0  0  0    Boston ph            1   0  0  0
Randolph 2b           0   0  0  0
Totals . . . . . . .  29  1  3  1    Totals . . . . . . . 33  2  11 2
One out when winning run scored . . . . . . .
```

```
New York# . . . . . .  000 000 100 -- 1
Chicago# . . . . . .  001 000 001 -- 2
Game-winning RBI -- Redus (3)
E -- Shields. DP -- New York 2, Chicago 1.
LOB -- New York 5, Chicago 10.
2B -- Karkovice (2), Gallagher, Ward.
SB -- Redus (14), Williams (4). S -- Manrique, Guillen.
```

```
                        IP#      H#     R    ER    BB    SO
     . . . New York
Guidry               4 2-3      6     1    1    2    1
Shields (L 1-3)      3 1-3      4     1    1    0    3
Righetti             1-3        0     0    0    0    1
Guante               0          1     0    0    0    0
     . . . Chicago
McDowell             8          3     1    1    2    6
Thigpen (W 5-5)      1          0     0    0    2    0
Shields pitched to 2 batters in 9th:
Guante pitched to 1 batter in 9th.
T -- 2:49, A -- 19,798
Umpires -- Home, Young; 1b, Evans; 2b, Tischida; 3b, Hendry.
```

To non-fans, the box score is meaningless statistics. But to knowledgeable sportswriters, it contains enough information to produce a lengthy written account of the game's highlights. The sports pages of many newspapers reprint the box scores in their entirety, or in shorter versions called *line scores*. TV news often uses the line scores in electronic graphics or titles to accompany the sportscaster's text. Very often, a news agency will transmit *only* the box score, without a separate written account of the game. Obviously, a sportswriter must know how to interpret it.

Almost all sporting events can be reduced to statistical versions for transmission to newsrooms. Thus, anyone wishing to specialize in sports broadcasting must learn how to decipher them. Space does not permit us to explain these statistical analyses here. We therefore urge you to seek knowledgeable help, perhaps by visiting local news organizations and asking questions of sports-desk staffers, or by checking with coaching personnel at a college athletic department. Statistics are the raw material with which sportswriters and reporters earn much of their living.

WEATHER

Like sports, weather reporting and forecasting has become a standard segment of local radio and TV news. And, like sports, it is a segment often filled, unfortunately, with cliché-ridden, substandard prose. On local TV especially, weather writer/anchors tend to be "personalities" rather than journalists, watched chiefly for their entertainment value.

All stations get their weather information from the same source, the U.S. Weather Service's local and regional offices. The forecast and hourly temperatures are carried alike to all newsrooms via the news agencies. So unless the weather is sufficiently harsh as to provide an actual news story, the forecast can be given in about 15 seconds. The weather segment of most local TV newscasts is thus an exercise in making a mountain out of a molehill. Stations employ "entertaining" weather anchors for competitive reasons; they are afraid, perhaps justifiably so, that dropping the weather segment will result in a significant loss of audience for the entire newscast.

So this section is not about how to become a stand-up comic/weather anchor. It is about how to avoid grabbing the nearest cliché such as:

```
        Better get out those umbrellas -- the weatherman says it'll

    rain tonight...
```

Please resist this temptation. Most of your listeners are wise enough to realize that if rain is forecast, they should probably carry an umbrella. And *who* is "the weatherman"? Is he related to the Sandman? Leave the silliness to the disk jockey. As for you, just keep it short and to the point:

```
     The weather forecast:  Possible rain tonight, with a low

around 50.  Clearing by morning, with a high tomorrow around 70.
```

Because the weather is often the closing item in a newscast, it is well to write it in such a way that it can be shortened or lengthened at a glance from the newscaster. That's because, while it's easy to begin a newscast on time, it's tricky to end it on time. A certain amount of flexibility is needed to enable the newscaster to "stretch" or "get off."

Therefore, the weather should be written (on a separate page, of course) something like this:

```
     The weather forecast calls for possible rain tonight, with a

low around 50.  Clearing by morning, with a high tomorrow around

70.  (Turning colder by Thursday, and more rain expected by the

weekend.)  At _____ o'clock, the airport temperature was

_____.  The humidity was _____ percent.  And the

wind was _____ at _____ miles per hour.
```

The blanks are filled in with the latest readings just before air time, and the material in parenthesis, as well as the hourly readings, may be read or deleted as time warrants. Many news departments have standardized format sheets for the weather; the blanks need only be penciled in on the way to the studio.

FINANCIAL NEWS

Like sports reporting, financial news reporting can get mired in statistics. Therefore, unless the newscast specifies otherwise, the stock report should be kept very short. It should include only the latest (or closing) Dow Jones industrial average, state whether trading has been "light," "moderate," or "heavy," and, time permitting, give the closing dollar price of gold in New York and the closing Nikkei (pronounced NEE-kay) average on the Tokyo Stock Exchange.

This limited information must often be extracted from a long financial report from a news agency:

```
PM-WallStreetNoon
     NEW YORK (AP)--The stock market gained more ground today,
following through on Wednesday's modest rally.
     The Dow Jones average of 30 industrials, up 10.80 points
Wednesday, climbed 10.00 points to 3,281.39 by noontime on
Wall Street.
     Gainers outnumbered losers by about 4 to 3 in nationwide
trading of New York Stock Exchange-listed issues with 824 up,
611 down and 644 unchanged.
     The dollar was mixed in foreign-exchange trading after a
rally on Wednesday.
     At the same time, analysts said stocks drew some support
from expectations of favorable inflation news. The Labor
Department reports Friday on the producer price index of
```

```
finished goods and next week on the consumer price index for
August.
     In today's economic news, initial claims for state
unemployment insurance rose 8,000, or a little less than
expected, in the week ended Aug. 29.
     National Semiconductor rose 7/8 to 12 in active trading.
The company reported earnings for the fiscal first quarter
ended Aug. 30 of 17 cents a share, compared to a loss in the
corresponding quarter a year earlier.
     Charles Schwab Corp. tumbled 37/8 to 185/8. Late Wednesday
the company surprised investors with a projection of a 50
percent decline in third-quarter profits.
     Gainers among the blue chips included Proctor & Gamble, up
11/4 at 483/8; Philip Morris, up 1/2 at 845/8; Aluminum Co. of
America, up 13/8 at 681/8; and international Paper, up 5/8 at
63.
     The NYSE's composite index of all its listed common stocks
rose .41 to 229.51. At the American Stock Exchange the market
value index was up .27 at 383.09.
     Volume on the Big Board came to 89.12 million shares at
noontime, up from 79.19 million at the same point Wednesday.
APTV-09-10-92 1223EDT
```

As the agency designations indicate, that interim stock report moved at 12:23 P.M. Eastern Time. Thus, for an upcoming newscast, the entire story would be boiled down this way:

```
     On Wall Street at this hour, stocks are headed for a second

straight day of moderate gains.  At noon the Dow Jones

industrials were up 10 points in active trading.
```

(:07)

Short and simple.

Closing stock averages for the day, including the price of gold, move in mid-afternoon, Eastern Time. Those are the figures to use thereafter.

Daily business news programs on CNN and PBS, as well as full-time financial news outlets on cable TV and radio, obviously require much more detail than in the foregoing bare-bones account. Their viewers and listeners tune in specifically to learn the statistics. For TV, writers key the scripted figures to identical figures appearing in electronic graphics and titles.

KICKERS

By its very nature, any newscast is overwhelmingly devoted to stories involving serious issues. Seldom is there any time for lighter human interest stories, except at the very end of a newscast or just before the local sports and weather. Such a lighter item is known in broadcasting as a "kicker."

Kickers are important psychologically—a way of saying to listeners that the world is not coming to an immediate end despite the bleak picture painted by the news stories they have heard so far. And for the newswriter/newscaster, writing kickers is a sort of release from the tension of writing sober, issue-oriented copy all day.

There are no firm rules on which stories make good kickers. However, there are a few rules on what *not* to use:

1. Kickers should never treat serious issues lightly.
2. Kickers should never make fun of people or beliefs.
3. Kickers should never be cruel to people, animals, or religious institutions.

Here, for example, is the type of story to *avoid* as a potential kicker:

```
          DENVER (AP)--A man angry about the haircut he received
     returned to the barbershop with a gun and killed the barber,
     police said.
          Robert Willis, owner of Barber Bob's Barber Shop in east
     Denver, was shot at least five times Saturday by a man whose
     hair he had cut earlier in the day, witnesses said.
```

Let's face it: That is the kind of story that lends itself to "sick humor." There's probably not a newsroom in the country where staffers wouldn't kid around by shouting outrageous comments to one another—or pinning the story on a bulletin board and adding a remark or two. But sick humor is not—repeat *not*—a fit subject for a kicker. Yes, the event was bizarre and the story is attention-getting. But a person *was killed!* That makes it a straight news story, not a kicker.

Kickers must be in good taste. While most can be funny, they need provide only a pleasant contrast to the serious news stories that precede them. They are the news department's way of saying, "Things may be pretty bad today—but here's something that isn't."

The following kickers from ABC Radio News illustrate the style and tone to aim for:

```
     A new weapon in the age-old battle between man and mosquito:

     Two scientists in New Delhi say garlic does the trick.  They've

     discovered garlic not only helps stimulate the human system and

     fight bacteria -- a little spray of garlic also kills the

     mosquito.  However, at the dosage they're recommending, it could

     kill your social life as well.


                                   -o-


     Eight million dollars is a lot of overtime -- but that's how

     much doctors at three university clinics in West Germany

     collected last year.  Officials decided they'd look into the

     matter, and they found an easy explanation:  The doctors were

     cheating.  They put in for extra pay for working on special days

     -- February Thirtieth...June Thirty-first -- days that don't

     exist on any calendar.
```

As you scan the news agency copy coming over the teletype machine or computer screen, some stories virtually leap out as possible kickers. They are offbeat, tasteful and usually uplifting. Here's one that's *literally* uplifting:

```
          MOUNTAIN VIEW, Cal. (AP)--Little DeAndra Anrig was flying
     her kite when it suddenly started to fly her, her parents say.
     It was just a short hop, but one the 8-year-old isn't likely
     to forget.
          A twin-engine plane caught the 200-pound nylon test line
     of DeAndra's kite, lifted her several feet off the
     ground -- over her father's head and almost into a tree -- and
     carried her about 100 feet, she said Tuesday.
          She let go and landed safely, but said she was still sore
     after two days' rest. The plane, meanwhile, is grounded
```

because of damage apparently caused by getting tangled in the
kite string.
    DeAndra and her parents, who live in the East Bay
community of Dublin, were picnicking with friends at the
Shoreline Park about 30 miles south of San Francisco and about
two miles from the Palo Alto Airport on Sunday and taking
turns flying a glider-type kite with a 12-foot wingspan.
    While it was DeAndra's turn, a plane descending for the
airport snagged the line, her parents said.
    "She said it was just a big jerk that lifted her into the
air," said DeAndra's mother, Debby. "It carried her right over
my husband's head. All he saw was a shadow going over his
head. I'm just thankful she let go.
    "We always said, 'Hold on tight. Don't let go, honey,'"
the mother said, recalling their advice on proper kite-flying
techniques.
    DeAndra said she was doing just that, until she saw what
was looming in front of her: "I thought that I was going to
hit a tree."
    Lenore Deaville, a pilot, was at the airport watching a
friend make her first solo flight. She said the pilot of the
twin-engine Rockwell Turbo Commander, Jake Uranga of Reno,
told her that "he was at 800 feet doing about 140 knots (160
m.p.h.) when this thing came at him."
    Uranga, who was flying a patient destined for Stanford
University Hospital, said he tried to avoid it, but couldn't.
He landed safely.
    An FAA official said one of the two propellers on Uranga's
plane suffered a 2-inch gash.

If your mental wheels have been spinning, you're probably ready to start rewriting this one. But a word of caution: One thing you do *not* want to do is use the same wording as the news agency writer, especially in the lead. There's no law against "stealing" a lead—but doing so is a violation of professional etiquette. It is much better to be original, to come up with your own version. A couple of possibilities:

    An eight-year-old California girl knows what it's like to be

Peter Pan, if only for a scary moment. The other day she found

herself sailing through the air when a small plane snagged the

line of a kite she was flying. Her parents say she held on and

was airborne for about 100 feet, dropping safely to the ground

just before she would have smacked into a tree.

    She's spent the past two days in bed...sore but otherwise

unhurt. As for the plane, a twin-engine Rockwell Turbo

Commander: It's been grounded with a damaged propeller, a gash

caused by the nylon kite line.

                  -0-

    Kite-flying may be a safe and sane thing to do -- but don't

tell that to 8-year-old DeAndra Anrig of Dublin, California.

DeAndra was flying a large kite the other day when a small plane

coming in for a landing at a nearby airport snagged the kite

line. DeAndra held on for dear life...and was airborne for about

```
100 feet.  Her parents say she let go and dropped safely to the
ground just in time to avoid hitting a tree.  She's still a
little sore, but otherwise okay —— which is more than can be said
for the plane:  It's been grounded with a damaged propeller.
```

If you are the type of person who just can't wait to sink your teeth into this story and devise your own version, the chances are good that you will become a successful broadcast journalist. If you can't have fun writing this kind of story, you may never have fun in a newsroom.

Warning: Writing kickers can be habit-forming. Limit yourself to only one per newscast.

HEADLINES

Broadcast news borrowed the term "headline" from print—and changed the term's meaning in the process. On radio and TV, a headline (or just "head" for short) is a one-sentence capsule version of a story. Many stations use headlines frequently and in various ways: as promos for upcoming newscasts (during breaks in entertainment programming), as introductions to newscasts, as recaps or previews during newscasts, or, on radio, every 20 minutes or in place of full newscasts (usually at half-past the hour).

Do not confuse headlines with "teasers" (which we'll get to in a moment). Headlines simply boil down the essence of the hour's (or day's) major stories into a series of rapidly delivered sentences or sentence fragments, one per story. They may be put in the present tense, the past tense, or the present perfect tense, depending on the style set by management. They are *typed on the same page* and slugged "HEADS."

KCAL-TV associate producer Stacy Scholder confers with director Chris Stegner about a "Newsbreak" (set of headlines) she has just scripted for telecast during a commercial break in entertainment programming.

On the news set, KCAL-TV anchor Jerry Dunphy delivers Scholder's copy on a hand cue from stage manager Frank Gervasi.

A set of present-tense heads for some of the stories used so far in this book might go as follows:

```
        Good evening.  In tonight's news...

        More than 50 people are hurt as a jetliner aborts take-off

in New York....

        Supreme Court nominee Douglas Ginsburg admits to having

smoked marijuana....

        Forest fires rage in southern Arizona....

        And...authorities uncover an alleged plot to murder the

mayor of San Antonio.

        Details on these stories...and other news...coming right up.
```

A headline might also be used to preview an upcoming story just before a commercial break:

```
        The president says "no" to a tax increase.  That story...and

more news...in a moment.
```

TEASERS

Headlines *reveal* the essence of news stories. "Teasers" *withhold* it. The distinction is important—and controversial.

Teasers are aptly named because they attempt to "tease" the audience into staying tuned, usually through a commercial break. Many news departments frown on teasers because they are a way of saying to the audience, "*We* know the news, but if *you* want to know it, you'll just have to sit through several minutes of commercials." That, these news departments say, is shoddy journalism and is not the sort of image they wish to project.

But, in the real world, fierce competition for ratings often intervenes. Top management may seek to "hook" listeners and viewers by employing teasers instead of headlines. Thus they are a fact of life in many newsrooms.

Using the same stories that were the basis for the foregoing headlines, a set of teasers might go this way:

```
            Good evening everybody.  In tonight's news....

            A near-disaster at a New York airport....

            A surprising revelation from Supreme Court nominee Douglas

      Ginsburg....

            Forest fires rage in the Southwest....

            And...an alleged plot to murder a big-city mayor.

            Stay tuned.
```

And as a segment break:

```
            The president's decision on a tax increase.  That story when

      we come back.
```

TRANSITIONS

In broadcast news, a *transition* (sometimes called a "tie-in" or "link") refers to the word or phrase connecting two news stories or two elements within a single story. Print's way of linking related developments is to combine them into a single story, a structure which, as we've seen, does not work well on radio or TV. As for unrelated stories, print merely places them in different columns or on different pages.

But a newscast has no visible "columns" or "pages." A newscast goes from beginning to end, leaving the audience with but two options: to stay tuned or to tune out. Thus, a newscast should "flow." Occasional transitions help the flow, softening the potentially jarring change from one story to another.

A few transitions are so standard that they long ago reached the status of cliché: *meanwhile, meantime, in the meantime,* and *elsewhere.* Because broadcasters sometimes write under extreme time pressure, they may grab for one or more of those clichés out of desperation. Given sufficient time, however, they prefer to write more inventive transitions.

The best transitions are those that specifically tie one story to another:

```
            Federal spending wasn't the only thing on the president's

      mind today....
```

(linking two distinctly different presidential actions on different subjects)

-0-

```
          While the Israelis remained adamant, the P-L-O was showing
     some flexibility....
```

(linking two different diplomatic developments)

-0-

```
     Arizona's loss was Nevada's gain....
```

(linking related stories in different geographical locations)

Remember that if you have to stretch for a transition, it may call too much attention to itself, thereby detracting from the details of the news itself. When in doubt, keep transitions simple:

```
          At the same time,...

          In other economic (medical, political, etc.) news...

          Also downstate (upstate, etc.)...
```

To reiterate a point we made in an earlier chapter, the Where element can often serve as a simple transition:

```
          In New York, Mayor David Dinkins said today...
```

-0-

```
          In Washington, the Labor Department reports...
```

Viewed out of context, such transitions may seem redundant. Yes, the Labor Department is always in Washington and the mayor of New York customarily speaks in New York. However, depending on the story that preceded it, a story connected with this sort of transition *sounds* smooth, and the newscast flows.

A word of caution: Do not get carried away with transitions. A few per newscast are enough. A well-written newscast may require no transitions at all, provided the writer has varied his or her approach among stories that are *inherently* related. For example, the following excerpt from CBS Radio News links three stories without specific transitions:

```
     (HONDURAS)

          Terrorists in Honduras holding 105 hostages say they will

     start killing their captives one at a time, starting two hours

     from now, if their demands are not met.  The terrorists are

     demanding freedom for some 80 political prisoners in Honduras,

     and softening of the country's three-month old anti-terrorism

     law.

     (BRUSSELS)

          Four people were wounded today in Brussels when a man with a

     machine gun opened fire on a synagogue during Rosh Hashanah

     services.  The gunman escaped.
```

(PARIS)

     French police have arrested 14 people and uncovered a cache of weapons and explosives in Paris. Officials say they believe the 14 are part of the terrorist group "Direct Action." That group has claimed responsibility for recent anti—Jewish violence in France.

                          (Rob Armstrong, CBS Radio)

    Note that those three stories, whose common thread is terrorism, could have been read *in any order*. If the writer had used a transition, the flexibility of story order would have been destroyed. Instead, each was written on a separate page to stand on its own and eventually linked with the others by placement (story order) rather than transitional words.

EXERCISES

1. Using the slug OLYMPICS TENNIS, write two versions of the following sports story: First, a one-sentence item for inclusion in a set of sports headlines; and second, a 30-second story for the sports segment of a regularly scheduled newscast.

    BARCELONA, Spain (AP)--Jennifer Capriati won the biggest title of her young career today by capturing the Olympic gold in women's tennis, and pronounced the whole experience "cool."
    The 16-year-old Capriati, exultant after beating top-seeded Steffi Graf 3-6, 6-3, 6-4 in a baseline slugfest, smiled and raised a triumphant fist in the air from the medals stand.
    "It was so emotional up there," said Capriati. "I had chills the whole time. I couldn't believe I was up there.
    "I still can't believe it. For two weeks I was watching other athletes up there who won gold medals and thinking, 'I bet that would be so cool to be up there.'"
    Capriati had earned three previous tournament crowns, none this year, and she has yet to reach a Grand Slam final.
    The decisive shot came in the next-to-last game--a crackling Capriati forehand winner down the line. It happened on break point and gave Capriati a 5-4 lead in the final set.
    In the last game, the third-seeded Capriati held serve at 15. After Graf hit a forehand into the net on final point, Capriati grinned, blew a kiss to her parents and held her arms aloft in celebration.
    "It was definitely one of my greatest matches in terms of fighting for everything, running down balls and really grinding it out," she said.
    Graf took consolation from receiving her silver medal.
    "It's definitely a bit of a disappointment," she said. "But there are times I felt much worse after a match. I still felt good standing up there" (on the medals stand).
    It was Capriati's first victory over Graf in five tries. Capriati, ranked sixth, has now beaten each player ranked in the top five.
    "This is a big step for me--proving to myself I can beat all of them," she said.
    Capriati prevented a German sweep of the day's matches. In the final of the men's doubles, Boris Becker and Michael Stich beat Wayne Ferreira and Piet Norval of South Africa, 7-6 (7-5), 4-6, 7-6 (7-5), 6-3.
    Capriati squandered her first 11 break points, including nine in the fifth game of the first set, which Graf won in 16 grueling minutes. Capriati finally broke for a 5-3 lead in the second set, and then she served out the next game at love.
    The defeat was the first for Graf in Olympic singles. She

won the tournament when tennis was a demonstration sport in
1984 and took the gold in Seoul in 1988. The loss also snapped
Graf's 17-match winning streak.

2. Slug the following story DEFICIT and write a 15-second version to follow a newscast's stock market
report:

        WASHINGTON (AP)--The federal deficit totaled $44.6 billion
in July, wiping out an unusual surplus from a month earlier,
the Treasury reported Friday.
        The gap was 9.2% larger than the $40.8 billion in red ink
in July of last year, and contrasted with a $3.8 billion
surplus in June. The black ink in June had been attributed to
quarterly tax payments.
        The July deficit boosted the imbalance so far in the
fiscal year that will end Sept. 30 to $272.3 billion, compared
to $218.3 billion at the end of the first 10 months of the
last fiscal year.
        Last month, the Administration forecast a deficit of
$333.5 billion for this fiscal year. It said it had lowered
its January forecast of $399.7 billion after Congress failed
to act on additional money for the savings and loan bailout.
        Still, the deficit would set a record if the forecast is
realized. The previous high was $269.5 billion in fiscal 1991.
        Revenues so far this year totaled $894.6 billion, up 3%
from the $868.5 billion raised in the first 10 months of last
fiscal year. But spending jumped 7.3% to $1.17 trillion.
        In July, revenues totaled $79.1 billion, down from $120.9
billion in June. Revenues totaled $78.6 billion in July of
last year.
        Spending in July reached $123.7 billion, up from $117.1
billion a month earlier, and compared to $119.4 billion in
July of last year.
        Individual income taxes last month contributed $35.1
billion to government revenues, down from $38.4 billion during
the same month of last year. Corporate taxes totaled $2.7
billion, up from $1.8 billion a year earlier.

3. Write a maximum 35-second kicker slugged CASH DASH based on the following news agency
story:

        SAN FRANCISCO (AP)--Three people apparently made off with
at least $460,000 after a crate of money bags fell off an
armored car Tuesday, police said.
        The unidentified individuals scooped up the cash-stuffed
bags and drove away after the crate, containing more than $1.5
million, fell out of a moving Loomis Armored Inc. truck when
the rear door flew open in the Mission District.
        The truck driver was unaware of the loss until he stopped
two blocks away after a motorist honked his horn and said the
truck's door was ajar, according to Police Officer Harry
Soulette, who was flagged down by the driver.
        By the time Soulette and the Loomis driver went back to
the crate, a crowd had gathered around the fallen bags. About
$1 million was recovered.
        Some people were putting the sacks back in the crate, but
a few had other ideas.
        "There was a gentleman from the post office grabbing bags
of money out of people's hands and putting them back in the
crate," Soulette said. "At least three people looked at him
and told him what he could do with his suggestion. . . .
Several people decided they were going to take advantage of
what happened, threw the bags into their cars and left."
        Witnesses were able to give detailed descriptions of three
of the people and their cars. If found, they could face felony
grand theft charges, police said.
        "My advice to them is to turn it in," Soulette said.

PART 2: RADIO NEWS

Is Anyone Listening?   8

At this point some of you may be thinking, "Radio? Why should I bother with radio? I want to work in *television*."

Well, chances are you *will* find work in television—eventually. But because of the crowded job market, you are first likely to serve a sort of apprenticeship, perhaps a long one, in radio. There you will discover what generations before you have discovered—namely that radio news is the parent of TV news, and the old-timer still has many important lessons to teach.

MURROW'S LEGACY

If you are under fifty, you may never have heard of Gabriel Heatter or H.V. Kaltenborn. Heatter and Kaltenborn were radio news commentators whose popularity peaked during and just after World War Two. In their day, they were every bit as well-known as John Chancellor and Bill Moyers are today.

If you are under twenty, you may never have heard of Eric Severeid. Severeid, who died in 1992, transferred the art of broadcast news reporting, analysis, and commentary from radio to television. He helped pave the way for Chancellor and Moyers.

Broadcast news techniques, you see, trace their history all the way back to the birth of radio, in 1920. The very first radio broadcast in the United States was a *news* broadcast: the 1920 Harding-Cox presidential election returns over Westinghouse station KDKA in Pittsburgh.

In its first two decades, radio news did not have a "broadcast style." Writing and presentation were in newspaper style— stilted, long-winded, laced with journalese. This was unsurprising, since the only existing training ground was in print journalism.

But as radio grew to rival newspapers and magazines as a reliable deliverer of news—and, of course, as a profitable advertising medium—the men (yes, they were all men in those days) of broadcast news began to evolve some of the writing and presentation techniques discussed so far in this book, especially brevity and informality. There were a number of early pioneers, men whose careers crested just before and during World War Two. But one man above all is credited with stamping broadcast news indelibly with the two qualities that most distinguished it from print: the ability to transmit the sound and the "feel" of events. That man was Edward R. Murrow.

By the outbreak of the war in Europe, Murrow, from his base at CBS in London, had assembled a network of correspondents across Europe who, by short wave, telephone, and transatlantic cable, reported not just the events of the war, but also its *sounds*. For the first time, American listeners could hear not just the voices of the reporters and the voices of Hitler, Churchill, Stalin, and Mussolini, but the actual sounds of bombs exploding, air raid sirens shrieking, anti-aircraft batteries pounding, and fighter planes roaring overhead.

Murrow's own broadcasts from London during German air raids stand even today as models of the art of broadcast reporting. Here's part of his first such live broadcast, delivered from the roof of the BBC building:

I'm standing on a rooftop looking out over London. At the moment everything is quiet. For reasons of national as well as personal security, I'm unable to tell you the exact location from which I'm speaking. Off to my left, far away in the distance, I can see just that faint red angry snap of anti-aircraft bursts against a steel-blue sky, but the guns are so far away that it's impossible to hear them from this location. About five minutes ago the guns in the immediate vicinity were working. I can look across just at a building not far away and see something that looks like a flash of white paint down the side, and I know from daylight observation that about a quarter of that building has disappeared, hit by a bomb the other night.

I think probably in a minute we shall have the sound of guns in the immediate vicinity. The lights are swinging over in this general direction now. You'll hear two explosions. There they are! That was the explosion overhead, not the guns themselves. I should think in a few minutes there may be a bit of shrapnel around here. Coming in, moving a little closer all the while. The plane's still very high. Earlier this evening we could hear occasional—again, those were the explosions overhead. Earlier this evening we heard a number of bombs go sliding and slithering across, to fall several blocks away. Just overhead now the burst of the anti-aircraft fire. Still the nearby guns are not working. The searchlights now are feeling almost directly overhead. Now you'll hear two bursts a little nearer in a moment.

There they are! That hard, stony sound.

Half a century later, a trio of CNN correspondents—Peter Arnett, Bernard Shaw, and John Holliman—could trace their professional lineage back to Murrow as they broadcast live from Baghdad during the Allied air attack against Iraq in 1991. If you thought the CNN coverage was riveting, imagine what radio listeners must have felt back when such live coverage was unprecedented!

Murrow delivered many such broadcasts, usually speaking extemporaneously. But he was a marvelous writer as well. One day he and a colleague were caught in the open during a German air raid. Listen to how he later described it to radio listeners:

It was like a shuttle service, the way the German planes came up the Thames, the fires acting as a flare path. Often they were above the smoke. The searchlights bored into that black roof but couldn't penetrate it. They looked like long pillars supporting a black canopy. Suddenly all the lights dashed off and a blackness fell right to the ground. It grew cold. We covered ourselves with hay. The shrapnel clicked as it hit the concrete road nearby. And still the German bombers came.

Notice the short sentences, the spare, simple language, the rhythm and flow of the whole. This was, and remains, the very model of the art of news broadcasting—in television as well as radio.

Ed Murrow went on to pioneer the development of television news and documentary techniques, and later was named head of the United States Information Agency by President John F. Kennedy. Murrow died a premature death from lung cancer (he smoked as many as four packs of cigarettes a day) in 1965. He is survived by an army of admirers, today an equal number of men and women, who still strive to emulate his work.

Although the technology of broadcast news has changed radically since Murrow's time, his overall concept of radio's use remains unaltered: Radio journalists seek to transmit not only the cold hard facts of events, whenever possible in the voices of the newsmakers themselves, but also the way things "look." Television may bring us pictures, but radio journalists become our eyes.

There is a tendency among today's broadcast journalism students—who, after all, have grown up in the age of television—to give short shrift to radio. Never having heard the writing and reporting

What CNN viewers saw during the initial Allied air and missile attack on Iraq in January, 1991. A video link was impossible at first, so viewers heard live audio coverage from CNN's Peter Arnett, Bernard Shaw, and John Holliman in Baghdad. Their reportage was in the tradition set half a century earlier by CBS's Edward R. Murrow during the London Blitz.

(Off-monitor photo courtesy CNN)

artistry of Ed Murrow, Robert Trout, or Edward P. Morgan (to name but a few), today's students are more attuned to the visual impact of television than to the pure power of words. Be that as it may, radio news, largely because of its closer ratio of humans to machines, remains an excellent training ground for developing abilities that can smooth the transition into television. And once you experience the relative freedom of expression that working in radio allows, who knows? You may decide to stay there.

DRIVE TIME = PRIME TIME

By the late 1950s, radio had lost most of its audience to television except at two distinct times of day: early morning and early evening. People may prefer watching "Murphy Brown" and "Cheers" reruns at night (TV's Prime Time), but they still listen to the radio while traveling to and from work.

The radio audience is especially large between 6 A.M. and 10 A.M. as people awaken, shower, dress, eat breakfast, and commute to work. Radio broadcasters refer to this time period as "Morning Drive Time" or "AM Drive." It is where radio concentrates its main efforts, including news coverage.

Of secondary (but still great) significance is the period from 3 P.M. to 7 P.M., known as "Afternoon Drive Time" or "PM Drive." Between these hours, stations once again concentrate their efforts, especially targeting commuters who are heading home by car and who are getting their first hearing of the day's news.

The rest of the time, roughly 16 hours out of every 24, plus weekends, most radio stations content themselves with a modest schedule of newscasts—or no newscasts at all. Until the 1980s, virtually all stations scrupulously devoted at least part of their broadcast schedules to news and other programming "in the public interest"—pursuant to the terms of their licenses issued by the Federal Communications Commission (FCC). But the FCC appointees of the Reagan/Bush era declined to enforce the regulations, and as a result, radio news and public affairs programming decreased radically. By the early 1990s, many of the nation's estimated 8,500 AM and FM radio stations had eliminated their news departments entirely. Many others had cut their news staffs to the bare bones.

Fortunately, news programming as a full-time format continued to hold its own, and in some cities grew even more popular. Today, there are all-news radio stations in most major cities, as well as numerous stations across the country which devote most of AM Drive and PM Drive exclusively to news.

FORMATS

We just introduced a word, "format," with which you should become familiar. Broadcasters use the term in two ways: to describe both a station's overall form of programming, and to specify the form of each broadcast. For example, stations playing country music are said to have a "Country and Western" (or "C and W") format; stations airing mostly call-in and discussion shows are said to have a "Talk Radio" format; other formats are "Soft Rock," "Hard Rock," "Easy Listening," "Golden Oldies," and so on.

At the same time, each programming segment has its own format. Each newscast has its format as well. The format is like a blueprint, meticulously designed to cover every aspect from beginning to end. For example, a five-minute hourly newscast (its length and air time are the first two aspects of its format) might typically be formatted this way:

- **News Open**—a snappy-sounding series of musical notes or audio tones (sometimes called "beeps") forming a familiar "signature" for the station or network.
- **Sign-on**—the first words spoken by the newscaster, usually stating the newscaster's name and the name of the station or network ("W-W-K-K news-on-the-hour, Joe/Jill Jones reporting," etc.).
- **Section One**—the first part of the newscast, containing the top one to five stories.
- **Commercial Cue**—a sentence or phrase to alert listeners that the news will continue after a commercial break ("More news in a moment" or "More news after this," etc.).

- **Commercial**—either one 60-second commercial or two 30-second commercials played back to back.
- **Section Two**—the balance of the newscast, including local weather, sports, and possibly a kicker.
- **Sign-off**—the newscaster's closing words, usually repeating his/her name and station/network's call letters ("Joe/Jill Jones, W-W-K-K News," etc.).

All-news radio can also be rigidly formatted. Here, for example, is a format for the Westinghouse ("Group W") all-news stations in New York, Chicago, Philadelphia, and Los Angeles. The format is repeated (with minor variations) every 20 minutes:

· Open:	time check, current temperature, station ID, anchor ID
· News Headlines:	top five news stories, mainly local
· Sports Headline:	one only
· Traffic Update:	from metro traffic service
· 1st News Segment:	first three headlined stories
· Commercial Break:	(2:00 minutes)
· 2nd News Segment:	remaining headlined stories plus other news
· Weather:	complete forecast and current temperatures
· Traffic Update:	from metro traffic service
· Commercial Break:	(2:00 minutes)
· Sports:	from staff sportscaster
· Commercial Break:	(1:00 minute)
· Fill to 20:00:	newsbriefs and/or kicker

Newscast formats can be designed in an almost infinite number of ways. In fact, they are changed frequently as part of management's drive to give a station's news programming a distinctive "sound" which listeners can distinguish from all the competing stations, and thus increase the station's share of the audience. A radio journalist who stays at a station for any length of time will probably experience many format changes. Finding the "right" format is a matter of constant tinkering.

Although Judy Ford of all-news KFWB, Los Angeles, is officially designated "anchor," she embodies the multiplicity of skills required in modern radio news. In addition to anchoring for up to 30 minutes at a stretch, she writes, reports (usually by conducting taped telephone interviews), and edits tapes. While on the air, she operates the studio's electronic machinery, controlling the sound levels and tape playback machines. She also has a computer terminal to keep herself updated on breaking stories carried by the news agencies—which she may have to ad lib at length.

Commercials

Radio news staffers do not write or schedule commercials. That task is kept strictly outside the news department and belongs to a station's traffic department (it's called "traffic" because it controls the flow of programming). However, newscasters must often *read* (announce) the commercials scheduled within their newscasts. Commercial sponsorship may even be built into the format itself:

```
       Good morning.  I'm Jack/Jill Jones with the latest W—W—K—K

    news...brought to you by McNulty Chevrolet...where Smilin' Ed

    McNulty always gives you the best deal on a new or used car.
```

In radio's Golden Age (the 1930s and 1940s), such commercial copy was usually read by a staff announcer, to safeguard the strict separation of news and commerce. Even today, some stations have the disk jockey or call-in host read the commercial copy while the newscaster sticks to the news. At most local stations, however, news staffers should not be surprised to find themselves required to read the plug for "Smilin' Ed"—and sound as if they mean it.

MEASURING THE MARKETPLACE

If we have seemed to be dwelling on the commercial aspects of radio, the business side, it's because you need to understand how broadcasters conduct their affairs, of which the news department is just one branch. Radio and television stations measure themselves and their audiences (for advertising sales purposes and by extension for news purposes) through a combination of signal strength and the population density of the local marketplace.

Signal Strength

Nowadays, much network radio programming is delivered to local stations via satellite. Individual stations then relay the signal (along with their own programming) to local listeners by means of radio waves emitted by AM or FM transmitters.

To begin broadcasting, and then to remain on the air, a station owner requires a license from the Federal Communications Commission (FCC), the agency that regulates radio and television in the United States. The FCC assigns each local station its specific frequency on the AM or FM bands (and in TV on the VHF or UHF bands). The agency also regulates the power and direction of each station's transmitter. This is a complicated matter because sound waves, notably on the AM band, behave erratically and fluctuate with atmospheric conditions, especially at night. Therefore, a station whose signal is precise and narrow during daylight hours may find that signal wandering at night, possibly interfering with signals from other stations. The FCC thus strictly limits the frequencies, directions, and power of transmitters in order to minimize the atmospheric chaos.

If your goal is to reach the largest possible audience, you obviously want as strong a signal as possible, in as heavily a populated area as you can find. The FCC, however, has set maximum AM transmitting power at 50,000 watts and has licensed relatively few stations at that power. (If you've ever been driving at night and used the "seek" or "scan" function of your car radio, you may have been surprised to hear a station located at the other end of the continent—undoubtedly one of the lucky 50,000-watters.) All other stations are limited to 25,000 watts, 10,000 watts, or considerably less, down to a low of 1,000 watts of daytime power and 250 watts at night.

What has all this got to do with broadcasting the news? The answer is that the size and quality of a station's news department is partly determined by the strength of the station's transmitter: The stronger the signal, the bigger the potential audience, the greater the potential profits (through the sale of commercial air time), and the bigger and better a news staff the station can afford to hire.

Broadcast Markets—The 1993 TV Market Rankings of U.S. Cities.

Rank	Market	ADI TV HH
1	New York	6,760,400
2	Los Angeles	4,962,300
3	Chicago	3,023,600
4	Philadelphia	2,659,700
5	San Francisco-Oakland-San Jose	2,236,700
6	Boston	2,121,400
7	Washington, DC	1,812,500
8	Dallas-Ft. Worth	1,803,200
9	Detroit	1,728,100
10	Atlanta	1,483,400
11	Houston	1,465,700
12	Cleveland	1,418,100
13	Minneapolis-St. Paul	1,400,500
14	Seattle-Tacoma	1,399,100
15	Miami-Ft. Lauderdale	1,301,900
16	Tampa-St. Petersburg	1,258,500
17	Pittsburgh	1,137,900
18	St. Louis	1,108,300
19	Sacramento-Stockton	1,073,700
20	Phoenix	1,040,300
21	Denver	1,031,700
22	Baltimore	973,000
23	Orlando-Daytona Beach-Melbourne	952,100
24	Hartford-New Haven	928,000
25	San Diego	909,500
26	Portland, OR	887,900
27	Indianapolis	881,200
28	Kansas City	772,700
29	Milwaukee	772,200
30	Charlotte	756,700
31	Cincinnati	756,400
32	Raleigh-Durham	751,100
33	Nashville	731,000
34	Columbus, OH	696,800
35	Greenville-Spartanburg-Asheville	666,400
36	San Antonio-Victoria	626,400
37	Grand Rapids-Kalamazoo-Battle Creek	623,000
38	Buffalo	613,900
39	Norfolk-Portsmouth-Newport News-Hampton	611,200
40	New Orleans	603,900
41	Salt Lake City	597,600
42	Memphis	595,200
43	Providence-New Bedford	571,500
44	Harrisburg-York-Lancaster-Lebanon	567,700
45	Oklahoma City	563,000
45	West Palm Beach-Ft. Pierce-Vero Beach	563,000
47	Louisville	545,400
48	Greensboro-Winston Salem-High Point	533,300
49	Birmingham	523,700
50	Wilkes Barre-Scranton	521,600
51	Albuquerque	519,000
52	Albany-Schenectady-Troy	506,400
53	Dayton	504,400
54	Jacksonville	475,700
55	Charleston-Huntington	471,200
56	Fresno-Visalia	456,500
57	Flint-Saginaw-Bay City	453,900
58	Little Rock	450,800
59	Tulsa	448,700
60	Richmond	441,800
61	Wichita-Hutchinson	422,700
62	Knoxville	415,700
63	Mobile-Pensacola	414,100
64	Toledo	405,900
65	Green Bay-Appleton	385,400
66	Austin, Tx	385,300
67	Roanoke-Lynchburg	383,700
68	Syracuse	382,000
69	Rochester, NY	373,400
70	Des Moines	372,700
71	Shreveport-Texarkana	368,300
72	Lexington	363,700
73	Omaha	358,000
74	Springfield-Decatur-Champaign	350,700
75	Portland-Poland Spring	343,300
76	Paducah-Cape Girardeau-Harrisburg-Marion	329,900
77	Las Vegas	328,900
78	Springfield, MO	321,700
79	Tucson	320,400
80	Spokane	315,600
81	Huntsville-Decatur-Florence	308,600
82	Cedar Rapids-Waterloo-Dubuque	300,800
83	South Bend-Elkhart	298,500
84	Davenport-Rock Island-Moline: Quad City	298,300
85	Chattanooga	292,000
86	Columbia, SC	291,300
87	Jackson, MS	287,600
88	Ft. Myers-Naples	284,700
89	Johnstown-Altoona	281,100
90	Bristol-Kingsport-Johnson City: Tri-Cities	280,700
91	Madison	276,300
92	Youngstown	270,000
93	Burlington-Plattsburgh	268,500
94	Evansville	260,000
95	Baton Rouge	253,300
96	Waco-Temple-Bryan	253,200
97	Springfield, MA	247,400
98	Colorado Springs-Pueblo	243,600
99	Lincoln-Hastings-Kearney	241,900
100	El Paso	236,500
101	Ft. Wayne	235,900
102	Savannah	234,400
103	Greenville-New Bern-Washington	228,900
104	Lansing	228,700
105	Charleston, SC	225,700
106	Peoria-Bloomington	218,100
107	Sioux Falls-Mitchell	218,000
108	Fargo	214,100
109	Santa Barbara-Santa Maria-San Luis Obispo	210,000
110	Montgomery-Selma	209,100
111	Augusta	207,200
112	Tyler-Longview-Jacksonville	206,400
113	Salinas-Monterey	206,300
114	McAllen-Brownsville	201,500
115	Tallahassee-Thomasville	196,600
116	Reno	195,400
117	Ft. Smith	191,800
118	Lafayette, LA	184,300
119	Traverse City-Cadillac	182,200
120	Macon	181,700
121	Columbus, Ga	181,400
122	Columbus-Tupelo	172,200
123	Corpus Christi	170,400
124	Eugene	168,700
125	Duluth-Superior	168,100
126	La Crosse-Eau Claire	167,900
127	Yakima-Pasco-Richland-Kennewick	167,500
128	Amarillo	167,400
129	Monroe-El Dorado	167,300
130	Chico-Redding	166,900
131	Bakersfield	164,000
132	Wausau-Rhinelander	162,500
133	Boise	158,400
134	Binghamton	158,300
135	Wichita Falls-Lawton	156,500
136	Rockford	156,300
137	Topeka	154,700
138	Terre Haute	154,100
139	Florence-Myrtle Beach	154,000
140	Beaumont-Port Arthur	153,900
141	Sioux City	153,400
142	Wheeling-Steubenville	152,800
143	Erie	150,500
144	Wilmington	148,700
145	Medford	137,900
146	Joplin-Pittsburg	137,500
147	Rochester-Mason City-Austin	135,500
148	Bluefield-Beckley-Oak Hill	135,000
148	Lubbock	135,000
150	Minot-Bismarck-Dickinson-Glendive	134,900
151	Columbia-Jefferson City	133,200
152	Odessa-Midland	133,000
153	Sarasota	131,600
154	Albany, GA	127,800
155	Bangor	124,400
156	Abilene-Sweetwater	107,900
157	Idaho Falls-Pocatello	107,800
158	Biloxi-Gulfport-Pascagoula	107,000
159	Quincy-Hannibal	103,900
160	Utica	102,500
161	Clarksburg-Weston	101,300
162	Salisbury	97,000
163	Panama City	96,900
164	Gainesville	91,000
165	Laurel-Hattiesburg	90,400
165	Palm Springs	90,400
167	Dothan	89,400
168	Watertown-Carthage	87,400
169	Rapid City	87,000
170	Elmira	86,500
171	Alexandria, LA	85,200
172	Harrisonburg	84,500
173	Billings-Hardin	83,800
174	Jonesboro	81,800
175	Lake Charles	81,300
176	Missoula	73,800
177	Ardmore-Ada	70,800
178	Greenwood-Greenville	69,900
179	El Centro-Yuma	68,600
180	Meridian	64,700
181	Jackson, TN	62,300
182	Great Falls	62,200
183	Grand Junction-Durango	60,900
184	Parkersburg	57,100
185	Tuscaloosa	56,600
186	Eureka	56,000
186	Marquette	56,000
188	San Angelo	49,400
189	Butte	48,400
190	Lafayette, IN	45,900
191	Bowling Green	45,800
192	Hagerstown	45,000
193	St. Joseph	44,800
194	Anniston	43,000
195	Cheyenne-Scottsbluff	42,400
196	Charlottesville	41,200
197	Casper-Riverton	40,200
198	Laredo	39,100
198	Lima	39,100
200	Ottumwa-Kirksville	33,600
201	Twin Falls	30,800
202	Zanesville	30,700
203	Presque Isle	30,400
204	Bend	29,900
205	Mankato	29,800
206	Flagstaff	29,700
207	Helena	18,700
208	North Platte	17,700
209	Alpena	15,600

The figures listed under "ADI TV HH" refer to the estimated number of "TV Households" within range of local broadcast signals. The rankings shift very slowly over the years, reflecting population patterns. Thus, cities in the Southwest and Southeast have been gradually rising in the rankings at the expense of cities in the Northeast and Midwest.

Source: Arbitron. Reprinted with permission.

Market Size

The other determining factor is the size of the local area itself. In broadcasting, size is determined not by geographical area but rather by population density. "Market size" thus refers to the potential listening audience and the number of radio (or TV) sets in a given area, not city limits or other geographical or geopolitical demarcations.

For example, the "Los Angeles market" does not mean the city of Los Angeles. It means the Los Angeles metropolitan area within reach of local radio and TV signals. The same is true of every metropolitan area in the United States. (See the chart on page 116 to find the "designated ranking" of your metropolitan area.)

For all purposes, including news, broadcasters break market sizes into three main categories:

1. *Major markets* are the country's 10 or 20 largest. They correspond for the most part to the country's largest cities. However, because of the standard of measurement just explained, some smaller cities, geographically close and thus yielding high population density, are served by the same stations; this boosts them into the major market category: San Francisco/Oakland, Dallas/Fort Worth, Tampa/St. Petersburg, and so on.
2. *Medium markets* are the next largest population areas: Indianapolis, Sacramento, Louisville, Portland, and so on.
3. *Small markets,* the most numerous category, are the least populated areas: Laredo, Peoria, Tallahassee, and so on.

As with signal strength, it's easy to understand the link between market size and news department size: the bigger the one, the bigger (usually) the other.

(Cable television measures its audiences somewhat differently. Cable TV signals are delivered by satellite or microwave relay to local cablevision operators who "package" them and relay them via coaxial cable to home cable boxes and TV sets. The local operators designate which channel will be assigned to each signal. Cable TV originators thus estimate their potential audiences based on the number of local systems relaying their signals, as well as on the ratings compiled by Nielsen or by Arbitron to measure what the audience is actually watching.)

But of course we are really talking about more than size. We are also talking about professional competency. Although there are many exceptions (No station of whatever size in whichever market has a corner on either excellence or, conversely, ineptitude), it is generally true that the larger the market, the greater the professional demands and the higher the pay. This accounts for the usual (but by no means required or unconditional) career track for broadcast journalists: small market to medium market to major market to network. Mistakes and lack of professionalism that can be abided at a lower level are not tolerated at a higher one.

Naturally, there are excellent news departments at all levels, just as there are poor ones. A broadcast journalist may find that he or she is perfectly content, personally and professionally, to remain at a station in a small or medium market. But the goal of the vast majority of young people entering broadcast news is to go as high, as far, and as fast as they can.

JOB TITLES AND DUTIES

The trend in radio news has been for staffs to become smaller. The advent of computer word-processing systems (so-called "electronic newsrooms") and automated production equipment has enabled management to lay off both editorial and technical personnel. Despite the cutbacks, however, U.S. radio still employed an estimated 20,000 news staffers in the early 1990s.

Radio news staffs vary in size from 1 (in the case of a daylight-only station in or near a major market or at a medium-power station in a medium or small market) to 50 or more (at all-news stations in major markets and at networks). The larger the staff, the more specialized the work of each individual staffer.

Except at networks, all-news stations in major markets, and at the relatively few big-city stations with large news departments, radio news staffers are now expected to "do it all": write, interview, report from the field, operate portable and console recording equipment, edit audiotape, and anchor newscasts while operating the audio control board (also known as the "console")—the amplifier/mixer controlling the flow of sound from microphones, tape playback machines, and remote locations in the field.*

Staff Newsman/Newswoman

Gathers and writes local news, assembles full newscasts (by culling world and national stories from the news agencies to accompany locally written copy), and reads them on the air. Conducts live or recorded telephone interviews ("foners") and edits taped excerpts for inclusion in newscasts. Covers stories in the field via mobile unit, portable tape recorder, and/or portable cellular telephone. Calls in stories both live and on tape. May have to read live commercial copy during own newscasts. (And, at the smallest stations, may have to substitute for a vacationing disk jockey, clean and refill the station coffee pot, log transmitter readings —and possibly perform janitorial chores as well.)

News Director

The boss. Hires, fires, and auditions all applicants. Nowadays, usually also writes and anchors newscasts, as well as setting work and vacation schedules, ordering new equipment, and generally trying to cover the news on a small budget (a process described by one news director as "trying to fit two quarts of linguini into a one-quart container"). Accepts ultimate responsibility for the entire staff's success or failure.

In larger news departments, the more specialized radio news positions are as follows:

Newscaster (Anchor)

Writes and announces scheduled newscasts, usually one every hour during an eight-hour shift, and possibly headlines on the half-hour as well. Often requires "good" speaking voice (deep and resonant for men, mid-range for women).

At all-news stations, an anchor is typically on the air for 30 to 60 minutes at a stretch, for a total of about 3 hours in a single work shift.

Reporter

Except at all-news and in major markets, an entry-level position. Armed with the aforementioned equipment of a staff newsman/newswomen, covers breaking news in far-flung locations and/or "beats" such as city hall, crime, sports, and the like. Demands for "good" voice quality not as stringent as for anchors.

Writer

Actually a misnomer. In addition to writing news stories, modern radio "newswriters" oversee and edit audiotape from reporters and closed-circuit network feeds, as well as work the phones and conduct recorded interviews. In other words, they do virtually everything *except* go on the air.

---

*Even in the largest news departments in the largest markets, the division of labor is rapidly disappearing. Traditionally, the most powerful guarantors of job protection and specialization have been the labor unions. However, faced with shrinking memberships because of layoffs facilitated by new technology, labor unions have had to compromise, acceding to management's demands that editorial personnel operate equipment formerly operated only by technical personnel.

This trend is also affecting television. Because a professional video camera now weighs only a few pounds, network and major-market managements say reporters no longer need to be accompanied by camera operators in all circumstances; big-city managements say reporters should now take the pictures as well as report the news (as is already the case in small markets).

Because this could lead to further layoffs, and because this raises profound questions about the very nature of newsgathering in modern broadcasting, it is an issue you should keep track of. Its outcome may well affect your eventual career.

Editor Rick Schroeder of all-news KFWB, Los Angeles, organizes his station's coverage into a format of 20-minute "blocks." He decides which stories to include in each block, their order of presentation, and which stories will include audiotape. Schroeder also decides how to *re*organize everything in case of late-breaking developments—a routine occurrence in all-news radio and TV.

Editor

Exists only at networks and all-news stations. Decides newscast content and story order, chooses which taped excerpts to include, and proofreads copy submitted by writers and anchors.

Producer

Found only at networks and all-news stations. A staffer may be assigned to "produce" (be in charge of) long chunks of programming necessitated by special events or major breaking stories, as well as weekly or monthly documentaries, panel and interview shows, news-in-review shows, and so on. A related job is segment producer at major-market Talk Radio stations.

To summarize: Staffers in modern radio news tend to be Jacks- and Jills-of-all-trades. Only when and if they reach major markets (or go into television) are they likely to specialize.

EXERCISES

1. Get to know what's on the radio! Choose any weekday and carefully scan the AM and FM bands in your area. Concentrate on the stations broadcasting news and news-related features. Familiarize yourself with the local and network news broadcasts, and note their various formats.

2. Choose a second weekday and listen carefully to the *style,* both writing and anchoring, of those local and network newscasters whose work appeals to you most. (Keep an ear open especially for essayist Charles Osgood on CBS Radio and commentator Paul Harvey on ABC Radio.) Try to identify the writing and presentation techniques we've described in this book, especially in the *leads* to news stories.

Sources of Radio News

9

Newspapers, magazines, radio stations, and television stations all compile their news from a variety of sources—frequently from the *same* sources. For example, all rely heavily on material gathered by their own reporters and by news agencies. The differences arise in the way they process this material and the way they shape it for presentation to the public.

Radio stations use three primary sources for gathering news:

1. News agencies (formerly called "wire services")
2. Network and syndicated news services
3. Their own reporters

We shall consider each of these sources in order.

NEWS AGENCIES

News agencies began in the nineteenth century, even before the invention of the telegraph (the news traveled by mail, by special messenger, and by carrier pigeon). News agencies were created by newspapers as cooperatives to share coverage of stories they would otherwise have had to cover with their own separate (and inadequate) reporting staffs. The first major news agencies were European: Havas (French), founded in 1835; Wolff (German), founded in 1849; and Reuters (British), founded in 1851. Of these three, only Reuters survives today as a major international news service.

In the United States, half a dozen news agencies came into existence, but only two dating from that early period still exist today: the Associated Press (AP), begun in the 1870s, and United Press (UP), founded in 1882. The Associated Press is a nonprofit cooperative financed by its many thousands of subscribers in print, broadcasting, government, and private industry. By contrast, UPI (United Press International, as it now calls itself) is a for-profit agency which sells its services to compete with AP. (During the 1980s and early 1990s, UPI was repeatedly on the brink of bankruptcy, undergoing a series of cutbacks, reorganizations, and ownership changes. It was uncertain, at this writing, how long UPI would continue to stay in business.)

Until modern broadcasting came along, perhaps nowhere in all of journalism was the competition to report the news *first* more fierce than among AP, UPI, and (on a worldwide basis) Reuters. The exploits of news agency reporters to outwit their competitors are legendary (including such "dirty tricks" as locking them in hotel bathrooms or getting them drunk). The advent of radio made this competition even more intense. Radio stations, with their unquenchable thirst for immediacy and their own inter-station rivalries, drove the news agencies to introduce services tailored specifically for the new medium. And, in the age of television, AP and UPI retooled yet again to exploit new technologies, replacing their old-style wires and daisy-wheel teleprinters with satellites, computers, lasers, and high-speed printers. Information that once traveled banded to the legs of carrier pigeons now travels at the speed of light. Thanks to news agencies and modern broadcasting, a news event virtually *anywhere* in the world is known virtually *everywhere* in the world in a matter of seconds.

In addition to their main menu of world, national, regional, and local news, news agencies today offer a wide variety of specialized services, including sports and financial news, as well as services tailored specifically for broadcast use, including audio and video material. Further, agency services are organized to "split" (subdivide) on a regional basis to better serve the needs of local clients. There's so much variety, in fact, that the type of news-agency material you encounter nowadays at one radio or TV station may be quite different from the type you encounter at a different station.

Nevertheless, there are two basic types of news-agency material with which you should be familiar, and we shall examine these at length.

The Main Service

Large radio and TV news departments subscribe to the main service of world and national news from both AP and UPI. Until recently, the main service was known as the "A Wire" (less urgent news and features were carried on secondary wires known as "B," "C," and so on). For broadcast users, the main Associated Press service, delivered to newsrooms either via computer or via high-speed printer, is called APTV; it couples world and national news with local and regional inserts. UPI offers a similar service. The stories each agency transmits on its main service are long and full of detail—written, in other words, *in print style*. This means they must be rewritten in broadcast style for presentation on the air.

Most of the print-model stories used so far in this book are from the main services. We have trimmed them of extraneous material to eliminate possible confusion. But in the workplace you will see them in their entirety, so it is important that you understand what you will be dealing with. Here is a lengthy chunk of untrimmed AP material as it "moved" (was transmitted) via teleprinter:

```
        A233
        U 1 BYLZYVZYV A0588
AM--Turkey--Quake, 1st Ld, a222, 230
Eds: Death toll climbs to 509. Survivors endangered by cold.
By Ismail Kovaci
Associated Press Writer
        ISTANBUL, Turkey (AP)--A major earthquake struck eastern
Turkey early Sunday and officials said at least 509 people
were killed. Newspapers said 50 villages were leveled, and the
death toll was expected to climb.
        About three hours earlier a quake rolled through the Hindu
Kush mountain range, 1,400 miles to the east on the border
between Afghanistan and Pakistan, shaking Islamabad and
reaching as far as India's Kashmir state. There were no
immediate reports of casualties or damage. More than 12 hours
later, a strong quake shook southwestern Japan, but no
casualties were reported.
        The devastating quake struck Turkey at 7:12 A.M. (11:12
P.M. EST Saturday) and was felt in mountainous provinces
bordering Iran, Syria and Iraq.
```

Nightfall and intermittent snowfall in several areas hampered rescue efforts. A local army corps mobilized all its soldiers to help survivors and clear debris in communities reached earlier in the day.

Dropping temperatures threatened thousands of homeless survivors in remote towns, local officials said. Temperatures of 35 degrees Fahrenheit were expected.

Authorities said the quake was believed to be centered in Erzurum and Kars provinces, where most of the damage was done, but it also shook the provinces of Bitlis, Mus, Dyarbakir, Bingol, Van and Malatya, according to the martial law command of the eastern region.

Journalists in: 6th graf

ap-ny-10-30 1738EST

A236

   B A BYLZYVVYX A0615
   AM--Obit--Lillian Carter, 30
Bulletin
   AMERICUS, Ga. (AP)--Lillian Carter, the mother of former President Jimmy Carter, died Sunday in Americus-Sumter County Hospital at age 85, officials said.
   More
ap-ny-10-30 1758EST

A237

   U 1 BYLZYVEEV A0572
AM--Missing Ship, 340
No Sign of Missing Oil Drilling Ship
   PEKING (AP)--Searchers turned up no further signs Sunday of an American oil drilling ship or its 81 crewmen, missing since a typhoon five days ago in the South China Sea.
   "Unfortunately, these searches are sometimes a long and hard job," said U.S. Air Force Senior Master Sgt. Bill Barclay at the West Pacific rescue coordination center on Okinawa.
   Early Sunday, four ships searched an area where a plane had spotted what might have been survivors, but found nothing, said Air Force Lt. Col. Jack Gregory of the rescue center.
   "It doesn't mean they aren't there: but we haven't found them," he said.
   Barclay said two U.S. Navy P-3 planes continued to take turns searching for the 5,926-ton Glomar Java Sea, which had been drilling for oil south of China's Hainan Island before Typhoon Lex hit it with 75 mph winds.
   The ship, carrying 42 Americans, 35 Chinese, two Singaporeans, an Australian and a Filipino, was doing the exploration for Arco China Inc., a U.S. company working under contract with China.
   The ship's Houston-based owner, Global Marine Inc., said in Hong Kong that the sighting of what might have been two or three survivors was made about 60 miles northwest of the drilling location.
   Gregory said three Chinese ships and a vessel belonging to Global Marine, the Salvanquish, went to the area.
   Earlier, China's official Xinhua news agency said China had sent four ships to find a life raft flashing distress signals in the area.
   There was no word from Chinese officials Sunday on any findings. There also was no report on a Chinese ship that went to investigate a large undersea object with sonar equipment and underwater television apparatus.
   The object, discovered near the drilling site with sonar equipment, was reportedly about 328 feet long, 164 feet wide and 66 feet high, about the size of the missing ship.
   So far, searchers have reported finding two fenders from the missing ship, more than 10 life jackets and an empty life raft.
ap-ny-10-30 1805EST

A239

   U A BYLZYVQYV A0617

AM--Obit--Lillian Carter, 1st Add, a236
,110
Urgent
    AMERICUS, Ga.: Officials said.
    Mrs. Carter had been at the hospital for about a week. The
former president and his wife, Rosalynn, had been at the
hospital for the day.
    "Miss Lillian," as her neighbors in Plains, Ga., called
her, lived on the fringes of politics for most of her life.
    Her father, Jim Jack Gordy, a postmaster, never ran for
office. But she recalled during an interview in 1976 that he
"was the best, biggest politician in this part of the world.
He kept up with politics so closely that he could tell you--
almost within five votes--what the people who were running
would get in the next election."
    More
af-ny-10-30 1810EST

A241
    U A BYLUIVZVT A0619
AM--Obit--Lillian Carter, 2nd Add, a239, a236,170
Urgent
AMERICUS, Ga.: next election.
    Mrs. Carter was offered her husband's seat in the Georgia
Legislature when he died during his first term in 1953, but
she declined.
    "I was too shocked by his death," she said later. "But I
think if later they offered the legislature seat to me again,
I would have taken it."
    A graveside service for Mrs. Carter will be at 3 P.M.
Tuesday at the Lebanon Cemetery in Plains.
    Mrs. Carter had 15 grandchildren and eight
great-grandchildren.
    She campaigned actively for her son when he ran for
governor of Georgia in 1970, but her role in his 1976
presidential campaign, when he lost to Ronald Reagan, was more
sedate. Her job was to care for granddaughter Amy, then 8, the
only Carter child left at home.
    It was the second death in the family in just over a
month. Evangelist Ruth Carter Stapleton, Carter's sister, died
Sept. 26 at age 54 after a months-long struggle with
pancreatic cancer.
    More
ap-ny-10-30 1824EST

A242
    U A BYLUIVBYL A0622
AM--Obit--Lillian Carter, 3rd Add, A241, A239, A236, 200
Urgent
AMERICUS, Ga.: Pancreatic cancer.
    In 1964, Mrs. Carter was a delegate to the Democratic
National Convention and was asked to serve as co-chairman of
Lyndon B. Johnson's local campaign headquarters.
    "At that time, people around here didn't like Johnson
because he was for blacks," she once said. "Anyway, I was
delighted to do it, took the job and the blacks had access to
the office over at the hotel just like the whites."
    Mrs. Carter was known for being liberal about race in an
era when most of her neighbors were exactly the opposite.
    A registered nurse, she used her knowledge of medicine to
help many poor blacks in Plains.
    Carter recalled that his mother "taught us by her daily
example to help the weak and handicapped even when it wasn't
the comfortable or socially acceptable thing to do."
    Born Aug. 15, 1898, in Richland, Ga., about 20 miles from
Plains, Mrs. Carter attended public schools there and studied
nursing at the now-defunct Wise Clinic in Plains. She earned
her nursing degree at Grady Memorial Hospital in Atlanta.
    She married James Earl Carter Sr., a peanut farmer and
businessman, in 1923.
ap-ny-10-30 1828EST

Now that you've seen it, let's make sure you understand it.

Each story, you will have noticed, begins with a number. In our material, the first number was "A233." Stories are numbered consecutively throughout the day. In the workplace, it is important *not* to trim or misplace a story's number because that number will be referred to in later additions, revisions, or corrections.

Just beneath the number A233 is "U 1 BYLZYVZYV A0588." That is an AP internal code and need not concern us.

The next line—"AM--Turkey--Quake, 1st Ld, a222, 230"—is broken down this way: "AM" means the agency is sending stories intended for the next morning's newspapers, known as the AM cycle. From midnight until noon, Eastern Time, it had been sending PM cycle stories intended for afternoon and evening papers. Obviously, the designations "AM" and "PM" are meaningless for broadcasters, who go with the latest developments regardless of news-agency time designation.

"Turkey--Quake" is the story's slug, and "1st Ld" (short for "First Lead") means this is the first complete and updated version of this story for the AM cycle. Later versions will be designated "2nd Ld," "3rd Ld," and so on.

"A222" is the number of the previously moved story which A233 updates. And "230" is the number of words in A233, rounded off to the nearest 10.

The next line (beginning "Eds: Death toll climbs . . .") calls writers' and editors' attention to the specific information updating the story and making it newsworthy.

Underneath is the AP reporter's byline. Then follows the story proper.

Now skip to the end of A233 where you find the words "Journalists in: 6th graf." This is a "pickup" line. It tells you that you will find the rest of the story by going back to the sixth paragraph of story A222, which begins "Journalists in . . ."

(In computerized newsrooms, where electronic reception of news-agency material is instantaneous, there is no pickup line; the text from A222 is picked up and retransmitted automatically.)

Now the final line: "ap-ny-10-30 1738EST"; "ap" stands for Associated Press; "ny" is the identification of the AP bureau through which the story was edited and transmitted, in this case New York; "10-30" is the date, October thirtieth; and "1738EST" is the time of transmission, based on a 24-hour clock, and the time zone: 5:38 P.M. Eastern Standard Time.

As noted, networks and local stations with large staffs appreciate this newspaper-style material even though it must be rewritten. The extreme detail, color, and background information provide newswriters, reporters, editors, and producers with story angles which enable them to write distinctive, attention-grabbing leads.

However, smaller stations usually lack the staff to do so much rewriting. They rely instead on news-agency services that are *already written* in broadcast style.

Broadcast-style Services

Broadcast-style agency material moves as a separate service. It includes none of the foregoing newspaper-style writing. But before examining its advantages and disadvantages, let's take a look at some of it. The following (abbreviated) AP "Newswatch" incorporates some of the stories from the main service:

```
V2307
R D
AP-19th Newswatch

Here is the latest news from the associated press:

    Officials in Americus, Georgia say that Lillian Carter--
mother of former President Jimmy Carter--has died at the age
of 85. Mrs. Carter had been in the hospital for about a week--
although there's no immediate word on the cause of her death.
It's the second death in the Carter family in just over a
month. The former president's sister--Evangelist Ruth Carter
Stapleton--died of cancer on September 26th.
```

```
          Authorities in Turkey report more than 500 deaths as a
     result of a major earthquake that struck early today.
     Newspapers say 50 of Turkey's villages were leveled. According
     to officials, cold and snow in many areas are hampering rescue
     efforts and are likely to cause more deaths.

          A scientist with the government's Hawaiian volcano
     observatory says Hawaii's Kilauea (Kih-luh-way'-uh) volcano is
     ready to erupt again. Kilauea's last eruption ended on October
     seventh. The geologist says molten rock continues to collect
     at the volcano's summit--and the next wave of volcanic
     activity could come at any time.

     V2309
     R D
     AP-19th Newswatch-Take 2

          Last week, the citizen-labor energy coalition was telling
     natural gas customers that they can look for their bills to
     rise an average of 21 percent this winter. Today, the consumer
     and labor organization says the study that produced the figure
     was wrong. The coalition says there were errors involving 20
     of the 80 cities studied.

          Hospital officials in Fort Lee, New Jersey report the
     death of pioneer animator Otto Messmer. He was 91. Messmer was
     the creator of "Felix the Cat"--although it was the studio he
     worked for and not Messmer who got the credit.

          The tiny village of Lijar in Southern Spain has apparently
     decided to let bygones be bygones. The villagers have signed a
     peace treaty with France--ending what was officially 100 years
     of war between the small town and the neighboring country. The
     whole thing started in 1883 when the king of Spain was
     insulted and hit with stones in Paris. The war was declared to
     defend the king's honor--and ended today with a festive
     ceremony.

     APTV-10-30 1841EST
```

A staffer at a small radio or TV station can simply rip that copy off the printer (or command a computer printout) and read it on the air as is, bypassing the rewriting process. But this is a mixed blessing, especially in a competitive environment.

The advantages of broadcast-style wire services:

1. The station saves money by not having to hire writers.
2. Staffers save time; they are able to assemble newscasts quickly.
3. The copy is easy to read at a glance—no complicated editorial directions to follow.
4. Staffers can devote full attention to covering and writing local news.

The disadvantages:

1. Every station airing the copy unedited sounds identical. You can switch to another station and hear the news told in exactly the same words.
2. Each story tends to have the same length. The news delivery thus sounds static and without variety. Many broadcasters believe this fails to hold the audience's interest.
3. Broadcast wires fail to exploit immediacy (broadcasting's inherent speed) because they are *slower* to move major-breaking stories. Go back to the initial newspaper-wire bulletin (A236) slugged "Obit—Lillian Carter." Note that it was timed off at 5:58 P.M. Now look at how it moved on the broadcast wire:

```
V2295
U A
AP-U r g e n t

Lillian Carter
     (Americus, Georgia)--Officials say Lillian Carter, the
mother of former President Jimmy Carter, died today in
Americus-Sumter County Hospital in Georgia at age 85.
APTV-10-30 1802EST
```

Note that that version was timed off at 6:02 P.M.—four minutes *later* than the newspaper-wire version. In radio news, those four minutes constitute the difference between getting the story on the 6 P.M. news and having to wait until the next newscast. And in TV news, the station with the newspaper wire can get the story on the air four minutes sooner than the station with only the broadcast wire. In competitive situations, those four minutes count.

4. Staffers at stations with only the broadcast wires find it next to impossible to be creative or original because they lack the color and detail with which to be inventive. For example, no further details on the Lillian Carter obit moved on the broadcast wire until 6:41 P.M.—39 minutes after its first report. But the newspaper wire moved sufficient details at 6:10 P.M. (in A239) to support the following rewrite:

```
     Miss Lillian Carter died a short time ago in Americus,

Georgia.  Her son, former President Jimmy Carter, was at her

bedside.
```

The writer was able to lift out this latter detail and thus make his or her station's version sound different and original—and do it half an hour *before* a staffer at a station without the newspaper service.

The reason for the delay in transmitting the broadcast version is that writers and editors of the broadcast service must await the newspaper service's version before they can start their work. Truly competitive broadcast news organizations can't afford to wait; they prefer to buy the newspaper service and rely on their own staffers to rewrite quickly in broadcast style in order to air the stories before their competitors.

Local News Agencies

Many large metropolitan areas have home-grown news agencies usually called City News or City News Bureau. These began as cooperatives among local newspapers and are now supported as well by radio and TV stations. Again, their purpose is to provide reliable coverage of local and regional events beyond the personnel limitations of any single news organization.

As a rule, extreme care must be taken in handling copy from such local agencies. Most of them operate on a shoestring. Typically, they serve as training grounds for print journalists who are just out of school and still wet behind the ears. The copy tends to be poorly written, unclear, inexact, and convoluted in the extreme.

That said, such city wires are also extremely valuable. They provide coverage of the nitty-gritty news stories that many big newspapers and broadcasters tend to neglect, sometimes to their dismay and regret: the "routine" homicide that turns out to be a VIP, the "routine" political campaign speech that turns out to be a bombshell, the "routine" court trial that reveals the appearance of a surprise witness, and so on.

In addition, city wires serve as conduits for the scheduling of events, from news conferences to rallies and marches. A single call to a city wire from an official or would-be newsmaker ensures that word of the upcoming event will get to just about every newsroom in town, enabling coverage to be planned ahead of time.

Handling News Agency Copy

As you've no doubt experienced by now, it can be very frustrating to have to boil down an interesting and colorful news-agency story to a broadcast length of 20 or 30 seconds: It seems such a pity to throw out all those juicy details! Eventually, you will learn to lessen the frustration by choosing different details for each of your broadcast versions. In a TV newsroom, you will write two or three versions of a story, each for a different broadcast. And in radio, you may write as many as eight or twelve different versions. So while no one story will contain everything you deem important, your output taken as a whole will usually cover all the important points. Sometimes, though, you'll just have to shrug and say, "I did what I could under the circumstances."

But beware of a trap. Because broadcast rewrites are typically so brief, you may get into the habit of reading only the first few paragraphs of a news agency story. You may think, "Why should I clog my head with details that I won't be able to include?" That's a dangerous frame of mind, because important details, especially local angles, are often buried deep in the body of a long story. Because you should always be looking for a fresh lead, an arresting detail, and/or a local angle, it is vital to read news agency copy *all the way through*. Remember, news-agency writers are in competition with other news providers, and their copy is often written in haste. In particular, you should watch out for the following:

1. *Casualty figures.* Do they add up? Do the numbers of dead and injured reported in the lead correspond to the numbers given in the body of the story?
2. *Names, titles, and identifications.* Has the news agency identified everyone correctly? Are officials identified by title and, where relevant, by state and by party affiliation?
3. *Unsubstantiated leads.* Do the facts of a story, as reported in its body, support the lead sentence or paragraph? Is there a quote or substantial paraphrase to back up the writer's interpretation of someone's remarks?
4. *Buried leads.* Did the agency writer pick the newsiest story element for the lead, or, in your opinion, did he or she "bury" it somewhere in the body of the story?
5. *Buried sources.* What is the real source of the news agency story? Is the reporting original, or is it based on a secondary source (such as a publication or independent study) identified somewhere in the body of the story? (The broadcast version should identify the true source.)
6. *Unnamed sources.* Are there tip-off phrases such as "It was learned today" or "According to congressional sources"? In other words, do you think the story is trustworthy? (If there is doubt, you should identify the news agency as the source: "AP reports that . . ." or "Sources quoted by the Associated Press say . . . ," etc.)

NETWORK AND SYNDICATED NEWS SERVICES

Let's say you are the owner/manager of a 1,000-watt AM radio station in a small market or in a fringe (suburban) area of a medium or major market. The low power of your transmitter and your limited potential for building a large audience (measured in total listenership), and thus your inability to charge high rates for commercials, preclude hiring a large news staff; you just can't afford it. Yet you are a responsible broadcaster in that you consider the news an important element in community life. So how, given your limited budget, do you go about providing a modest, yet balanced diet of local, national, and world news?

First you hire two staffers for your news department—a news director and one other person of the news director's choosing. The two of them will concentrate on gathering, writing, and announcing local news. They will probably work six-day weeks (to cover at least part of each weekend day) and dovetail their shifts Monday through Friday in order to begin local coverage during AM Drive and end it following PM drive.

Next, you decide to buy a regional broadcast-style service from AP or UPI to provide your two-person team with news from nearby areas and from the state capital. But you decide you don't want them ripping and reading world and national items because that's what your competitors across town are doing, and you don't want to sound exactly like them.

So you decide to affiliate your station with a network or syndicated news service: You negotiate a contract with CBS Radio News, ABC Radio News, AP Radio News, UPI Audio—or any of a dozen other suppliers—to carry their network news on your station. Very likely, the network will provide an hourly newscast containing network commercials but with a "hole" in the middle or at the end where you can insert your own local news and a local commercial. In return, the network or syndicator will pay you a tiny fraction of the money it makes through sale of the network commercial time. On your part, you agree not to compromise the network's integrity by delaying the news broadcast or by deleting any portion of it sold to commercial sponsors.

Now everybody's happy: you, because you've got your professional national, world, and local news (as well as a package into which to insert your local commercials), and the network or syndicator, because it has now extended its voice into your market, thereby increasing its own audience for the national-brand commercials it wants to sell.

Closed-Circuit Feeds

Included in the package you've negotiated with the network is a schedule of closed-circuit feeds of news reports, features, and actualities. ("Closed circuit" means that the material is transmitted to affiliated stations but not directly to listeners.) The material is fed ("to feed" = "to transmit") at fixed times several times a day, perhaps as often as every hour, and is recorded for eventual inclusion in locally originated newscasts.

Because this taped material requires special handling by radio journalists, we shall be devoting major attention to it in coming chapters. For now, suffice it to note that a precise description of its components—an "audio advisory"—moves *in advance of transmission,* either via teleprinter or via computer terminal (depending on the station's electronic system). Here's a brief portion of an hourly audio advisory from AP's broadcast service:

```
AP-Network 1:32ped, Wed Sep 23

Auto Theft (COPY: upcoming)

218-w-40-Cap Hill-(Dick Uliano w- Cong. Chas. Schumer, D-

NY)-Key NY Dem. urges Cong. to pass tough legislation on car

theft. (needs hard lead)

219-a-15-(Charles Schumer, at news conf.)-"your car"-parts

marking is critical deterrent to car theft.

220-a-16-(Charles Schumer)-"as well"-he'll fight

automakers over his proposal that car parts be marked.

221-a-11-(Det. Sgt. Clarence Brickey, Md. State Police, at

news conf.)-"thieves involved"-police need auto parts "I-D-ed"

to solve crimes.

Syria-Israel (COPY: V3513)

222-v-34-NYC-(Barry Schweid)-U-S, Syrian envoys talk

Mideast peace, land.
```

To explain the foregoing requires us to introduce a few terms with which you may not be familiar. But we'll try to keep the broadcast news jargon to a minimum—at least for now.

As the top line indicates, the hourly closed-circuit feed was scheduled at 1:32 P.M. Eastern Daylight Time on Wednesday, September 23. The numbers beginning each paragraph—218, 219, etc.—are the item numbers of the taped material sent since midnight. Each number is followed by a letter: either a, v, or w. "a" stands for *actuality,* the voice of a newsmaker; "v" stands for *voicer,* a report not containing an actuality; and "w" stands for *wraparound* (abbreviated as *wrap*), a report containing an actuality.

Following is another number—40, 15, 16, and so on. This is the precise length, measured in seconds, of each tape.

Voicers and wraps are then identified by location—in the foregoing cases, "Cap Hill" (Capitol Hill—the U.S. Congress, Washington) and "NYC" (New York City, where the U.N. is headquartered). Unless specified otherwise, the reporter's location will be the last words on the tape: "Dick Uliano, Capitol Hill" or "Barry Schweid, New York."

The material in parentheses specifies the names of the reporters and/or the newsmakers.

Note that the descriptions of the actualities are preceded by two words in quotation marks— "your car," "thieves involved," etc. These are the final words of the actualities, known as *outcues.*

And finally, note the parenthetical words "needs hard lead" in item 218. This means that the report can not be aired without an intro from the anchor telling the hard news, because the taped report itself does not open with it.

Okay, this sounds a bit complicated. Patience, please. By the end of the next few chapters, we hope to make this—and a lot more—as clear as day.

LOCAL REPORTING SOURCES

To state the obvious: The most important source of a station's local news is its own reporters—their talent, intelligence, curiosity, drive, capacity for hard work, their "nose for news." Without talented local reporters, all the paraphernalia of broadcast news—microphones, recording gear, mobile units, cellular telephones, police and fire scanners (not to mention TV cameras, microwave transmitters, satellite dishes, etc.)—*all* of it is worthless. As we noted in the Preface to this book, broadcast journalism depends on brain power, not merely on electronic wizardry.

It is a fact of life that local broadcast reporters are at a disadvantage compared to their newspaper colleagues. The latter usually outnumber the former by a wide margin. That's because a higher proportion of broadcast operating expenses goes for equipment rather than newsgathering personnel, whereas the opposite is true at newspapers. Be that as it may, even a small broadcast news staff can outhustle and outreport its print competition by following diligent work habits:

1. Set up a regular telephone routine of checking with the police department, the fire department, city hall, and the clerk of the municipal court. Develop reliable sources at each location to keep yourself informed of ongoing and upcoming activities.

2. Make sure the newsroom fire and police radio scanners are always on. You may find them distracting at first, but your ears will soon grow accustomed to picking up anything unusual.

3. Keep background files of all continuing stories, including newspaper clippings as well as your own stories. In case of breaking news, you may have to find background information in a hurry.

4. Make sure all local maps, street guides, government directories, and telephone books are up-to-date. You may have to go somewhere or reach someone in a hurry.

5. Make a habit of entering important telephone numbers in a newsroom computer file or desktop Rolodex, as well as in your own "little black book." (However, keep personal sources private; share them only with trusted colleagues on a case-by-case basis.)

6. Socialize with newsmakers. A journalist's day is not over at the end of a formal work shift. A certain amount of "shmoozing" with officials and community leaders, perhaps at a bowling alley or at an outdoor barbecue, is part of the job. The object is to build personal relationships that may result in getting the inside track on news stories.

Of all these habits, #1 is the most important in terms of maintaining a reportorial edge. Police do not always use their radios when something is breaking. The mayor doesn't always alert the news media when he or she is about to do something. Newsmakers don't routinely give out their telephone numbers.

In other words, you can't sit around waiting for the news to come to you. You must hustle for it. The way events normally break in the news business is that *one single reporter* learns something, and then other reporters jump on the bandwagon. For building a career it the news business, it would be nice if that first reporter were *you*.

EXERCISES

1. If you do not have access to APTV or its UPI equivalent, arrange to visit a radio station, television station, or local newspaper that subscribes to one or the other. Ask to take home a printout, a carbon copy, or a thermal-paper copy of at least two continuous hours' worth of agency material. Study it at length, noting its organization and editorial designations. Familiarize yourself thoroughly with such material—because in a professional broadcast newsroom you will be expected to scan one or two hours of it very quickly, perhaps in a matter of minutes.

2. Find out if a local press club, press association, or other organization publishes a media resource guide (listing important local telephone numbers for city hall, hospitals, police precincts, and so on). If possible, obtain a copy to use as a starting point to build your own file of local reporting sources.

Audiotape I: Actualities 10

Modern broadcast news owes much of its style and content to the invention of portable sound and picture recording equipment. Once such gear became readily available, facilitating news coverage at the scene of events, broadcast journalists altered their writing and presentation techniques to exploit the new technology. The transformation began in radio—which is where we, too, shall begin.

In 1961, a portable audiotape recorder featuring professional-quality sound reproduction weighed more than 20 pounds and cost more than $1,000. By 1971, a recorder of the same quality weighed about five pounds and cost about $100. By 1991, a professional-quality recorder weighed less than a pound and cost less than $50. If the trend continues, you may soon find one as a giveaway in a Cracker Jack box.

So ubiquitous and affordable have tape recorders become that it's difficult to imagine news coverage without them. Not long ago, print journalists scoffed at broadcast reporters who carried tape recorders, preferring to rely instead on their shorthand notes. Then their editors heard the *accurate* quotes on radio, in the newsmakers' *own* voices, and decided their reporters could learn something after all. Nowadays, many print journalists feel disadvantaged without their tape recorders.

The adroit handling of a tape recorder and the ability to integrate taped excerpts into reports and newscasts are fundamental skills *demanded* of today's radio journalists. On average, one-third to one-half of every newscast is on tape, either in the form of actualities (the voices of newsmakers or the natural sounds of events) or reports voiced by staffers in the field.*

The art of integrating news copy and tape to tell the news is what makes electronic journalism radically different from print journalism. Nothing of what follows has its equivalent anywhere in newspapers or magazines.

---

*In TV news, actualities are called *sound bites* and reports are called *packages*. We will stick with radio terminology until we come to the chapters on TV news.

TYPES OF ACTUALITIES

Voices of Newsmakers

Nothing conveys the "feel" of a news event on radio as well as the voice of someone who took part in it or witnessed it. True, writers can be very skilled at paraphrasing. But what writer could convey the emotional power of the Reverend Martin Luther King, Jr.'s "I have a dream!" speech? The faraway yet breathtaking essence of Neil Armstrong's "small step for a man, giant leap for mankind" remark as he set foot on the moon? The forced monotone of Richard M. Nixon's "I shall resign the presidency effective at noon tomorrow"?

Those words, those sounds, are lodged deep within our individual and collective memories not only for their substance, but also for the way in which we heard them. In particles of magnetic tape or imbedded in computer chips, they are now preserved for all of human history.

At first glance, voice actualities appear to be the equivalent of print's direct quotes. But they are not, and it is misleading to consider them as such. Quotes in print have no "voice" or "image." They are disembodied, appearing only as ink on paper. As such, a direct quote in print, preceded or followed by an identification of who said it, seems to flow in context. But on the air, the quote and the identification of the speaker are heard and seen as *two voices and/or pictures,* two different sounds and/or pictures emanating from two different electronic sources. Unless handled in a special way, they might not seem to flow; instead, they might seem jarring or incongruous.

Before detailing how to make writing and actualities flow, let's examine the actualities themselves. How do you choose them? What standards guide their selection and use? Answering these questions is tricky, because, in the last analysis, each case must be decided on its own merits. But by and large, there are six standards by which to judge actualities:

1. *Informational Content.* This is by far the most frequent basis for selection. Almost every speech, news conference, or interview contains one or more portions, brief excerpts, which reflect the crux of the remarks as a whole. Journalistically speaking, the crux is overwhelmingly the "what" or the "why," perhaps both. In short, the *main point* (or points) of a spoken context is what most often makes the best actuality (or series of actualities).

2. *Colorful Details.* Sometimes the main point of a spoken context can be stated more quickly and clearly by the newswriter than by the speaker. In such cases, the colorful or quirky remark might make the better actuality. Suppose that the president of the United States, in a speech somewhere, proposes a long series of controls on the food industry to guarantee the purity and safety of food products on supermarket shelves. And suppose his recitation is so long-winded and boring that a newswriter could summarize the proposal in two sentences. Good-bye, actuality. But suppose that the president had ad-libbed, "You know, the only reason I'm making these proposals is because I found a staple in my Corn Flakes this morning," followed by audience laughter. Suddenly, you've got your actuality: that remark, *including* the audience reaction.

3. *Emotional Impact.* Very often the flavor or weight of a set of remarks is carried not so much by the words as by the speaker's tone of voice or facial expression. Someone's reaction to a piece of good or bad news is a frequent example. If you ask the winner of a multi-million-dollar state lottery for his or her reaction, you are obviously going to hear words to the effect, "I'm very, very happy." But the tone of voice or facial expression will tell you just *how* happy; the words themselves mean little without their emotional coloring.

4. *Sound Quality.* Except in rare cases (as when a piece of tape is of historic value or, in television, where the picture itself is important), actualities must sound clear technically. Every word must be understandable. The voice or accent can't sound mushy or "off-mike."

   Obviously, you can't control the quality of the receiving equipment used by the audience. But at the point of transmission (that is, the newsroom or studio), there must be no straining of ears or shaking of heads over the text of an actuality. In radio, a common standard for judging sound quality is to ask the question, "Will this be understood over a commuter's car radio while driving at 55 miles an hour in moderate traffic?" If the answer is no, the tape should not be used.

In television, the text of a hard-to-understand actuality may be presented simultaneously on the screen in an electronic graphic or title.

5. *Picture Quality*. On television, an actuality may consist of silence—or at least a lack of spoken words. A facial expression or emotional reaction (such as laughter or tears) can speak volumes. A handshake between two former enemies is an actuality (even though some news departments, instead of labeling it a "sound bite," refer to it as NATSOT; more on this later). So is a punch thrown in anger. Or a public official stonily refusing to reply to a question.

6. *Length*. There is no "best" length for an actuality. By that we mean that each actuality depends on context (cf. the five preceding standards) and therefore has its own inherent "best" length. Further, you can't control the way people express themselves (beyond editing the tape afterwards); therefore, some actualities will be short, others long.

As we've noted repeatedly, however, broadcast news prizes brevity. Thus, the shorter an actuality, the better. As a rule of thumb, no actuality should run less than 6 seconds in radio; it takes a second or two for listeners to "digest" the second voice. But on television, where the picture of the speaker immediately establishes a new presence, the modern trend is to use actualities as short as 4 seconds, the time required for a single pithy remark.

Natural Sound

Sometimes the best actualities are not words in the form of prepared or ad-lib remarks. Sometimes they are the natural sounds of events, such as chanting, singing, sirens, police bullhorns, railroad cars clacking on rails, machinery in operation, computers beeping, and so on. In television, "natural sound" also means "natural picture." We can watch people doing something, performing some action; they need not be saying anything. Or we can watch a building collapse, a rocket blast off, or a child eating an ice cream cone. When President Ronald Reagan signed a bill making the third Monday in January a national holiday in honor of Rev. Martin Luther King, Jr., the crowd of onlookers in the White House Rose Garden spontaneously began singing "We Shall Overcome"; the natural sound and picture of the crowd in song was a memorable actuality on both radio and television, more telling than anyone's prepared remarks.

Broadcast reporters and producers are always on the lookout for such natural sounds and pictures, which are recorded "in the clear" (that is, without spoken commentary) and then incorporated into stories and newscasts.

In television news, natural sound is designated NATSOT—short for "natural sound on tape." In radio, natural sound is often called "wildtrack audio."

Q/A

"Q/A" is short for "question and answer." It is an actuality that includes the reporter's voice (or voice and picture) as well as the newsmaker's. A typical Q/A actuality opens with a newsmaker's remark, continues with a reporter's follow-up question, and ends with the newsmaker's reply. Q/A's inherently run longer than simple actualities, and, as a general rule, they are used only if both parties' remarks are succinct or if the interview from which they are excerpted is a newsmaking exclusive.

There is a second type of Q/A that does not even include the voice of a newsmaker. It is composed either entirely of a reporter's voice (or voice and picture) or of a combination of the reporter and an in-studio staffer. For example, a reporter at the scene of an event may be interviewed (by phone in radio, by satellite in TV) by a colleague (a writer, producer, or even the anchor) about what he or she has witnessed. The interview (a form of debriefing) may be broadcast live, but more often it is taped; excerpts are then edited for broadcast. In radio, the edited Q/A may in fact be just the reporter's "answer," typically a firsthand description or assessment. In television, Q/A typically runs longer and does include a portion of both ends of the conversation. It has become a common practice in TV news to follow a reporter's recorded package with a live Q/A portion in which the reporter delivers later information or responds to the anchor's questions on story angles not covered in the package itself.

INTERNAL EDITING

Content

The content of taped actualities is an editorial decision in the same way that print journalists decide which of their notes to include in a story and which to reject. Journalists, *not* the newsmakers, control the structure and content of their stories in all media.

This means freedom to edit out extraneous remarks, as long as such editing *does not distort the speaker's meaning or intent.* Clearly, internal editing demands a high degree of journalistic integrity. Former President Richard Nixon once declared, "I am not a crook." Any journalist who edited out the word "not" would deservedly have been fired on the spot.

More than likely, the case will be something like this: Mayor Smith says,

> The tax bill is a sham from stem to stern. *Now wait a minute, folks, let me answer this question.* It takes money from the poor and puts it into the pockets of the rich.

Clearly, the second sentence (in italics) is an interruption of some kind and not a part of the mayor's train of thought. You as a journalist would edit that sentence out, butting together the first and third sentences into a single actuality.

Of course, internal editing can get much trickier. Suppose that the mayor had said.

> The tax bill is a sham from stem to stern. *Its proposal at this time is a blight on the citizens of our fair city, a stain on our civic pride, a caving in to greedy instincts.* It takes money from the poor and puts it into the pockets of the rich.

This time the radio journalist has a choice: to use the remark unedited *or,* for the sake of brevity, to edit out the second sentence. Again, the meaning is not distorted.

However, suppose Mayor Smith had said,

> The tax bill is a sham from stem to stern. *And the property assessment indicator is no bargain, either.* It takes money from the poor and puts it into the pockets of the rich.

Much as you might like to edit out the second sentence, you can't do it honestly. That's because the "it" at the start of the third sentence could refer to the tax bill, the assessment indicator, or both. You just don't know for sure. So your choices are to use the actuality in its entirety, or not to use it at all.

Internal edits need not be confined to single sentences. A remark from one part of the text may be butted to a remark that came minutes later (but not hours or days), as long as the resulting actuality is faithful to the sense of the remarks as a whole. We can't stress this too strongly. Responsibility in tape editing is at the heart of broadcast journalism.

Inflections

Sometimes you won't be able to edit an actuality for the most desirable content. That's because human speech patterns won't always let you.

All human languages rely, to varying degrees, on rhythms and inflections to help convey meaning. Some Oriental languages rely on inflections so heavily that, in Chinese, for example, one word can have four or five different meanings, depending on its tonal inflection.

English, on the other hand, uses inflections sparingly, usually at the end of a phrase or sentence. The sentence, "You are going," ends in a *down* inflection. But if we add a question mark, "You are going?" the inflection is now *up,* indicating doubt or that something is to follow.

Many speakers tend to ramble, unsure of where the thought or sentence will end. Such speakers end their sentences with unnatural *up* inflections. The result, in tape editing, is that it's hard to find a place to end the actuality without letting it go on to an undesirable length. For the sake of flow and normal speech patterns, actualities should end with *down* inflections. In other words, natural speech rhythms should be retained in editing and ending actualities. Otherwise, they sound unnatural, in fact, sound "edited."

Most beginners discover the inflection problem through trial and error. But they soon develop an ear for inflections and can predict in advance whether a certain edit will work.

WRITING TO TAPE

To understand the way radio (and television) journalists prepare stories containing taped actualities, let's begin at the beginning—with a text spoken by a newsmaker in real-life circumstances.

Choosing Actualities

Although the setting of the following is Los Angeles, the story was covered by all national networks; you may remember hearing it in your local area.

On Thursday, September 24, 1992, at 5 P.M. Pacific Time, Los Angeles's five-term mayor, Tom Bradley, addressed a group of city officials and political supporters at a downtown hotel. His remarks were broadcast live on the city's two all-news radio stations and on four of its eight English-language TV stations. All other stations, as well as the network news bureaus, recorded Bradley's statement for later use as actualities. As for context, the 74-year-old mayor was speaking six months after the Los Angeles riots triggered by the acquittal of four white police officers on charges of brutally beating a black man named Rodney King. Bradley's text:

> For 50 years—as police officer, councilman and mayor—I have loved and served Los Angeles. I grew up in her schools. I raised my family in her neighborhoods and raised my voice in prayer in her churches. I fought for her, protected her, boosted her. I sought trade for her marketplaces and jobs for her people. I listened to her varied voices. I encouraged her children to reach for the stars. I sought justice and opportunity for all.
>
> I owe all that I am to this wondrous city and to all of you. And to the best of my ability I have tried to repay that debt.
>
> In 1973, Los Angeles gave life to my impossible dream. She cast aside appeals to fear and bigotry and elected me the first black mayor to serve as mayor of a major American city. At that moment, Los Angeles proved some people wrong: the people who said that a black man couldn't go to college, couldn't rise through the ranks of the police force, couldn't attain the highest public offices. As I walked the streets of this city and this nation, I saw sparkle in the eyes of children of all races who identified my victory as their victory. I'll never forget when it hit me: I was living proof to our sons and daughters that their futures had no limits.

When I first entered office, I saw only a tiny part of our diverse community represented in the halls of government. I am proud to say I changed that.

As I look back, I take great pride because, together, we accomplished wonders. We revitalized a decaying downtown, built a great international airport, transformed our harbor into the nation's leading port, energized culture and the arts, established equal opportunity programs, furthered economic development, helped clean our water and air, and built new housing and rapid transit.

I'll never forget the naysayers crying that the Olympics would bankrupt the city. (. . .)

Now those naysayers warn that we cannot stop gang violence and serious crime on our streets. I believe we can. We can expand our L.A.'s BEST after-school program to every classroom, giving kids real alternatives to gangs and drugs. And in the November election, we can put 1,000 new officers into community-based policing.

I'll never forget those who cautioned me against taking the political risk of reforming the Police Department. But we knew what had to be done. (. . .)

Challenge and change will always face us. Change allowed me to knock down the old doors of prejudice. Change allowed me to break new ground, forge new alliances and open new paths. I, as much as anyone, understand the need—and the time—for change.

The decision I am about to share with you has been the most difficult of my life. I have made it with just one thought in mind: what is best for Los Angeles and her people.

The time for change has come. I have served a record five terms as your mayor. Others should now have the opportunity and responsibility to bring their vision to bear on the future of this great community. I am prepared to pass the torch to new leadership.

Nine months of service remain before I retire as mayor. During that time I will devote all of my energy to making Los Angeles a better, safer, fairer and more just place to live. When I finally stand down I intend to be standing tall for the great causes of my life.

The greatest cause of all is learning to live with one another. Racism is America's greatest evil. We in Los Angeles must be the first to slay that demon.

Our children must learn that education is more than math, history and English; it is learning to respect the differences of race, religion and culture. The April unrest tore at my heart, and I will not be at peace until we have healed our wounds and rebuilt our neighborhoods. Let us all pledge to make Los Angeles a beacon of mutual respect, justice and tolerance.

I thank all of you for your boundless support. Your friendship has sustained me.

At the end of each of my days, I have gone to sleep knowing that I did my best, and that I did what I believed to be right. Tonight I know I am doing what is right for Los Angeles—and, my friends, what is right for Los Angeles is right for me.

The first decision broadcast journalists must make is the same as *all* journalists must make: to decide what the *news* is. That's easy in this case: Mayor Bradley announced his retirement.

The next decision is to choose actualities pertaining to this major point. The most obvious actuality is the retirement announcement itself:

BRADLEY #1

"The time for change has come. I have served a record five terms as your mayor. Others should now have the opportunity and responsibility to bring their vision to bear on the future of this great community. I am prepared to pass the torch to new leadership."

(runs :16)

So much for our actuality with key informational content. But we must now choose additional actualities, using our judgment as to news value, colorful details, and emotional impact. In the context of the city's riots, few would argue against Bradley's comment on racism. Thus:

BRADLEY #2

"The greatest cause of all is learning to live with one another. Racism is America's greatest evil. We in Los Angeles must be the first to slay that demon."

(runs :09)

In fact, that aspect of Bradley's remarks is such a strong actuality that we might decide to use a second version of it, containing his allusion to the riots, by making an internal tape edit:

BRADLEY # 3

"Racism is America's greatest evil. We in Los Angeles must be the first to slay that demon. (. . .) The April unrest tore at my heart, and I will not be at peace until we have healed our wounds and rebuilt our neighborhoods."

(runs :14)

Because we may air this story many times over the next few hours, and because each version must be fresh, we need at least one more actuality. We could choose from among Bradley's remarks about past accomplishments. But, as we've seen, the past—background—does not fit the style of broadcast news. Instead, we need something that addresses the present or looks to the future. Thus:

BRADLEY #4

> "Nine months of service remain before I retire as mayor. During that time I will devote all of my energy to making Los Angeles a better, safer, fairer and more just place to live. When I finally stand down I intend to be standing tall for the great causes of my life."

(runs :18)

Please note our working method: First we decided the news. At this point, a print journalist could immediately begin to write his or her story, interweaving text and quotes. We broadcasters, on the other hand, can not begin writing until *after* we have chosen our actualities. That's because, when we do write, we must tailor our language to suit the specific text of a given actuality.

Lead-ins and Tags

Once we have selected an actuality, we proceed to write news copy both before and after it. The components of this type of copy have specific names, which are the same in both radio and television.

The introductory copy *preceding* an actuality is called a *lead-in* (pronounced LEED-in). A few stations call it an "intro"—but the correct, universally understood term is lead-in. The copy *following* an actuality is called a *tag*.

Thus, a radio news story incorporating an actuality has the following structure: lead-in/actuality/tag. (As we shall see in later chapters, this basic structure often applies in television as well.)

The term "lead-in" is especially apt because the copy is supposed to "lead listeners in" to the taped voice or natural sound. In other words, listeners must not be surprised by the tape; they must be expecting it because the written copy prepared them for it. Lead-ins thus have two functions:

1. To open a news story.
2. To set the stage for the tape.

Tags also have two functions:

1. To re-identify the voice or sound we've just heard.
2. To finish the story or to carry it one step further.

At many stations, the modern practice is to dispense with a tag if (1) the voice is familiar to the audience (such as the president, the governor, or the mayor), and/or (2) the final words of the actuality make a natural end to the story. However, the vast majority of radio and TV news organizations insist that all stories with taped elements must have tags.

So much for the radio-news jargon (at least for a few moments). Let's apply the structure, beginning with BRADLEY # 1, which we will be preparing as a 35-second story for the 6 P.M. News (that is, the first hourly newscast following the event's occurrence) on a network or station outside Los Angeles. The text once again:

BRADLEY #1

> "The time for change has come. I have served a record five terms as your mayor. Others should now have the opportunity and responsibility to bring their vision to bear on the future of this great community. I am prepared to pass the torch to new leadership."

(runs :16)

Because this actuality in and of itself tells the crux of the news, our lead-in need not contain very much information. It need merely set up the specific text. Some examples:

> Mayor Tom Bradley of Los Angeles is stepping down. Bradley
> told a group of supporters a short while ago that it's time to
> elect a successor:
>
> -0-
>
> Los Angeles Mayor Tom Bradley, the first black man elected
> to run a major American city, is announcing his retirement:
>
> -0-
>
> Twenty years is a long time to run a city, and tonight, Los
> Angeles Mayor Tom Bradley said it's been long enough:

Note that none of the above lead-ins contains the wording "time for change" or "record five terms as mayor." Why? Because that specific wording is *in the actuality*. To have used those words in the lead-in would have been redundant. In other words, if *you* write the same words as the actuality, you obviate part of the reason to use the actuality in the first place. Once edited, you can't change the text of the tape—so you have to choose different wording in your copy.

Each of our sample lead-ins runs about 6 seconds. The actuality runs 16 seconds. The cumulative total is 22 seconds. Since this is supposed to be a 35-second story, we have only 13 seconds left for our tag. Some possibilities:

> Bradley, the first black man elected head of a major
> American city, said racism remains the nation's greatest evil.
> He said his city's main challenges are to fight gang violence and
> to rebuild after last April's riots.
>
> -0-
>
> Bradley said Los Angeles must rebuild itself in the wake of
> last April's riots, and he called racism "America's greatest
> evil." The 74-year-old mayor's current term expires next June.
>
> -0-
>
> Bradley thanked Angelenos for, as he put it, casting aside
> fear and bigotry to elect a black man as their mayor. And he
> called on America to overcome racism -- which he termed the
> nation's greatest evil.

If you have not been doing so all along, please reread those lead-ins and tags *with* the text of the actuality. Do you hear how we have integrated copy and tape into a smoothly flowing whole? We have given the newsmaker time to make a point in his own words, and we have used our words to summarize a few of his other points—and at no time have we left listeners wondering, "Now what the heck was *that* all about?"

Now let's try another version, with a different actuality, this time as a 30-second story for the 7 P.M. News:

> BRADLEY #2
>
> "The greatest cause of all is learning to live with one another. Racism is America's greatest evil. We in Los Angeles must be the first to slay that demon."
>
> (runs :09)

This brief actuality requires us to tell more information in the lead-in. But because we only have 30 seconds total, we still have to "write tight." Examples:

(lead-in)   Los Angeles Mayor Tom Bradley is resigning. Elected nearly 20 years ago as the first black mayor of a major American city, Bradley says it's time for a change. But he says major challenges still face his city and the entire nation:

(tag)   Bradley also said Los Angeles must end gang violence and rebuild itself from last April's riots.

-0-

(lead-in)   Tom Bradley says he'll be stepping down as mayor of Los Angeles. Bradley was elected nearly 20 years ago...as the first black mayor of a major American city. Tonight, Bradley thanked voters for overcoming bigotry THEN -- but warned it's still a problem NOW:

(tag)   Bradley said he'll devote his remaining nine months in office to rebuilding the city from last April's riots.

Once again we have covered the main points, partly in the newsmaker's words and partly in our own.

Leading with an Actuality

Before moving on, let's try something a little more difficult—a version which *opens* with an actuality. There are four basic requirements for choosing this method: 1) The opening actuality must be very short, pithy, and of good sound quality; 2) the voice must be well known to the audience; 3) the voice must be identified immediately after the tape; and 4) the story should lead the newscast so that the opening actuality plays immediately after the sign-on. Unless these basic requirements are met, the audience will likely become disoriented.

Bearing this in mind, here is a version tailored for a local Los Angeles station. It incorporates an abbreviated actuality, which we shall call BRADLEY # 5, followed by interceding copy (known as a *bridge*) linking it to a second actuality, then a tag:

(sign-on)   This is Jill Jones, KWKW News.

(actuality)   BRADLEY #5

"I am prepared to pass the torch to new leadership."

(runs :03)

(bridge)   Mayor Tom Bradley a short time ago, as he announced his
retirement. Bradley has been in office five terms, spanning 20
years, the first Afro—American elected to head a major American
city. He said race remains an issue:

(actuality)   BRADLEY #2

"The greatest cause of all is learning to live with one another. Racism
is America's greatest evil. We in Los Angeles must be the first to slay that
demon."

(runs :09)

(tag)   Bradley will remain in office until his current term expires
next June.

That entire story runs about 30 seconds. Until the 1990s, this would have seemed rather short for a lead story containing actualities. But the inexorable trend has been toward shorter and shorter stories with shorter and shorter actualities—as well as shorter and shorter radio newscasts altogether. Until the Reagan-era deregulation, many stations routinely carried several newscasts each day running 15 minutes or longer (in addition to a regular schedule of 5 minutes every hour). Now such practices are increasingly rare.

SCRIPTING

Broadcast news scripts do not include verbatim transcripts of taped portions. To include them would be cumbersome and time-consuming. But scripts do contain directions, identifications, and timings for each taped portion. These are called *cues*.

Incues and Outcues

Continuing with our lesson in broadcast news jargon: The first two or three words of a taped actuality (or tape of any kind) are called the *incue*. The last two or three words are called the *outcue*. Thus, the incue of BRADLEY # 1 is "The time for . . .," and the outcue is " . . . new leadership." The incue of BRADLEY # 2 is "The greatest cause . . .," and the outcue is " . . . that demon."

In addition to the slug and time placements with which you are by now familiar, a scripted tape insert is indented, bracketed, and identified by cut number, exact running time, and outcue. Hence the script for one of our 6 P.M. stories would look this way:

```
Bard, 9/24, 6p                          BRADLEY
```

```
        Mayor Tom Bradley of Los Angeles is stepping down.

        Bradley told a group of supporters a short while ago that it's

   time to elect a successor:


                   BRADLEY #1

                   RUNS:   :16

                   OUT:   "...new leadership."


        Bradley, the first black man elected head of a major American

   city, said racism remains the nation's greatest evil.

        He said his city's main challenges are to fight gang violence and

   to rebuild after last April's riots.
```

In a computerized newsroom (using BASYS), one of our 7 P.M. scripts would look this way:

```
┌─────────────────────────────────────────────────────────────────┐
│ PG____   SLUG___BRADLEY_____   CT#_2__  VO_____  SND_:09_  CUME __:31__ │
│ SHOW_7p_  COPY_:22_   WTR__Bard_____   ANC__Smith__   DATE/TM_9-24-92__ │
└─────────────────────────────────────────────────────────────────┘
```

        Los Angeles Mayor Tom Bradley is resigning. Elected nearly 20 years

ago as the first black mayor of a major American city, Bradley says it's

time for a change.

        But he says major challenges still face his city and the entire

nation:

                    BRADLEY #2

                    RUNS: :09

                    OUT: "...slay that demon."

        Bradley also said Los Angeles must end gang violence and rebuild

itself from last April's riots.

It is vital that these cues be accurate and in their proper places on the script page. The purpose is to prevent technical or announcing errors due to misplaced cues.

Remember, too, that outcues must reflect the final *sound* of the tape—such as laughter or applause—in addition to the final words. That sound is part of the "feel" of an actuality and adds presence. It may also allow the anchor to resume his or her delivery *over* it—hence the term "voice-over."

The following, for example, is a story scripted to allow the tag to be a simple reidentification over applause. It incorporates the following actuality:

                        SPIELBERG #1

            "They both have the desire and the need to communicate, often to
            'phone home' (laughter), to understand the care and the love, regardless of
            nationality. This film is dedicated to all such children, of all ages, in all the
            world. Thank you very much." (applause)

                                            (runs :22)

```
Diehl, 10/14, 3p                    SPIELBERG                     :35
```

```
     A special honor today for Steven Spielberg, who directed the

summer box-office smash "E-T."  Spielberg was in New York, where he

received the United Nations Peace Medal.

     In accepting the medal, Spielberg compared the U-N with E-T:


          SPIELBERG #1

          RUNS:  :19

          OUT:  "...very much." (APPLAUSE)


Movie Director Steven Spielberg.



                                        (Bill Diehl, ABC Radio)
```

Note that the Spielberg actuality cannot stand on its own. Its incue begins with the pronoun "they." Thus, the lead-in not only had to identify the speaker and establish the context, it also had to spell out who "they" were. Otherwise, the actuality would not have made sense.

MULTIPLE ACTUALITIES AND BRIDGES

Now let's take a closer look at the more complex scripting required for stories involving two actualities with a bridge of copy tying the two together. Here's a verbatim transcript, followed by the radio-news script itself:

```
(lead-in)      The government's new off-shore oil and gas leasing plan came

               under fire today at a hearing on Capitol Hill.  Leading the

               attack was Democratic Senator Walter Metzenbaum of Ohio:
```

(actuality 1)   (Metzenbaum) It would seem to me that the program to lease 200 million acres a year for five years is absurd. And its only conceivable result will be the most monumental giveaway in the nation's history: vast and immensely valuable public resources leased out at bargain basement prices, and in all probability leased out to the largest corporations in America.

(bridge)   But Interior Secretary James Watt said Metzenbaum and others
were off-base in their criticism of the leasing plan:

(actuality 2)   (Watt) There's a basic lack of understanding that what we're talking
                                                 about is the far-out lands under the oceans — not the coastal beach areas.
                                                 And too many people have, without understanding or intentionally without
                                                 understanding, have made comments and conclusions that are not accurate
                                                 or fair.

(tag)   Watt, who was testifying before the Senate Energy
Subcommittee, said the plan would create jobs, strengthen
national security, protect the environment, and reduce the
nation's dependence on foreign oil.

                                                                (George Engle, ABC Radio)

Engle, 11/4, 1130a   LEASE HEARINGS   (1:10)

The government's new offshore oil and gas leasing plan came under
fire today at a hearing on Capitol Hill. Leading the attack was
Democratic Senator Walter Metzenbaum of Ohio:

        METZENBAUM #2

        RUNS: :23

        OUT: "...corporations in America."

But Interior Secretary James Watt said Metzenbaum and others were
off-base in their criticism of the leasing plan:

        WATT #3

        RUNS: :20

        OUT: "...accurate or fair."

Watt, who was testifying before the Senate Energy Subcommittee,
said the plan would create jobs, strengthen national security, protect
the environment, and reduced the nation's dependence on foreign oil.

In a concise, one-sentence bridge, the writer/anchor has reidentified Metzenbaum while simultaneously setting up the context of the Watt actuality. Often it may take two sentences to write a bridge, especially if the two actualities being linked are not addressed to the same point.

SCRIPTING NATURAL SOUND

Scripting natural sound ("wildtrack audio") requires additional cues to ensure that the actualities and news copy interplay coherently. Here's a verbatim transcript of what radio listeners heard:

(actuality 1) (CHANTING) "Win, Jesse, win,...win, Jesse, win...

(bridge) (VOICE OVER) To the chant of "Win, Jesse, win," civil rights

leader Jesse Jackson announced today he's a candidate for the

Democratic presidential nomination. (TAPE OUT) Jackson says that

he is running for office to affirm his belief that leadership has

no color or gender.

(actuality 2) (Jackson) I seek the presidency because there is a need to inspire the young to hold fast to the American dream, and assume their rightful place in the political process.

(tag) With Jackson in the race, there are now 8 announced

candidates for the Democratic presidential nomination.

(Ann Taylor, NBC Radio)

Beginning with natural sound is an abrupt way to open a story. The anchor's voice must come in quickly to provide context. Also, the writer must be certain that the *preceding* story does not end with an actuality; that would be *too* abrupt.

The following is the script of the story. Note the wording and location of the cues telling when and how to play the opening tape and when and how the anchor should begin reading. These make clear that the opening actuality, although edited to run 15 seconds, will only be played "in the clear" for a few seconds; the rest is played under the anchor's voice. And the opening copy *repeats* a key phrase, just in case some listeners could not immediately understand what they were hearing:

```
Taylor, 4/4, 12p                          JACKSON            :40


(OPENS W/TAPE:  ESTABLISH & FADE)


                    CHANTING #1

                    RUNS:  :15

                    OUT:  (CHANTING) "Win, Jesse, win!"
```

```
        (VOICE OVER) To the chant of "Win, Jesse, win," civil rights

leader Jesse Jackson announced today he's a candidate for the

Democratic presidential nomination.

        (TAPE OUT) Jackson says that he is running for office to affirm

his belief that leadership has no color or gender:


                    JACKSON #4

                    RUNS:  :14

                    OUT:  "...political process."


        With Jackson in the race, there are now eight announced

candidates for the Democratic presidential nomination.
```

SCRIPTING Q/A

As noted previously, part of a reporter's interview, debriefing, or eyewitness account of an event may be excerpted for use as an actuality. Here's what we're talking about:

```
(lead-in)        A few moments of high drama today...amid the hours of tedium

                 at the occupied Polish embassy in Bern, Switzerland.  A diplomat

                 the terrorists did not know was hiding in the building all this

                 time...got away...with some help from Swiss police.  ABC's Bob

                 Dyke, who's been covering the story in Bern, says it began to

                 unfold when police units showed up at the embassy building in

                 force:
```

(actuality, Q/A)
> (Dyke) A van with blankets over the window drove away. Later, we learned that police had rescued from inside the embassy someone, uh, who was not a hostage, but had managed to hide away in the building when the compound was seized last Monday.

```
(tag)            Correspondent Dyke says photographers had spotted the man

                 several hours earlier when the man held a piece of paper up to

                 the top floor window.  But police asked reporters not to mention

                 it so the terrorists wouldn't find him.  They didn't.  He's now

                 been identified as Polish diplomat YO-seff SO-zee-ak...his post

                 at the embassy unknown.
```

(ABC Radio)

The Q/A is scripted in exactly the same fashion as any other actuality: by cut name and number, running time, and outcue.

Note, however, that if *two* voices are heard in the tape (such as a reporter *and* a newsmaker), *both* must be identified in the lead-in.

INFLECTIONS AND DOUBLE OUTCUES

In our previous discussion of editing techniques, we noted the desirability of ending actualities on a down inflection. The same applies to lead-ins.

Let's say we have an actuality of the president of the United States speaking the following text:

> "The world cannot tolerate this kind of behavior. It amounts to international piracy. We will ask the United Nations for a resolution demanding a Chinese withdrawal—an IMMEDIATE Chinese withdrawal."

Now suppose we phrase our lead-in this way:

```
        President Jones reacted angrily today to the Chinese seizure

     of a disputed island in the South China Sea.   The president said:
```

If you read that aloud, you'll hear that your inflection ends "up" on the word "said." It would end "up" even higher if we'd phrased it, "Said the president."

What's wrong with that? Well, maybe nothing—unless there's a long pause between your voice and the start of the tape. That silence is known as *dead air.* Broadcasters regard dead air the way campers regard poison ivy: they avoid it whenever possible. Nevertheless, dead air does occur occasionally—and when it does, its disorienting effect is mitigated by using down inflections. Therefore, try to avoid up inflections at the end of lead-ins. Make the lead-in an entire sentence instead of a fragment.

Now look at that actuality once again. Note that the final words—"Chinese withdrawal"—are *repeated.* This is called a *double outcue,* and unless the script contains a warning, the anchor might come in too soon with the tag copy. Here's how to script the warning:

```
        OUT:  "...Chinese withdrawal."  (DOUBLE OUTCUE)
```

The scripted notation "DOUBLE OUTCUE" in parentheses and capital letters lets the newscaster and studio technician know that the final words of the actuality will be heard twice.

EXERCISES

1. Using the Bradley transcript on pp. 135–37 and the actuality BRADLEY #4 on page 138, write a 40-second story for the 8 P.M. News. Slug it BRADLEY RESIGNS.

2. Using the following news agency story and actualities, write a 40-second story for 12 Noon (slugged MIA'S), incorporating any *one* of the actualities.

```
        WASHINGTON (AP)--Henry Kissinger on Tuesday denounced as
     "a flat-out lie" the allegation that he and others knew U.S.
     servicemen were left behind when the war in Southeast Asia
     ended two decades ago.
        Two people who made such suggestions Monday were
     Kissinger's colleagues from the Nixon administration--defense
     secretaries James R. Schlesinger and Melvin Laird.
```

But the former secretary of state and national security adviser acknowledged that even as he negotiated peace with the North Vietnamese, he recognized they had not provided an adequate accounting for missing Americans.

And in a sometimes hostile exchange with members of a Senate committee, Kissinger didn't rule out the possibility that some Americans survived after U.S. soldiers were withdrawn from the jungles of Southeast Asia in 1973.

"I think it's improbable any are alive today," Kissinger said. "I have always kept open the possibility in my mind there were some in Laos."

Kissinger's intensely defensive, sometimes combative testimony came under oath before an extraordinary hearing by the Senate Select Committee on POW-MIA Affairs.

The bipartisan panel is trying to answer lingering questions about the fate of missing soldiers and airmen two decades after the conclusion of the Vietnam War, which divided the nation.

Kissinger testified a day after other former Nixon officials, including Schlesinger and Laird, said they believed some American prisoners were still in Vietnam or Laos after the withdrawal of U.S. troops and the 1973 release of 591 prisoners of war. The former defense secretaries cited reliable reports of more POWs, particularly in Laos.

Kissinger said neither man ever expressed those views at the time.

"If we had known, if we had heard this, we would have acted on it," Kissinger said.

He bitterly disputed suggestions "that when President Nixon announced that all prisoners were on the way home, he or his aides knew that many were left behind."

KISSINGER # 1

"No Administration official knew that there were live Americans kept in Indochina. American prisoners may have been kept in Vietnam by a treacherous enemy in violation of agreements and human decency. But no one was left there by the deliberate act or negligent omission of any American official."

(runs :20)

KISSINGER # 2

"American prisoners may have been kept in Vietnam by a treacherous enemy in violation of agreements and human decency. But no one was left there by the deliberate act or negligent omission of any American official."

(runs :15)

KISSINGER # 3

"I think it's improbable any are alive today. But I have always kept open the possibility in my mind there were some in Laos."

(runs :07)

KISSINGER #4

"The turn that this investigation has taken, to concentrate on American failings rather than Vietnamese transgressions, pains me greatly."

(runs :07)

3. Write a second MIA'S story, this one for 6 P.M., running 45 seconds, using *two* of the actualities.

4. President Bill Clinton, following a practice by his predecessors Ronald Reagan and George Bush, has been delivering a 5-minute radio commentary every Saturday morning, starting at 6 minutes past the hour. Find out which station in your area carries the president's remarks and at what time, and arrange to record the broadcast. Then, in a real-life test of your abilities, select one actuality running 10 to 20 seconds and use it in a story running no longer than 40 seconds. (The hard part is that your story must be ready for broadcast by half past the hour. In other words, you will have only 19 minutes to decide the news value, choose your actuality, and complete your script.) You may be able to compare your work against a professional's by tuning to a network newscast beginning at half past the hour or at 55 minutes past the hour.

Audiotape II: Reports

11

Reports, either written and assembled in the newsroom or at the scenes of events, constitute the second major type of broadcast newswriting requiring the integration of audiotape.

As we've seen, modern technology permits reporters to exploit broadcasting's immediacy by going live, sometimes ad-libbing, perhaps with the aid of a few hastily scribbled notes. Most reports, however, are recorded for playback during later newscasts. And despite the hectic pace of broadcast news, reporters often have some time to organize their thoughts and choose their words carefully.

Before proceeding, we should note that reports differ in radio and television. Radio reports are short, running around 40 or 45 seconds on average. A TV report (called a "package") typically runs between 1½ and 2 minutes. A radio report focuses on a single aspect (or element) of a story, at a single location. A TV report covers many aspects at many locations.

Because of these differences, we shall concentrate, for the time being, solely on the structuring and writing of radio reports, as well as the lead-ins to them.

TYPES OF REPORTS

First our customary vocabulary lesson:

A radio report (or "spot") that contains only the reporter's voice telling a story is called a *voicer*. No actuality or sound of any other kind is included.

A report containing one or more actualities is called a *wraparound,* or just "wrap" for short. The name derives from the structure: The reporter's voice "wraps around" the actuality. A wrap's basic structure is thus lead-in/actuality/tag/sign-off.

Still another basic type of radio spot is called a *ROSR*—pronounced "RO-zer"—short for "Radio On-Scene Report." A ROSR is simply this: A reporter in the field talks into his or her tape recorder, either extemporaneously or from prepared notes, describing a scene or event as it occurs before his or her very eyes. In other words, the reporter acts as if he or she is going live, trying to capture the color and feel of an event. This running eyewitness narrative is then fed (transmitted) back to the newsroom, where 30- or 40-second chunks of it are excerpted and aired in the same manner as a voicer or wrap.

Sign-offs

Every spot, whether voicer, wrap, or ROSR, concludes with a sign-off. Sign-offs in broadcasting are roughly the equivalent of a combination of a newspaper byline and dateline—roughly but not exactly. For one thing, sign-offs do not contain the date. They do contain at least two elements:

1. The reporter's name
2. The reporter's location

> ```
> ...Pye Chamberlayne, Washington.
> ```
>
> (UPI Audio)

> ```
> ...Jack Vail, New York.
> ```
>
> (UPI Audio)

And most sign-offs contain a third element:

3. The reporter's news organization

> ```
> ...James Wooten, ABC News, Washington.
> ...Peter Arnett, CNN, Baghdad.
> ...Andrea Mitchell, NBC News, at the White House.
> ```

Whenever possible, sign-offs emphasize the *closeness* of the reporter to the story:

> ```
> ...Susan Spencer, CBS News, with the president in New
> Orleans.
> ...Forrest Sawyer, ABC News, with American forces in Kuwait.
> ```

There are strict rules about expressing proximity to a story. Obviously, the president of the United States was not looking over Susan Spencer's shoulder as she filed her report. The two weren't in the same room, maybe not even in the same building. But Spencer (and the rest of the White House press corps) had followed the presidential party throughout the day. Their assignment was to cover the president, to be with him whenever permitted by the White House staff. Thus her sign-off "with the president" is correct. If Spencer had merely rewritten news agency copy—in fact had not been "with the president" to witness any of his activities—she could *not* use those words in her sign-off.

> ### Rule: No reporter may ever sign off from where he or she has not been in connection with a story.

The reporter need not be at that location at the moment of filing the story. But the reporter must have been there to cover it, at least in part.

And in fact many spots in radio are merely rewrites from news agency copy or are based on telephone interviews. In those cases, the sign-off contains the reporter's name, news organization, and *city*. No further specification is legitimate. No reporter must ever give the impression of having been somewhere he or she has not in fact been.

There are a few other twists to sign-offs. The general public is largely unaware of them, but they are understood inside the industry.

One is a matter of professional standing. Only a full-time staff member of a news organization may use the name of that organization unqualifiedly in a sign-off. Nonstaff reporters, such as part-time "stringers" or local staffers of independent or network-affiliated stations, must include the word "for" in the sign-off:

```
...Jeff Grant, for CBS News, Newark, New Jersey.

...JoAnne Nader, for NBC News, Boston Heights, Ohio.
```

These two sign-offs are examples of local reporters who, either by volunteering or by request, got their voices onto network newscasts. For this they were paid a fee by the network.

You may have noticed a few other sign-off variations. For example, a network customarily including a reporter's location in the sign-off may occasionally have the reporter *omit* the location altogether:

```
...Garrick Utley, NBC News.

...Lynn Sherr, ABC News.
```

or

```
...Ralph Begleiter, CNN, reporting.
```

Nonspecific sign-offs such as the above indicate that the reporter was *not* at the scene of the story and did *not* cover it in person. He or she merely *voiced* the report based on material obtained from a different location or source—a report that may in fact have been written by someone else (possibly a newswriter or producer not permitted to go on the air). Even so, such wording follows the rule never to sign off from where a reporter has not actually been in connection with a story.

Still another variation has arisen from the budget cutbacks of the late 1980s and early 1990s. It has become prohibitively expensive to blanket the world with staff correspondents. Before the cutbacks, networks would unhesitatingly send correspondents to wherever news was breaking. Nowadays, to save money, they often have staff correspondents based in major media centers write and voice reports based on material supplied by other news organizations, instead of having them travel to the scene. Thus, if a news event breaks, say, in France or in Belgium, a correspondent based in London might file the report, signing off:

```
...Martha Teichner, CBS News, London.
```

or

```
...Bill McGlaughlin, CBS News, Hong Kong.
```

(in reporting a story taking place elsewhere in Asia)

Note that this still follows the rule never to misstate a reporter's actual location.*

Note also that sign-offs to *newscasts* are not subject to the rule of stating location. In local radio, it's assumed that the newscaster is in town and in the studio, not announcing from a vacation cottage in Acapulco. And in network radio, although most newscasts originate from New York or Washington, the practice is to omit the location in the sign-off as a kind of gimmick to make the news organization seem omnipresent—sort of like saying, "If we don't tell 'em where we are, maybe they'll think we're everywhere."

To sum up: sign-offs to reports must be accurate. It is unethical to "invent" a sign-off.

STRUCTURE OF SPOTS

To attempt to tell exactly how to write a radio news spot would be just as impossible as telling how to construct a snowflake. Each is different. Writing (hence, journalism) is an art, not a science.

However, we can offer guidelines regarding the content and structure of spots in general. And this much we can state unequivocally: It is impossible to tell the history of the world in 45 seconds. So don't even try.

Beginners have a tendency to think that their spots must be comprehensive, must trace the history of an event from its early beginnings, through its current developments, and on to an analysis of its possible ramifications. That is far, far too much territory for a radio spot. Instead, the focus must be kept narrow, on the current developments. History (background) should be kept to a minimum— only enough, in fact, to make the current developments clear. And the analysis should be kept out altogether or confined to the telling of what will (or might) happen next. (And we do mean *next*—not down the road a decade or two.)

Specifically,

1. Spots should be limited in subject matter. A spot should deal only with the story immediately at hand: its facts, limited background, and significance. Spots should *not* deal with related stories; related developments will be treated in separate stories scripted by the newswriter/ newscaster and/or by other reporters in their own spots. Limit the content to what *you* have seen or learned.

2. Spots should be limited geographically. A spot should treat events that occur at the location stated in the sign-off or close to it—*not* events occurring elsewhere. Again, events elsewhere, however related, will be treated in spots from those locations, not yours.

Okay, we're ready to examine the structure and style of the various kinds of spots. To do so, we'll use an actual story, but, for the purposes of demonstration, to put you in the role of a reporter/writer in a lifelike situation, we'll have to give you a new identity and move you to another location.

We'll call you "Jim/Jill Deadline." You are a staffer at KQKQ Radio (a fictional station) on the island of Maui, Hawaii. Shortly after 2 P.M., the newsroom police and fire radios alert you that an airliner has made an emergency landing at Kahului (Ka-HOO-loo-ee) airport. You grab your tape recorder, jump into a station vehicle (equipped with a 2-way transmitter), and rush to the airport. It is immediately clear that you have come upon a major news story, of importance to a national and international audience as well as to your local one. Your first task is to go on the air live (via your vehicle's transmitter) to describe what you see. Your station, recognizing that this is a major story, will send other staffers to help cover it while you rush to interview anyone and everyone you can find to help you piece the story together.

---

*The staff cutbacks and resulting modifications in signoffs are only one aspect of the worldwide reorganization of TV news-gathering resources. For example, no single network could hope to compete globally with London-based Reuters Television, whose 400 camera crews make it the world's largest TV newsgathering agency. It is far less costly to pay Reuters a licensing fee, and then have a staff correspondent re-edit the tape and write an original narration.

And here, as represented by the following news agency copy, is what you learn:

```
PM-Jet Blast, 2nd Ld--Writethru: 1021
One Person Missing, 60 Injured In Jetliner Explosion
    KAHULUI, Hawaii (AP)--A mysterious explosion ripped open
an Aloha Airlines jet "like a convertible" at 24,000 feet,
injuring 60 people and tossing a flight attendant to her death
before the pilot landed safely.
    The Boeing 737, with one of its two engines aflame and
about 15 to 20 feet of its cabin exposed, flew for 25 miles
after the blast and made an emergency landing at Kahului
Airport at 2 P.M. Thursday (8 P.M. EDT), airline officials
said.
    "There was a big bang when it happened and everybody
looked up and we were looking at blue sky," said passenger
Bill Fink of Honolulu.
    The cause of the blast was unknown, said Kevin Morimatsu,
a spokesman for the state Department of Transportation.
    The National Transportation Safety Board was sending
investigators to the scene and FBI agents were sent from
Honolulu to determine whether the blast was caused by a bomb,
said FBI spokesman Robert Heafner.
    Another passenger, Alice Godwin of Boulder City, Nev.,
said she put on a life jacket and put her head between her
knees. "I sang all the hymns I knew," she said. "That kept me
busy."
    "Everybody screamed," said Dan Dennin, also of Honolulu.
"However, it was very brief, the panic. . . . The rest of the
plane was intact, and we did not go into any unusual attitudes
or anything like that. I think that people realized the plane
was still flying and they quickly went about the business of
doing whatever they could do to save their lives."
    Mark Eberly, a ramp supervisor at the airport, said he
dropped to his knees in shock as he watched the plane land
with one of its engines smoking and a section of the top
missing. "I saw hair flying in the wind and arms dangling," he
said.
    Craig Nichols of Pocatello, Idaho, said after the plane
came to a stop on the ground, he saw "some really mangled
people (passengers)," including one with an arm almost
severed.
    "It looked like a normal landing with the whole top of the
plane gone," he said, adding that the damage began behind the
cockpit,"clear down to the windows," and extended to the rear.
    "It looked like a convertible," said Joe Ronderos of Los
Angeles.
    "It was like somebody had peeled off a layer of skin. You
could just see all the passengers sitting there," said George
Harvey, area coordinator for the Federal Aviation
Administration in Honolulu.
    "I give credit to the pilot. He brought that plane down so
smoothly. It was just like riding in a Cadillac," said
passenger John Lopez, 40, of Hilo.
    "I've had worse landings in normal aircraft," Dennin said.
    Sixty people were taken to Maui Memorial Hospital and 12
were admitted, two in critical condition and four serious,
said Dr. Charles Mitchell, emergency room director. Injuries
included burns, bruises and cuts, he said.
    The missing flight attendant, identified as Clarabelle B.
Lansing of Honolulu, was probably ejected by the blast or
blown out of the plane by the wind, said Clifford Hue, another
FAA area manager.
    "I think the stewardess (Mrs. Lansing) had just picked up
the microphone to start talking" when the explosion occurred,
Fink said.
    Fink and Dennin said some of the passengers hung on to
another standing flight attendant so she would not be sucked
out of the plane, and they praised the cabin crew for helping
calm the passengers.
```

The U.S. Coast Guard mounted a search that included a
cutter, a C-130 search and rescue aircraft and two
helicopters, said Coast Guard spokesman Petty Officer Jeffrey
Crawley.
     However, searchers found no trace of Mrs. Lansing, or the
missing section of the plane, he said.
     The explosion occurred southeast of Maui while the plane
was at an altitude of 24,000 feet, the airline said. It said
the 110-mile flight from Hilo on Hawaii Island to Kahului
carried 89 passengers, five crew members and an air traffic
controller from Hilo Airport.
     Passengers reported hearing an explosion in the forward
part of the plane, apparently around the first-class section,
said assistant hospital administrator Alan Lee.
     "They told me there was a loud, sudden explosion and the
roof of the plane literally flew off," said Mitchell.

VOICERS

Hard Leads

Your first spots (the first of what may be dozens before very long) will be *voicers*. Because almost anything you report at this time will be listeners' first hearing of the story, you will concentrate on the hard information—the Who, What, When, and Where. Thus, you will structure your first voicer much like a traditional news story, giving the latest information at the top. An example:

```
JET BLAST #1


     An Aloha Airlines jet made an emergency landing here this

afternoon after a midair explosion blew away part of the

passenger cabin.   Officials say a flight attendant was killed,

and 60 of the 95 people aboard were injured.

     The Boeing 7-37 was on an inter-island flight from Hilo to

Honolulu, flying at 24-thousand feet.   Passengers say an

explosion blew the roof off the forward passenger cabin, causing

a momentary panic.   Somehow, the pilot managed to fly the

stricken aircraft 25 miles to a safe landing.

     Officials identified the single fatality as flight attendant

Clarabelle Lansing of Honolulu.   They say she was apparently

blown out of the plane by the explosion.

     For the moment, officials are unable to say what caused the

explosion.   But an investigation is under way.

     The injured were taken to Maui Memorial Hospital, where two

are listed in critical condition.

     Jim Deadline, KQKQ News, at Kahului airport.

                          (runs :48)
```

There's nothing fancy about that spot. The writing is bare-bones. As the character Joe Friday used to say on the old "Dragnet" program, "Just the facts, Ma'am."

This is what's known as a "hard" spot with a "hard lead." That means the spot stands by itself as a story. It needs no preceding information to put it in context. It stresses immediacy wherever possible, making frequent use of the present tense to report what is happening "now."

It thus contains information that may become dated very quickly—such as the total number of deaths (the two people in critical condition might succumb at any time) and the cause of the explosion (which may also be learned very shortly). A spot containing material that can quickly be rendered inaccurate by later information is said to be "unprotected"; it is "unprotected" against fresh details.

Thus, a hard, unprotected spot is meant to go on the air as quickly as possible, before events overtake it. As long as a reporter/writer is in a position to update and transmit fresh details, the "hard lead" approach is the right one.

However, because you cannot gather information and go on the air simultaneously, you can tailor at least some of your spots to cover the time you spend gathering and preparing fresh material. The tailoring process is called "soft leading."

Soft Leads

The structure of this second type of spot is very different from the foregoing hard lead. It is called a "soft lead" because it *begins* by assuming that the audience has *already heard* the hard news from the anchor. In other words, the reporter/writer assumes the anchor will tell the audience that there has been an apparent explosion on the airliner and that X number of people have been killed or injured.

In addition, you would write the spot in a "protected" manner. That is, you would make *no reference* to story elements that might change very quickly. Therefore, you would *not* give the total number of casualties, the condition of survivors, or speculation about the cause of the explosion. Instead, you would confine yourself to those story elements that cannot change because they are in the past. This "protects" your spot, permitting your station to air it in a later newscast while you are busy rounding up fresh information.

(*Note:* If you wanted to protect your spot for a longer time, from a period of several hours to as long as overnight, you would also leave out any reference to the day or time of day—no "today," "this afternoon," "tonight," "yesterday," etc.)

A typical soft-lead, protected voicer would go this way:

```
JET BLAST #2

     The explosion took place at an altitude of 24-thousand feet,

while the jetliner was en route from Hilo to Honolulu.

Passengers said there was a "big bang" and then, suddenly, the

top of the forward passenger cabin simply wasn't there.  They

said there was momentary panic, but when they realized the plane

was still flying, they calmed down enough to buckle themselves

in.

     With two of the plane's engines aflame and part of the

superstructure missing, the pilot managed to guide the stricken

plane 25 miles here to the airport.  An airport employee said he

gazed in stunned amazement as the jetliner came in for an
```

emergency landing. Clearly visible, he said, were passengers

with arms dangling, their hair flying in the wind.

The explosion's one immediate fatality was flight attendant

Clarabelle Lansing of Honolulu. Officials say she was literally

blown out of the plane.

Jill Deadline, KQKQ News, at Kahului airport.

(runs :48)

A soft-lead, protected spot such as this offers some clear advantages in addition to providing breathing space. It enables the writer/reporter to concentrate on the details that make a story vivid for listeners. Precious time not spent on the basic facts, which can be left to the anchor, becomes available for color and quotes. And that's especially important when actualities are included—because they eat up time.

WRAPAROUNDS

During the breathing space afforded by having sent the foregoing protected voicer, you (as "Jim/Jill Deadline") have been busy preparing some wraparounds. You have chosen the following actualities from interviews recorded at the airport:

PASSENGER #1 (Dan Dennin, of Honolulu, passenger)

Everybody screamed. However, it was very brief, the panic. The explosion happened, the rest of the plane was intact, and we did not go into any unusual attitudes or anything like that.

(runs :11)

PASSENGER #2 (Dan Dennin again)

I think that people realized the plane was still flying and they quickly went about their business of doing whatever they could do to save their lives. I think we flew for almost 15 minutes with half an airplane, so we were all well aware of what was going on.

(runs :14)

PASSENGER #3 (Alice Godwin, of Boulder City, Nevada, passenger)

We all prayed. As long as those engines were running, the more secure I felt. I sang all the hymns I knew. That kept me busy.

(runs :09)

In a story of this nature, which goes under the heading of "near-catastrophe," the entire news industry—news agencies, newspapers, news-weeklies, network radio and television, local radio and television, etc.—throw vast effort and resources into the competition for news, sounds, and pictures. Within moments of a story like this breaking on the wires, editors, reporters, and producers will be calling anyone they can think of who might shed light on how it could have happened. In this case, calls flooded the Boeing company in Seattle, the main office of Aloha Airlines in Honolulu, as well as the Federal Aviation Administration (FAA) and the National Transportation Safety Board (NTSB) local and regional offices.

In short, a lot of people will have a lot to say, and the news media will be busy reporting it.

Jim/Jill's role in all this is to concentrate on those story angles that he/she is in the best position to report. In this case, which is perfectly typical in such situations, Jim/Jill had access to surviving passengers at the airport.

So Jim/Jill's wraps might go this way:

```
JET BLAST #3

     They were scared, very scared.  Passenger Dan Dennin of

Honolulu says the explosion caused momentary panic:

          PASSENGER #1

          RUNS: :11

          OUT: "...anything like that."

     Another passenger, Alice Godwin of Boulder City, Nevada,

says she tucked her head between her knees:

          PASSENGER #3

          RUNS: :09

          OUT: "...kept me busy."

     Maybe it was the prayers.  Maybe just a skilled pilot.

Maybe both.  Whatever it was, the plane -- what was left of it --

landed safely.

     Jim Deadline, KQKQ News, at Kahului airport.

                         (runs :43)

                            -0-


JET BLAST #4

     If it had been a movie, it might have been called "Terror at

24-thousand Feet."  But it wasn't a movie.

     Torn off was a 20-foot section of the jetliner's front

passenger cabin.  One passenger said when he looked up, all he

could see was blue sky.

     Another passenger, Dan Dennin of Honolulu, said there was a

moment of panic, but then everyone recovered:

          PASSENGER #2

          RUNS: :14

          OUT: "...was going on."
```

```
          People on the ground who watched the plane come in could

     scarcely believe their eyes.  And the passengers could scarcely

     believe their luck.

          Jill Deadline, KQKQ News, at Kahului airport.


                              (runs :44)
```

Both versions are protected soft leads. They can be used and reused as desired, with other reporters and writers updating the hard, breaking information as it becomes available.

ROSRS

At some point, Jim/Jill might have started talking into his/her tape recorder, to voice some of the things that might occur to almost anyone witnessing such an unusual event. And the resulting ROSR might have gone like this:

```
          I'm standing near the Aloha Airlines jetliner, and it's hard

     to believe a plane with this much damage could fly at all, much

     less 25 miles from a height of 24-thousand feet.  A 20-foot chunk

     of the fuselage is missing, blown out in the explosion.  Two

     engines are charred by fire.  The front passenger seats are

     exposed to the open air.  It must have felt like riding in a

     Ferris wheel gone out of control.  But of course, this was no

     amusement park ride.  It's amazing so many survived.
```

The purpose of a ROSR is not so much to impart hard facts—although it can do that—as to provide listeners with the feel of an event. In this case, the truly unusual thing is that there was only one death in this bizarre event. But a death is a death, and you can't very well report "only one death" as good news. In all likelihood, someone among the passengers or spectators on the ground would say in the course of an interview, "It was a miracle more people weren't killed . . . ," and that could have been broadcast as an actuality. Without that, there remains only the reporter to act as a surrogate on behalf of the audience. A ROSR or Q/A thus becomes an effective way to give voice to eyewitness reportage.

Take a look at a couple of ROSRs that were broadcast on network radio. The first is by a CBS reporter accompanying Israeli armored units on an assault against Palestine Liberation Army forces in Beirut, Lebanon:

```
          I'm with a forward Israeli tank unit...rolling forward in

     the center of West Beirut...(gunshots)...tanks are coming

     up...(tanks firing)...heavy machine guns on the tanks (machine

     gun firing) trying to pick out sniper positions in the buildings

     above us.  Israeli troops back against the walls of this street,
```

```
amid the rubble...thick black smoke rising just in front of the

tanks (tank shell explosions).  The tank's now charging forward,

turret swinging...(machine guns and sniper fire)...firing toward

sniper positions, the machine guns opening up.  Its twin firing

its heavy cannons into the buildings ...thick smoke clouding

everything in front of us.  Israeli troops here with us against

the walls of the buildings... (more tank fire).  Larry Pintak,

CBS News, with the Israelis in West Beirut.


                         (runs 1:03)
```

Not long afterwards, an NBC reporter sent a ROSR while accompanying Israeli forces out of Beirut. No gunshots or exploding shells this time, but the steady rumble of army vehicles is heard in the background:

```
     I'm standing beside a column of Israeli soldiers who're

beginning their individual pullout of West Beirut.  This has been

going on now for several days...but tomorrow, all of the Israelis

are supposed to be out of this section of the city, which was

once a stronghold of the Palestine Liberation Army ...(sirens).

Their pullout has been controversial.  The multinational

force...has refused...to come in until the Israelis get out of

West Beirut.  But another French unit arrived today, after

another 350 French paratroopers came in yesterday.  Ike Seamans,

NBC News, West Beirut.


                         (runs :39)
```

HARD VERSUS SOFT LEADS

The concepts of hard leading and soft leading are sometimes difficult for newcomers to understand. But understand them you must, because reporters are expected to write both kinds of spots for every story they cover (in TV as well as radio). And, back in the newsroom, writers and anchors must know how to integrate them into newscasts.

The single hard-lead voicer we've looked at so far was unprotected. It had to be aired quickly, or it would have become out of date. But we don't want to leave the impression that all hard-lead spots should be left unprotected or that, conversely, all soft-lead spots should be protected. In fact, the styles may be mixed at the discretion of the reporter/writer and the editor/producer.

As further illustration, here is a pair of network radio voicers on the same story, the first hard-led, the second soft. The writer was Richard C. Hottelet, formerly of CBS News:

#1 (HARD LEAD)

The Arab states, which have been talking about expelling
Israel from the current session of the General Assembly, have now
decided to pull back. Instead of challenging Israel's
credentials in a routine vote next Monday, the Arabs and others
will express reservations about Israel's presence in drastic
terms. They will denounce Israel as a member which violates
international law and specifically refuses to obey numerous
Assembly resolutions on Palestinian rights and withdrawal from
occupied territory. Many Arab and Islamic states, as well as
African and Western countries, were appalled by the idea of
trying to expel Israel. They saw it derailing a Middle East
process which may just be starting to move again. And some of
the Arabs argued privately that it could only heal the breach
between the Reagan administration and the Begin government. Most
did not have the confidence to make these points publicly, but
they seemed to have sunk in. Unless the radical Arabs go back to
the original idea, or Iran picks it up next Monday, the issue
appears to have been shelved for this year. Richard C. Hottelet,
CBS News, United Nations.

(runs 1:03)

#2: (SOFT LEAD)

Two weeks ago, radical Arab states proposed that Israel be
thrown out of the current session of the U-N General Assembly.
The idea was to call for rejection of Israel's credentials when
the report of the Credentials Committee comes up for approval
next Monday. The proposal stirred up a storm. Most Western
countries saw it as unwarranted and illegal distortion of the
spirit and letter of the United Nations charter. Washington
served official notice that if Israel were excluded in this
fashion, the United States would walk out with it and, more than
that, would withhold American payments to the United Nations'
regular budget. Since the United States pays 25 per cent or more

```
of the U-N's expenses, this would have been a disastrous

political as well as financial blow to the organization.  Many of

the Arab states, and of the larger Conference of Islamic

Countries, opposed the action of expelling Israel, especially at

a time when Arab leaders are consulting with the United States

about plans for peace in the Middle East.  This afternoon, the

Arab group of nations at the U-N decided NOT to try to reject

Israel's credentials, but simply to express their reservations

about Israel's presence.  Richard C. Hottelet, CBS News, United

Nations.


                          (runs 1:09)
```

Spot #1, the hard lead, tells the latest information in the very first sentence. Spot #2, the soft lead, defers telling the latest information until the very last sentence.

But that sentence in spot #2 contains the words "this afternoon." This dates the spot, leaving it unprotected after a few hours. Thus, CBS Radio aired it quickly, at 3 o'clock in the afternoon.

Spot #1 is protected. It contains no reference to the day or time of day. It could thus be held for later use. And in fact it was: CBS Radio aired it at 8 o'clock the next morning.

Now we're ready to examine why the hard/soft distinction is important to the technique of integrating spots into newscasts.

LEAD-INS TO SPOTS

Spots do not exist in a void. Because they represent a second sound source (the first source being the voice of the anchor of the newscast), usually on tape, they must be integrated into newscasts in the same way as actualities. In other words, they require carefully written lead-ins to make them flow.

The exact wording of a lead-in to a spot depends both on the overall content of the spot and on its opening words. Listeners must be prepared both for the new voice *and* for the context in which it is speaking. Neither must come as a surprise. Writers must tailor the language of their lead-ins to suit the opening language of the reporter.

Here is the news department's working method:

1. A reporter covers a story.
2. The reporter writes one to three spots on the story and feeds (transmits) them to the newsroom.
3. The editor (or producer) gives the hardest spot, the one with the freshest information, to a writer or writer/anchor for inclusion in the next newscast, reserving the other spot(s) for later newscasts.
4. The writer or writer/anchor tailors the lead-ins to fit the content and opening wording of the spots.

Now we come to the importance of the hard/soft distinction:

1. If a spot begins with a hard lead, the lead-in should be soft. In other words, if the reporter tells the important news in his or her first sentence, the writer's lead-in should *not* do the same.

Instead, it should tell just enough to key the listener's attention and understanding. If the lead-in and reporter's first sentence are both hard, the result is needless repetition; to the listener, it sounds as if the people in the newsroom weren't paying attention.

2. Conversely, if the reporter begins his or her spot with a soft lead, deferring the hardest news till the end or omitting it altogether, then the lead-in must be hard; it must state the latest, most important news. If the lead-in and reporter's opening are both soft, it will take too long for the listener to learn what the real news is—or never learn it at all.

You could almost reduce this to a formula:

Soft-led spot requires hard lead-in.
Hard-led spot requires soft lead-in.

But enough lecturing. Let's see how this works in practice—beginning with the lead-ins to the foregoing two Richard C. Hottelet spots:

```
                    At the United Nations, Arab nations have backed away from

               their campaign to oust Israel from the General Assembly.   The

               story from Richard C. Hottelet:

                         HOTTELET #2

                         RUNS: 1:09

                         OUT: "...CBS News, United Nations."
```
                                                    (lead-in by Stephanie Shelton, CBS Radio)

The spot began soft, so the lead-in was hard.

```
                    Here in New York, the United Nations has apparently been

               spared a crisis that Richard C. Hottelet says could have put it

               out of business:

                         HOTTELET #1

                         RUNS: 1:03

                         OUT: "...CBS News, United Nations."
```
                                                    (lead-in by Dallas Townsend, CBS Radio)

The spot began hard, so the lead-in was soft.

Note that the lead-in tells the name of the reporter. That prepares listeners for the new voice. Most lead-ins also tell the reporter's location.

(A few news departments follow a format of *not* identifying the reporter or his or her location in the lead-in. Writers in such newsrooms are instructed to make the lead-in and reporter's opening words flow without this information. This approach risks leaving listeners disoriented—which is why most news departments don't do it that way.)

Now let's tailor lead-ins to suit the spots filed by our alter egos, "Jim/Jill Deadline." We are at the station, putting together the next newscast, and we get JET BLAST #1. We listen to it and realize that it has a hard lead—Jim tells the hard news up front. All we need to do is set the stage:

A jetliner made an emergency landing at Kahului Airport a

short time ago. Jim Deadline is there with details:

        JET BLAST #1

        RUNS: :48

        OUT: "...at Kahului airport."

Half an hour later, we air spot #2. The text of Jill's spot leaves it up to us to give the basic information in the lead-in:

At least one person was killed and 60 injured this afternoon

aboard an Aloha Airlines 7-37. As we hear from our Jill

Deadline, the plane made an emergency landing at Kahului airport

after being damaged in midair:

        JET BLAST #2

        RUNS: :40

        OUT: "...at Kahului airport."

Please go back and read the lead-ins and spots together. Do you see how we've made them flow? We have figuratively taken listeners by the hand and led them through the story, making sure they don't get lost along the way.

Before doing the lead-ins for spots #3 and #4, let's say it is now around 11 P.M., many hours since the mishap. We can safely assume that all but a handful of the audience have heard (or seen, or read) the story by now. We are eagerly awaiting new developments. And we get them: Over our news agency printer (or CRT) comes the following update:

```
     AM-Jet Blast, 5th Ld
Investigators Seek Cause of Mid-Air Explosion of Jetliner
Eds: LEADS with 7 grafs to UPDATE with comments from press
conference targeting structural failure as likely cause. Picks
up 5th graf, "The Federal . . ."
     KAHULUI, Hawaii (AP)--A structural failure, not a bomb,
likely caused the "big bang" that ripped open an Aloha
Airlines jet, injuring 61 people and apparently sucking a
flight attendant from the cabin to her death, a federal
official said Friday.
     The Boeing 737, which was cruising at 24,000 feet on an
island hop from Hilo to Honolulu, made a safe emergency
landing at Kahului airport Thursday, after flying about 15
minutes with 20 feet of its upper fuselage just behind the
front passenger door torn away to the floor. Witnesses said
one engine was on fire.
     "There was a big bang when it happened and everybody
looked up and we were looking at blue sky," said passenger
Bill Fink of Honolulu.
     At a news conference late Friday night, a member of the
National Transportation Safety Board said investigators
believed the cause of the accident was a structural problem
with the aging jet.
     "I think it's fair to say the focus of the investigation
is on the structure itself, the hole itself, and what if any
causes might have been to create hull fractures or hull
fatigue," said NTSB member Joseph T. Nall.
```

Obviously, this updates our story in a major way. The injury toll has risen by one, but, more important, authorities report a likely cause of the incident. Even so, we can still use the protected spots from "Jim/Jill." Here's how:

```
       A federal investigator says it was probably structural

  failure that tore open that Aloha Airlines jet.  The official

  says the investigation is now focusing on what he called "hull

  fracture" or "hull fatigue."

       One person was killed and 61 injured in what passengers

  described as a mid-flight explosion.  Our Jim Deadline was at

  Kahului airport shortly after the jet came in for an emergency

  landing.

            JET BLAST #3

            RUNS:  :43

            OUT: "...at Kahului airport."
```

Even after midnight, we can still use our final spot. We use the lead-in copy to retain our immediacy; the spot itself is undated, and therefore protected. Thus:

```
       "Structural failure."  That, investigators are now saying,

  is probably what caused yesterday's near-catastrophe on an Aloha

  Airlines jetliner.  One person died, and 61 were injured, in what

  passengers described as a mid-flight explosion.  Our Jill

  Deadline talked with many of them after they landed safely at

  Kahului Airport:

            JET BLAST #4

            RUNS:  :44

            OUT: "...at Kahului airport."
```

TAGS TO SPOTS

Normally, there is not (repeat *not*) a tag after a spot. That is because the sound source (the reporter) includes his or her own reidentification in the form of a sign-off, which makes a natural break from one story to the next. Structurally, the spot amounts (or should amount, if it's been written correctly) to the last word in the newscast on the specific story element it concerns.

Occasionally, however, there may be a late-breaking development that updates a spot in a significant way. A news agency, for example, may report new information between the time a spot was filed and the time it is to go on the air. In such a case, the newsroom must choose between two editorial options:

1. Junk the spot and substitute a fresh spot or writer-written version containing the new information.
2. Play the spot and update it with a tag.

The choice depends on the individual case. If, logistically, it is a relatively easy matter to get an updated spot by air time from the reporter, so much the better; the new spot will simply be substituted for the old. If, however, the reporter is unavailable (for example, he or she may be covering another story by then), or if time is very short (which is often the case), and the original spot is well written and otherwise rich in content, then a tag is in order.

Suppose, for example, that a reporter covering a union meeting on whether to strike says, in concluding the spot, "Results of the strike vote are expected shortly." And just before air time, AP sends a bulletin announcing the result of the vote in favor of a strike. This is quite clearly a major update. To include the information in the lead-in to the spot would negate any reason for using it, because it ends with dated information. So instead a tag would be written to this effect:

```
        And, we've just received late word that the union HAS voted

    to strike.
```

To repeat, the use of such tags is rare. Newsrooms would rather not use them at all, preferring to have the latest word from the reporter. Unfortunately, for logistical and technical reasons, it isn't always possible.

OVERNIGHTS

Let's say you are working the PM shift in radio—3 P.M. to 11 P.M. or 4 P.M. to midnight. Unless you're at a network or exceptionally well-staffed local station, you will turn out the lights as you leave the newsroom, because the AM shift won't be in for four or five hours yet. The news agency machines will be left running, but for all intents and purposes, the news department will be closed overnight.

All right, in walks the AM shift. They check the wires. But what do they do for fresh tape? There's been no one to prepare it, right?

Wrong. *You* prepared it before you left last night. How? By writing and recording a spot or two on events that occurred late in your shift. You tailored them specifically for use during AM Drive by rewriting the "when" element to suit the circumstances.

Suppose, for example, that you covered a fire that was brought under control at around 10 P.M. In your spots that evening, you spoke of "tonight's fire" and concluded by saying that "Officials suspect arson and have begun an investigation." Fine. But in your overnight versions, which are simply called "overnights" or "o'nites," you must change the wording to correspond to the projected time of broadcast. You might say

```
        Arson investigators this morning are looking into last

    night's fire on the West Side...
```

or

```
        Arson is one possible explanation fire officials are giving

    for the fire that destroyed a warehouse on the West Side...
```

Yes, the AM shift could simply have rewritten fresh copy from the overnight wire service material. But that's not what your news director wants. What he or she wants is fresh *tape* to enliven and enrich newscasts, tape that only *you* as the reporter of the story can provide.

EXERCISES

1. Using the following news agency copy, write two *voicers* slugged ANDREW #1 and ANDREW #2, each running no longer than 45 seconds. Sign off your name and "Miami."

Make ANDREW #1 a *hard lead* for the 8 P.M. Sunday News. Date it, leaving it unprotected after an hour or two.

Make ANDREW #2 a *soft lead,* protecting it for possible use after midnight.

> MIAMI (AP)--Hurricane Andrew surged relentlessly toward southern Florida on Sunday and forecasters warned it would be one of the most powerful storms to hit the United States in decades. More than 1 million residents were told to flee.
>
> The hurricane ripped into the Bahamas on Sunday afternoon with 120 mph winds, heavy rain and surging tide. The outlying eastern islands of Abaco and Eleuthera were hit first. There were four reported deaths.
>
> "It's on a dead course for South Florida. I hoped I would never experience this," said Bob Sheets, director of the National Hurricane Center in suburban Coral Gables. "We've not seen anything like this in the past few decades."
>
> Winds were fluctuating between 135 mph and 150 mph as the storm approached Florida's coast, Sheets said, adding that with luck, Andrew might hit land at the lower speed.
>
> Forecasters had feared Andrew could reach Category 5--the worst category with winds topping 155 mph--as it crossed the Gulf Stream to Florida, but that appeared less likely when the storm weakened slightly.
>
> Gov. Lawton Chiles issued a state of emergency and activated National Guard forces as Andrew grew to a Category 4 storm, the same as Hurricane Hugo in 1989.
>
> "I'm prepared for the worst," said Jim McDermott, 65, who left his Florida Keys home to spend Sunday evening at a Red Cross shelter."Those coconuts are like cannon balls. They can blast through concrete at that speed."
>
> In Dade County, which includes Miami, many shelters were full by mid-evening. Organizations that had promised medical services for the shelters had failed to show up, said emergency director Kate Hale, who pleaded for medically trained volunteers.
>
> Meteorologists reported shortly after 6 P.M. EDT that the eye of the hurricane passed over the northern end of Eleuthera in the Bahamas with gusts up to 120 mph.
>
> Landfall in southern Florida was expected between 6 and 8 A.M. EDT Monday, hurricane specialist Max Mayfield said. Up to 10 inches of rain was forecast.
>
> In the Bahamas, government news spokesman Jimmy Curry said he received a report of four deaths on either Abaco or Eleuthera.
>
> Newly sworn-in Bahamian Prime Minister Hubert Ingraham urged calm and directed people to story shelters. Getting information from the Bahamas was difficult Sunday as many phone lines were down.
>
> Only two known Category 5 hurricanes have hit the United States: Hurricane Camille, which devastated the Mississippi coast in 1969, killing 256 people, and the 1935 Labor Day hurricane that hit the Florida Keys and killed 405 people.

2. Now write a protected *wraparound,* slugged ANDREW #3, running no longer than 1 minute (:60) and incorporating *two* of the following actualities—one of the Bob Sheets cuts plus the Jim McDermott cut:

Bob Sheets #1

"It's on a dead course for South Florida. We've not seen anything like this in the past few decades."

(runs :07)

Bob Sheets #2

    "I hoped I would never experience this. We've not seen anything like this in the past few decades."

(runs :08)

Bob Sheets #3

    "It's on a dead course for South Florida. I hoped I would never experience this. We've not seen anything like this in the past few decades."

(runs :12)

Jim McDermott #1

    "I'm prepared for the worst. Those coconuts are like cannon balls. They can blast through concrete at that speed."

(runs :09)

3. Write anchor lead-ins for all three spots. Be careful to tailor each lead-in to the specific hard/soft nature of each spot.

Audiotape III:
Interviewing, Editing,
Field Reporting

12

FONERS

A great advantage of radio news is that newsmakers can be interviewed by telephone and their remarks reported immediately, either live or on tape. Radio is thus much speedier than television in assembling and airing breaking news. Despite tremendous advances in live TV transmission capabilities, television news is often reduced to emulating radio while awaiting reception of relevant pictures.

Every radio journalist has a favorite story about getting the ideal phone interview: the gunman holding hostages inside a bank, the public figure gone into hiding following reports of a major scandal, and so on. Such scoops are rare, but they illustrate the goals of radio journalists: to reach the right person, to reach that person *first,* and to reach that person *exclusively.* In real life, it seldom works out that way, but it's always worth a try.

Tape-recorded telephone interviews are called *foners.* This bit of radio-news jargon takes the verb *to do,* as in "do a foner" or "I did a foner with Alderman Smith."

Federal and state laws generally permit the tape-recording of telephone interviews *only with the subject's permission,* either tacit or expressed. You *must* inform a prospective interviewee that you wish to tape the conversation, thus giving him or her a chance to decline. Some news departments require the subject's permission to be expressed clearly on the tape before allowing the interview to proceed.

Naturally, there are some exceptions. If perchance you *do* reach the gunman holding hostages (which at some news departments might violate a policy of noninterference in criminal matters where lives are threatened), you are obviously not going to begin the chat by asking, "Please, sir, may I pretty please have your permission to tape this interview?" Someone who is clearly breaking the law at the time you reach him is not going to sue for invasion of privacy.

Equipment

There are certain technical problems in doing foners. The first involves the sound quality of the phone lines themselves, which, despite recent fiber-optics technology, is often poor—when compared, that is, with live or studio-quality sound. Some telephone sound quality has actually been growing *poorer* because of the proliferation of cheap, gimmicky telephones and the overcrowding of circuits. Thus, radio news departments use specialized equipment to record optimum-quality telephone sound.

The recording phone itself is a separate line bypassing the switchboard and is located in a studio adjacent to the newsroom or in a relatively quiet nook near a console recorder. The handset is equipped with a "push-to-talk" button or switch, which, unless activated, kills the handset microphone, thereby shutting off extraneous noise on the reporter's end. Users must press the button or flick the "talk" switch whenever they want their questions heard and recorded.

The recording line number (large news departments often have more than one) is unlisted and unpublished, and is engraved in the minds of newsroom personnel; it's the same number reporters use to phone in their reports and actualities from the field.

(In a pinch, a portable cassette recorder with a phone recording attachment can be used to do foners. But the resulting sound quality is often very poor and thus "UFB"—unfit for broadcast.)

Reaching the Subject

Since foners are often done in connection with breaking stories, speed is of the essence. If you linger in trying to reach a newsmaker, chances are you'll get a busy signal because the competition has reached the newsmaker first. So you've got to move fast.

As mentioned earlier, you will have compiled your own private list of names and telephone numbers, your own "little black book." The newsroom, too, has its Rolodex file of important and frequently called names and numbers, which each staffer is expected to correct and update as changes warrant.

On breaking stories, however, such sources may be of no help. You'll have to find new numbers—and find them *quickly*. Elementary as it may sound, you should lunge for the telephone book instead of calling Directory Assistance. The phone book is quicker than "Information," which is mainly of help only in learning new listings or numbers outside your calling area. If the phone book proves of no help, *then* call "Information." If that's no help either, or if there's no answer at the subject's home or office numbers, call known relatives or associates of the subject for possible leads to his or her whereabouts.

There's also the Reverse Directory (also called the "Crisscross" Directory) published by phone companies in many cities, listing residential, building, and business numbers by street address rather than alphabetically. All you need to know is the approximate address of a person or place; you can then use the street index to find the specific address and phone number.

Here's an example of how radio staffers can use the Reverse Directory to do effective foners. Let's say that a fire breaks out on the far side of town. You are the only staffer on duty at the time; there is no one to go to the scene. The newsroom fire radio has announced the address or approximate location of the fire. You check the Reverse Directory for telephone numbers of businesses or residences *across the street* or *near* the fire. Then you call those numbers to tape "eyewitness" accounts of the fire from people within sight of it.

INTERVIEWING TECHNIQUES

Preparation

The first thing to do upon reaching an interview subject is to identify yourself by name and station call letters. There must be no misrepresentation; this is a matter of ethics, if not law. Then you explain briefly why you are calling (most times it'll be obvious) and ask permission to tape-record the conversation.

That's the easy part. The next part—conducting the interview itself—is truly the highest art of journalism. Many times, two questions—"What happened?" and "What do you think about it?"—will suffice. But at other times, when you are talking to people who may have something to hide or who you suspect are being less than truthful or forthcoming, the ability to conduct a fruitful interview (from your point of view) can spell the difference between getting a story and missing it.

Although we are about to suggest some guidelines for interviewing, we must say ahead of time that interviewing is a talent developed over time and with much practice. Fortunately, there is no shortage of role models available for you to emulate, even as you develop your own abilities—in particular Mike Wallace ("60 Minutes," CBS), Ted Koppel ("Nightline," ABC), Robert MacNeil, Jim Lehrer ("The MacNeil/Lehrer NewsHour," PBS), and Larry King and Judy Woodruff (CNN and syndicated radio). And on local radio, almost every market has one or two talk or telephone call-in hosts who consistently bring out (or wring out) the best and most newsworthy in their interview subjects.

What unites these and other effective interviewers, first and foremost, is their *knowledge of the subject matter*. They come *prepared*. Nothing turns off an interviewee more quickly or more thoroughly than an interviewer who does not know what to ask.

Broadcast journalists, while inherently generalists because of the hopscotch nature of the news business, must nevertheless prepare themselves for every interview. On the workaday level, this may mean no more than reading every available bit of news-agency and newspaper copy before placing a call. But the preparation must be done. You must have a pretty firm idea of what questions to ask.

Avoiding "Yes-No" Questions

Remember that what you are seeking in a foner is not just newsworthy information, but information that can be excerpted as actualities. Therefore, questions that can be answered by a simple "yes" or "no" should be avoided.

If (for example) you ask Senator Piltdown, "Do you think the tax bill will pass?" you will likely get a one-word answer (well, maybe not in the case of Senator Piltdown). So instead, you should phrase the question, "What will happen to the tax bill?" or "How do you assess the tax bill's chances?" Such phrasing forces the interviewee to be more forthcoming and give an answer that may be used as an actuality.

Similarly, in interviewing witnesses to events, do not ask, "Did you see the bridge collapse?" Instead ask, "What did you see?" and "What did it look like?" You must oblige people to use *their* words, not parrot yours.

(Sometimes, no matter how hard you try, all you'll get are one-word answers. In such cases, actualities may be excerpted as Q/A.)

Sticking to the Point

It goes without saying that your questions should stick to the subject matter; that's why you called. More difficult, though, is getting the *interviewee* to stick to the point. Some people express themselves poorly. Others may be nervous about being interviewed by reporters. Still others may be reluctant to answer your questions, refusing to be pinned down or preferring to utter self-serving comments on matters closer to their hearts than to yours. (There's the story of the Texas politician who, when asked his stand on the Equal Rights Amendment, replied, "Some of my friends are for it, some of my friends are against it, and I never disappoint my friends.")

You should not let people get away with evading questions. Politely but firmly, you should repeat the question, remarking if necessary that the interviewee's previous reply was unresponsive.

Many people in the public eye, especially politicians, have considerable experience in dealing with reporters and the media. Many of them know your technical requirements as well as you do, as well as the questions you are likely to ask. Such people are very skilled at using the media for their own ends. They have certain points to make, and will make them no matter what you ask or how many times you ask it. In such cases, it is well to remember that *you* are conducting the interview; if the interviewee (who *agreed* to be interviewed) doesn't want to answer your question, make him *say* he doesn't want to answer it—on tape.

Listening

It seems elementary to have to mention this, but failing to *listen* to a person's answers is a common cause of flubbing interviews. If you are not listening carefully, if instead you are contemplating the wording of your next question, you may miss the most newsworthy part of the interview, and thus miss the ideal chance to ask a follow-up question.

Almost every broadcast news staffer has a personal horror story of "letting the big one get away," and almost always the reason was failure to listen carefully (or failure to prepare for the interview by reading background material). Such disasters can usually be avoided. Here's how:

Jot down a few questions in advance of the interview. But do *not* look at your written questions during the interview *unless* your mind suddenly goes blank or the interview is not proceeding smoothly. Those written questions serve as a kind of crutch to be used only in an emergency. But having them around frees you to concentrate on what the interviewee is saying instead of mentally thrashing about for what to ask next.

Handling "Difficult" Interviewees

Now about those nervous or inexpressive interviewees: Herein lies much of the art of broadcast interviewing, for it is often necessary to put people at ease or flatter their egos before they will open up. There may be a certain amount of shamelessness involved in getting people to give you the information you want in the form you want it. But it goes with the territory.

Sensing trouble ahead, you might, for example, begin a foner with small talk and gradually work the conversation into the subject matter you really want to cover. Or you could phrase your questions as an appeal for help, reminding the interviewee that he or she is the expert, while you, a mere reporter, need educating.

You can appeal to the interviewee's ego, his or her sense of self-worth, by mentioning how much you are enjoying the talk because he or she is making things so much clearer than other interviewees.

Shameless flattery? Trickery? Yes, in a way—but perfectly legitimate. The person did agree to be interviewed and is free to stop at any time.

What you must never (repeat, *never*) do is misrepresent your credentials.

"Good Tape"

After some practice doing foners and interviews in the field, you will develop an ear for a good actuality—"good tape"—even as the words are being spoken and recorded. A broadcast interviewer must learn to listen closely for both information *and* good actualities. The corollary is that he or she must also be able to recognize "bad tape" in order to shift gears in the course of an interview.

Some people ramble on and on. Others use specialized jargon or technical language your audience may not understand. Still others mumble indistinctly just when they're telling you what you want to hear. In such cases, where you fear the remark will not make a good-quality actuality, you should ask the question again, perhaps phrasing it a bit differently. You may have to "play dumb," saying you don't quite understand. Or, on rare occasions, you may simply explain that you've got a technical problem with the answer, that listeners won't understand unless the answer is phrased better or more concisely. This is *not* telling a person what to say or "staging the news." It is merely a technical requirement of the medium, in the same way that a print reporter may ask someone to speak more slowly in order to be quoted more accurately.

With a nervous or rambling interviewee, you'll find nine times out of ten that the second time such a person says something, it makes "better tape," because, in effect, the remark has been re-hearsed. (With an experienced interviewee, however, the *first* time something is said usually makes the better actuality because it sounds more spontaneous.)

Remember, the real payoff of foners and taped interviews in the field is not only gathering information in a form *you* can understand, but also in a form your *audience* will understand.

"Off the Record"

Each news organization has its own specific rules regarding off-the-record interviews, that is, remarks which, by agreement with the interviewee, you will not attribute to him or her. Whatever the rules of your news department, it is expected in radio that you will *turn off your recorder* for anything stipulated "off the record." Obviously, a tape recording would be a "record," solid proof of the remarks of which you promised there would be no proof.

There's no *law* saying you have to turn your recorder off. But if you don't, it may be the last time you'll ever hear from that particular source and, once the word gets out, the last you'll hear from many such helpful sources. Like so much in the news business, this is a matter of professional ethics.

You should be aware that in some states, courts have ordered reporters to divulge their sources, and that some reporters have been held in contempt of court and actually sent to jail for refusing to do so. Other courts have ordered broadcasters to turn over their unused (unaired) portions of tape— known as *outtakes*—for use in trials. By and large, broadcasters have refused to allow this, saying to do so would do great harm to the interview process.

These are issues of vital interest to journalists in all media. This book, which is designed as a practical guide for fledgling broadcast journalists, does not have space to chronicle such matters, except insofar as they may affect writers and reporters on the everyday working level. Suffice it to say that journalistic ethics, while often established by individual news departments, may ultimately be a matter of personal choice—and personal courage.

EDITING PROCEDURES

In foregoing chapters we examined how to choose and edit actualities, as well as how to package reports. Now we look at how to prepare taped material for broadcast.

Equipment

Some radio news departments still do studio editing by cutting and splicing quarter-inch (¼″) reel-to-reel tape running at 15 or 7½ inches per second (ips), a system which has been around since the 1950s and which is still the method of choice in commercial production. Cassettes of eighth-inch (⅛″) tape running at 1⅞ ips (the worldwide standard which came along in the early 1960s) are reserved for field reporting.

Nowadays, though, manual editing has given way to electronic editing in most news departments, with eighth-inch cassettes and quarter-inch cartridges as the standard. Reel-to-reel machines are still used as backup equipment for cases when electronic editing is too difficult.*

Carts and Labels

Whatever the original recording medium, edited actualities and reports are dubbed onto cartridges of quarter-inch tape. Simply called "carts," these are similar to the 8-track stereo cartridges you used to find in electronics stores before the advent of noise reduction systems (Dolby, etc.) for eighth-inch audiotape cassettes and the invention of compact discs (CDs). Radio-news carts are different in that the tape inside each cart is on a continuous loop, the length of tape differing with each cart. Some carts thus run as short as :10, others as long as five or ten minutes. If an actuality runs, say, :18, it will be dubbed onto a 20-second cart. Once played, the measured tape loop automatically re-cues itself at the incue of the actuality.

Each cart is *carefully* labeled. On the label are:

1. The *name* of the newsmaker or reporter speaking
2. The *place* at which he or she was speaking

---

*Electronic editing—dubbing from one tape machine to another without cutting and splicing the tape—is actually less precise than the older method. A precise edit often requires sufficient tape length and surface area to permit a clean pickup of a wanted sound or deletion of an unwanted one. Fast-moving quarter-inch tape meets this requirement. But eighth-inch tape is too small to be manipulated. It can't be cut and spliced. Thus, an editor must rely on a good ear and a quick finger to make an acceptable electronic edit. It doesn't always work. Either an actuality must be "cleaned up" by dubbing it to quarter-inch tape for manual editing, or the news department must live with the "dirty" version.

After securing permission from an interviewee, KWFB reporter Paul Lowe records an interview via telephone.

Immediately thereafter, Lowe electronically edits several actualities from the interview onto audio carts.

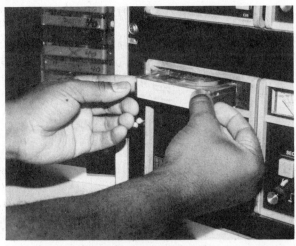

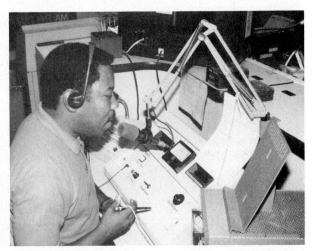

Lowe carefully labels each cart with the date, the name of the speaker, the number of the actuality, its precise running time, and its outcue.

Lowe chooses one of the actualities for use in his own wraparound aired live from the newsroom . . .

. . . and delivers the remaining carts to editor Sue Stiles, who distributes them to other staffers . . .

. . . including anchor John Brooks, who airs one of Lowe's actualities within moments of receiving it during his air shift.

3. The *number* of the cut
4. The *exact running time* (in seconds)
5. The *outcue*

This is all vital information for any newswriter, newscaster, or engineer who handles the cart. And the bigger the news department, the more vital the label information, because the cart will pass through just that many more hands. No one should ever arrive at the start of a shift, pick up a cart presumed for a newscast, and have to wonder, "Now what the heck *is* this?" So, in the preparation of cart labels, as in the preparation of news copy itself, neatness and precision count.

Carts that are ready for broadcast are delivered either directly to the studio where they will be played back or to the anchor of the upcoming newscast, who will hand-carry them to the studio just before air time.*

RUNDOWNS (LOGGING TAPE)

In addition to foners, radio news staffers are routinely assigned the job of recording and monitoring long stretches of potentially newsmaking material (such as presidential news conferences or network closed-circuit feeds). In addition to the notes they must take as journalists on the newsworthiness of the material, they must also note the location of potential actualities and be able to relocate them quickly anywhere on the bulk tape. This process is called *logging* a tape (or a feed) and the "log" itself is called a *rundown*. To do this efficiently, a staffer must obviously have a reliable reference point and a method of measuring the tape accurately. That is why professional recording equipment comes with a precise *tape counter*.

The counter is calibrated either by number or by clock-time. The counter must be "zeroed"—reset to zero—at the start of each reel or cassette and then not touched until editing is completed; otherwise, the reference point would be lost and the rundown notes worthless.

A zeroed number counter looks like this: **0000.**

A zeroed clock-time counter looks like this: **00:00.**

The number counter advances consecutively from 0001 to 9999. The clock-time counter advances the same way a digital clock or stopwatch does, in minutes and seconds, from 00:01 to 59:59.

Logging a good (that is, accurate and efficient) rundown comes with concentration and practice. Each broadcaster evolves a system best suited to him or her. Some log by hand, others use a typewriter or computer keyboard. As a practical matter, though, it's a good idea to learn how to log a rundown by hand—because you can't always count on there being a typewriter or computer handy.

One good method is to use a legal pad. On the extreme left, before the margin line, write your tape-counter readings. On the left side of the page proper, write your notes on possible actualities, including their incues. And on the right side of the page, write your notes on newsworthiness and news content. The rundown page thus contains a column of counter readings on the extreme left, an adjacent column of incues, and an adjacent column of notes. When the feed is completed, you can quickly assess its news value, decide on an actuality, and rewind directly to its location so that it can be dubbed onto a cart.

Logging rundowns may sound complicated at the moment, and there's no doubt they require concentrated effort. But in the professional workplace, they are an essential part of the routine. Their purpose is to enable your station to avoid wasting time by having to listen to an entire tape a second time in order to find just one or two actualities. The ultimate goal is to get your story on the air accurately—and ahead of the competition.

*Radio news carts and cart editing, both manual and electronic, are likely to be obsolete by the year 2000. In their place will be computerized systems such as "D-cart," invented in Australia and already in use at ABC News. With D-cart, taped material is digitized as it is fed onto a hard disk; actualities can then be edited on-screen at any networked computer terminal (with a mouse-like control pad) for preview and/or playback.

Bear in mind that logging rundowns in radio is easier than in television, where, in addition to everything else, you also have to log information about picture values.

FIELD REPORTING

Reporting for radio is not as complicated, technically speaking, as reporting for TV; you only have to worry about the sound. Nevertheless, radio reporting requires a thorough understanding of the tools of the trade.

Tape Recorders

Like doctors with their paging devices and beat cops with their sidearms, radio reporters are never without their cassette tape recorders. A recorder becomes virtually an extension of the reporter's arm, a tool ready for use at a moment's notice, and without which he or she cannot function properly. Staff reporters always take their recorders home after work because they never know when they'll be called upon to rush directly to the scene of a breaking story.

In this book we shall not be recommending specific makes or models of electronic equipment. However, we do specify certain minimum features and techniques to enable professional or semi-professional results. Audiocassette recorders for use in radio newsgathering, no matter how sophisticated their control configuration, will not automatically record the crisp, clear sound required for broadcast quality. Their successful use depends on the ability of their users to handle them properly.

Regardless of brand name or cost, any cassette recorder for professional broadcast use should have the following *minimum* features:*

1. A directional or semi-directional hand microphone (with or without a remote control switch)
2. A tape counter (for fast location of actualities)
3. An output jack (usually labeled "Earphone" or "Monitor")
4. An input jack (usually labeled "Auxiliary Input"; on some models, the microphone input will serve this function)
5. A shoulder strap (to free the hands for holding the mike and taking notes)
6. An earphone (for private listening in the field via the output jack)

The following additional features are helpful:

7. A battery-level indicator (to show when the batteries are growing weak)
8. A "Cue/Review" function (to permit speedy relocation of incues and outcues)
9. A "Pause" control (to permit precise stopping and restarting)

Audiocassettes

Audiocassettes for professional use must be of high quality. Cheaply made, inexpensive cassettes break or malfunction easily, causing you to lose a potentially important recording.

Cassettes should be a maximum of 60 minutes in length (30 minutes per side). Longer cassettes (lasting 90 or 120 minutes) have transport systems that cause jamming or stopping in small, battery-powered machines.

It is not necessary to use top-of-the-line, high-bias tape cassettes, which are designed for the home stereo buff. Normal bias ("low noise") cassettes are sufficient for news purposes.

Batteries

Always use long-lasting alkaline, lithium, or rechargeable nickel cadmium batteries, *not* standard or so-called "heavy duty" batteries. Only premium batteries have enough strength and staying

---

*Do not—repeat, *not*—use a *micro*cassette recorder. Only use recorders that take standard-size audiocassettes.

power to serve reliably in the field. (But beware of rechargeable batteries, too. They require frequent recharging, and the charge dies quickly instead of fading gradually like alkaline batteries. Thus they are risky when recording a lengthy event, and the battery-level indicator must be monitored closely.)

Field Testing

Before leaving on assignment, a reporter should test his or her recorder thoroughly to avoid a malfunction in the field. Here's a checklist:

1. Make sure that the batteries are fresh. Do *not* rely solely on the battery-level indicator.
2. Make sure that the recording and playback heads are clean and demagnetized. If they are dusty or dirty from tape particle buildup, clean them with a cotton swab (a "Q-tip" will do) dipped in head cleaner solution or denatured alcohol.
3. Record something and play it back. Speak (do not blow) into the microphone, and verify that the tape transport system is moving smoothly. If the playback sounds mushy or distorted, change the batteries and cassette, and repeat the test. If you still do not get crisp, clear sound, get a different recorder; the one you've been testing probably needs professional maintenance.

Backup and Accessory Equipment

In addition to the gear just listed, full-time radio reporters carry an array of backup and accessory items enabling them to record under a variety of conditions and to feed the material back to the station over a telephone line. These items are compact, light, and fit easily into a small shoulder bag, where the recorder itself may be stored when not in use. This accessory gear should include:

1. A spare set of fresh batteries
2. Several spare cassettes
3. A patch cord for recording from a mult-box or other tape recorder (discussed shortly)
4. An acoustic coupler for telephone transmission (discussed shortly)
5. A roll of adhesive tape (discussed shortly)
6. A small clamp (discussed shortly)

Each item of standard and accessory equipment has an important use which may not be apparent to the novice reporter or student reading this book, so we shall explain why each is necessary and how it is used.

MICROPHONES

Many portable cassette recorders are manufactured with a built-in microphone, usually along one edge of the recorder. Most professional radio reporters do *not* rely on this built-in mike. For one thing, it would require them to hold and move the recorder itself during recording; this is unwieldy, no matter how compact the recorder. But more important, the built-in mike is omnidirectional: it records sound indiscriminately from all directions. Thus, it is likely to capture and enhance unwanted background noise, instead of just the desired sound.

That's why professionals prefer a small hand mike which, when plugged into the recorder, overrides (disconnects) the built-in mike. Most hand mikes are directional or semi-directional. That means they must be pointed *at* the desired sound source. The result is sharper, clearer sound.

If the hand mike has a remote control switch, the switch should always be left in the "on" position, and the recorder's main controls used for on/off operation. That's because the remote switch does not control the recorder's full circuitry. In the "off" position, it merely pauses the transport system but doesn't turn off the recorder itself; left unattended, this will drain the batteries. Thus, to avoid accidental battery drainage, it is better to rely on the recorder's master controls only.

Automatic Volume

Most modern recorders are equipped with an automatic volume feature (often abbreviated as AGC, for "Automatic Gain Control"), freeing the user from having to adjust the sound level during recording. However, this feature is at best a mixed blessing because it does not operate like the human ear. AGC cannot distinguish between wanted and unwanted sounds. The circuitry automatically boosts the machine's sensitivity to weak sounds and lowers it to loud sounds.

But suppose you *want* the weaker (that is, less loud) sound? That's where the hand mike proves useful once again. Its directionality permits you to point it close to the specific sound source you wish to record and thus eliminate much of the unwanted sound. The recorder itself, being dumb, can't make editorial decisions. Without a human hand and ear to guide it, the machine records all sounds indiscriminately.

Mike Placement

Beginners sometimes think that a cassette recorder mike will record a speech or news conference from across the room. Thus placed, what it will record is mush. Because of the features already described, it'll give equal attention to the speaker's voice, the person coughing next to you, your own breath and heartbeat, and the power lawn mower chugging along outside the window.

In short, microphones must be held or placed *close* to the desired sound, which is usually someone's mouth, frequently the reporter's own. Depending on the quality of the microphone and the recorder, and the amount of ambient noise, the optimum mike-to-mouth distance is from *6 to 18 inches*. Any closer will overemphasize the speaker's popping of *P*'s and spitting of *S*'s, and any farther away will put the voice "off-mike" (rendering it "echoey" and indistinct).

Clamps and Adhesive Tape

In most situations, a reporter will hand-hold the mike, aiming it back and forth at whichever mouth happens to be speaking. But at other times, the mike must be *affixed* in a semi-permanent position. That's where a clamp or adhesive tape comes in handy.

Reporting assignments often involve covering a speech or news conference at which the speaker is either sitting at a table or standing on a podium behind a lectern. Although some hand mikes come with a collapsible stand allowing them to be placed at a toward-the-mouth angle on a flat surface, the stand won't work on a lectern, which is slanted. Thus, the mike must be clamped or taped in a suitable position (aimed toward the speaker's mouth).

In practice, there are usually other broadcast reporters at such assignments, all with the same mike placement problem. So as a matter of common interest they agree among themselves to help each other with taping or clamping their mikes. If there is a "house" mike (set up by whoever manages the premises), the radio reporter has only to tape his or her own mike to it.

Recording from Loudspeakers

Recording from loudspeakers is to be *avoided* whenever possible. A loudspeaker is only as good as the sound system connected to it. Frequently, house sound systems and loudspeakers, being designed to amplify sounds over large areas, have undesirable sound quality in the bass register and are full of static. Such sounds captured by your own microphone will be of only marginal broadcast quality. That's why broadcast reporters make every effort to arrive at events *early,* in plenty of time to set up their own microphones.

(In certain circumstances, whether because of crowded, chaotic conditions, lack of permission to set up sound gear, or your own late arrival, you will have no choice but to record from a loudspeaker. If so, you should hold the mike close enough to the loudspeaker to capture that sound only, eliminating as much as possible the sounds from other sources, such as applause or the comments of people nearby.)

The best sound quality for broadcast news is in the *treble* register, the opposite of the bass register of most large loudspeakers. So if your recorder has a tone control (which is inoperative in the Record mode), it should be turned to *full treble* during playback.

PATCH CORDS

There is still another way of recording certain events, one that bypasses your own microphone altogether. But for this you'll need what's called a "patch cord," enabling you to plug your recorder directly into someone else's equipment.

Patch cords have been pretty well standardized with eighth-inch plugs (also called "Sony plugs") at each end. However, some news organizations still use equipment requiring pin plugs (also called "RCA plugs"), and a few others use European-made gear requiring DIN plugs. So a patch cord has to be suited to your own equipment.

A patch cord may be used in two ways: One way is to link your recorder (through the Auxiliary Input) with a *mult-box* (short for "multiple plug box"). A mult-box is part of the sound system permanently installed in conference rooms and auditoriums which are frequently used for news conferences or speeches. It is designed to accommodate radio and television journalists who might otherwise be so numerous that their separate mikes "bury" the speaker behind a wall of microphones.

The second use of a patch cord is to connect two tape recorders. For example, a fellow reporter could agree to let you "patch into" his or her recorder (via his or her Output jack and your Auxiliary Input jack). The two linked recorders both capture the same sound through the first reporter's microphone. Or, a patch cord may be used to dub a copy of a tape from one machine to another.

ACOUSTIC COUPLERS (FEED CORDS)

An acoustic coupler—or "feed cord"—enables a reporter to transmit his or her tape-recorded material back to the station via telephone or two-way car radio transmitter. One end of the coupler attaches to the Output (or Monitor) jack of the cassette recorder, the other to a telephone or to an Auxiliary Input jack of the two-way radio. This device is the *only* means of sending broadcast-quality taped sound back

What the well-equipped radio reporter carries on the job: tape recorder, hand microphone, mike stand, extension cable, patch cord, acoustic coupler, audiocassettes, spare batteries, adhesive tape, a clamp, and occasionally (but not shown here) a portable cellular telephone.

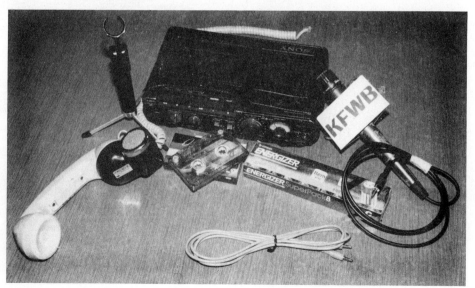

to the studio. (You can *not* hold up the recorder's tiny speaker to the phone mouthpiece; the sound quality will be entirely UFB.)

The design of acoustic couplers has evolved over the years to accommodate newer types of telephones. Most do not require opening the phone to attach the coupler. Instead (in one type of standard model), a rubberized coil slips over either the mouthpiece or earpiece of the handset. Although many acoustic couplers automatically override the microphone in the phone's mouthpiece, some do not, in which case it is necessary to clamp one hand firmly over the mouthpiece in order to shut out extraneous noise.

MOBILE UNITS

Radio reporters are their own chauffeurs, possibly at the wheel of a "mobile unit." At many stations, staff reporters are given personal use of mobile units in order to respond to the inevitable 3 A.M. calls to cover fires.

Although a mobile unit used in radio news may be a small van painted with the station's call letters, more often it is merely an ordinary car or station wagon which has been equipped with a two-way short-wave radio, a short-wave handset so the reporter can keep in touch while out of the vehicle, and/or a portable cellular telephone.

A radio reporter "going live from the scene" is usually talking via the two-way, either while sitting in the driver's seat or via the handset or cellular phone while covering "the action." At other times, he or she may use the mobile unit as a "nomadic studio" from which to feed tape.

FEEDING VOICERS, ACTUALITIES, AND WRAPS

Whenever you call in from the field with reports or actualities, you will be using your station's recording number. On the answering end will be either a fellow staffer or a broadcast technician. Whoever it is, do *not* engage in small talk. There may be other reporters trying to phone in or other

Before heading to his first assignment of the day, KFWB reporter Charles Sergis checks the equipment in his mobile unit: two-way radio, cellular telephone, patch cord, and acoustic coupler.

staffers waiting to do foners. You mustn't tie up the recording line. So state your business and get on with it.

When you are reporting live from the scene of a breaking story, you will be wearing an earphone so that you can hear the newscaster cueing you or asking you questions. At most other times you will be feeding material which is being recorded at the station for inclusion in upcoming newscasts. Your call will originate from the mobile unit, a pay phone, or (better) a private phone located someplace quiet. You will have your copy written and your tapes cued up, ready to feed.

Although each station follows slightly different procedures, here, generally, is how you will go about it:

Feeding Voicers

1. Identify yourself.
2. State that you are feeding a voicer, and briefly tell its subject matter.
3. Tell its approximate running time. This is important because the person on the other end will attempt to record the spot directly onto cart, thereby skipping the step of dubbing from bulk tape. (The console machine may be running anyway, as a backup.)
4. Await the instruction to "give a level." This refers to the sound level of your transmission, which must be set properly on the studio recording gear.
5. Go ahead with the level by delivering the first two sentences of your spot *at the volume and tone of voice you will use in actual delivery.* (The purpose is to set the actual level, not the rehearsal level; so they must be the same.)
6. Await instructions, if any, to speak louder or softer. Once the level is set, you will be told to "count down and go."
7. Precede your spot with a *countdown.* This means that you start by saying, loudly, clearly, and in tempo, "Five-four-three-two-one." Then you pause a beat (about half a second) and go directly on with your voicer. The countdown, which is used for spots in TV as well as in radio, enables the recording technician to know when to start the cartridge machine. Without a countdown, such coordination would not be possible. The technician will hit the Record button during your half-second beat. Thus, it's essential that the countdown be done in cadence.
8. If you "bobble" (make an error in delivery or pronunciation) anywhere in a *short* spot, pause a few seconds, then do it over from the top, *including* a new countdown. (The cart is "blown," and the operator will have to insert a fresh one.) If you bobble in the *first half* of a long spot, again, do it over from the top with a new countdown. But if you bobble in the *second half* of a long spot, pause a few seconds, then resume *from the start of the sentence in which you bobbled.* (The technician will edit the spot together before transferring it to cart.)
9. After your sign-off, *remain silent.* Give the technician a chance to kill the Record circuitry before you talk.
10. Do not hang up until the engineer confirms that everything has been received "loud and clear."

At first glance, this process may seem complicated and time-consuming. In fact, it is precisely the opposite. It is designed to ensure good sound quality and avoid delays due to technical error.

Feeding Taped Voicers

Sometimes you won't be able to find a quiet phone. You may have to call from an outside pay phone on a busy street, or from an inside phone where your voice might disturb other people. In such cases, it's best to record your voicer on your own tape recorder, then feed the tape back to the studio. This procedure is slightly different from feeding live voicers.

Before calling in:

1. Record your spot in a quiet place, *with* a countdown. (Do not record in a washroom or other small space with hard walls; the sound will bounce off the walls and give the recording a "fishbowl" effect, a sort of echo.) Record your spot as often as you like (until you're satisfied), but the countdown must be on the tape just before the "keeper" (the version you are going to feed).

2. Attach your acoustic coupler to the phone. Cue the cassette to the countdown. Now you're ready to call in.

After calling in:

1–4. Same as for live voicers.

5. Play the first 10 seconds of your recorded spot. Adjust the level if necessary, as instructed by the technician.

6. Await the instruction to "re-cue and go."

7. Rewind your recorder to the start of the taped countdown, pause, then play the countdown and spot in their entirety.

8. After the sign-off, do *not* stop your tape machine immediately because this would cause a loud click back in the studio. Again, give the technician a chance to stop his or her own recorder.

9. And, again, await the "all clear" before hanging up.

Feeding Actualities and Wraps

Feeding actualities proceeds exactly like feeding taped voicers, except, of course, that there is no countdown; the level is given by playing the first few seconds of the desired cut. Feeding wraparounds, however, can be complicated for newcomers because it requires both manual dexterity and the ability to deliver copy without bobbling. What you attempt to do is read your lead-in live, play your taped actuality, and resume live with your tag and sign-off as you simultaneously shut off your recorder. Few radio reporters can do this without considerable practice.

(If a station's engineering staff is large enough, a reporter can feed the lead-in, actuality, and tag/sign-off separately; a technician can then assemble the wrap while you go about your reporting business. Unfortunately, there are few stations nowadays with sufficient staff to permit this.)

Here's the procedure:

1. Attach the acoustic coupler and cue the actuality before calling in.

2. Go through the identification and description procedures listed earlier.

3. Give levels *both* on yourself *and* the tape. The technician will have you adjust the tape level until it corresponds as closely as possible with your live announcing voice.

4. Carefully re-cue the taped actuality to the incue and press the Pause button. (The Pause control, when released, restarts the tape transport system more quickly and cleanly than the on/off circuitry.)

5. Array your copy comfortably in front of your eyes.

6. Poise a finger above (but not touching) the Pause control.

7. Count down and go, releasing the Pause control at the end of your lead-in, and pressing it again at the end of the actuality at the same time as you continue with your tag and sign-off copy.

8. Remain silent until the "all clear."

FINDING A TELEPHONE

According to figures compiled by the Paris-based world trade organization GATT (General Agreement on Tariffs and Trade), the United States has more telephones per capita than any other country in the world. However, American reporters sometimes wonder, If that's true, why can't you find a phone when you really need one?

They are referring to the fact that calling in a story is sometimes more difficult than covering it. So many reporters (from all media) cover major stories nowadays that they literally have to scramble for the telephones. Networks routinely hire flunkies just to monopolize the few available telephones for their own reporters. Sometimes, they even install their own phones.

Cordless phones and portable cellular phones have alleviated the problem to a degree. But cellular phones are expensive, and not everyone operates on a network budget. Yet everyone wants to be first on the air, and you can't be first on the air unless you're first to the phone. Thus, radio reporters, who more than anyone rely on the telephone to transmit their particular form of news coverage, must always be on special lookout for available telephones. They must know where the phones are—and be prepared to compete in the mad dash for them once an important news development is announced.

MEANWHILE, BACK IN THE STUDIO . . .

A reporter's day is not done when he or she is through covering stories in the field. There is still work to do back at the station.

Specifically, reporters are expected to write and record voicers and wraps for use later that evening, again after midnight, and again during the next morning's AM Drive. It is at this point that reporters must understand how to protect their spots against becoming dated, as well as the difference between hard leads and soft leads.

The reason this material is prepared in the studio is to ensure that any actualities, especially those used in wraps, are of good sound quality. The actualities phoned or radioed in from the field sound comparatively tinny or flat—a price that had to be paid for speed. Now, however, the emphasis is on *quality,* both in writing and in recorded sound.

Since the reporter will no longer be writing and recording at the actual scene of a story, it may be necessary for him or her to change the sign-off. Some stations are firm in ruling that to use an on-scene sign-off, the reporter must actually *be* at the scene at the time. Therefore the sign-off must end only with the reporter's name and the station's call letters. However, other stations allow reporters to retain the on-scene sign-off, even though they are now back in the studio, as long as they *were* on the scene at some point. As we shall see, this latter procedure is more typical of television than of radio.

AND NOW A WORD FROM . . .

. . . the brain.

In this chapter we have dealt more with technical matters than with news content. In a way, this reflects the reality of a newcomer's first experiences in a broadcast news department. Inevitably, he or she becomes swept up into "our way of doing things."

And, in truth, no one is born doing countdowns and hooking gadgets into telephones. There is undeniably a modicum of technical proficiency required of broadcast journalists that is not required of their print counterparts.

But technical proficiency comes in a few short weeks or months. That is the *easy* part of broadcast news. More difficult and more important, by far, is developing writing talent and the editorial sense required of a good journalist: the ability to transform complicated reality into clear, concise language to inform and enlighten one's fellow citizens. *That,* we would argue, is a lifelong undertaking.

EXERCISES

1. Using the following news-agency copy as your point of departure, do foners in your area as a means of localizing and updating the story. (If you do not have access to a recording phone, use a cassette recorder with a telephone pickup attachment; such an attachment—a short cable which is really an elementary type of acoustic coupler—can be purchased at most electronics stores, including Radio Shack.) Choose an actuality (or two) from your recorded interviews and incorporate it (them) in a 45-second (:45) story aimed at your local audience. Slug it EXERCISE.

```
        NEW YORK (AP)--The American Heart Association on Wednesday
declared lack of exercise a major risk factor for heart
disease, ranking it with smoking, high cholesterol and high
blood pressure.
        The Association has long said that physical inactivity
raises heart disease risk, but the scientific evidence has
recently grown strong enough to call it a major risk factor,
the Association said.
        Even modest physical activity will lower a sedentary
person's risk of heart disease, the artery-clogging that sets
the stage for heart attacks, specialists said at a news
conference.
```

   (If this assignment is given to a large number of students simultaneously, it would be prudent for classmates to agree among themselves to call different local organizations for separate angles. Otherwise, the local chapter of the Heart Association is likely to be overwhelmed.)

2. Write a 45-second *voicer* incorporating the information you've gathered by phone, and feed it *live* to the recording phone from a different phone.

3. *Record* the voicer on cassette and feed it to a recording phone. (You will need a real acoustic coupler for this.)

4. Write a second spot, this time a 45-second *wraparound*. Record your lead-in and tag/sign-off separately. Then feed *both* your reportorial copy *and* the actuality to a recording phone. (Again you will need an acoustic coupler.)

Radio Newscasting

13

Radio newscasting requires proficiency in all the writing and tape-integration techniques we've covered thus far—plus two others: the ability to oversee and shape an entire broadcast *(producing)* and the ability to communicate clearly and authoritatively by voice *(performing)*. Thus, an apt subtitle for this chapter might be "Putting It All Together."

As we shall see, television news is a group activity. Modern radio news, on the other hand, is largely an individual endeavor. Except at networks and all-news radio stations (where large staffs combine and coordinate their activities), a single person writes, edits, and announces a newscast—not just one newscast, but often six, eight, or even twelve newscasts per shift. He or she must be able to work fast under constant pressure. Very often, it's a matter of sink or swim. This chapter is aimed at helping you keep your head above water.

PRODUCING

It is well to bear in mind the *nature* of most radio news in the United States (and overseas, too), which is overwhelmingly the reporting of late-breaking developments, told briefly. Although most newscasts are short, they come hard and fast—every hour or half-hour, depending on the station—a fresh "edition" as many as 24 or 48 times a day. Each newscast is different, consisting of a different mix of stories of different lengths, rewritten, updated, and handled differently from hour to hour.

Thus, it is necessary to approach the producing of radio newscasts with an attitude different from newspapers and television, whose "editions" are longer but fewer and farther between. One cannot expect from a single short radio newscast the same sort of "definitive" treatment of the day's news as from a single edition of a newspaper or a single telecast. Instead, a day's radio newscasts must be regarded as a whole for any true assessment of quality of coverage.

This is important psychologically as well as journalistically. A newswriter/newscaster need not feel that he or she has failed if an important story gets only 10 seconds on one newscast, as long as it receives adequate time on a different newscast. Radio newscasts are trade-offs whose value can only be assessed in the aggregate.

All of which is not to say that a single newscast, however ephemeral its nature, cannot be a creative, skillful, tasteful, sensitive, and perceptive account of the day's news. Quite the contrary. Those are precisely the qualities to strive for.

LENGTH AND STRUCTURE (FORMAT)

In Chapter 8 we described a typical format for a five-minute hourly newscast. Here it is again, but in a slightly different form, showing its starting time "at the top of the hour":

Section 1	**Section 2**
· Sign-on at 00:00:00	· More secondary stories (local or non-local)
· Lead local or non-local story	· Local sports (if any that day)
· Related stories (if any)	· Local weather
· Secondary stories (local or non-local)	· Sign-off at 00:05:00
· (COMMERCIAL: 1 × :60 or 2 × :30)	

As you can see, the format dictates the newscast's length and structure: its total air time; the precise hour, minute, and second it must begin; the amount, length, and placement of commercials; the inclusion and placement of standard items (such as stocks and the weather); and the precise hour, minute, and second it must end. However, *everything else* about it—the number of stories, their lengths, their placement (story order), the mix of local and non-local stories, which stories will contain audiotape and in what lengths—is up to the writer/anchor. He or she thus has *complete editorial control*. How he or she exercises this responsibility is guided by three main considerations:

1. To tell the *latest* news.
2. To tell the *most important* news.
3. To maintain listener *interest and attention*.

Consideration #1 is a matter of keeping up with breaking events via the news agencies, local news sources, and reporters in the field.

Consideration #2 is a matter of news judgment and experience.

Consideration #3 is a matter of ability to write and communicate in broadcast style.

All three are equally important and require unremitting alertness and concentration.

READING IN

A newscaster's shift usually begins two hours (but sometimes only one hour) before his or her first scheduled newscast. The time must be put to good use.

The first task is to "read in," that is, to scan the latest several hours' worth of news-agency copy and audio advisories, read the station's four or five preceding newscasts, check the locations and story assignments of the station's field reporters, and become familiar with the taped actualities and reports already "in house." This may be the newscaster's only opportunity to set aside interesting feature stories and possible kickers; later, once the grind of writing hourly newscasts has begun, there will barely be enough time to keep up with breaking events.

During the reading-in process, the newscaster should be selecting stories for possible inclusion in upcoming newscasts. In newsrooms with news-agency teleprinters, this will involve tearing off individual stories and arranging them in an organized fashion (such as dividing them into piles of "local," "domestic," and "foreign"). Since news-agency copy continues to build up endlessly and thus clutter one's work space, it is a good idea to throw out immediately any copy which will definitely not be used.

In computerized newsrooms, selected stories should either be printed out or saved to the staffer's own file to avoid having to do a time-consuming computer search to relocate them later.

(Computerized newsrooms have an advantage in that virtually all essential information is available at a few keystrokes. You don't have to run around to find the scripts of old newscasts, the reporters' assignment schedule, or the type and availability of tape; it's all right there in the computer, each in its own file, along with the breaking news, sports, weather, and stock reports via the news agencies. And if reporters are equipped with laptops and modems, they can file information directly into the system from the field.)

Once the writer/anchor has selected the stories for inclusion in the first newscast (and possibly the second as well), he or she can begin writing. A good place to begin is with the kickers and interesting features; there might not be time to write them later. Stories about breaking news events should be saved for the very *last* because the details are constantly changing; writing them too soon may mean having to rewrite them hurriedly just before air time, a redundancy of effort that can usually (but not always) be avoided.

STORY COUNT AND LENGTH

Only in rare cases—perhaps a few times a year—will an entire newscast be devoted to just one or two stories of overwhelming importance. At all other times, the 4 minutes available for news (in our model format) will contain a total of from 6 to 10 stories (not counting the weather).

Deciding how much air time each story is "worth" is a matter on which reasonable men and women will differ. There is no such thing as an "optimum" length, since "length" is relative to the structure as a whole. What *can* be said definitively about story lengths is that they should *vary widely* within each newscast. When experienced producers speak of the "flow" of a newscast, they are referring to the fact that, for better or for worse, a newscast is a kind of "show." Sameness of length results in a dull show. And a dull show risks losing listeners.

Writer/anchors should thus make a deliberate effort to vary the running times of the stories they have chosen for each newscast. And they should decide the length (running time) of each story *before* writing it. As actually written, a story may come out a few seconds short or a few seconds long of the target, but the end result will be to vary the pace of the newscast.

CHOOSING A LEAD STORY

Deciding the lead story of a newscast—a decision often made only moments before air time—usually provokes the most heated discussion in the newsroom. Again, reasonable men and women will differ, and differ strongly.

Much of the time, of course, the lead story will jump out and grab you by the throat. Stories with great immediacy, importance, or impact virtually "tell themselves."

But at other times, on slow news days, you could literally begin digging into the waste basket to find a lead story, hoping against hope that it was buried in a piece of news-agency copy you overlooked or rejected.

There is an unfortunate tendency in some news organizations, on slow news days, to "hype" stories out of proportion to their true importance, to use overly dramatic language such as "war of words" or "dropped a bombshell" when there was neither hostility nor air raid. This technique, almost always employed for strictly commercial reasons to attract an audience, debases the English language and, in the long run, debases listeners' trust in the offending station's news team.

So what to do if there's no clear or obvious lead story? Well, some newswriter/newscasters flip a coin. However, certain other solutions are much better. One is to lead with a human-interest story instead of with a hard news story, especially if the former involves health, medicine, or everyday science (a new household invention, for example). Another is to lead, in a general way, with the weather, returning to the specific forecast at the end of the newscast.

Whatever the merits of one possible lead versus another, it is well not to waste too much time in deciding. Remember, if you lead with story "A" at 10 A.M., you can lead with story "B" at 11 A.M. One newscast is just one *installment* of the news, not the day's definitive record.

Still another way to resolve the problem of stale or slow news is to rewrite stories to stress what is *about* to happen or what is *expected* to happen. This technique works best during early-morning newscasts, especially when there have been no major news developments since the previous evening. Sometimes, what is *going* to happen is more immediate and newsworthy than what has already happened.

STORY PLACEMENT

Following selection of the lead story, the rest of the stories are not just thrown together helter-skelter. Instead, they are grouped in some sensible or logical way so that, as much as possible, they flow one to another until they come to a natural break. Modest transitions may be required either between groups of stories or between stories in a group. But if stories are clearly written at the outset, only a slight pause between them by the newscaster will be sufficient.

The intention to group related stories should be in the newswriter/newscaster's mind even as he or she writes the newscast. This makes it possible to write smooth transitions and to order the newscast by grouped rather than individual stories, without getting caught short for time just before air.

There are several bases on which to group stories:

1. *By subject matter,* such as labor relations, politics, economic news, medicine, science, and weather, among others
2. *By geography,* such as U.S. region, Western Europe, Eastern Europe, the Far East, the Middle East, and so on
3. *By newsmaker,* such as Congress, the Supreme Court, the president, governor, or mayor taking different actions on different matters

Remember that grouped stories, however related, should still be typed one story per page. This is to permit the sudden deletion, if necessary, of just one story and the subtraction of that story's running time from the total.

TAPE PLACEMENT

There is a sort of Eleventh Commandment in radio newscasting: "Thou shalt use tape." Based on studies of listening habits and patterns, commercial station managements are convinced that audiences quickly become bored with "static" newscasts, that is, where the only thing heard is the voice of the newscaster. So they instruct newswriter/newscasters to include tape in every newscast, the object being to enliven the "sound" of the news as well as its content. The risk in such a policy is that, depending on circumstances, the tape available may not be newsworthy—in which case its use amounts to cosmetics only. Management's answer to such criticism is, "If you don't like the tape you've got, do foners until you *are* satisfied." So one way or another, there *will* be tape in just about every commercial newscast.

In structuring a newscast, the rule is not to use all the tape in the same place. Rather, it should be divided among newscast sections. Our model newscast, with its two sections, would ideally have one piece of tape in each section, not two in one and none in the other. It doesn't matter if the total tape is two actualities, two reports, or one actuality and one report. The point is to vary the newscast's pacing, both in story length and in tape placement.

"FILL" (PAD AND PROTECTION)

As you've no doubt noticed, radio and TV news does not always air as smoothly as planned. Technical foul-ups—"glitches"—occur often. Mislabeling, inattention, or plain carelessness can lead to a tape mix-up. Or the tape mechanism itself can fail. Be it human or mechanical, the failure can force the newscaster to "bail out" to fill an uncomfortable silence.

To minimize the damage, experienced newscasters go into the studio prepared for disaster. They always bring more news copy than normally necessary. This excess copy is called "fill"—because it fills the empty time, the silence, caused by human or mechanical error.

There are two types of fill copy. Extra copy of a nonspecific nature, stories of varying lengths that can stand on their own, is called "pad"; it "pads out" (lengthens) a newscast that would otherwise be too short because of the lost tape time.

The other type of fill is designed to replace a specific story lost because of tape failure. Called "protection," this copy is a scripted version of the story that was to have played on tape. If the tape fails to play as scheduled, the newscaster reads the protection copy as smoothly as possible, ad-libbing a transition from the preceding lead-in.

In modern radio news, the writing of protection copy is characteristic only of networks and the largest local stations, places with staffs given enough time to prepare for most eventualities. Elsewhere, staffs are too small and the workloads too heavy to allow for such niceties. At the same time, no newswriter/newscaster can risk going on the air completely unarmed. Thus, fill copy in the form of a pad is a must.

The best time to write fill copy is at the start of a work shift, immediately after reading in. Select at least three stories of marginal interest—stories you consider newsworthy but not as important as the day's other news—and write them for a total of 60 seconds. Vary their running time (say 15, 15, and 30 seconds) because you can't know in advance how much air time you may have to fill. Set the fill copy aside, but remember to bring it with you to the studio for your first newscast. Once it's there, leave it there. (At the end of your shift, you might have the courtesy to offer it to a hard-pressed colleague.)

SPECIAL TECHNICAL MATTERS

Scripts

Broadcast scripts are never stapled or clipped together until *after* they've been aired. The pages must be kept loose. That's to permit the newscaster to slide the pages noiselessly as they are read on the air. It also permits him or her to drop or rearrange pages at will either before or during a newscast.

Slug and Time Placement

There is a practical reason for insisting that slugs and times be written in the *extreme* upper edge of a page. A newscast script is customarily held in one hand, slightly fanned vertically. This permits the newscaster to see at a glance, without fumbling pages, which stories remain and how long each runs, in order to get off the air on time.

Backtiming

Okay, you've written a terrific kicker. It runs 20 seconds. You want to end the newscast with it, just before sign-off. How do you *ensure* you will begin reading it on time, in order to get off the air on time?

By "backtiming" it. You *subtract* the time of your kicker from the time you must be off the air (00:05:00):

$$
\begin{array}{r}
:05:00 \\
-\quad\ :20 \\
\hline
=\ :04:40
\end{array}
$$

You write and circle the notation   (BY :04:40)

in the upper right corner of the copy page. This reminds you at a glance of the latest time you may begin reading the story and still get off the air on time.

The technique of backtiming may be used for the weather or any other item with which you want to end a newscast. It may seem a bit complicated to you now, but after a few months on the job, you'll be doing double and triple backtiming, just to give yourself a challenge.

PERFORMANCE SKILLS

The final—and most subjective—element in assessing newscasts is the newscaster's ability as a *performer*. This is the "show-business" element of broadcast news, and there is no escaping it. Broadcast management customarily refers to on-air personnel as "talent"—as if to imply that it doesn't require talent to write, edit, or produce. But that's the reality, and anyone wishing to make a career as a news anchor or major-market or network correspondent must pay attention to developing performance skills.

Diction

We have noted elsewhere the need to know correct pronunciation. To this we must now add *enunciation,* the ability to articulate clearly and distinctly. Formerly, this was known as "having good diction." Newscasters simply cannot afford sloppy diction.

Unfortunately, by the time you are old enough to read this book, you are already at an age when your speech habits have become firmly set. It is only with considerable effort and constant practice that you will henceforth be able to correct any flaws. There is no time to waste. And you will need qualified supervision. That old orator's ploy of rehearsing with a mouthful of gravel doesn't work if you're alone; besides, you might swallow the gravel.

Voice Quality

This is the element of performance that you can do the least about. The human voice goes through a series of changes as one grows to adulthood. The change is more noticeable in men's voices than women's, going from a boyish alto to a tenor, baritone, or bass. In women, the voice remains at a higher pitch altogether, finally settling into a lyric soprano, mezzo soprano, or contralto. By the time you are of an age to read this book, your larynx and resonating chambers will have stopped growing, and your voice quality will remain basically unchanged for the rest of your life. For newscasting, the most "desirable" voice qualities are in the lower two registers, both in men and women. Sorry, you lyrics and altos, but that's the way it is.

Fortunately, the days are long gone when "golden tonsils" or a booming basso profundo were required of anyone who wished to get on the air. Broadcasters, especially news departments, have of late relaxed some of the old strictures, including some of the silly ones. It was long thought, for example, that people would not accept women as newscasters or reporters, since they didn't sound "authoritative" or "in charge." This has, of course, proved to be utter nonsense, with the result that performance standards have altered for men as well as women. Now the overriding prerequisite is the ability to communicate clearly.

Accents

Due in large part to network broadcasting, U.S. regional accents and speech rhythms are not as diverse as they once were. The voices that one hears on radio and TV, in any part of the country, tend to be speaking "standard American."

Nevertheless, many natives of New England, New York, New Jersey, Boston, Chicago, the Mid-South, and the Deep South are immediately recognizable by their accents. There is nothing wrong with accents in news broadcasting—as long as they are moderate and do not call such attention to themselves that they detract from the communication of news content. Thus, accents that are thick and that permeate a person's speech are not acceptable, except at the smallest local station level, where most listeners share the same accent.

The most "desirable" accent is no accent at all, which is clearly impossible, but by which is meant the "standard American" mentioned earlier, a voice whose region cannot be determined. (The comedian George Carlin, in a monologue parodying radio announcers, begins by saying, "Hi, I'm from Nowhere.") Natives of the Upper Middle West and the Pacific Northwest come closest, by birthright, to speaking the "standard American" sought by broadcast executives.

Practice

Most people don't really know how they themselves sound. They hear their own words in a sort of "re-resonated" fashion, the sounds reaching their auditory senses both from the interior and the exterior. Listeners hear only the exterior sounds—your "real" voice.

So the first step in developing and improving your voice and diction is to discover how you really sound. And for this, you need a good tape recorder, hooked up to a good loudspeaker. Everybody sounds tinny over the minispeaker in a portable cassette recorder.

It is natural to be apprehensive or shy about recording yourself at the start. Fine. The point is to get started. Lock yourself in a room and record yourself reading some broadcast-style news copy (*not* newspaper articles). Listen to the tape. Go over it sentence by sentence. Are you communicating? Are you stressing the right words? Are your inflections natural? Or do you sound forced, unnatural, stagy? Re-record the copy as often as you must until *you yourself* are satisfied.

Then, and only then, should you seek a second opinion. And, because these matters tend to be subjective, a third opinion. And not just *any* opinions. Opinions must come from qualified persons— people who understand vocal structures, habits, and diction, ideally people who also understand news broadcasting.

And, then, having lost your reticence, practice some more. Join the staff of your campus or corporate closed-circuit radio station so that you can begin delivering regular newscasts.

The important thing, if you hope to become a professional (i.e., paid) radio or television newscaster, is to starting working toward it *now*.

EXERCISE

1. Using the model format described in this chapter, write a 5-minute newscast as it might be broadcast on your campus or other local radio station. For raw material, use either same-day news agency copy or the latest edition of your local newspaper. Assume you will have two pieces of tape: a 45-second report on your biggest local story and a 15-second actuality of a newsmaker quoted in one of your world or national stories. Remember that the amount of news copy you must write is reduced by one 60-second commercial and by another 60 seconds of newstape. Thus, you will need to write only 3 minutes of news copy—plus, of course, a few "fill" stories.

   (*Note:* Even though you are new at this, you should be able by now to write and assemble the entire newscast in less than two hours. Bear in mind that in a professional radio newsroom, you would typically have less than one hour to do it—in addition to other duties such as doing foners and editing tape.)

Is a Picture Worth a Thousand Words?

14

On a recent Tuesday in early summer, of all the stories of national interest, two stood above the rest: At 1:30 A.M., Eastern Daylight Time, a 100-foot section of the Connecticut Turnpike Bridge, near Greenwich, collapsed. Several cars and trucks plunged into the Mianus River 70 feet below, killing three people.

Some 14 hours later, in midafternoon, the U.S. Senate, by a vote of 50 to 49, defeated Congress's first-ever attempt to change the Constitution to allow the 50 states to make their own laws on abortion.

On almost every journalistic basis, print or broadcast, the second story was the more important. No issue had so excited the public interest, was as fiercely debated, as abortion. Only a few days before the Senate vote, the U.S. Supreme Court had affirmed that the Constitution forbade the federal and state governments from banning abortions. The powerful "Right-to-Life" lobby, representing the views of many millions of Americans, had proclaimed that the only remaining alternative was to change the Constitution. The vote in the Senate, which fell 17 votes short of the required two-thirds majority needed for constitutional amendments, was a huge defeat for the antiabortion forces.

The bridge collapse in Connecticut, while especially tragic for the victims, and while indicative perhaps of the unsafe state of many other bridges across the United States, was simply not in the same class. And, by broadcast standards, it was, by early evening, already stale news; it had been on the air since early morning in newscast after newscast and was front-paged in afternoon newspapers. The abortion vote, on the other hand, was fresh and immediate news—a major story with which to lead the evening TV newscasts.

And yet, at 6:30 P.M. Eastern Daylight Time, the first feed of the "CBS Evening News" opened this way:

Good evening...

For the want of some pins, the

bridge was lost. That was the

speculation today, as

authorities investigated the
fatal, pre-dawn collapse of a
major highway bridge section in
Connecticut, outside New York
City. And, officials said, the
accident points up a threat that
spans the continent. We have
two reports, beginning with
Richard Wagner:

Wagner's taped report, narrated over aerial and ground views of the collapse aftermath, explained that several steel "pins" (actually rods 7 inches in diameter and 10 inches long) had apparently come loose, unlinking a center section of the bridge and allowing it to break away. The second report promised in the lead-in was on the wider problem of the precarious condition of bridges all across the United States, some in need of urgent repair at enormous cost, at a time when public funding was virtually nonexistent. In other words, the reporter was implying, there might be another bridge collapse at any time, perhaps far more deadly than the present one.

There followed a 60-second commercial break. *Then* came the abortion story, more than six minutes into the newscast. It was a 40-second "reader"—no videotape.

The issue here is not the merits of the bridge story. It was clearly important and deserved major coverage. And CBS did a first-rate job, detailing the story clearly and graphically. The lead-in itself (cited above) shows a love for language; the first sentence is a literary reference to the seventeenth-century British poet George Herbert *("For want of a nail . . ."),* and the bridge metaphor—"threat that *spans* the continent"—is a nice touch.

CBS also told the abortion vote story clearly and succinctly. But why did the story not *lead* the newscast? Because *pictures* of a collapsed bridge, especially as taken from a helicopter, are far more spectacular and dramatic than are sketches from the Senate floor, where cameras were not permitted at the time.

The issue is *not* a matter of "right" lead or "wrong" lead. No doubt many "CBS Evening News" staffers would have preferred to lead with the Senate vote; such matters are always discussed, sometimes heatedly, until the executive producer makes a final decision.

No, the issue here is the *nature of the medium.* TV news thrives on *pictures.* It always tries to tell a story *visually.* This makes it relatively hard to *show* a story about a Senate vote and relatively easy to *show* a story about a bridge collapse. The drama of the *visual* elements is inherently unequal.

It is absolutely essential to understand the primacy of pictures in television news because it pervades not just what viewers see, but also what they don't see: how the news is covered.

GETTING THE PICTURES

Situation:

An early spring thaw, coupled with heavy rain, causes severe flooding in a Midwestern state. Whole communities are cut off by road and by rail. Telephone and electric lines are down. You are a TV news reporter, and you and a camera operator are assigned to cover the flood. The only way into the flooded area is by helicopter. But the only chopper available is a two-seater, one seat reserved (obviously) for the pilot. If you were a print or radio reporter, in you'd climb. But in TV, that single available seat must go to the camera operator. You yourself, temporarily grounded, may have to write your eventual narration based on a debriefing of the camera operator, viewing the videotape, and reading news-agency copy. In other words, the demands of TV news coverage have placed a higher premium on the camera's single eye than on your two.

That situation is not hypothetical. It happens repeatedly in TV news, where the rule is *the camera comes first*. And not only is the camera first in, the videotape is first out. Forced to make a choice between pictures of an event or a reporter's account of it, TV news producers will always choose the pictures.

Thus, in the world of television news, the answer to the question posed in this chapter's title is a resounding *yes!*

A (VERY) BRIEF HISTORY OF TV NEWS

Although television was invented before World War II, the U.S. Defense Department co-opted all cutting-edge electronics for the war effort. Thus, TV's commercial development had to await the mid- and late 1940s.

Hard to believe as it may seem today, most people in broadcasting in those days thought that TV could never compete with radio as a news medium. And, if you saw the way early TV newscasts looked, you'd probably have agreed with them. The technology was rudimentary: TV screens were small (seven to ten inches, as measured diagonally), the image was fuzzy (and of course in black and white), and what viewers saw (for 15 minutes, then the standard length of a news telecast) was a newscaster sitting in front of a desk microphone, reading from a hand-held script, and occasionally holding up (yes, *holding up*) news-agency wirephotos or pointing to a spot on a globe; on the rare occasions when newsfilm was available, it was usually shown 24 or 48 hours after the event. In short, it was a kind of delayed radio newscast performed in front of a studio camera under bright lights. No wonder they thought it would never fly!

The temptation is to say, "And the rest is history." But in reality, TV news as we now know it developed gradually, in response to ever-newer technologies. By the mid-1950s, portable 16-mm sound-film equipment was in widespread use. The equipment was bulky and required a three-person team: a camera operator, a sound technician, and an electrician to set up or hold the lights. Nevertheless, by the late 1950s and early 1960s, the new gear and the advent of commercial jet aircraft had enabled TV news broadcasters to show events on the same day of their occurrence, and sometimes within hours.

The late 1950s and early 1960s also marked what proved to be the dominating influence on TV news: more people were now watching it than were listening to radio. The major networks and, to a lesser degree, local stations fought for higher ratings by competing for news audiences as well as entertainment audiences. Newscasts were expanded to 30 minutes. Color was introduced and quickly displaced black and white. High-speed color newsfilm came along, as did darkroom equipment which enabled news departments to process their own film (instead of sending it to outside labs) and thus get it on the air even more quickly.

The 1970s saw the introduction of portable video cameras and videotape cassettes; tape, which did not have to be processed, gradually displaced film. Then came communications satellites, mini-cams, and transportable microwave transmitters. By the late 1970s, virtually all stations were peppering their newscasts with live reports from the scenes of events, often from halfway around the world. Network newscasts were scheduled more frequently. Local stations expanded their newscast schedules to one hour, and in some markets to two, three, or even four hours.

Paying for all this electronic gadgetry and the personnel needed to operate it was an expensive proposition. By and large, it cost more to produce a competitive newscast than could be earned through the sale of commercial time on it. Much of TV news was thus a "loss leader"—an exercise in deficit-spending aimed at winning prestige and viewers for a network's or local station's entertainment programming, which remained highly profitable.

But the 1980s brought radical changes. First and foremost was the rise of cable TV. Suddenly, viewers had dozens and dozens of choices. Atlanta-based Turner Broadcasting alone introduced two 24-hour news channels, CNN and CNN Headline News, which also sold to independent stations the right to air CNN's visuals. The result was a fragmentation of the audience. Millions of viewers switched to cable or independent stations, and, for the first time, the broadcast networks and their affiliated local stations, which had experienced nothing but growing audiences and growing profits, now began to *lose* audiences. Their profits shrank. Ownership changes and financial restructuring quickly followed, and a new ethic was imposed on TV news departments: *"Henceforth, ye shall not lose money."* Automated equipment was acquired to replace technical personnel, and news staffs were cut, as were operating and expense budgets.

Thus, in the 1990s, most television news is treated more or less like other forms of programming: if it loses money, it is rethought, reorganized, and rebudgeted until, at the very least, it breaks even. As we noted elsewhere, it is often cheaper to pay a user fee to a common supplier of newstape than to send one's own reporter and camera operator for exclusive coverage.

But there has been a plus side to this bottom-line financing. Because news and news-related programs are cheaper to produce than most prime-time entertainment programs, the 1990s have been seeing a rash of "news-magazine" shows, both network- and independently produced, between the hours of 8 P.M. and 11 P.M. (7 to 10 P.M. Central Time). By and large, such programs (including the syndicated "tabloids" such as "Hard Copy" and "Inside Edition") are produced and presented by people who got their training in daily TV news coverage. Indeed, it is usually considered more prestigious to work on a network or cable news-feature program than on the Evening News. (Just ask the folks at "60 Minutes.")

JOB TITLES AND DUTIES

To expand on something we mentioned in an earlier chapter: TV news is a group activity. In print and in radio, a journalist works essentially alone, whether writing, reporting, or newscasting; colleagues may be involved at various stages, but the final product (a story or a newscast) is essentially the work of a single person.

But in television, what eventually appears on the screen is the work of many people. A reporter's package is actually the combined efforts of an assignment editor, a producer, a reporter, a camera operator, and a tape editor—and, at larger stations and networks, possibly those of a field producer, sound technician, writer, and assistant producer as well. This is not to mention the contributions of a graphic artist, an electronic titling operator, the studio crew of camera operators, technical director, and Teleprompter operator, plus the control-room crew of director, switcher, audio technician, and so on. That is a *crowd*. In round numbers, a TV news staff outnumbers a radio news staff by about ten to one. The capital investment in equipment is higher by an even greater proportion. Compared to radio, TV news resembles the classic definition of a camel as "a horse designed by a committee."

Obviously, not everyone is suited temperamentally to function in such an environment. Cooperation and reliance on others are absolutely essential. The iconoclast, the curmudgeon, the churl can function quite safely (if insecurely) in print and in radio. But in television such a person's professional life may be short, unhappy, or both. An even disposition and a high boiling point are important qualities in TV news personnel.

So is stamina. The working hours in most forms of journalism are long, sometimes grueling. But nowhere are they longer or more arduous than in television. Print and radio reporters can gather stories by phone. TV reporters must go to the scene. Thus, to the time spent in purely journalistic functions such as researching, covering, and writing a story must be added the traveling time to and fro, the editing time, and the time to protect any breaking angles for late-night or next-morning newscasts. It is routine for TV news personnel, especially reporters and camera operators, to work 12, 14, or even 18 hours a day, often without enough time off to sit down to a proper meal.

Anchors, producers, and writers often work long hours as well, especially during coverage of major breaking stories. In TV, there always seems to be a "crisis" of one sort or another, whether due to a lost microwave signal, to a misplaced tape cassette, or to an unexpected event at location X when the minicam is set up at location Y. "Scrambling" to cover the news is virtually a daily occurrence.

In mentioning these matters, it is not our intention to discourage you from choosing a career in TV news. Rather, by painting a realistic portrait of what occurs behind the normally calm facade of what the public sees, we are trying to give you a balanced foundation on which to make your own decision.

You see, the wonder of TV news, with so many cards stacked against it, is that most of the time it works so well.

In the following breakdown of TV news jobs and titles, it is important to remember that strict specialization occurs only at networks and at local stations in major markets. In most medium markets and in virtually all small markets, job duties overlap considerably, with staffers expected to fill a variety of roles (except in top management).

News Director

As in radio, the news director is the boss of the news department, responsible for overseeing editorial operations and personnel. The ND hires and fires staff, draws up work schedules, and tries to cover the news within the budget set by station management.

(In large markets, where millions of advertising dollars are at stake, the ND usually lacks independent power to hire the station's principal news, weather, and sports anchors; the final decision on that usually goes to the station's chief executive officer, the general manager.)

Assistant News Director

A position typically existing only in large markets. The AND's chief concerns are setting the work schedules, overseeing expenses, inventorying supplies and equipment, and sifting through job applications and audition tapes—thus freeing the ND from many bureaucratic duties and allowing him or her to concentrate on news coverage.

Executive Producer

Another position reserved to large markets and networks. At local stations, the EP assumes many of the day-to-day editorial responsibilities of the ND, especially those that concern coverage of major stories and the planning of "news specials" such as election returns. At networks, each newscast has its own EP; he or she is completely in charge, answering only to the network's president of news and the director of news operations.

Producer

The boss or "editor" of a local newscast. The producer is responsible for deciding story selection, story order, and story length, overseeing the work of reporters, camera operators, writers, and tape editors. The producer also chooses electronic graphics and is present in the control room during the telecast to supervise any last-minute changes.

Associate Producer

Another position generally found only in larger markets. As the title implies, the AP assists the producer in all the aforementioned tasks. The AP is also customarily responsible for writing the "newsbreaks" that precede the telecast, as well as the various headlines or teasers that air during the telecast.

Assignment Editor

Also known as "assignment manager." He or she runs the assignment desk, the hub of the news department. The assignment desk is usually staffed 24 hours a day. Its manager is responsible for keeping track of scheduled and breaking news events, and dispatching reporters and camera operators to cover as many of them as logistically possible.

This is a high-pressure position because the AE can neither control events nor magically create extra reporters or camera crews. He or she is thus engaged in a precarious guessing game, warily parceling out the available staff to this location or that, hoping that the day's biggest stories won't occur at precisely those locations which he or she has neglected.

The assignment desk—such as this one at WMAQ-TV, Chicago (photographed before the station moved to new quarters)—is the hub of a TV news department. It is equipped with fire and police scanners; several telephone lines; a two-way radio link with reporters and camera crews in the field; a paging system; fax machines; cellular phones; banks of monitors tuned to live minicam units and competing stations; local maps, street guides, and airline schedules; and the newsroom's most complete listings of important telephone numbers.

The AE is usually a long-time resident of the market with a thorough knowledge of its geography and its "pulse." To be able to estimate travel time to and from story locations, assignment editors must know the streets and freeways, the traffic patterns, the flight schedules at local airports, the locations of hospitals, police stations, fire stations, the city morgue, and all government buildings.

The assignment desk's Rolodex of names and telephone numbers is the most complete repository of news sources and contacts in the entire department.

Planning Editor

A major-market position, elsewhere another function of the assignment desk. The planning editor is the equivalent of a newspaper's futures editor, responsible for keeping track of coming events weeks or even months ahead, and keeping producers apprised well in advance. The planning editor also sifts through the hundreds (and sometimes thousands) of pieces of mail and faxes that pour in every day from people and organizations seeking news coverage: government agencies, private industry, politicians, lobbying organizations, charitable fund-raising groups, irate citizens, and so on.

Reporter

The foot soldier of the news department. At some large news departments, reporters may have specific beats such as city hall, health and medicine, entertainment, or consumer affairs. But most TV reporters at all levels are general-assignment (G-A) personnel who are sent to cover breaking events of all kinds.

Reporters are given shift schedules, but they are likely to be called in early by the assignment desk to cover breaking news. On more "relaxed" days, they receive scheduled assignments, research them, make phone calls, set up interviews, and assess possible shooting locations. Except in small markets (where reporters usually operate the cameras themselves), they then proceed with camera operators to those various locations to shoot videotape and piece story elements together. They may remain in the field to report late developments "live" during the telecast. Otherwise, they return to the station to write a narration and, together with a tape editor, combine their narration with taped excerpts to form a finished "package" whose targeted running time will have been predetermined by the producer. (In small markets, reporters usually edit the tape as well.)

Although G-A reporters respond mainly to specific assignments from the producer and the assignment desk, they are expected to come up with their own story ideas. All producers and news directors prize reporters who are self-starters. (Remember what we said about hustling and career-building in radio!)

Camera Operator

Also known as photographer, photojournalist, or "videographer." Another foot soldier, but armed with heavier firepower.

Camera operators are responsible for gathering a story in the technical sense, that is, that the videotape is properly framed and shot to *show* the story. In the field, the reporter tells the camera operator what he or she wants, and the camera operator decides if the requested shot is technically possible. In other words, the two *work together*, the reporter controlling content, the camera operator controlling form.

(As we've noted, small-market reporters shoot and edit their own videotape. Now that cameras have become so small, medium- and major-market station managements have been pressing to have *their* reporters operate them as well. As we shall see, this threatens to have profound effects on the way TV journalists are able to cover big-city news and is therefore being resisted fiercely by most news-gathering employees and their labor unions.)

Sound Technician

A holdover from the days when TV news relied on film rather than tape. It was the film-sound technician's job to set up microphones (at news conferences, rallies, and the like) and to ensure that the recorded sound was clear and undistorted. With the advent of minicams, major markets and networks have switched from three-person camera crews (the third person was an electrician) to two-person crews, each member of which is equally qualified to operate the camera or monitor the sound. In smaller markets, a single camera operator monitors both sound and picture: Unless the microphone is mounted on a podium or held by the reporter, the operator relies on a directional microphone mounted on the camera.

Anchor

Except for the news director, anchors hold the most important jobs in the news department. They are usually paid accordingly (except in small markets).

The high status and relatively high pay of news anchors is a fact of life which many broadcast journalists dislike and deride. Specifically, they dislike the fact that management will hire anchors whose journalistic skills are not readily apparent. While it's true that many local news anchors can neither write well nor find their way to city hall, it is equally true that, by and large, they possess the ability to communicate the news to a large audience.

Like it or not, people tend to judge TV news (and decide whether or not to watch) by the personalities of the anchors. People are likely to say, "I was watching Rather last night," or "I saw Brokaw," instead of, "I was watching the CBS Evening News," or "I saw NBC Nightly News." While Dan Rather and Tom Brokaw are both outstanding journalists, it is the drawing power of their ability to communicate, an aspect of their public personalities, which keeps people watching and thus keeps them at the anchor desk.

Unfortunately, there aren't many Rathers or Brokaws around. On the local level, where managements often must choose between outstanding journalists and outstanding communicators, their allegiance to their companies' owners and investors compels them to select as anchors only those who can command an audience, regardless of journalistic credentials. Sometimes it's a matter of looks. Sometimes it's a matter of voice. Sometimes it's a matter of warmth. No one can say precisely what "it" is, but that "it" exists can be demonstrated by a glance at the ratings—a measure by which anchors may dive as well as thrive.

Anchoring is thus a precarious job. Anyone wishing to become a news anchor is well advised to become a solid journalist first. The pay may not be nearly as high out of the anchor chair, but a reporter or producer's career lasts a lot longer.

Weekend Anchor

A position whose importance varies with the size of the market. In small markets, the weekend anchor may well turn out to be any news department employee who happens to be available on a given day. In medium markets, the weekend anchor slots are customarily rotated among staffers who work as reporters during the week.

In major markets and at networks, weekend anchors also report during the week. However, a weekend anchor slot at this level is often treated as a steppingstone to a full-time prime anchor position. The competition is fierce—almost as fierce as for the prime anchor slot itself.

Writer

As a distinct category of editorial employee, newswriters make their appearance starting at the medium-market level and come into their own in major markets and at networks. One of their main tasks is, quite obviously, to write news stories and lead-ins under a producer's supervision. Often they work with reporters to put a package together and to script the proper cues for graphics and titles.

Equally important, however, are their newsgathering and clerical functions: Writers are not only expected to transform print-style copy into broadcast style, they are also expected to "work the phones" to dig for their own angles—in other words, to act as desk-bound reporters. Their clerical function is to keep track of (that is, carefully log) all incoming feeds, whether live or on tape, so that specific visual material can be located quickly for inclusion in a written story or reporter's package. Writers are responsible for correctly identifying all people and places appearing on aired tape.

In terms of career paths, producers and other newsroom executives are usually recruited from among the ranks of writers.

Videotape Editor

A VTR editor is responsible for the finished form of taped material. A camera operator, not knowing what camera angle or position will turn out best, may "take" the same shot several times. The VTR editor chooses the best take. Therefore, he or she must know not only how to operate sophisticated equipment quickly and skillfully, but should also have a command of cinematic techniques which make one scene flow into another. There can be great art in this, and in Hollywood they give Oscars for it.

Field Producer

A sort of advance scout for a reporter and camera crew. Many stories require preparation over a period of days, weeks, or even months. Staff reporters, meanwhile, may be tied up covering breaking events. Consequently, a field producer does research, scouts locations, and sets up interviews.

Field producers exist only at networks and in major markets. Next to that of reporter, a field producer's job is the most peripatetic in the news department: he or she is always on the go. Occasionally a field producer will gather, write, and edit an entire package, which will then be voiced by a reporter. (No extra pay, but another rung up the career ladder.)

Unit Producer

(Another major-market and network job.) Just as a reporter may be assigned to a specific beat, so too, may a producer. Together they will investigate and prepare stories in their area of competence. Typical beats utilizing unit producers are health and medicine, consumer affairs, entertainment (mainly movie reviewing), and the investigative unit.

Researcher/Librarian

If a news staff is large enough, it may employ one or two researchers to do much of the time-consuming investigative drudgery: poring over documents to ascertain property ownership (called a "title search"), studying legal documents and judicial rulings, verifying statistics, analyzing historical records, doing telephone canvasses, and so on. The work can be extremely interesting during a major investigation to uncover wrongdoing, but mostly it involves trips to the municipal archives, the public library, the county court building, the station's tape library, the computer workstation, and so forth. A researcher position may lead to a writing position.

Tape Librarian

The videotape library is a TV station's "morgue." Taped reports and sound bites are periodically archived after broadcast so that staffers can quickly locate "file footage" (often the only visuals immediately available for use in connection with a breaking story). In large news departments (where the amount of archived videotape is often so great that it requires a vast storage area), a staff tape librarian is on hand to update the file catalog and to deliver to the newsroom specific cassettes of file footage requested by producers, reporters, writers, and VTR editors.

Desk Assistant (or Production Assistant)

As in radio, the job was known as "copy boy" until it became inadvisable to address anyone wearing a skirt as "boy." This is the lowest rung of the newsroom ladder. Much of a DA's day is spent in routine chores such as changing the ribbons in teleprinting machines, assembling and delivering scripts, answering telephones, dashing to McDonald's or Burger King, and so on.

But wait: This is not necessarily a dead-end job. In fact, many students gladly take internships as summer-replacement or full-time desk assistants in major and medium markets in order to observe and to learn. Indeed, they do get to witness every facet of the TV news business firsthand. The catch is, to be able to begin *doing* any of those facets, they usually find they must leave town for a smaller market.

With occasional exceptions at individual stations, all the aforementioned personnel are employees specifically of the news department. But TV news personnel work daily with employees of various other departments, especially graphic artists, electronic titling operators, Teleprompter operators, master control technicians, studio crew (camera operators, technical directors, stagehands, and the like), and control-room crew (director, assistant director, audio switcher, and so on). *All* such personnel contribute mightily to getting the news on the air in the way the producer desires, especially the control-room director, who is in overall technical charge of a newscast and who consults regularly with the producer starting well before air time.

CAREER PATHS

Building a career in broadcast journalism is much different from doing so in medicine, the law, or nuclear physics. A journalist's period of formal schooling is much shorter, the professional qualifications much less defined. The only equivalent of, say, a budding lawyer's bar exam is the writing or reporting audition a broadcast journalist must pass in order to win his or her first job. From then on, it's largely a matter of track record.

As we've noted repeatedly, the competition to enter radio and TV news, especially TV, is fierce at all levels. Nevertheless, there is a traditional career path which works for most newcomers most of the time: It is to begin in a small market, work one's way up to a medium market, thence to a major market, and finally to a network or type of specialization.

The pay in small markets (and in many medium markets) is very low. You would expect that to be the case, given the limited budgets of small-town broadcasters and the generally low experience level of their employees.* Therefore, you might not expect the job competition to be quite as fierce as in larger markets. But it *is*. It is *tough sledding* out there. Writing ability and radio-reporting ability are the absolute minimum requirements, each or both of which is tested by having to pass an audition.

Newcomers are also faced with an almost complete lack of choice about *which* small market they would prefer. They must be prepared to accept a job halfway across the country on very short notice. From then on, they might find themselves moving to a different locality every couple of years, taking their opportunities wherever they find them.

That's the bad news. The good news is that starting in a small market is not the only path to a career. Taking a job as an intern, desk assistant, or researcher in a larger market can sometimes lead to an opportunity to try out as a writer or field producer. Just being present when the opportunity arises is half the battle. The other half, of course, is being able to exploit the opportunity when it arises by performing the work satisfactorily. Unfortunately, *watching* a field producer at work is not the same as actually *doing* the work.

Another career path is through specialization. There is always a need for reporters and producers who can knowledgeably cover sports, medicine, the police, the court system, or consumer affairs. Many cable TV outlets devote themselves almost entirely to one or more of these areas.

There is also a need for investigative reporters with legal training who know how to penetrate bureaucracies and uncover factual information. The major networks, CNN, and many local stations have investigative units whose work is kept secret even from their colleagues in the newsroom until just before air time.

Unfortunately, broadcast news is a poor training ground for specialized or investigative reporting; its overwhelming need is for generalists. Investigative and specialized reporting skills are thus better learned at newspapers and magazines. When a big-city TV news department decides to hire such a specialist, it is likely to do so without major regard for his or her broadcasting credentials. Print reporters who know their beats intimately can sometimes jump to television without paying dues at small-town stations.

Still another path is working overseas. If, for example, your goal were to become a foreign correspondent, you might be wasting your time in a small or medium market in the United States, where you would learn little or nothing about covering foreign news. You might be better off packing a camcorder and suitable clothing and heading straight for a foreign location that is frequently in the news. Again, being on the spot is half the battle. Rather than relying solely on staffers, U.S. and Canadian networks routinely hire "stringers" (part-time employees hired on retainer or on a per-diem basis) who are often relatively young and inexperienced—provided that they have some knowledge of the local language and customs, and/or personal contacts who can facilitate news coverage.

However, this is an option that should *not* be undertaken lightly if your intended destination is an area torn by war or civil strife. Obviously, such areas are highly dangerous. At the very least, you

---

*On the other hand, some small-town news departments employ people with vast experience who are there by choice rather than happenstance. Typically, they are people who worked in major markets or at networks and who disliked living and working in big, noisy, crowded, expensive cities. So they resigned and opted for the life of a bigger fish in a smaller, calmer, less expensive pond.

As for pay, broadcast news salaries generally rise in proportion to the size of the audience. Although viewing patterns have been changing since the advent of cable TV, small-market stations still have the smallest audiences, and therefore the lowest pay. The major networks (ABC, NBC, and CBS) still command the largest news audiences and thus offer the highest pay. Salaries generally rise according to the following pattern:

1. small markets and local cable (lowest)
2. medium markets and network cable
3. major markets and syndication
4. major networks (highest)

Salaries in radio news tend to be smaller than in TV news, at all levels.

CNN foreign correspondent Peter Arnett reporting from Iraq during the Gulf War in 1991. Although foreign correspondence is one way for newcomers to bypass the small- and medium-market rungs on the career ladder, the work is often hazardous and should not be undertaken lightly. As if reporting under wartime conditions were not sufficiently daunting, Arnett and CNN found themselves the target of right-wing criticism in the U.S. for "airing enemy propaganda." However, the vast majority of U.S. officials and journalists supported Arnett, and he won several awards for outstanding reportage.

(Off-monitor photo courtesy CNN)

should inquire about conditions before making a decision. You might also contact potential employers to learn if indeed they might hire you as a stringer if you got there on your own.

Lastly, it should be mentioned that training in broadcast news can lead to employment in other fields, especially advertising and public relations. People who write and produce commercials or who write and produce promotional campaigns (for products, services, politicians, corporations, government agencies, and so forth) use many of the same techniques as broadcast journalists. Of course they use them in a highly partisan manner, since that is what they are being paid for—advocacy rather than education or enlightenment. Nevertheless, most of us need to make a living and not all of us can choose to be saints. Advertising and public relations generally offer higher pay than broadcast journalism, except for on-air personnel in major markets or at networks.

Well, all that is for the future. At present, we are more concerned with examining the tools of the TV news trade. On, then, to the next chapter.

EXERCISE

1. Do 50 sit-ups, 20 push-ups, and 10 chin-ups. Start building your stamina for working in TV news!

Picture and Script Components $\qquad$ 15

TV NEWS FORMATS

Here's that word again: *format*, used to describe the shape and structure of a newscast. Because TV newscasts run much longer than radio newscasts, their formats are much more complex. A radio newscast contains predominantly hard news. A TV newscast, while containing much hard news, especially at the top, has time for features, sports, weather, and sometimes editorial comment. Telecast format and content are thus the focus of intense planning and, as developments warrant, frequent revision.

Almost everywhere in the U.S., TV news is formatted in blocks running 30 or 60 minutes. This is true at all levels in all markets, whether in small towns, big cities, networks, or all-news cable. For example, a station in New York with 3 hours of local news from 4 P.M. to 7 P.M. formats each hour separately. Each hour is planned and presented as a separate newscast with its own producer, writers, and anchors. Stories from staff reporters and other sources are rewritten and repackaged for each 60-minute block.

We'll examine the various components of the medium, beginning with the absolute basics.

PICTURE COMPONENTS

The most fundamental component of video journalism is, of course, the TV screen itself. The screen is called the *frame*. It has a specific "geography" enabling video journalists to describe where to place various picture elements.

Picture Area

The frame can be split in half vertically (as shown in Figure A, p. 204), the sides described as "left" and "right." This is important when it comes time to show two things happening simultaneously (called "split-screen").

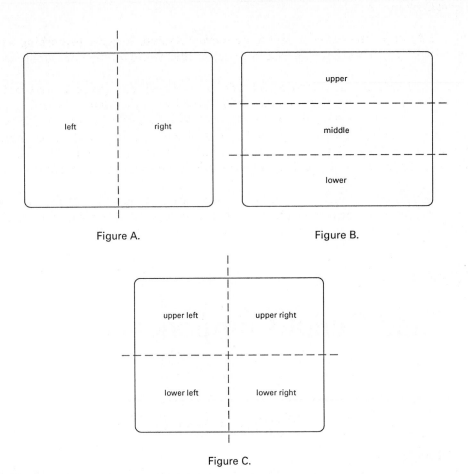

Figure A.   Figure B.

Figure C.

Another way of splitting the frame is into horizontal *thirds* (as in Figure B) known as "upper third," "middle third," and "lower third." Identifications of *people and places* generally go in the *lower third* and identifications of *source material* ("file footage," dates, and so on) in the *upper third*.*

Figure C shows the frame split into *quadrants* known as "upper left," "upper right," "lower left," and "lower right." Electronic *graphics* are generally placed *upper left* or *upper right*. Graphics and titles may also be placed *full screen*.

The significance of all this side-side, up-down, left-right is that it describes how TV journalists fill the frame, in other words, how they *show* various elements of a news story.

The most basic way to fill the frame is with the head and shoulders of the news anchor:

*Bear in mind that there is no absolute standardization in TV news. Practices vary from newsroom to newsroom. For example, some news departments identify people in the lower third and places in the upper third.

The type of electronic equipment also varies widely, as does the terminology to describe its use. In this book we are using the terms encountered most frequently in TV newsrooms across the country, or terms that are altogether generic.

This is called a *full-frame anchor shot* or an *anchor closeup*. It shows us nothing but the anchor as he or she delivers the news from the center of the frame. There are no additional visual elements of any kind.

News stories presented this way, without videotape (but with the graphics and/or titles we'll get to in a moment) are called *readers* or *tell-stories*. Their written style *follows the style of radio news* in all major respects. In fact, were it not for the anchor looking into the camera (actually he or she is reading a script off a Teleprompter), this would *be* radio news. It doesn't show us anything but the anchor's face. Its use in modern television is thus limited to a conscious effort to establish intimacy between anchor and viewer, or to provide a brief visual change during an on-camera bridge between stories.

Except in very small markets, at least two cameras are trained on the anchor. In major markets and networks, three or four cameras are present. One camera is consistently used for anchor closeups, another consistently for shots which make more graphic use of the medium.

ELECTRONIC GRAPHICS

This shot places the anchor at screen left and inserts an electronic visual called a *graphic* in the upper right. (The shot can also be reversed, with the anchor on the right and the visual in the upper left.) The insertion of the graphic (in this case a map) is accomplished via computer-assisted electronic devices. As a journalist, you do *not* need to know how the devices work. But you *do* need to know that they are capable of inserting on the screen *whatever visual elements you choose*. In other words, the choice of what to put into that electronic window is an editorial decision made by a writer or producer.

Electronic graphics can be maps (to show the location of a story—the Where element); still photos of people or places (to show the Who, What, or Where elements); still frames extracted electronically from videotape; flags; corporate or governmental logos; charts; graphs; drawings; or original creations from a station's graphic arts department made on request of the newsroom. In short, they can be virtually anything a writer or producer feels will clarify, enhance, or pinpoint some element of the story being delivered by the anchor. Further, more than one graphic can be used per story; the first graphic can illustrate something in the lead sentence, the second graphic a later element, etc.

However many graphics are used, it is important to remember that an "over-the-shoulder" graphic occupies a relatively small area of the screen and must therefore not be too complicated or attempt to show a lot of detail; viewers might be forced to squint or be otherwise distracted from listening to the news copy itself. If it is important to show a detailed graphic, then it may be shown full-screen. This gives viewers a chance to study the visual details even as they absorb the facts of the story.

Tell-stories using graphics are subject to slight modifications in broadcast style. First, because maps can be used to show a story's location, it is often unnecessary to specify that location in written copy as precisely as in radio. (To cite an example from a story we used earlier: If brush fires are raging "near the Arizona-Mexico border," it is not necessary to name the nearest well-known city, because viewers can *see* the location on a map used as a graphic.)

Second, it is unnecessary to describe a newsmaker's attitude or expression if viewers can see the expression in a photograph used as a graphic. (For example, it is unnecessary to write, "A smiling Governor Smith signed the new law this afternoon . . . ," if we can *see* the governor smiling.)

Electronic Graphics

Graphic artist Levi Braverman of KCAL-TV, Los Angeles, "draws" an electronic graphic on a computerized machine called a "Paint Box." Newswriters and producers request specific graphics, sometimes including text, to highlight key story elements.

During KCAL's newscast, the graphics are inserted full-frame or in an electronic "window" in an upper quadrant (either right or left, depending on which anchor is on-camera), or, as shown here, by merging the two electronic images in a process called Chromakey.

In short, graphics often allow you to tighten your written news copy—to avoid redundancy by omitting the obvious.

ELECTRONIC TITLES

Electronic titles insert *textual* material (words and numbers) into the picture, usually in conjunction with graphics and/or videotape.

Electronic Titles

KCAL-TV's Monica Mendoza types the texts of electronic titles into a computer-assisted machine called a character generator. Because titles are meant to be read by viewers as they simultaneously hear the news, Mendoza adheres to print style rather than broadcast style.

Titles—identifications of people and places, file tape, attribution, credits, etc.—are inserted electronically into the TV picture during newscasts. The style of fonts and positions in the frame vary with each news department.

(CNN/Headline News; WBBM-TV, Chicago; CNN/Headline News)

Created by computer-assisted machines called *character generators,* titles are used to identify people and places, itemize lists, give statistics, and spell out direct quotes. They are also used in conjunction with full-screen graphics, typically in giving the weather forecast and the sports results. As noted earlier, text used in titles and graphics *reverts to print style:* "$1 million" instead of "one million dollars," and so on.

As we shall see, electronic titles enable writers to omit additional words from copy accompanying videotape. In tell-stories, however, titles do *not* replace details in written copy. Rather, they augment that copy by specifying significant details *at the same time* as those details are being related by the anchor. For that reason, the text seen in titles must *closely match* the spoken text. (For example, titles enable viewers to see and hear direct quotes simultaneously. But if the anchor's version of the quote and the title's version do not match, viewers may become confused, which is just the opposite of the intended effect.)

SCRIPTING

Please review the rules for copy appearance that appear on pp. 13–17. From now on, we shall be using model scripts that correspond to proper TV style and appearance (with video cues on the left, news copy on the right, and so forth).

(Those of you using computers will have to reformat your tabs and margins. A professional newsroom computer system does this by a macro command entered by a single keystroke. Another one-key macro command reformats the style bar at the top of the screen to account for differences in format and timing.)

As journalists, we remain concerned chiefly with our words, the way we tell the news. But TV scripts also contain specific instructions (called *cues*) for all audio and video components, that is, news copy, graphics, titles, and videotape. This makes scripts appear complicated at first, but there's a reason for it: In radio, there's usually just one copy of the newscast script, for the newscaster (although sometimes a carbon copy goes to a technician who may be running the control board). But in TV news, many pairs of eyes must see the script. Full copies of it go to the anchor, the producer, the control-room director, the technical director, and the Teleprompter operator. In some news departments, additional copies go to the titling machine operator and the videotape playback operator (although these technicians may receive only a technical rundown instead).

It is thus vital that all cues be in their proper places. It is just as vital that the news copy, the part the anchor concentrates on, be neatly typed (or printed out in letter quality). A radio anchor can squint and squirm and no one may be the wiser. But a TV anchor's contortions to decipher a messy script, while possibly amusing to viewers, will not endear the writer to the anchor, the producer, or the news director.

To keep things as simple as possible, we will use generic terms to express cues, that is, we shall cue a graphic by calling it *graphic,* cue a title by calling it *title,* and so on. We do this because

Even in fully computerized newsrooms, hard copies of TV news scripts go to many people both on- and off-camera. Here, KCAL-TV production assistant Stan Peters and intern Tina Santos assemble the scripts for delivery to the director, the producer, the anchors, and the newsroom archives.

professional graphics and titling equipment is manufactured by many different companies, and depending on the specific equipment it uses, each news department has its own terms for cues. The important thing is to understand the concept. Once in the workplace, you will quickly adapt to the news department's specific terminology.

Naturally, the off-monitor photographs accompanying model scripts in this book do not appear on actual scripts. We include them to show you the type of TV picture that results from a specific cue. Short of hopping from campus to campus with a van-load of electronic gear, it's the best we can do.

One other thing before we proceed: You are about to encounter new forms—repeat, *forms*. Computers now enable graphic artists and titling operators to achieve special effects such as animation, color changes, variable fonts, and so on. To nontechnicians, these forms appear complicated, and at first you may feel that they divert your attention from the substance, namely the words you must write to tell a news story simply and clearly. If so, that is an accurate reflection of the real world of TV news; video journalists can get so wrapped up in the technology that they lose sight of the goal, which (as we've stated repeatedly) is to inform and enlighten. So take your time. For now at least, getting it right is better than getting it fast.

KCAL-TV director Chris Stegner studies his copy of the script for the Six-Thirty News. Although last-minute changes and late-breaking stories may disrupt some of Berglund's careful planning, he wants to ensure that the newscast flows smoothly from the technical point of view.

Scripting Full-Frame Anchor Shots

As we've seen, the simplest TV news picture shows only the anchor as he or she reads a story on-camera. This shot is so standard that it does not require a specific video cue. In the absence of a cue for a graphic, title, or tape, the shot will be taken automatically. However, because most stations now use more than one anchor, it is necessary to specify which anchor is to deliver the story. This is accomplished by typing the anchor's name in the video column, adjacent to the start of the story in the audio column.

A sample script:

Smith, 2/27, 8a   ISRAEL

Charles: Israel says one of its

warplanes was shot down today

while attacking guerrilla bases

in Lebanon. The plane was one of

four Israeli jets making an air

raid on Syrian-controlled

positions in the mountains around

Beirut.

("Sunday Morning," CBS News)

This is just about as simple as a TV news script gets. Note that the writer's name, the date, and the hour of the newscast go in the upper left corner of the video column. The slug goes in the upper right corner of the video column. The story's running time, rounded off to the nearest :05 (five seconds) and circled, goes immediately under the slug. The audio column (containing the news copy) remains uncluttered.

(In computerized newsrooms, writers enter these various elements in a template or style bar, and the computer program automatically places them in the proper script positions during printout. The exact running time is also calculated automatically, provided that taped components are correctly entered in the template.)

Scripting with Graphics

The inventiveness and originality of graphics depends both on the writer's imagination and the resources of his or her news department. At small stations and at larger stations with small news departments, the choice is limited to the graphics already on file, usually procured through companies that mail them out on a weekly basis. In large news departments and at networks, original graphics are made to order by staff graphic artists. A lead time of an hour or more may be required for an original graphic.

A lot of care and preparation goes into a graphic element that may appear on the screen for only a few seconds. Indeed, it may take the writer longer to arrange for the graphic than to write the story it's to be used with. That is a normal condition in TV newswriting. At small stations, the writer simply combs through the file of prepared graphics and chooses the one that comes closest to his or her needs.

Whatever a station's resources, there will often be a number of choices available for each story. Let's say the story is that the U.S. House of Representatives cuts the defense budget. Among the choices for graphics might be

· A photograph of Capitol Hill
· A photograph of an aircraft carrier
· A photograph showing some other type of military force or personnel
· Lettering saying "Defense Budget Slashed" or something similar
· A generic drawing showing an element of military might, such as a rocket or bomber in flight

And so on. You can probably think of several more possibilities. The main thing is that the graphic must somehow highlight the subject of the story. In so doing, it should neither contain too little information (such as wording like "Congressional Action") nor too much information (such as the exact dollar amount by which the budget was cut). The point is to enhance the anchor's words, not to detract from them by providing more detail that can be absorbed at a glance.

As for scripting, this, too, is usually straightforward and simple. Unless specified otherwise, the graphic will appear automatically in the upper right or upper left (depending on the news department's practice), over the anchor's shoulder. All that need be included in the video column is the cue "graphic," followed by a word or two describing it:

```
Jones, 2/27, NN                    NOBEL
```

```
graphic -- Nobel Prize               An American won the Nobel

                                     Prize for chemistry today, giving

                                     the United States a clean sweep
```

```
                                     of this year's Nobel science

                                     Prizes.  The winner in chemistry:

                                     Henry Taube (TOW-bay) of Stanford

                                     University.



                                     ("NBC Nightly News")
```

Tell-stories using more than one graphic can be tricky. The visual changes should not come so fast as to be disorienting to the audience. Also, changes should follow both the written story structure and logical thought processes, which move from the general to the specific.

To change from one graphic to the next, script the video cue precisely adjacent to the line of copy where you want the new graphic to appear:

Smith, 10/9, EN   ECONOMY

graphic -- The Economy

graphic -- indicators

    The Commerce Department today reported its main economic forecasting gauge rose nine-tenths of one per cent last month. That's the thirteenth straight monthly increase for the index of leading indicators, and it pointed to continuing moderated recovery. The report said five of the available ten indicators rose in September.

("CBS Evening News")

As noted earlier, if you want the audience to be able to scrutinize a graphic in detail, it should be shown full-screen. This requires a slightly longer video cue: adding the word FULL right after the word "graphic." Here's how it looks properly scripted:

Bard, 5/12, 6p   QUAKE

graphic -- earthquake   Walter:

    A major earthquake has struck the northwestern United States, killing two children, injuring an unknown number of people, and causing widespread damage in parts of Idaho.

```
graphic FULL -- map
```

The quake was centered near
the small town of Challis, Idaho,
and was felt in seven surrounding
states and Canada. It measured
seven points on the Richter scale
-- a reading that usually means
very severe damage. Several
small towns in Idaho are
reportedly devastated, and two
people are missing. The child
victims were crushed when a
drugstore wall collapsed right
on top of them. Rescue teams are
being sent tonight to remote
areas of the state.

(WBBM-TV, Chicago)

Scripting with Titles

Graphics, especially full-screen graphics, are often accompanied by electronic titles, the former serving as background for the latter. As with graphics, titles must be prepared well before air time. There is seldom enough time while a newscast is in progress for the titling operator to type out the texts that will appear on-screen; instead, the texts are entered into the character generator's memory bank, then recalled and inserted at precisely the point indicated in the script.

There is not enough room on the script itself to include the verbatim text of a title, nor is it necessary to do so. All that's needed is the video cue "title" scripted adjacent to the specific line of copy where the title will appear. It may also be necessary to specify its location on the screen. Most titles accompany videotape, and as we shall see, their customary position is *lower third*. This would also be the customary position for a tell-story including, say, a telephone number announced by the anchor.

More typical, however, is the case of full-screen graphics and titles to augment statistical information being cited by the anchor. In this case, it is necessary to add the word FULL in the appropriate video cue, as well as a two- or three-word description of the text of each title. The following script shows how to change and combine graphics and titles, one cue at a time:

graphic -- hunger

New evidence of an emerging health crisis in America -- hunger.

graphic FULL -- Hunger in America

title -- 30 million

A congressional study by Tufts University concludes 30 million Americans experience some form of hunger -- defined as a condition where health is threatened because a person doesn't get enough nutrition. That's up 50 percent from 1985.

title -- 6 million

The study also found that six million Americans who live in poverty don't get food stamps. A bill is pending in Congress to increase the number of people who get the government subsidies.

title -- 5 million

And the study found five million people who live above the poverty line and who are ineligible for assistance...also experience hunger because of budget restraints.

(CNN/Headline News)

Our sample scripts so far have begun with the anchor sharing the screen with a graphic, then switching to full-screen graphics and titles. Although that is typical of most nontape stories, it is not always the case. Some stories may *open* with full-screen graphics and titles, then return to showing the anchor. Other stories, especially short ones containing statistics, can be presented *entirely* without seeing the anchor. An example:

```
Bard, 3/24, 5p          STOX

                          :10


graphic FULL -- NYSE        Walter:     On Wall Street today, stock

title FULL -- closing stox              prices were lower.  By closing

                                        time, the Dow-Jones Industrials

                                        were down more than 18 points.

                                        The average share lost 30 cents

                                        in trading that was active.


                                        (WBBM-TV, Chicago)
```

To summarize, here are the things TV newswriters generally know in advance: the desired length of a story (as specified by the producer), the identity of the anchor, the nature of the opening and succeeding graphics, and the possible need to include specific information in one or more titles. Writers must then:

1. Gather information on the story, whether in news-agency copy, consulting with a reporter, working the telephones, doing research, or any combination of these.
2. Script the story by coordinating the important story elements with the graphical and titular elements.
3. Decide the specific text for the title(s) and place an order for it with the titling operator, supplying him or her with the *exact* wording and appearance as they are to look on the screen. (In large news departments, there are special forms which the writer must fill out when ordering graphics and titles.)
4. Submit the written script to the producer, complete with news copy, cues, and running time. (In computerized newsrooms, the writer "sends" the completed script either to the newscast file, to the producer's file, or to both.)

Perhaps *now* you have an idea of why the ability to write news copy in broadcast style must be second nature to TV news professionals!

EXERCISES

1. Slug the following story VAN CRASH and write a 25-second tell-story, using a map pinpointing Sweetwater, Texas, as an upper-quadrant graphic:

> Team's Outing Ends in Tragedy
>   MIDLAND, Texas (AP)--The young boys and girls of the
> Midland Boys Club had spent the last week practicing for an
> out-of-town softball tournament, but their trip ended in
> tragedy.
>   Five lost their lives and 12 others in a Boys Club van
> were injured, four of them critically, in a collision Friday
> with a tractor-trailer near Sweetwater in West Texas. The
> truck driver also was injured.
>   "It's truly a miracle any of them are alive," said Nolan
> County Sheriff Jim Blackley.
>   Midland Boys Clubs officials Saturday thanked people in
> the community for their sympathy and response during the
> tragedy.
>   "In particular, we are grateful to those who we do not
> know, whose faces we have not seen, those who provided swift
> medical attention to our children," said Chuck Clarkson,
> chairman of the board of the Boys Club.
>   Trooper David Gonzales said the van was nearly alongside
> the Coca-Cola truck when the van driver apparently dozed off
> and swerved onto a grassy median. The driver, attempting to
> regain control, oversteered the van directly into the path of
> the truck, Gonzales told The Dallas Morning News.
>   Gonzales said the van, with 17 passengers, was overloaded.
> He said there should have been no more than a dozen
> passengers.
>   The van was returning from a softball tournament in
> Abilene earlier in the day. Clarkson said the tournament was
> to cap the summer program for underprivileged youth in
> Midland.
>   "They had been practicing pretty hard for the softball
> tournament, and they were really excited about it," he said.
>   A memorial service was planned for Sunday afternoon.
>   The driver of the van and nine occupants remained
> hospitalized Saturday in hospitals in Lubbock and Abilene. The
> truck driver was released Saturday, but refused interviews.

2. Slug the following story TRIDENT PROTEST and write a 20-second tell-story using two upper-quadrant graphics:
   1. the words "Protesters Arrested"
   2. a photo of a Trident submarine
   (Be careful. The choice of which graphic to use first depends on your decision how to lead the story.)

> USS Pennsylvania Launched, Protestors Arrested
>   GROTON, Conn. (AP)--The U.S. Navy Saturday launched its
> 10th Trident nuclear-powered submarine, the USS Pennsylvania,
> as police arrested dozens of anti-war protesters.
>   "This ship is part of the strongest military deterrent
> force ever assembled," Rep. Joseph M. McDade, R-Penn, said at
> the launching at the Electric Boat Division of General
> Dynamics Corp. "This boat allows us the luxury of having no
> doubtful engagement."
>   The Pennsylvania, after it is fully equipped and
> outfitted, a process that normally takes at least a year, will
> be the second ship in its class to carry the more accurate
> Trident II missiles. Each of the 24 missiles carries 10
> nuclear warheads.
>   The boat, which was christened by Marilyn Kay Garrett,
> wife of Navy Undersecretary H. Lawrence Garrett III, will have
> a crew of 154.

   The Ohio Class Trident submarines are the largest and most powerful in the Navy fleet and are the heart of the U.S. sea-based nuclear deterrent. The boats measure 560 feet long and displace 18,750 tons.

   The program was initiated in 1974, with the first ship, the Ohio, commissioned in 1981. Congress has approved funding for 15, of which eight are in service.

   Fifty to 75 anti-war protesters demonstrated at the shipyard, and Joan Cavanagh, a member of the Coalition To Stop The Trident, said 32 people were arrested after they lay down in front of the gates.

   A dispatcher with the Groton City Police Department said more than 20 people had been arrested on disorderly conduct charges as of Saturday afternoon and would be released on their own recognizance.

Videotape I: Components, Sources, and Editing 16

At last we come to what modern TV news is mainly about: pictures that *move*.

In a way, as basic a picture as a full-frame anchor shot contains movement; after all, the anchor *is* seen to be breathing, blinking, and, of course, talking. The appearance of graphics and titles in various parts of the frame also constitutes a type of movement, roughly equivalent to flipping a series of still pictures. But what is really meant by "moving pictures" is videotape shot at the scenes of events and edited flowingly to show the "action."

VIDEOTAPE TECHNOLOGY

In its early days, TV news relied for visuals on the black-and-white still photographs (called "wire-photos") sent over the newspaper wires, and on black-and-white 16-mm movie film shot by bulky and expensive sound cameras and by hand-held silent cameras with three-lens turrets; this was the type of equipment used by the newsreels which, before the growth of television, accompanied feature films in movie theaters.

Camera operators required stamina, sturdy legs, muscular arms, and a strong back. The cameras were eventually made smaller, but the switch to color film initially required brighter lighting (as well as costlier processing equipment); thus TV news crews still resembled pack animals as they traveled from location to location. By 1980, videotape had replaced film in virtually all TV newsrooms in the United States, and by 1990, newstape had become the standard worldwide.*

Early video cameras and ancillary sound gear were heavier than film cameras, so pumping iron was still part of a camera crew's preparation for work. But by the late 1980s, professional video gear had become so relatively lightweight and easy to operate that camera crews no longer needed extra muscles. This was a very positive development for equality of opportunity because camera operators nowadays are just as likely to be women as men.

---

*From the mid-1970s through the mid-1980s, newstape technology was called "ENG" (Electronic News-Gathering) or "EJ" (Electronic Journalism) to distinguish it from film technology. However, since tape is now the single standard, it is no longer necessary to give it a fancy name.

Even though video cameras themselves are now relatively small, TV news crews are frequently loaded up with other electronic gear, enabling them to transmit a live signal over long distances. In order for television to match the immediacy of radio, a TV crew must use a microwave transmitter with a directional dish antenna. This requires a van instead of a car. And if the crew wishes to go live over immense distances, it must have a satellite uplink transmitter requiring even a larger vehicle— all this in addition to cameras, sound gear, a tripod, lights, cables, and editing gear, plus space for ham-and-cheese sandwiches. Such fully equipped road hogs (some are the size of motor homes) are called "SNVs"—Satellite News Vehicles. Networks and some major-market stations have them—but at enormous cost; depending on configuration, the price tag can be upwards of half a million dollars (the sandwiches are extra). Most news departments thus either rent them or make do without them, relying instead on vans or panel trucks converted into mobile units.

Satellite News Gathering (SNG)

KCAL-TV technician Mark Davis checks the dish of the station's satellite news vehicle. The SNV carries editing equipment as well as an uplink transmitter and power generator, and can broadcast live or on tape from anywhere in the world.

CNN international assignment editor Donna Liu and co-workers coordinate satellite feeds in the network's newsroom in Atlanta. While expensive, satellite technology has evolved so rapidly that its relative cost has decreased, enabling local stations to send reporters and camera teams to far-flung locations that were once the exclusive domain of the major broadcast networks.

(Photo courtesy CNN)

Because of the relentless pace of technological change, it is risky to predict what video gear will be like next year or the year after (except, of course, to say that it will be smaller). But very likely it will resemble the equipment in use in the early 1990s: either a system geared to the ¾″ U-matic tape standard first introduced in the 1970s; a system geared to the ½″ professional Beta standard introduced in the 1980s; and/or a semi-professional version of the 8-mm (¼″) consumer camcorder format known as "Hi8," first introduced by Sony Corporation. These standards are *not* compatible with consumer video systems such as VHS, VHS-C, Beta, or 8-mm; consumer video must be dubbed onto professional video before it can be edited for broadcast.

Regardless of standard, videotape technology works the same way. In Record mode, sound and picture are encoded in magnetic particles on the tape's surface. Editing and Playback modes read this code to reconstitute the images and sounds. Sound and picture are recorded on separate "tracks," enabling tape editors to rearrange them independently of one another.

Video Cameras

Camcorders for sale nowadays at local electronics stores are often loaded with features that make amateur videography relatively uncomplicated: automatic focus; automatic exposure (to compensate for changing light conditions); a power zoom lens; automatic white balance (to stabilize the color saturation); and a built-in microphone with automatic gain (volume) control. Some consumer camcorders even have titling circuitry to insert the date and time of day into a corner of the frame. All in all, pretty snazzy.

It may surprise you to learn, however, that *professional* video cameras do *not* have all these automated features. Their electronics, including computer chips and circuitry, are far more sophisticated. Their parts are precision-tooled out of metal rather than stamped out of plastic. They are built to withstand harsh weather conditions and occasional rough handling. They require constant care and maintenance. If they were made as "automatic" as consumer camcorders, the quality of the sound and picture would be vastly reduced. That is why when you are watching TV at home you can always spot the "amateur" video. It is simply not as sharp and clear as professional video; the colors are rarely true-to-life, and the sound is often mushy or indistinct. Professional camera gear requires experienced operators to constantly monitor and adjust its performance to maintain optimum quality. (It's true that TV news often shows amateur video nowadays—but only when no professional-quality video happens to be available.)

Ancillary Field Gear

In addition to a camera with sound and picture circuitry, professional TV news crews routinely carry:

· Two or more microphones to allow mixing of sound sources during recording
· A tripod to ensure that the camera will not move and the picture will remain steady during long takes
· A camera-mounted light (battery powered) to work along with the camera in low-light conditions
· A second, stand-mounted light (AC powered) for formal, long setups in low-light conditions
· A backup battery pack to replace a rechargeable battery that runs down during shooting
· A roll of adhesive tape for affixing microphones and for attaching small items (photographs, documents, etc.) to vertical surfaces to permit closeup (macro) photography.

(It's not hard to see why TV field crews often refer to themselves as pack animals.)

SOURCES OF VIDEOTAPE

TV news departments rely on many sources for the videotape they include in their newscasts:

1. Local staff and free-lance camera crews
2. Network and/or cable newscasts
3. Network, cable, or syndicated closed-circuit feeds
4. Group or regional pools
5. Government or industry handouts
6. Amateur video

Local Crews

Most of the videotape shown on local newscasts comes from staff camera operators dispatched to myriad locations in the local viewing area. A small-market station may have only two or three cameras, often operated by reporters. (It is not unusual for a small-market reporter to conduct an interview or speak on-camera by mounting the camera on a tripod, framing the shot, turning on the camera, then running around in front of it to do the interview or on-camera text.) Medium-market stations may have as few as 5 cameras or as many as 15, each run by a single operator. Major-market stations may have as many as 20 camera crews (each consisting of two technicians), and networks and all-news cable broadcasters have double, triple, or quadruple that number.

As part of the budget and staff cutbacks of the late 1980s, many local stations have come to rely on free-lance suppliers for coverage of "routine" fires, road accidents, and petty crime, especially between the hours of midnight and six A.M. The free-lancers shoot these events "on spec" (without guarantee of payment) and offer it to all stations equally. If the tape is used, they are paid a fee by each user.

Network and Cable Newscasts

The news broadcasts of ABC, CBS, NBC, and CNN are, in effect, the United States' "national newspapers." Their broadcasts, especially CNN's, are now seen in many other parts of the world as well.* Their influence is enormous, and the competition among them is fierce. Each wants the most dramatic video, each wants exclusives, and each wants to be first on the air with major news developments.

Until CNN came along, the traditional networks often held back their "most dramatic" videotape for their evening broadcasts, each of which is watched by an estimated twenty million viewers. Their local affiliates in the East and Midwest thus had to await the network evening news to "lift" the best video, thereby having to make do with less than the best for their own early news broadcasts. In competitive terms, this did not matter much as long as independent stations (non-network affiliates) had no access to excellent visuals either.

But CNN never held back its best video; the very essence of CNN's programming is to air newstape as quickly as possible. And when CNN (along with a number of other non-network suppliers) decided to make this material available to any station that agreed to pay a user fee, the independents jumped at the opportunity. Now *they* had speedy access to dramatic tape—often to the competitive disadvantage of the network affiliates. The affiliates complained to their respective networks, loudly. The result is that the networks no longer hold back dramatic visuals: they transmit their "best"

*Despite the relative decline in network viewership due to the growth of cable TV, the weekday evening half-hour newscasts of ABC, NBC, and CBS averaged (in 1993) around 15 million viewers *each*. Compare this with around 1.5 million viewers watching CNN at the same time of day. (The preceding figures applied only in the United States. Abroad, CNN was clearly the audience winner. Its broadcasts were being carried in at least 135 countries.) A fourth network, Fox, was planning to debut a nightly newscast by the mid 1990s.

newstape to local affiliates just as soon as they can. Local stations re-edit the tape to suit their own needs.

Closed-Circuit Feeds

As in radio, a closed-circuit feed in TV means a transmission sent to participating stations for their own use instead of for direct broadcast. At least twice a day—but more frequently if news events warrant—each network feeds its affiliates a package of video material including graphics, sound bites, reports, and unnarrated clips (called "NATSOT"—short for "Natural Sound On Tape"). Local producers and writers utilize the closed-circuit material for their own stations' versions of world and national news.

In the 1980s, satellite technology made it possible for a large number of group (multi-station) owners such as Westinghouse and Post-Newsweek, as well as independent suppliers, to package video material and transmit it on a same-day basis to any station willing to buy it (a business method known as "syndication").

The availability of this syndicated material had reached such proportions by the early 1990s that the market became saturated. Supply outstripped demand, and many suppliers went out of business.

Pools

Whenever possible, stations like to cover stories with their own personnel. But, like the nineteenth-century newspapers which established news agencies to serve their common needs, local TV stations sometimes combine their resources to share coverage and expenses on a regional basis. In broadcasting this is known as "pooling" (as in "pooling one's resources"). Stations in the pool agree to share the expenses of the originating station, which feeds its material to the others, usually via satellite, at a predetermined time of day.

A typical pool arrangement would call for coverage of an action by a state legislature, the pooling stations not having had sufficient advance warning to dispatch their own reporters and camera crews to the state capital.

Handouts

More and more, we live in a video-oriented society. Business and industry have long recognized this, and latterly so has government. Many private companies and government agencies now provide videotape of their activities, offering it as handout material (that is, free of charge) to TV news departments. Sometimes handout material is the only possible source of visuals, as is the case, for example, of on-board activities on the space shuttle, live pictures and tape of which are provided by NASA. Another example would be a drug company providing tape of a laboratory experiment.

Because such handout material is proprietary (that is, the originator owns the copyright), and because no journalist has independently guaranteed its authenticity, TV news departments (1) retain the right to edit the material any way they see fit, and (2) *always identify its source*. The attribution is usually accomplished by means of an electronic title inserted in a portion of the frame (such as "NASA tape" or "tape courtesy of Johnson & Johnson"). This "visual sourcing" tells viewers, in effect, "We cannot vouch for the authenticity of what you see here. We got it from the source named on your screen. We show it because it is the best illustration we could find of the story we are telling."

Amateur Video

Hard to believe as it may now seem, TV news departments used to *reject* amateur video out-of-hand. They were dissatisfied with its generally poor quality, of course, but there was another reason as well: Except in emergencies, it was a matter of policy (and of pride) to use only newstape shot by staff crews, professional free-lancers, or network and pool providers. But then came the staff cutbacks

Video Attribution

Reporter Cindy Vandor and VTR editor Kimberly White of KCAL-TV, Los Angeles, view cassettes of file tape to locate visuals for background elements of Vandor's package. After dubbing, they return the archived tapes to the station's tape library.

On the air, archive footage is labelled by electronic title either by specific date or by a generic term identifying it as file tape. Titles are also used to identify the source of proprietary videotape—that is, tape furnished by private, corporate, or governmental sources outside the news department.

(CBS News; WMAQ-TV, Chicago; CNN/Headline News)

of the late 1980s, concurrently with the proliferation of consumer camcorders. All of sudden, local stations came to rely on the alertness of amateur videographers to shoot tape which could be used on the news (and the networks came to rely on their affiliates to pass this tape along). Hence it is not uncommon nowadays for stations to *solicit* amateur video on a pay-for-use basis.*

VIDEOTAPE EDITING

Professional videotape comes packaged in cassettes of varying lengths, usually from 20 minutes to one hour (professional tape-transport circuitry moves much faster than consumer tape circuitry, which is another reason for the superior quality of professional video). In addition to sound and picture tracks,

---

*While we're on the subject, here's a tip: If *you* ever shoot amateur video that a local station wishes to put on its news, be very careful to specify, *in writing,* that the tape is for that station's *local use only.* Stations routinely pay a fee for permission to use amateur video, the dollar amount depending on the size of the market. But unless you specify otherwise, the station will simply *give* the tape to its network or *resell* it at a profit. Any resale money (which can total many thousands of dollars) should go to the person who shot the tape, or at least be shared with that person on a fifty-fifty basis. But as a legal matter, this must be specified in writing.

The infamous "Rodney King video" that eventually led to brutality charges against four Los Angeles police officers, and whose acquittal by a state-court jury triggered the 1992 L.A. riots, netted its amateur videographer the sum of $500 from the local station to which he sold it. But his failure to stipulate the terms of the station's resale rights meant that he did not receive one penny of the many thousands of dollars he could have earned when the station shared the video with stations and networks worldwide. He later filed a lawsuit to be awarded payment from the tape's many, many users.

the tape also contains a *time-code track,* a built-in reference based on a 24-hour clock, enabling precise logging and speedy relocation of selected scenes. (If the camera operator has neglected to activate the time-code circuitry, the code is placed on the tape the first time it passes through an editing deck.)

In the editing process, the cassettes of "raw tape" (as it is known; other terms are "bulk tape" and "field tape") are placed in a computer-assisted editing deck which displays the time code along with the sound and picture. Under the guidance of a producer, writer, or reporter, the VTR editor selects scenes from the raw tape, one scene at a time, by noting the time code reference of each. Then the story is built onto a separate cassette, scene by scene, to form the version that will be incorporated into a newscast, whether as a simple sound bite, a longer tape to be narrated by the anchor, or a reporter or producer's package.

The selection of scenes and their order of presentation are *editorial decisions* in the same way as the selection of words and story structure to tell the news. The choice is thus up to the producer, reporter, or writer. However, *esthetic* considerations, such as how the picture "looks" and whether the scenes "flow," are the responsibility of the VTR editor. This is another of TV's group activities where cooperation is an essential ingredient, especially under the time constraints of a busy newsroom. (Bear in mind that a small-market staffer may be editing *solo.*)

Before examining the challenges of videotape editing, we should consider a few overall technical matters that guide the way camera operators shoot tape and the way VTR editors edit it.

The TV Cutoff

The next time you watch an old movie on television, pay particular attention to the credits. You may notice that the titles seem to be off-center, either left or right. Or entire lines of titles may not be wholly visible on your set, "lost" at the top or bottom of the frame.

This is because the feature movie you are watching was made for showing in a movie theater. The movie's makers knew that every bit of the frame would be projected onto the screen. Modern movie-makers, however, realize that their movies may eventually be shown on television, so they design the credits to occupy the central position of the frame. That's because they know all about the TV cutoff.

In television, the signal passes through many different steps before reaching the home screen. And at each step of the way, a little of the image is lost along the outside perimeters. And as a TV set itself gets older, its picture tube deteriorates, resulting in more picture loss along the outside edges.

This picture loss is estimated to amount to about 10 percent of the total frame. Thus, it must be compensated for both when shooting tape and later in the selection of scenes. The TV camera operator must frame the picture about 10 percent *smaller* than the movie camera operator. And the tape editor must not choose scenes containing important action or visual elements too near the edges of the frame, where they may not be seen by viewers at home.

Dubbing

The second overall technical consideration is the sharpness of the picture. It goes without saying that the picture should be as sharp and clear as possible, since, again, some quality is lost in the various stages of transmission. But in editing tape, picture quality deteriorates with each successive dubbing. The original tape, the tape on which the pictures were shot, is called the "first generation." The tape onto which the edited version is built from the first generation is called the second generation. With modern professional equipment, there is very little loss in quality from the first generation to the second. However, if a second generation tape is used as the raw material for a re-edited version, the resulting third generation will show considerable loss in quality; the pictures will begin to look fuzzy and the colors less vivid.

This happens especially with network material recorded by local stations for inclusion in local newscasts. The final edited local tape may be a fourth or fifth generation, possibly resulting in a picture of truly marginal quality or the equivalent of radio's UFB, unfit for broadcast.

At most stations, the standards of picture quality are very high. So whenever possible, air tapes should be edited from first-generation cassettes.

SHOT COMPOSITION

TV journalists borrow many terms from moviemakers to describe the various ways to frame a scene and to adjust the camera during photography. It is important to understand this vocabulary.

In the first instance, it is the people in the field—reporters and camera operators—who must understand picture composition, for it is they who provide the raw material for writers, producers, and tape editors. However, these last, too, must understand picture composition and terminology to make the best use of the raw material. Moreover, a TV journalist must at least know what his or her colleagues are talking about, whether or not he or she is ever involved in editing or shot selection.

In TV news, as in movies, there are five basic shots describing the *distance* between the lens and the subject being photographed:

· ELS—Extreme Long Shot
· LS—Long Shot (also called Wide Shot)
· MS—Medium Shot
· CU—Closeup
· ECU—Extreme Closeup

ELS.   An ELS is the widest, most comprehensive view possible of a location or event. An ELS is what a movie director might use to show two armies marching toward another on a field of battle or to show a lone horseman crossing a vast plain. Such views depend on a large screen to be effective and, therefore, are almost never used in TV news with its small screen, where the soldiers might look like ants and the lone horseman like a misshapen blade of grass.

LS.   Long Shots, however, are used briefly but frequently. A shot of a building, or a stadium, or a street serves to establish the location of an event. In fact, LS's are often called "establishing shots." As you watch videotaped TV reports, you will notice that an LS is customarily used at the beginning and then again to establish a radical change of location. These shots are short because, as with the ELS, it is hard to make out details from such distance on the small home screen.

MS.   This is the most frequent shot used in TV news, the one that best captures the action. A Medium Shot is close enough to the subject to show detail, yet far enough away to show what the subject is doing. It shows both the person or persons performing an action and the person or persons being acted upon.

CU.   Closeups are the second most frequently used shots in TV news. CU's are used for interviews. We see just the head and shoulders of the person being interviewed or just the head and shoulders of the reporter conducting the interview. The lower third of the frame, under the subject's chin, leaves room for an identifying title without blocking the face.

ECU.   As the name implies, this shot moves the camera in even closer. During interviews, for example, the ECU is the somewhat "artsy" shot that shows just the person's head, usually while the person is in a state of deep emotion. Some stations and camera operators overdo this shot, to the detriment of what the person is saying; the viewer becomes preoccupied with the texture of the interviewee's eyebrows rather than with his or her words. ECU's also serve to show small objects or documents closely enough so that any printed matter can be read. Such shots are also called *Inserts,* because the shot is "inserted" at a specific point in which the script refers to the object or the text of the material being shown.

CAMERA MOVEMENTS

Let us specify at the outset that during news photography, the camera itself should move *as little as possible,* to avoid jarring the image. Whenever possible, the camera should be mounted on a tripod.

Calling the Shots

An Extreme Long Shot (ELS) of one wing of the KCAL-TV, Los Angeles, newsroom. An ELS shows an entire location, covering a wide area.

A Long Shot (LS) narrows the frame somewhat—but still shows most of the location. Typically, an ELS or LS is used as an "establishing shot" at the beginning of an edited sequence.

A Medium Shot (MS) tightens to show what specific people in the scene are doing (in this case, KCAL-TV reporter Cary Berglund and newswriter Margot Merin preparing news stories). An MS is the customary framework for showing "action" in TV news coverage.

A Closeup (CU) shows a single person or object. CU's are used for interviews, speeches, news conferences, and so forth. The shot leaves enough room in the lower third of the frame to insert an identifying title under the speaker's chin.

An Extreme Closeup (ECU) comes in even closer on a person's face. A camera operator may occasionally tighten to an ECU to show someone's intensity of feeling. CU's and ECU's are also used for insert shots to show small objects, documents, still photographs, etc.

However, it is sometimes necessary to move the camera or adjust the lens in order to keep the action squarely in the frame. Here are the terms describing these movements.

Zooms

In a "zoom," only the lens moves. A zoom lens gets its name from its ability to reframe a shot either closer to or farther from the subject being photographed. To *zoom in* means to enlarge the subject by framing the shot closer. To "tighten" or "come in tighter" are other ways of expressing it. To *zoom out* means the opposite: to "widen" on the subject.

Zooms should be used as little as possible and only to reframe the action during unpredictable events. The reason is that a scene can *not* be edited smoothly in the middle of a zoom—a phenomenon that you will eventually see for yourself.

Pans

A "pan" describes a lateral swivel of the camera as it follows the action or swings to show what is happening at a different part of the same location. To *pan left* means to swivel the camera to the left, and to *pan right* means the opposite.

Like zooms, pans are to be used *rarely,* because they can't be edited in the middle. Typically, pans are planned shots used as visual transitions.

Tilts

While pans refer to lateral camera movements, "tilts" refer to swiveling the camera up and down. To *tilt up* means to swivel (point) the camera upwards, and to *tilt down* means the opposite.

Tilts should *almost never* be used. Not only are they difficult to edit, but tilts can literally make some viewers become nauseated. Once again, the editing difficulty of tilts is something you will no doubt come to appreciate once in the editing room.

To repeat, shots involving camera movement are to be used only when absolutely unavoidable. In 90 percent of news photography, it is the *subject* which moves, which provides the "action"—*not* the camera.

JUMP CUTS

A *jump cut* occurs when you edit together *(butt)* two moving pictures of the same person or action. The butted images appear to "jump" unnaturally. Editing videotape is thus more difficult than editing audiotape, where only the sound is involved.

This is something you actually have to see to appreciate. But by way of verbal illustration, let's say you have videotape of the president saying,

Senator Piltdown is single-handedly responsible for the defeat of the housing bill. (sudden coughing fit)

Uh, excuse me. (clears throat) But I promise him I've only just begun to fight. I'm sending Congress a new

housing bill next week.

Naturally, you'd want to cut out the coughing fit. And in radio, using audiotape, you'd have no problem. You'd simply cut after sentence 1 (" . . . housing bill.") and pick up with sentence 3 ("But I promise . . . "). You've got a nice, newsy actuality, which the coughing fit would have destroyed.

But editing the videotape picture is quite a different matter. Remember, we are looking at the president in closeup. Suppose at the end of sentence 1 his head is turned to the right. Now suppose that at the start of sentence 3 his head is turned to the left, the president having turned his head somewhere in the videotape we cut out.

Edited together, the sound bite will *sound* fine. But *visually* it will appear that the president has broken his neck, suddenly, instantaneously jerking his head from right to left. In short, it will be quite obvious that something has been cut out. And it will disorient viewers to the extent that many will no longer be listening to the content, but instead will be wondering who screwed up and how. In short, this is a major distraction which must be eliminated by finding alternative video.

CUTAWAYS

A jump cut is literally covered up by a short scene called a *cutaway*. The term comes from the expression "to cut away from the main action." In movie-making, a cutaway is called a "cover shot." Here's how it works in the aforementioned example.

The tape editor butts the two desired parts of the president's remarks, making sure the edit *sounds* right (according to the criteria we examined in radio editing). So much for the audio portion of the edit. To cover the jump in the picture, the editor searches for a short scene *not* showing the president—perhaps a shot of reporters taking notes or a shot of other TV cameras trained on him— and lays the video track of that shot *over* the jump cut. *Voilà!*—a sound bite that sounds right *and* looks right.

But wait a moment: Where did those other shots come from? After all, we had only one camera. How could it simultaneously be taping the president, the reporters, and cameras watching him? The answer is, it couldn't. The shots were taken *at different times*. During the president's remarks, the camera remained trained on him in order not to miss any potentially newsmaking comments. The cutaways were shot either before or after the president's remarks *with the express purpose of providing editing tools*. In the editing room, the cutaways were carefully logged by time code in order to be relocated speedily for insertion as needed.

So engrave this on your memory: *Next to the action itself, cutaways are the most important shots in TV news.*

Some of you may be thinking, "Hey, isn't a cutaway *posed*? Isn't that *staging the news?*" Posing, perhaps. Staging, no. Cutaways are indispensable tools of TV news production. If they are occasionally posed, they must show the kinds of actions (or reactions) that actually occurred during the main action itself. (Reporters *did* listen. They *did* take notes. TV cameras *were* present.)

In other words, as long as a cutaway is a faithful re-creation of an actual scene, no staging is involved. However, re-creation of the main action itself *is* staging, and it is absolutely forbidden. The penalty for staging is dismissal.

There are, of course, degrees in this—gray areas, if you will. Suppose that you and your camera arrive late to a mayoral news conference. May you ask the mayor to repeat his key remarks for the benefit of the camera? And if the mayor agrees to do so, is it staging?

We don't know. The answer depends on the policies of your news department and the perceived importance of the mayor's remarks, as well as the perceived importance of your audience seeing and hearing them from the mayor's own mouth.

We do know this: it is absolutely, positively, unethical staging for you to request somebody to do something on camera that he would not do privately. That would be like writing a movie script, handing it to a potential newsmaker, and saying, "Here—act this out." Strictly forbidden.

Okay, back to cases: There are two broad types of cutaways:

Reaction Shots

These are shots of the reporter listening to a speaker's or interviewee's remarks. Of necessity (the camera cannot be in two places at once), they are posed shots. Reaction shots are also known as "Reverse Angles" because, in order to tape them, the camera has had to move to the interviewee's point of view (POV), usually a 180-degree switch showing the reverse of the main shot.

(More on this, including procedures and camera angles, can be found in Chapter 19 on "Shooting the Story.")

Action Accelerators

The other broad type of cutaway is used to compress time. As we've seen over and over, time is a very precious commodity in broadcasting, so whenever we can eliminate or compress repetitive action, we do so.

Let's say you're writing a story about a swimming competition among preteenagers at a local YMCA or elementary school pool. The videotape shows the participants jumping in, swimming to the far side, kicking off, and then returning to the near side where the camera captures them at the finish. Total elapsed time: 2 minutes.

Two minutes is an eternity for a story like this. The problem is how to show the highlights while reducing the air time and maintaining the visual flow. What you might do is begin with the swimmers jumping in and swimming a few strokes, edit in a cutaway of spectators urging them on, return to the race as the swimmers kick off on the far side, edit in another cutaway, perhaps of a coach with a whistle in her mouth, then return to the race at the finish line. Total running time: 20 seconds.

Where did those spectator and coach cutaways come from? The camera operator shot them during another heat. Were they posed? No. Did the editing give the impression that all the scenes were occurring during the same heat? Yes. But were virtually the same cutaway scenes occurring during *every* heat? Yes. Therefore, the edited tape is an accurate representation of what did occur.

That is the way TV news stories are shot. It is the way they *must* be shot to allow writers and tape editors to represent reality and present news content within the constraints of a limited, yet reasonable, amount of air time.

As you can see, this is no easy task, especially for the reporter and camera operator, both of whom must be thinking not only of capturing the main action, but also of how that action can be accelerated, edited down to its highlights. What is finally shown on the news is not reality. It is video journalists' *version* of reality. It is no wonder, then, that working in TV news requires the highest standards of integrity and responsibility.

Logging

Tape editing also involves a lot of clerical work. Logging videotape requires an agile hand. That's because, in addition to making notes and time-code references on story details and possible sound bites, the staffer must also note the *visual* details of the tape, including where to find the cutaways.

At a major-market station, writers may spend their entire workday on just three or four stories involving tape. Writing the actual script (*the news,* let's not forget!), while it is certainly the most important part of the job, may take up the least amount of time. The bulk of the time is spent logging tape, supervising editing, ordering graphics and titles, and making sure that all these elements come together at air time.

At small-market stations, the individual workload is heavier, but there is also a higher tolerance of carelessness and error. However, it is those staffers who can do the work *without* carelessness and error who advance in their careers.

EXERCISES

1. Whether or not your course includes a lab section where you can observe and practice the aspects of videotape editing mentioned in this chapter, you will benefit from taking a closer look at the network and local TV news broadcasts you have by now made it a habit of watching. Set your VCR to record some of these broadcasts, then play back the stories that include videotape. Using the Still Frame or Slow Motion function of your VCR, identify zooms, pans, closeups, long shots, medium shots, and so on.

2. Now look at the tape again. This time try to identify the editing techniques, especially where cutaways may have been inserted to cover jump cuts.
    Note also the *structure* of the edited tape. Well-edited tape should follow one of two basic patterns: Either it should start with a "dramatic" shot and hold on it for a while, or it should go from the general to the specific, starting with an establishing shot of a location and then cutting to closer details.

Videotape II: Writing and Scripting

17

Newswriting with videotaped story elements is perhaps the highest craft of TV journalism, and for many newcomers, the hardest to learn. That's because, as we've seen, moving images cannot be rearranged and juxtaposed—edited—as freely as still images. Therefore, *language* must be adapted to suit a particular sequence of movement. Newswriters must choose words that complement, explain, and put in context the moving pictures seen by the audience.

Sometimes, writers fight a losing battle in this. Studies have repeatedly shown that given a conflict between pictures and words, viewers consistently trust the pictures more than the words. This is unfortunate because pictures do *not* speak for themselves. The camera's lens captures only a small portion of reality. Without the proper words to put the camera's limited view in context, TV journalists risk leaving the audience with a distorted view of the news, and therefore a distorted understanding of the real world. Writing to videotape is thus a skill developed and honed through constant practice.

WRITING TO TAPE

We trust that by now you have made considerable progress in broadcast-style writing. Your work thus far in radio newswriting and in writing to graphics and titles should have prepared you for what follows. As you will see, writing to videotape sometimes follows radio's basic structure of tell-story, lead-in/actuality/tag, or lead-in/report. But moving pictures often impose a severe limitation:

> ***The cardinal rule of writing to moving pictures is that***
> ***news copy and pictures must be correlated. Not***
> ***identical—correlated.***

News copy delivered on-camera by an anchor or reporter is free from competing visual elements. Thus, it need not be tied to specific pictures because there are none on the screen (except, perhaps, for certain of the upper-quadrant graphics we looked at in the preceding chapter). But once the screen is fully occupied by a graphic, title, or moving pictures (whether live or on tape), the freedom of expression is lost. Copy must refer to what we are seeing, *at the time we are seeing it.*

This correlation between sound and picture is often called "referencing." News copy properly keyed to TV pictures is said to be "referenced." *Un*referenced copy is substandard; it disorients the audience.

This is absolutely fundamental. And it explains why so much money, time, and effort are spent on getting the right pictures in the first place. If the pictures show the elements of a news story specifically, the writer can combine tape editing and language to tell the news in whichever order and structure he or she thinks does the job best.

But things don't always work out that way. The "right" pictures aren't always on hand. Thus, the writer must find some way, some language, to tell the right news while incorporating the taped visuals that are available.

One option, of course, is not to use the tape at all if it doesn't show exactly what the writer wants to tell. However, in the real world (which is vastly different from the academic world), this option is rarely exercised. The name of the game is to exploit the medium's visual aspect whenever possible. In practice, this means going with whatever tape happens to be available (as long as it's related to the subject at hand). And for the writer, this means tailoring language to fit the situation.*

For example, let's say that Senator Piltdown, during a tight race for re-election, visits your town briefly as part of a whirlwind campaign swing. His visit amounts to little more than a quick stop at the airport for a speech at the terminal (the kind of "photo opportunity" politicians love to stage for the exposure it gets them in the local media). You have picturesque tape of the good senator waving as he exuberantly emerges from the plane and walks down the ramp. You also have excruciatingly dull tape of the senator's remarks (Piltdown is no Demosthenes). Your best picture is the ramp footage, so you are going to use it as a visual introduction, followed by a bite of Piltdown.

Your challenge is this: It takes 12 seconds for Piltdown to get down that ramp. That's how long the tape runs. You could shorten it from either end, but not in the middle (which would result in a jump cut making it look like Piltdown *fell* down the ramp). But you'll need every precious second for your lead-in copy. So 12 seconds is what you've got—use it or lose it. That means you must write precisely 12 seconds of copy to cover the playing time.

And that copy should *not* say, "Senator Orotund Piltdown smiled and waved exuberantly as he arrived in Ourtown today" because everyone can *see* him smiling and waving. Why be redundant? And it should *not* say, "Senator Orotund Piltdown said today" because we see him *smiling, waving,* and *walking down stairs,* not *saying*—a glaring mismatch of sound and picture.

You must somehow relate what we *are seeing,* the arrival, with what we *are about to see,* part of the speech, as you tell the news. Here's one way to do it:

```
                                Senator Orotund Piltdown,

                                arriving in Ourtown

                                today on part of a campaign

                                swing, pressed the issues that

                                show him gaining in the opinion

                                polls: higher defense spending

                                and a crackdown on welfare

                                fraud.
```

The boldfaced words explain the context of the picture we are seeing, and the rest of the words set up the sound bite that follows (which is on defense, welfare, or both). All the words together take 12 seconds to say. Bingo.

---

*It is absolutely forbidden to *misrepresent* a piece of tape (or still photograph, for that matter). For example, you may never show tape of a demonstration that took place the day before yesterday and say in your copy that this was "today's" demonstration, even though today's demonstration may have been very similar to the earlier one. This would be completely unethical and, in fact, could be grounds for a station's ownership to lose its FCC license.

The dictum never to misrepresent extends to even the smallest things. If your copy talks of "wheat fields" and if you only have tape of alfalfa fields, you may not use the tape, even though the chance of viewers catching such a discrepancy is remote. "Truth in packaging" may not apply strictly to advertising, but it applies absolutely to TV news. No exceptions.

Now no one claims this is easy. It takes much trial and error. But after much practice, TV newswriters and reporters develop a kind of sixth sense for "writing to time." They are able, after looking at a tape just once, to tell a tape editor, "Give me eight seconds of this, four seconds of that, six seconds of this, then a bite on the incue 'Mary had a little lamb,' to the outcue 'lamb was sure to go' "—and then go back to their desks and write the proper amount of copy without ever again looking at the tape.

This sort of newswriting cannot be haphazard. It requires discipline. It requires the writer to assess all the available elements—story points, picture, sound, plus the allotted air time—*before* sitting down to write.

Once at the keyboard, there are two general methods of correlating sound (copy) with picture (tape): scene-by-scene and as a flow.

Scene-by-Scene

This technique, which is easier to learn and is frequently used by field reporters to help guide tape editors in the choice and order of scenes, employs a key word or phrase that corresponds *precisely* with the appearance of a given picture:

```
VIDEO                              AUDIO

(victim's house)                   The victim lived in this house

                                   on Crescent Drive...


                                            -0-


(suspect's photo)                  Police identified this man --

                                   31-year-old Orotund Piltdown

                                   Junior -- as the prime

                                   suspect...
```

The copy need not contain the demonstrative adjective "this" or "these"; the mere mention of a specific name or place will suffice. The technique requires a specific picture to appear at a specific time. For this reason, it is disliked by many "creative" tape editors who resent writers and reporters, in effect, editing their pieces for them. So be it.

As a Flow

By far the more difficult, more creative, and ultimately more satisfying technique is writing that lets thoughts and subject matters flow seemingly effortlessly one to another. In this technique, the references to specific pictures are more oblique, more off-handed, more like conventional storytelling.

```
VIDEO                              AUDIO

(victim's house)                   From the outside, there was no

                                   hint of what had taken place

                                   in the victim's basement

                                   rec-room...


                                            -0-
```

```
(suspect's photo)                            And the man in custody

                                             tonight, 31-year-old Orotund

                                             Piltdown Junior, is said by

                                             neighbors to have been one of

                                             the victim's frequent

                                             visitors...
```

Do you see the difference in styles? Scene-by-scene writing makes the audio-visual linkage the main business of the sentence. Flow writing makes the linkage seem incidental.

"Writing Away"

Now that we've stated the case strongly for tying news copy directly to the taped visuals, let us devote a few words to the inevitable exceptions. Sometimes, the most effective way to tell a story on TV is to let the picture speak for itself, or at least to let it show things not specifically described in the narration. Here, as an example, is some narration for a closing item (kicker) to a newscast:

```
(anchor on-cam)                              And finally, there was an

                                             honored guest at today's

                                             commencement ceremonies at

(tape)                                       State University.  Patty

                                             Cake, who followed a special

                                             curriculum on full

                                             scholarship, was graduated

                                             "magna-cum-banana."  Patty had

                                             an outstanding academic

                                             record.  Never once did she

                                             bite a professor.  It's not

                                             known if Patty will attend

                                             graduate school.  It's not

                                             even known what she'll do with

                                             the rest of her diploma.

(anchor-on-cam)                              Patty Cake was part of a

                                             language-learning experiment

                                             underwritten by the American

                                             Zoological Society.
```

Well, it's pretty clear from that copy that Patty Cake isn't human. But it *deliberately* doesn't tell you that she is a young chimpanzee or what is happening in the videotape. Here's what viewers *see:* the anchor introducing the story, then tape of Patty, wearing a cap and gown, being led by her trainer as she is handed a diploma and a banana, hugging her trainer, and then taking a bite out of the diploma instead of the banana, followed by the anchor back on-camera (no doubt chuckling or smiling).

This kind of writing is called "writing away" (that is, "away" from the precise pictures). It deliberately uses language as a counterpoint to the pictures. Neither element, neither audio nor video, can stand on its own—the video because it doesn't tell us the context, the audio because it doesn't describe the pictures. But *together* they make effective storytelling on TV.

Of all television writing techniques, "writing away" is the most fun. But, as with many things that are fun, it's easy to overdo it. Thus, you should use the technique very rarely, and *only* when there is a strong picture.

"VISUAL LOGIC" (SEQUENTIAL WRITING AND EDITING)

In early chapters, we saw how and why the structure of broadcast news stories must follow a straight line instead of jumping back and forth. And in Chapter 7, in a baseball story illustrating sportswriting, we showed how this technique might be adapted for television. The adaptation was necessary because edited videotape contains its own "visual logic" reflecting the natural order of the real world. It would have looked idiotic to show a ninth-inning game-winning hit and *then* go back to show action from earlier innings. The tape had to be edited in chronological order; thus the accompanying news copy had to follow the same order.

Many TV news stories are so brief—around 20 or 25 seconds—that the matter of sequential writing and editing is not of major concern. Because they want to seize viewers' attention, producers routinely instruct writers to begin with the "most dramatic" video, usually an "action" shot (of demonstrators, a natural disaster, fire, etc.), and then stay there. When no such "action" exists, another basic technique for handling brief stories is to open with an establishing shot, then cut to a medium shot or closeup. But in handling longer stories, especially those detailing events occurring over several hours or several days, we must be careful to respect the natural order.

To illustrate more fully, let's say we are doing a story on the space shuttle for the Late News. Throughout the day, we have received videotape of the following events, listed in the chronological order of their occurrence:

- · The shuttle astronauts eating breakfast
- · The astronauts boarding the shuttle
- · The lift-off from Cape Canaveral
- · The shuttle separating from the booster rocket
- · The shuttle in orbit
- · The astronauts getting a phone call from the president
- · The astronauts conducting on-board experiments
- · The astronauts eating dinner

After getting his or her lead paragraph out of the way, a print writer would be free to recount these events in any order, jumping back and forth, interweaving at will. He or she could, for example, describe the astronauts' dinner and then immediately contrast this with what they had for breakfast. Or the print writer could tell how calm a certain astronaut appeared, then tell how nervous that same astronaut had been before the launch.

But the TV newswriter who wishes to show any or all of these events on tape has no such freedom of movement. That's because to reverse the natural order of things, to show people eating breakfast right *after* dinner or someone preparing for space flight on the ground *after* we've already seen him or her in space, causes viewers to shake their heads in dismay. It *looks* odd to see things out of sequence, and *seeing* is what TV news is mainly about.

So here's a guideline for writing and editing: *Unless there's a compelling reason to do otherwise, always edit videotape in a natural sequence, and write your narration accordingly.*

Sequential writing and editing takes two forms: temporal and spatial. The foregoing space shuttle story, for example, can be told flowingly either by respecting a strict *chronological order,* showing things in the same order in which they occurred in real life, or by *location,* starting with what happened on the ground and then with what happened in space. Either way, however, there is *no going back.* Once we eat dinner, it's too late for breakfast. Once we're in space, it's too late to prepare ourselves for the launch.

Note that in either case, it is not necessary to show everything. You can pick and choose from the available tape, just as you can from the available facts. But once you do choose, you should follow the sequential order just described.

A typical handling of this story for TV would have the anchor open on-camera or with a graphic telling the latest or most important development, then go into tape for mission highlights seen and told chronologically, and then finally back to the anchor for a tag or the next story.

SCRIPTING WITH ANCHOR VOICE OVER (AVO)

The most typical type of TV news script involving videotape is where the anchor reads news copy while viewers watch a taped sequence; the tape's sound track is played at low volume to provide "presence," and electronic titles are inserted as needed. Tape used in this fashion is called AVO—the standard TV term for Anchor Voice Over.

Typically, an AVO script opens with the anchor on-camera, with or without a graphic, and then cuts to the tape. An example:

Smith, 9/18, 5p   EARLY SNOW

AVO (:20)

title -- Billings

Carol: It's still officially summer

for four more days -- but you

might not be able to convince

the residents of southwestern

Montana of that.

It SNOWED there today -- and

it snowed a LOT. At last report,

as many as 17 inches were on the

ground in south-central Montana,

14 inches in the suburbs of

Helena.

The snow was part of a

fast-moving storm out of Canada

that hit Montana, Wyoming,

Colorado, and Washington -- where

the temperature only yesterday

was 60 degrees.

(WMAQ-TV, Chicago)

Note the positions of various script elements: Writer's name, the date, and hour of the telecast in the extreme upper left; the story's slug in the extreme upper right of the audio column; and the *total story time* (on-camera copy plus AVO copy) just under the slug, rounded off to the nearest :05 and circled. (Newsroom computer systems put these elements in their proper places automatically.)

The video cue "AVO" tells the director where and when to roll the tape. It is immediately followed by the tape's running time, in parentheses. The title cue tells the director when to insert the title (in this case at the start of the tape).

(Note also that taped sequences are customarily edited to run at least 5 seconds longer than the time stated in parentheses. The extra 5 seconds are called "pad" and provide a visual buffer in case of an accidental delay in switching.)

(Because anchors can't watch the monitors without taking their eyes off the news copy, it is optional to place *brackets* around AVO copy. The brackets tell anchors when they are off-camera. Absence of brackets tells them they are on-camera.)

Just as typical of this type of script are stories told *entirely* AVO, that is, without the anchor appearing on-camera at all:

Bard, 9/9, 730p   HAITI PROTEST

AVO (:20)

title -- Wash, D.C.

Former tennis star Arthur Ashe

was among 95 people arrested

outside the White House today

during demonstrations against

U-S policy on Haitian refugees.

A protest leader charged the

Haitians are being shut out of

the United States because they're

black.

Those arrested were fined 50

dollars each -- then they were

released.

(CNN/Headline News)

Here's how the writer worked: He or she viewed all the raw tape on the Haiti demonstration, then requested a VTR editor to edit 20 seconds of AVO (plus :05 pad), beginning with Arthur Ashe's arrest* and then showing other arrestees. Then the writer scripted the story, making sure to mention Arthur Ashe at the top, because that's where viewers would see him. That's the typical working method: tape editing first, then copy written to match the edited tape. (However, given enough time and a wealth of visuals, some stories, especially reporters' packages, may be written first and the tape edited to match the script.)

Wipes

An additional AVO script element is required when two AVO stories are presented back-to-back. Each story is written on a separate page, but the end of first page contains the cue "WIPE." This tells the director to switch directly to the next tape without cutting back to the anchor. Here's a two-story example:

Bard, 9/9, 8p   NAVSTAR LAUNCH

AVO (:20)   A Delta-Two rocket blasted off

title -- Cape Canaveral   from Cape Canaveral, Florida,

                                             today and launched a military

                                             navigation satellite into space.

                                             The 65-million-dollar NavStar

                                             satellite is the fifteenth to be

                                             launched since 1989. The U-S Air

                                             Force hopes to build a system of

                                             24 NavStar satellites to guide

                                             jets, ships, submarines, and

                                             tanks.

WIPE

---

*It is worth noting, perhaps, that Arthur Ashe took part in this demonstration despite being in the final stages of AIDS (he died a few months thereafter). CNN/Headline News did not mention this because, as perhaps the mild-mannered Ashe would himself have been the first to say, his illness was unrelated to the subject of the news story.

Bard, 9/9, 8p   SHUTTLE

AVO (:25)

title -- Space Center

And the countdown is on for the 50th space shuttle mission. Endeavour's liftoff is scheduled for Saturday morning.

The seven-member crew includes the first black woman, the first Japanese person, and the first married couple in space.

The seven-day space lab flight is a joint venture with the Japanese Space Agency. Among other things, astronauts hope to study how frogs and tadpoles would do in space.

(CNN/Headline News)

SCRIPTING WITH SOUND BITES

A script containing a taped sound bite is a little more complicated. It requires an additional cue in the video column: SOT, short for "Sound on Tape," telling the director that instead of the anchor talking, the tape sound alone is to be played. The precise running time of the bite goes in parentheses.

Because it is necessary to tell both the director and the anchor precisely when the anchor should resume following the bite, the bite's outcue is scripted in the audio column, either bracketed or set off by horizontal lines. The TV script page does *not* contain a verbatim text of the sound bite, but merely the cues necessary to get it on and off the air smoothly.

To permit you to fully grasp the content of the following model script, here is the text of the sound bite it incorporates:

(Louis Sullivan, Health and Human Services Secretary in the Bush administration)

"I'm here to, uh, tell the American people that the Congress has yet to act, to even schedule hearings on the President's proposals that have already been sent to the Hill. Everyone, uh, knows that we must reform the malpractice situation—we must have tort reform. Everyone complains about the burden of, uh, paperwork in the system, that is smothering the activities of our hospitals, our doctors, our other, uh, health-care professionals. Everyone knows we must make insurance more available to our citizens. There can be no argument about, uh, that. So why doesn't the Congress act?"

(runs :37)

```
Bard, 9/9, 7p              SULLIVAN

                             (1:00)


    graphic -- Sullivan                    The President's point man on

                                         health held an unusual news

                                         conference on the lawn of the

                     U-S Capitol today -- to blast

                                         Democrats for politicizing

                                         medical reform.

                                             Health and Human Services

                                         Secretary Louis Sullivan

                                         complained Congress isn't paying

                                         attention to President Bush's

                                         health care proposals:

    SOT (:37)

    title -- Sullivan
                                         --------------------------------

                                         ENDS:  "...the Congress act?"

                     --------------------------------
```

```
Lynne on/cam                                          But Sullivan admitted the

                                                      Administration still hasn't
```

```
                                                      drafted the centerpiece of its

                                                      proposals -- a plan to help 35

                                                      million working poor to buy

                                                      health insurance.


                                                      (CNN/Headline News)
```

The circled time just under the slug—1:00—is the total running time of the story, derived by adding the tape time (:37) to the copy time (:25), rounded off to the nearest :05. Thus: :37 + :25 = 1:02, rounded off = 1:00.

The title cue did not express a precise time, so the director automatically "took" it at the top of the bite. However, if the bite had been edited and a cutaway used to cover a jump cut, it would have been necessary to script a precise time for the title cue in order to prevent the title from inadvertently appearing over the cutaway instead of the speaker's face.

Note that this particular script identified the speaker both in copy and by electronic title. But generally, it is only necessary to use one or the other of the two methods instead of both. TV staffers overwhelmingly prefer to identify speakers by electronic title only, thereby gaining a few extra seconds to tell something else in the news copy itself.

Note also that this script ended with an on-camera tag. The writer felt it was necessary to add context to the speaker's politically partisan remarks. But in television, as opposed to radio, it is often unnecessary to tag a sound bite, especially if the end of the bite marks a clear end to the story or provides a link to the following story.

SCRIPTING WITH AVO AND SOUND BITES

Much more typical than scripts with sound bites only are scripts combining sound bites with AVO. Unavoidably, such scripts are more complicated because each video cue must include a specific time. Here's why.

VTR playback operator Kate Williams loads and plays edited video-cassettes during a KCAL-TV newscast. The contents of each cassette have been carefully timed, allowing the director to order graphics and/or titles inserted at precisely scripted intervals.

A newscast's stories utilizing videotape are edited onto separate cassettes, one cassette per story. By the time a newscast goes on the air, a stack of cassettes, each clearly labeled and timed, has been assembled near the playback machines, ready to be loaded and played at the director's command. Once a tape starts, it *continues to play* to the end of the edited material—no stopping, pausing, or rewinding. Therefore, the only accurate way for all concerned to know the precise time to cue a script element is to keep a cumulative (or "running") time of the entire tape from start to finish. The reference point is the start of the tape, which is clocked as zero (:00) seconds. Every cue thereafter is given *cumulatively*. Once the director starts his or her stopwatch at :00, the timing does not stop until the end of the tape. The watch is then zeroed again in readiness for the next tape. Thus the writer or VTR editor must keep a careful record of the proper times for each cue.

Perhaps the best way to demonstrate this is by showing an example. The following script includes this sound bite:

(Dep. Chief Dave Clark, Des Plaines Fire Dept.)

"When the crews arrived on the scene, we had a fire in the basement. Uh, the basement was full of smoke. We spent the first half an hour just evacuating the building. We got maybe 75 to 80 people out of the building."

(runs :16)

Jones, 10/2, 6p   FIRE

graphic -- map   Ron: Suburban fire officials are

   trying to determine the cause of

                                                 this morning's multi-alarm blaze

                                                 in northwest suburban Des Plaines

                                                 -- a fire that destroyed a

AVO (:55)   36-unit apartment building.

title -- Des Plaines   Five Des Plaines policemen, a

   volunteer fireman, and one

                                                 resident were treated for smoke

                                                 inhalation. No one was seriously

                                                 injured.

title (at :10) -- this morning   The pre-dawn blaze started in

   the basement of the building, and

                                                 spread rapidly through stairwells

                                                 and heating ducts, up through the

                                                 roof. Some residents were

trapped for a while by the smoke
and flames. They had to be
rescued by firemen using ladders
going up to the stories and
balconies:

SOT (:22 to :38)

title (at :25) -- Clark

ENDS: "...of the building."
           (DOUBLE OUTCUE)

FIRE -- 2

AVO (:38 to :55)

Those residents left
homeless by the fire were housed
in a temporary shelter put up by
the Red Cross at a grade school.
By early afternoon, most of the
burned-out families had been
relocated at nearby motels or
put up with friends and
relatives.

Ron on/cam

Officials are looking into the
possibility that the fire may
have been set.

(WMAQ-TV, Chicago)

Okay, let's look at that script more closely.

· Once again, the circled time under the slug is the total running time of the story, derived by adding the tape time (:55) and the copy time (:05 at the start + :03 at the end = :08) for a combined 1:03, rounded off to 1:05.

· The first cue—"AVO (:55)"—starts the tape and tells how long it runs. The director's stop-watch is now running from zero.

· The next cue—"title--Des Plaines"—is without a time indication, so the director will take it over the very first scene, as intended.

· The next cue, however—"title (at :10)--this morning"—tells the director precisely when to insert the next title: at 10 seconds into the tape.

· The next cue—"SOT (:22 to 38)"—tells everyone that our 16-second sound bite begins at 22 seconds into the tape and runs until 38 seconds in.

· The next cue—"title (at :25)--Clark"—tells precisely when to insert the identifying lower-third title.

· Now check the audio column. Note that the audio outcue contains the warning "DOUBLE OUTCUE" because the closing words, "the building," are repeated in the space of a few seconds. As in radio, anchors must know precisely when the taped sound is done and when they should resume reading.

· Note that our old friend the arrow is back in the lower right of the page. As in radio, it indicates the story continues onto another script page.

· Note that page 2 of the script bears only the slug and the page number in the extreme upper left. That's all that's necessary.

· The final cue—"AVO (:38 to :55)"—reminds the director that the AVO continues until :55, by which time he or she must return to the anchor shot, or go on to the next story.

(Okay, take a deep breath—there's more.)

Although standard practice is to identify all people appearing in sound bites, there are some exceptions. For example, depending on the context, a story may require only very brief comments from a number of people whose names are not really germane to the telling of the story. In such a case, the bites are butted together, and the scripted audio outcue is of the *last bite only*. Here's an example, incorporating the following bites:

(passenger #1)

"I could see it. I was sitting at the window. We flew right through a huge flock of sea gulls. We hit one in front, and one went right into the engine."

(passenger #2)

"Well, I think we're pretty lucky. We're on the ground—both feet."

(runs :18 total)

Smith, 10/14, 6p   NEAR MISS

Mike: Some air travellers heading

               out of Chicago got to their

               destination a little late today

-- but it could have been a whole lot worse.

    An Air Florida jet had to make an emergency landing at Midway Airport, just minutes after taking off for Miami. A flock of birds, also heading south, somehow got sucked into one of the plane's engines:

AVO (:37)

title -- Midway

SOT (:12 to :30)

ENDS: "...both feet."

AVO (:30 to :37)

    No one aboard the plane was injured. The passengers were bussed to O'Hare Airport for a later flight to Miami.

(WBBM-TV, Chicago)

    In modern television, sound bites can be extremely short, lasting as little as 3 or 4 seconds apiece. Naturally, the content must lend itself to this rather abrupt treatment. It may seem foolish to spend hours (counting traveling time) to tape an interview and then to use only 4 seconds (or none) of it, but that's the way it works out sometimes. Many news managements like bites to be kept short because this gives "movement" to a piece that might otherwise appear static. "Keep it moving" is the advice they give writers and reporters, by which they mean "Keep the viewer's attention."

NATSOT and Video Outcues

What about when a sound bite ends not with talk (words) but rather with natural sound and picture (NATSOT)? As in radio, the outcue must indicate the actual closing *sound*—such as applause, cheering, laughter, and so on. The cues should be placed in *both* columns, video and audio:

```
     SOT (:06) (cheering)          _____

                                   ENDS: (cheering)
                                   _____
```

Sometimes (but rarely) a bite will end not with sound but rather with video only—such as with someone shrugging or gesturing emphatically. In this case, too, descriptive cues should be placed in both columns, especially the audio column to tell the anchor that he or she should be watching the monitor instead of listening for an audio outcue:

```
     SOT (:22) (video out, smile)  _____

                                   ENDS: (VIDEO OUTCUE)

                                        (smiles derisively)
                                   _____
```

SCRIPTING LEAD-INS TO REPORTS

In major markets and at networks, writers script the anchor lead-ins to reporters' packages. In medium and small markets, reporters generally script their own lead-ins. Either way, an anchor lead-in to a report serves the same function in television as in radio: to "lead" the audience into a story's key elements.

A TV lead-in introduces the subject of the story and identifies the reporter while preparing the audience for what it is about to see and hear. Lead-in copy is either hard or soft, depending on the reporter's opening copy (see Chapter 11).

A typical lead-in ends with a throw line such as "Joe Doaks reports" or "We get details from Jill Jones." But good writers try to weave the reporter's name and/or location into story elements that pique the audience's attention. Here, for example, are competing network lead-ins to packages on cocaine use by major league baseball players:

```
Another big-league baseball
player is in the news tonight --
not because of what he did ON
the field, but because of what
he did OFF the field.   Former
Kansas City Royals pitcher Vida
Blue, once one of baseball's
best, pleaded guilty today to
```

possession of cocaine. He joins
three other Royals in the
cocaine lineup. And, as Jim
Cummins tells us tonight, there
may be others:

("NBC Nightly News")

-0-

It's a world apart from the
World Series -- an underworld of
whispers and pointed fingers and
illicit drugs. But it's in the
courts now, and, as Frank
Currier reports, the scandal of
"diamond dust" continues to
spread:

("CBS Evening News")

Cue Sheets

TV writers do more, however, than script package lead-ins. They also script *cue sheets* that contain the cues for titles, graphics, and timings. To examine this process more closely, we need to go back a few steps to the text of a reporter's package. Like the text of a sound bite, a reporter's text does *not* appear verbatim in a TV script. But you'll need to see a complete text in order to follow what happens during scripting. The following package is by Irv Chapman of CNN Business News:

(file tape)

Four years ago, a group of
Kentucky eighth-graders were
returning from a field trip, when
a drunk driver collided with
their school bus. Its gas tank
ruptured and caught fire.
Twenty-four children died --
including Shannon Fair.

(SOT, Shannon's mother)

"For the families who have been devastated by these tragedies, we are not a family any more as we were then, and things will never be normal for us."

(news conference)

The Fairs sued Ford for building a defective school bus -- settling out of court after four years of litigation. They came to Washington to oppose a bill that they feel would make it harder to sue.

(Groen factory floor)

Louis Thomas manufactures kitchen equipment in Chicago. The price of his pots and kettles includes the cost of defending his firm against law suits.

(SOT, Louis Thomas)

"I settled a liability case for several thousands of dollars, even though there was no culpability on our part, because it was cheaper to do it that way than to defend and spend perhaps between 25 and 50 thousand dollars in fighting for us, the defendant."

(Thomas in Congress)

Thomas came to Washington to try to cut down on his lawyers' fees.

(SOT, William Coston)

"What this bill tries to do is to put the money in two different sets of pockets -- one, in the research and development labs of the manufacturers, so they can design better products -- safer products -- and second in the pockets of the victims.

(Senate floor)

The bill would create one national product liability standard, superseding 50 state laws.

(on/cam closer)

Although a provision to limit the amount of damages awarded was removed from the bill, the issues are still contentious -- and the vote could be close.

Irv Chapman, CNN Business News, Washington.

The CNN writer assigned to that package had to script both a lead-in and a cue sheet specifying all relevant cues. They went as follows:

Bard, 9/9, 830p   PRODUCT LIABILITY

graphic -- Prod. Liability   The Senate began debating a

                                        controversial subject today:

                                        product liability lawsuits.

                                             One report suggests those

                                        cases make more money for

                                        lawyers than plaintiffs. Yet,

                                        Irv Chapman reports the suits

                                        have their defenders:

SOT (1:39), Chapman package

(GO TO CUE SHEET)   -------------------------------

                                        ENDS: "...News, Washington."

Bard, 9/9/ 830p   PRODUCT LIABILITY

(CUE SHEET)

at :02, title -- May 14, 1988

```
        at :46, title -- Janey Fair
```

```
        at 1:06, title -- William Coston
```

```
        ENDS at 1:39 -- "...CNN Business News, Washington."


                                        (CNN/Headline News)
```

That script and cue sheet were relatively uncomplicated. But in modern TV news, many packages (as well as tell-stories and AVO stories) make extensive use of animated graphics and titles with multiple fonts in addition to "live-action" visuals. Scripting can become extremely complicated—so complicated, in fact, that it is properly the subject of an advanced course in video production.

EXERCISE

1. The following news agency copy, AVO, and sound bites constitute your raw material to write a TV script running a maximum of 1:15. Slug it GALLAUDET and be sure to familiarize yourself with all the available copy, sound, and picture elements before selecting those you wish to include in your story.

```
        WASHINGTON (AP/UPI)--Gallaudet University's board of
    trustees today chose I. King Jordan to be the first deaf
    president in the 124-year history of the school for the
    hearing impaired, and announced that board Chairwoman Jane
    Bassett Spilman has resigned.
        Jordan, dean of the school's college of arts and sciences,
    was chosen to replace Elisabeth Ann Zinser, a hearing woman,
    who resigned early Friday after protests from students seeking
    a deaf leader had virtually paralyzed Gallaudet's campus.
```

Spilman, who had come under fire from protesters for her handling of the crisis, will be replaced by Philip W. Bravin, one of the four deaf members on the board.

In a clean sweep for student protesters, Bravin announced that the board of trustees will form a task force to study composition of the board and institute a plan to ensure that a majority of the school's 20-member trustees panel is deaf. There will also be no reprisals against student protesters, Bravin said.

News of Jordan's selection was received with joy on Gallaudet's campus. There was pandemonium in the campus gym, where about 200 students had gathered throughout the day as the board met in a nearby hotel.

Before becoming dean of Gallaudet's largest undergraduate department in 1986, Jordan, 43, served as a psychology professor at the school. He becomes the seventh president of the nation's only liberal arts college for the hearing impaired.

Jordan's appointment comes after a tumultuous week in which clamor for a deaf president grew from an isolated campus protest to a national platform for deaf rights.

Students forced school officials to cancel classes Monday when they blocked all entrances to the campus and prevented faculty and staff from entering. Throughout the rest of the week, students boycotted classes, and on Wednesday, more than half the school's faculty voted to back the protesters.

AVO shows the following elements:

· Gallaudet campus exteriors
· Students in campus gym applauding at news of Jordan's selection
· File tape of students blocking campus entrances
· File tape of faculty meeting
· Still photograph of Jordan

Available opening graphics include:

· "Gallaudet Student Victory"
· Jordan photo
· Gallaudet campus photo
· "New Gallaudet President"

Available sound bites and running times:

I. KING JORDAN (at hotel where his appointment was announced):

1. In this week, we can truly say that we, together and united, have overcome our reluctance to stand for our rights and our full representation.

(runs :10)

2. The world has watched the deaf community come of age. We will no longer accept limits on what we can achieve.

(runs :09)

3. I must give the highest of praise to the students of Gallaudet for showing us all exactly how, even now, one can seize an idea with such force of argument that it becomes a reality.

(runs :13)

JANE SPILMAN (at same hotel, announcing her resignation):

1. I took this step willingly. In the minds of some, I've become an obstacle. I am removing that obstacle.

(runs :07)

PAUL SINGLETON, Gallaudet graduate student (in campus gym):

1. We love it. We know now the university is going to be ours.

(runs :05)

2. He (Jordan) is the perfect president, the perfect selection.

(runs :04)

(Remember to insert electronic title cues wherever necessary.)

Reporting I: The Assignment 18

Television news reporters are on call 24 hours a day. They are expected to be reachable any time, anywhere. Even when away on vacation, they had better be *far* away, because when a major story breaks, vacation schedules are as worthless as three-dollar bills.

Nowadays, the paging device you hear go off in a public place is just as likely to be worn by a TV reporter as by a doctor. A 3 A.M. wake-up call is as likely to be a summons to cover a fire as to deliver a baby.

News events, like babies, are not born according to nice, convenient schedules. And TV reporters are more likely than print or radio reporters to have their personal lives disrupted because of TV's need for relevant pictures. Videotape of the aftermath of an event, while a standard element of news coverage, is rarely good enough in the competitive world of broadcasting. The pictures are wanted *now*. The interviews are wanted *now*. The reporter's pager is beeping *now*.

Unfortunately, many people try to get into TV news reporting because, deep down, they have the same emotional desires as many actors and models: to be loved, to become "famous," to receive adulation, to get preferential treatment at restaurants and hotels—and the other "perks" of work performed in the public eye. Such people quickly discover, however, that TV news reporting is nine parts preparation and hard work and one part show business. Either they accept preparation and hard work, or they drop out.

That preparation begins long before reporters receive their daily assignments. Their news directors expect them to be "tigers," the sort of self-starters we mentioned many chapters ago, people who stay on top of the news and who cannot wait to tackle fresh angles. They are expected to originate their own story ideas instead of waiting for something to happen.

Then, once they are on the job, the working atmosphere is one of ceaseless competition—not just against reporters at other stations, but also among reporters at the *same* station. Landing the major, lead story of a television newscast is like landing on a newspaper's front page: You don't always land there by accident; you have to outhustle your colleagues. And if Reporter Smith can't handle an assignment, it'll be given to Reporter Jones, and soon Smith may be looking for a job in another line of work.

Now that we've presented the tough-as-nails side of the job, we really must be fair and present the pleasant side as well. Sure, the pay is good (in major markets and at networks), and it's nice to get preferential treatment at restaurants. But when you get right down to it, the pleasant side is this: There are few professional rewards, few feelings, like having covered and presented an important story well—the feeling of exhilaration at having been *the link* between momentous events and the public's perception of them.

Usually, such accomplishments are recognized by one's peers rather than by the public. Only one's peers know the long odds, the tension, the preparation, the hard work, that went into the final product. A simple "Well done!" from the news director is worth any amount of preferential treatment by waiters.

PREPARING THE STORY

Preparing and gathering coverage for television is a vastly different enterprise from what transpires in either print or radio. A print reporter can "work the phones" and immediately thereafter begin to write the story. A radio reporter can also work the phones, recording foners for actualities where appropriate, and be ready to air the story in short order. But when a TV reporter works the phones, his or her job is just beginning.

Sometimes, before handing reporters their assignments, the assignment editor or an assistant may have done some of the groundwork, arranging for permission for the camera team to attend an otherwise private event, jotting down phone numbers of important people involved in the story, and noting their various locations and travel plans. But likely as not, reporters themselves will have to track down this information.

In working the phones, TV reporters are seeking *two types* of information: (1) details of the story itself and (2) details of the *visual possibilities* of each story element. They may quickly learn what the story is all about, but now they must arrange for pictures and interviews to *illustrate* the story. They must decide not only whom to interview but also *where* the interviews should take place.

Interviews of people sitting in offices make for dull viewing. A factory owner's or manager's office may be plush, but it is still just an office. The interview should thus be arranged on the factory floor, where the setting *shows* the production process. The reporter needs to know ahead of time what the picture is likely to show, whether there's enough light, and whether it's likely to be too noisy to record clear sound.

Sometimes, of course, office interviews are unavoidable. Some executives and officials are simply too busy to allow a disruption of their schedules merely to accommodate a TV camera. Just the same, TV reporters should always strive to arrange interviews at suitable, picturesque locations. A doctor taped at a clinic is better than a doctor taped in an office. An attorney taped outside a courtroom or court building is better than an attorney taped in a law office. A politician calling for increased Medicare benefits is better taped at a nursing home or "senior-citizen" gathering than at a news conference.

It is a truism that "news is people." No one knows this better than TV reporters, who consistently try to show people in the visual framework of the story. This is nothing less than the main goal of television news coverage. Newspapers can quote people at length. Radio can bring us their voices. Only television can show them to us in a setting which serves as a visual framework of a story's context. Which is a better, more "journalistic" picture: an auto mechanic peering out from under a jacked-up car or an auto mechanic on a coffee break?

In short, even before leaving the station, TV reporters must have a pretty good idea not only of what the story is, but also how they will tell it and what it will look like. Things may not work out exactly as foreseen, but reporters nevertheless should clearly have thought through the pictures they will need, element by element and location by location.

Although we've perhaps made this sound terribly organized, almost as if taping the story elements were a mere formality, that is seldom the case. Often, the picture you want is inaccessible. Often, interview subjects refuse to go on-camera. Often, nobody's home or you get a busy signal. Often, when someone does answer, the reply is "No comment." Often, planning ahead is impossible because the story is breaking and the reporter and camera operator must fly out the door. Often, it's likely to be a hit-or-miss proposition. Like much of life itself, TV newsrooms often operate in chaotic conditions—cowboys trying to round up stampeding cattle.

A reporter's challenge is to impose order on this chaos whenever possible. Planning ahead increases the reporter's chances of returning with a well-photographed, well-scripted story. If coverage doesn't pan out in TV terms, the story may end up as a 30-second reader instead of a 2-minute package. One way or another, it gets on the air. Whether it gets on the air with the reporter's name on it is due partly to luck, but mostly to the reporter's own skill, drive, and hustle.

SHOOTING THE STORY

Technical matters such as camera operation, setups, shooting angles, and so on will be discussed in following chapters. At this point, however, we should note that at most stations the reporter's and camera operator's overall approach to gathering story elements in the field is to get the job done *quickly* whenever possible. Only networks and fully staffed major-market stations can afford to allow reporters and cameras to linger on assignments. Much depends, of course, on the nature of a story. But overall, the approach is to work fast in order to free up the camera for other assignments.

In small and medium markets, reporters and camera operators routinely cover several stories a day, with each camera operator shooting tape for more than one reporter. The quicker the tape is shot, the quicker a reporter writes and records his or her narration, the quicker the tape gets back to an editing room, the quicker the newscast can be assembled, and the fewer the last-minute headaches for the producer.

Such speedy field coverage is sometimes referred to by TV journalists as working "down and dirty." The term is pejorative; reporters and camera operators would prefer to remain at a location long enough to get the best possible story angles and the best possible pictures. Unfortunately, the logistics of TV newsgathering at most local stations usually preclude such an approach. Faced with a dallying reporter/camera team, more than one frustrated assignment editor has been known to exclaim, "Come on, folks—this is *news,* not art!"

PUTTING THE PIECES TOGETHER

While in the field, the reporter calls in periodically to discuss with the assignment editor and the producer the progress of the shooting. The producer wants to know if the story is working out and, if so, how much air time the reporter thinks it will require. They discuss the story briefly, and in the end it is the producer who decides if the reporter will "package" the story and how long it will run, or if the newscast will go merely with some AVO and perhaps a sound bite.

If the decision is for a package, the reporter will either write and record a narration (called *track;* short for "sound track") in the field or return to the station to do it. Naturally, it is more comfortable back at the station. More than likely, the camera will be wanted elsewhere, and the reporter will indeed be able to return to the newsroom, get some coffee, sit at a desk, gather his or her thoughts, and compose a nicely written track.

Often, however, that proves to be wishful thinking. The reporter may be instructed to wrap up the story quickly, before heading with the crew to a new location. The reporter may thus have to scribble out a narration in the field, perhaps leaning against a fender of the news van or sitting on a curb—environments not entirely conducive to creative thought.

Once the track is written, and before it is recorded (on a separate videocassette), the reporter calls the producer to read the copy aloud for the producer's approval. At least that's the way it's *supposed* to work. But as we noted in an earlier chapter, this simple measure of editorial control is often lacking. Time may be short, or the producer may distracted by other matters. The reporter may thus record his or her copy unproofed and unedited. This is how errors of fact and of grammar get into what you sometimes hear on local TV newscasts. Once a narration is on tape and sent back to the station for editing along with the pictures, there is no simple way to correct it; the reporter and crew are miles away and perhaps miles apart. Thus, the producer is faced with an unhappy choice: whether to use the narration complete with errors, or to junk the package and substitute writer-written AVO. And producers in local TV are extremely reluctant to junk packages that have cost so much time and effort to obtain.

Reporter David Jackson and producer Kerry Brace of KCAL-TV, Los Angeles, discuss the length and structure of Jackson's package for the Six-Thirty News. Reporter Jackson makes requests and recommendations; producer Brace makes the final decisions.

Jackson then records his track (narration) for VTR editor George Brown. The two of them will edit Jackson's package jointly, Jackson supervising and Brown operating the editing console. (If Jackson were working in a smaller market, he would likely shoot, record, and edit the package himself, without the aid of staff technicians).

This lack of editorial control over reporters' copy recorded in the field is endemic in television at the local level. Reporters at networks and major-market stations are expected *not* to make such errors as a condition of continuing employment. In other words, a reporter who consistently writes badly or whose narrations repeatedly contain factual errors is fired. It's as simple as that.

GOING LIVE

Nowadays, reporters routinely stay in the field to go live during the newscast via minicam and microwave. Live coverage works best when an event is still going on at news time. More typical, however, is the situation where the story is basically over and the reporter is merely required to do a live tag or live opener and tag/sign-off—and perhaps answer a few questions from the anchor (Q/A).

Here is how a typical "live shot" proceeds technically. The reporter writes and records a *protected* narration for the pictures already shot. That much of the package is sent back to the station (by microwave or special courier) for editing. The reporter then prepares opening and closing copy which

Going Live

A van equipped for live remote transmission features, in addition to the normal recording and accessory gear, an adjustable microwave transmitter (powered by a gasoline-fed generator), heavy-duty cables, and two-way radio links to both the master control room at the station and the main transmitting tower which relays the minicam's signal.

WMAQ-TV, Chicago

Reporters going live from the field wear an earphone through which they can hear both the live program audio and the director's instructions. Usually the earphone wire is worn under the jacket or taped to the reporter's back so that the viewers can't see it.

WMAQ-TV, Chicago

WBBM-TV, Chicago

he or she delivers live, on cue, around the taped portion which is played from the station. (Radio reporters will recognize this as a type of wraparound—just one of the reasons why working in radio can be good training for TV.)

This sounds complicated, and, quite frankly, it *is* complicated, not to mention nerve-wracking. In addition to coordinating the segment with a staffer back at the station (by discussing picture elements and sound bites, and by exchanging precise roll cues shortly before air time), the field reporter must be "wired in" during his or her live segment, not just to the newscast itself (Program Audio), but to the director's commands as well (via IFB—Internal Frequency Broadcast). While delivering live on-camera copy, the reporter must simultaneously be listening to the director's or producer's instructions via an earphone.

WRAPPING UP

The reporter's day is not finished after recording his or her narration or going live during the Early News. There's still the Late News to worry about. Whether in the field or back at the station, the reporter consults with the Late News producer to determine if there should be (1) a late angle for that show or, failing that, (2) a rewritten version of the Early News package.

In the first case, the reporter will grab a sandwich (maybe, if there's time) and head back to the field along with a camera operator to continue working the story. In the second case, the reporter writes and records a fresh version of the package—a *protected* one that will stand up overnight for possible replay the next morning during a local cut-in in network news programming. (To reiterate the rules for protecting copy: The reporter does *not* mention the date or time of day and *omits* details subject to short-term change, such as casualty figures; all such details are left for the anchor's lead-in, which will be written shortly before air time.)

Producer Kerry Brace takes her place in the KCAL-TV master control room at the start of the Six-Thirty News. Often, late-breaking developments force her to change the newscast significantly while it is on the air. She must remain unruffled while coordinating live coverage from various field locations with control-room personnel—often a complicated, nerve-wracking procedure.

Then the reporter can go home. At least for a while. As we said at the start of this chapter, reporters are on call 24 hours a day.

INFLUENCING EVENTS

On the evening of March 4, 1983, the assignment desk at WHMA-TV in Jacksonville, Alabama, received repeated phone calls from an unemployed factory worker named Cecil Andrews. Andrews said he was going to stage a "personal protest" against joblessness in America later that night. Without explaining the nature of his protest, he insisted he wanted a WHMA-TV camera to be there.

At around 11 P.M., a WHMA crew, comprised of two young station employees, rendez-voused with Andrews in the town square. They were the only news media representatives present.

Andrews, visibly disturbed, told them he was going to douse himself with lighter fluid and set himself on fire. *That* would be the form of his "protest against joblessness." Not knowing whether to believe Andrews, the WHMA crew set up its camera and turned on a light.

As the videotape rolled, Andrews proceeded to carry out his "protest." For 37 seconds, as the fire ignited and spread through Andrews's clothing, the camera crew continued to tape. Then, when Andrews became literally engulfed in flames and began dashing around the square in panic, the TV crew joined passersby in a frantic effort to save the man's life. Someone finally aimed a garden hose at Andrews and quenched the fire. Andrews was rushed to a hospital with critical burns over much of his body.

The next day, WHMA and its two young staffers found themselves at the center of a storm of controversy. Had Andrews nearly killed himself only for the camera's benefit? Would he have carried out his misguided "protest" without the camera's presence? (He later said he would have.) Should the camera crew have just stood there, continuing to record events as Andrews burned? Should they even have set up their camera and turned on a light? Without getting details of Andrews's plans over the phone, should the station even have sent its camera crew to meet with him?

These are not easy questions to answer. The camera crew later explained their behavior by reminding questioners that while they were indeed appalled at Andrews's actions, they had been trained as journalists never to intervene or influence events. They said they were able to overcome that training only when it became clear that Andrews had not completely thought out the consequences of setting himself afire and clearly did not wish to die.

With 20/20 hindsight, it is easy to conclude that WHMA should never have let itself be lured into providing a forum for an apparent lunatic. But that begs the question. The reality of a society permeated by television is that cameras will inevitably seek out the lurid and the bizarre. Attention seekers know this. And, to a degree, cameras *automatically* influence events.

The WHMA case may have pushed the matter to extremes, but as any TV reporter or camera operator can testify, the camera's mere presence causes people to alter their behavior. The changes may be subtle, as when people casually rearrange their hair or straighten their clothing; or they may be pronounced, as when attention seekers wave and clamor "Me! Me!" This is a special problem for TV journalists, who can tolerate subtle changes in behavior but who abhor major ones that can influence the flow of news events.

Typically, the camera's presence triggers an apparent reflex action among many people, especially youngsters, to wave and shout. Some teenagers go so far as to dash to wherever the camera is pointed, plant themselves squarely in front of the lens, and wave "hello" to the world. Such activity is annoying in the extreme, but it is basically harmless. Reporters and camera operators must deal with it almost daily, not by threatening bodily harm to the perpetrators (who, in any event, outnumber the camera team), but by asking politely but firmly for their cooperation. If that doesn't work, then a camera position must be found that effectively blocks the offenders' access to the shot.

As the WHMA episode demonstrates, all that is a minor problem next to the possibility of the camera causing distortion of events, or in effect, causing the events to happen. Most people these days know the power of television. They presume—sometimes rightly—that pictures of their activities on the Six O-'clock or Eleven O'clock News can lend credence and validation to those activities. This leads many people and organizations to stage "news events" (typically called "photo opportunities") *with the main intention* of garnering TV coverage. This occurs frequently at political or issue-oriented rallies and demonstrations: A group of pickets or demonstrators may swing into action only when they see the camera approaching.

Experienced reporters and camera operators must know how to deal with these situations. For one thing, they should keep the camera out of sight until they have assessed the true nature of an event, to make sure that the scene is not being staged for their benefit alone. Since local TV reporters' faces quickly become known in their communities, it is sometimes best for *them* to stay out of sight, too—until the event is actually under way.

Many times, in the end, the camera does roll on such staged events. But in those cases, it is the reporter's duty to explain the circumstances in his or her narration: "In an event apparently staged more for TV cameras than for the public . . . ," and so on. Admittedly, local reporters do not always do this, thus, in effect, bending themselves to the organizers' purposes. But we believe they *should* do it; they should explain the context to viewers. What it comes down to is a matter of journalistic ethics.

The camera is supposed to remain "neutral" at all times. But as the WHMA episode so graphically demonstrated, this is easier said than done. In the last analysis, therefore, the reporter's eye is more important than the camera's—despite the emphasis television news places on pictures.

STAGING

So much for events staged by publicity-hungry newsmakers. What about events staged by TV news crews?

First, "staging" is a term widely misinterpreted by people who do not understand the technical requirements of television. Most people do not know the necessity for cutaways in the editing process. To them, such posed shots can seem to be a form of staging.

So what we're dealing with is largely a semantic problem. All TV news is "staged" in the sense that a camera must be manipulated in an attempt to record reality. The camera lens does not see what the human eye sees. The camera's range, its focus, is much narrower. Thus, the TV picture is essentially the reporter's and camera operator's *interpretation* of reality, in the same sense that a newspaper story is the writer's interpretation of reality, rather than a verbatim record. The TV reporter, like the print reporter, is supposedly a trained professional and thus presumably a better judge than the average citizen of what is truly newsworthy. He or she decides what to show because that's the kind of decision that he or she has been trained to make.

That said, however, it is absolutely, positively *unethical* to *recreate* an event solely for the camera's benefit *unless the viewing audience is expressly told of this fact.* Viewers must never be led to believe that they are seeing a real event when in fact it is a staged one. That's the true meaning of "staging."

A vivid example of staging was provided in 1992–93 when the NBC newsmagazine "Dateline NBC" broadcast a story alleging design defects in General Motors pickup trucks. The broadcast alleged the trucks' fuel tanks were mounted in a position where they could rupture in a moderate-impact collision; the spewing gas could then catch fire, possibly killing the driver and passengers. NBC's videotape of crash tests it had commissioned for the broadcast showed a GM truck bursting into flame following impact. What NBC failed to tell viewers, however, was that incendiary devices had been mounted under the tested trucks to *ensure* that the gas would catch fire. In other words, the tests were rigged in order to guarantee visually dramatic results.

Several months later, General Motors sued NBC for defamation (libel). GM disclosed "Dateline NBC's" fakery publicly, and, as part of an out-of-court settlement (reportedly costing NBC more than one million dollars), NBC News was forced to admit the deception and to issue a public apology. NBC News also launched an investigation into how and why its own firm internal guidelines against staging and misrepresentation had been ignored. As a result, three of the program's senior staff members were forced to resign, including the executive producer.

Executives and staffers throughout the profession were appalled by the "Dateline NBC" episode, and they vowed to review their own internal procedures to ensure that similar episodes would never recur.*

But how do the issues of staging and misrepresentation apply to the actions of individual reporters and camera crews in the field? Here, as reported by news agencies, is a case in point:

```
        ROSTOCK, Germany--Police said Sunday that authorities may
take legal action against some foreign television crews
accused of paying German youngsters to give the straight-armed
"Hitler salute" in Rostock on Saturday.
        Officials would not identify the television channels but
quoted residents as saying they were American and French.
```

If true, the reported action of TV crews would constitute a gross violation of ethical standards. At some news organizations, such behavior would be grounds for instant dismissal.

To repeat, telling someone how to behave for the camera's benefit is staging. Don't ever do it.

"Transportation"

Sometimes, for perceived purposes of tape editing, it may be necessary to ask someone to repeat a *minor* action that the camera missed, such as entering or leaving a building or vehicle, pointing to a document or object, and so on. For example, let's say you wanted to show someone boarding a bus, first as seen from the street, and then as seen from inside the bus. Since the camera can't be in two places at once, it would be necessary to shoot the first part of the sequence from street level, then ask the passenger to get back out of the bus while the camera crew got on, then ask the passenger to reboard in order to be shown from inside.

Such "staged" shots are for the purpose of providing tape editors with what's known as *transportation,* a visual method of getting from one place to another in a series of scenes. Whenever such shots are deemed necessary, the reporter or camera operator should explain their purpose to the person or persons being taped, thus leaving no doubt in anyone's mind about "staging."

Bear in mind that transportation shots apply to actions that a subject *actually* takes in the

---

*The "Dateline NBC" incident occurred at a time when public confidence in the news media was relatively low. Large numbers of readers and viewers had always been critical of such weekly tabloid newspapers as *The National Enquirer* and such syndicated broadcasts as "A Current Affair," which they considered sensationalistic. But an opinion poll published in 1993 by the *Los Angeles Times* showed a growing number of people perceived *all* news media outlets as more or less sensationalistic, replacing substance with fluff and hard news with soft features.

Ironically, the "Dateline NBC" story on GM pickup trucks *was* a hard news story; the carmaker had just lost, and was appealing, a multi-million-dollar product liability suit in a wrongful death case involving the very issue NBC was investigating. As one executive of a competing network put it, "NBC was onto a good story, but it shot itself and the story down by its improper, unethical, and wholly unnecessary rigged video."

normal course of events. In no case should a reporter or camera operator request that a subject perform an action that he or she would not normally have taken.

THE RIGHT TO KNOW VERSUS THE RIGHT TO PRIVACY

This is a real dilemma. On the one hand, TV reporters try their best to get a story and the pictures to illustrate it. On the other hand, people in the news may not want their pictures taken; perhaps they are emotionally ill-equipped to deal with the camera's presence or fear legal repercussions from public remarks.

Situation: A child is killed in a car accident. The mother is almost hysterical with grief. Should she be interviewed on camera, even with her consent? Should she ever be asked, "How do you *feel?*"

Situation: A man is indicted for embezzlement. Although an indictment is merely an accusation, not a conviction, the man does not want to be photographed or interviewed. Should he be taped anyway, against his wishes, perhaps as he attempts to shield his face from the camera?

Once again, those situations are not hypothetical. The moral quandaries they cause among TV reporters and camera operators are faced day in, day out, in the normal course of news coverage. Which should prevail, the public's "right to know" (that is, *see*) or the individual's "right to privacy"?

Reporters and jurists have been debating this issue ever since the establishment of a free press. But nowhere is the debate more intense than as it regards TV coverage, because *pictures carry emotional weight.* Somehow, the person refusing to defend himself on-camera against an accusation "looks guilty," even though he is merely exercising his constitutional right to remain silent so as not inadvertently to incriminate himself.

So what to do, given TV's intense, inescapable demand for pictures? We are not so foolish as to attempt definitive answers. We know that each case must be weighed on its own merits. However, there are some legal considerations and taping techniques that may help you in deciding:

1. The law says that you may take pictures of people in *public places,* with or without their consent. On *private property,* you may *not* take pictures without the owner's or proprietor's consent. However, if you are standing on public property, aiming your camera at private property, it is the property owner's responsibility to protect his or her own privacy.

2. Even on public premises, secure permission from interviewees and participants whenever feasible. This is a matter of common courtesy. It also results in better interviews. A person's tacit or verbal consent puts him or her in a better frame of mind to handle your questions.

3. Refrain from attempting to interview emotionally overwrought people (such as the grief-stricken mother). Never put yourself, by dint of your very presence, in a position of contributing to another person's pain or sorrow. Wait until such people have recovered their equilibrium. In any case, tape shot *from a distance* with the zoom lens will adequately *show* a person's sorrow. What more could his or her words add in most cases?

4. Do not hound reluctant or reticent people with the camera. You can be forceful, even pushy, but don't be a bully. You have all seen shots where the camera literally chases someone down the street or has caught someone in ambush. Don't do it. So-called "ambush journalism" is frowned on, if not outright forbidden, in all reputable news departments.

Okay, having read all that, don't be surprised if your producer *insists* that you break one or more of those guidelines. The nature of competition is such that the producer is under enormous pressure to have pictures equal to if not "better" than those of competing stations. And, of course, the producer is far removed from the anguished mother's tears and does not have to share the reporter's and camera operator's discomfort at facing her in person.

Most TV news producers are decent human beings who, especially in well-managed and journalistically sound news departments, see no need to include emotionally overwrought videotape in their newscasts. But a few others, realizing that such tape has a very strong visual and emotional appeal for many viewers, will insist that you shoot it occasionally.

In the end, here is yet another area in which you yourself will eventually define your own ethical limits.

EXERCISES

Assume you are a reporter or field producer. The producer of the Six O'Clock News hands you the following story, slugged SECONDHAND SMOKE, and instructs you to use it as the takeoff point for a local package:

```
        WASHINGTON (AP)--Exposure to secondhand smoke accounts for
tens of thousands of serious respiratory ailments each year in
young children, especially infants, the Environmental
Protection Agency reported Thursday.
        The report reiterated a position taken by the agency in a
draft report a year ago that said substantial evidence shows
nonsmokers are at risk of cancer from secondary tobacco smoke.
        The EPA findings, the product of more than a year of
analyzing scores of scientific studies, were submitted to the
agency's Science Advisory Board for review. The science panel
endorsed a preliminary draft a year ago but asked that the
section on children's health risks be strengthened.
        The 600-page report said there are "consistent findings"
in the studies to conclude that young children, especially
those 19 months old or younger, face a substantial health risk
if exposed to secondhand tobacco smoke.
        According to the EPA researchers, exposure to so-called
"environmental tobacco smoke" contributes to between 150,000
and 300,000 serious respiratory ailments, including pneumonia
and bronchitis, among young children and infants annually.
        While children under 18 months old face the greatest
risks, older children also are likely to be affected, the
study said. Between 7,500 and 15,000 of these cases are
serious enough for the child to be hospitalized, the
researchers said.
        The EPA study said that exposure to secondary tobacco
smoke also "exacerbates" asthmatic symptoms in many of the
country's 2 million to 5 million asthmatic children and that
children in households where there are smokers are more likely
to become asthmatic.
        The Tobacco Institute, which represents the tobacco
industry, questioned the EPA researchers' conclusions, arguing
that they did not take into account many other potential
factors, including diet and quality of medical care, that may
increase the likelihood of respiratory illnesses in children.
```

1. Compile a list of the local agencies, organizations, and people you might interview in connection with this story, as well as the locations where you might conduct the interviews.
2. Compile a second list, specifying locations for shooting videotape to illustrate the story's main points, and telling what you expect such tape to show.
3. Draw up an outline of how you would organize the story for presentation on a local newscast, beginning with the anchor's lead-in, and then the package itself, element by element, from start to finish.

Reporting II: Shooting
The Story

19

"READY WHEN YOU ARE, MR. SPIELBERG"

One thing you'll find if you spend any time among TV news people: they love to go to movies. And afterward they like to discuss not only a film's plot but also how it was *shot*—what techniques and camera angles the director and cinematographer used to show various scenes. The TV staffers are thus engaging in a normal propensity to talk shop during nonworking hours.

For better or for worse, a TV reporter is a kind of very junior Steven Spielberg, directing his or her own minimovie on every assignment. The difference, of course, is that the TV reporter's "plot" is fashioned out of reality instead of make-believe, and therefore the reporter must stick to fact rather than invent fiction. A TV reporter's package is nonetheless a *story*. It should have a beginning, a middle (perhaps several middles), and an ending, with a continuity to make its various elements flow smoothly from incue to sign-off. While he or she may not shoot the actual pictures by running the camera, a TV reporter must oversee those pictures at every step of the way, consulting with the camera operator to make sure each story element is shown to best advantage.

By the time they reach college, some young people display a well-developed "visual sense"; through coordination of hand, eye, and aesthetic values, they are able to regard a scene and decide how best to represent it on a stage, drawing board, or video screen. Such people are "naturals" for the theater, painting, photography, movies, TV shows—and TV news. Because their minds already hold the conceptual ability to assess a scene, they find that learning the formal descriptions—long shot, closeup, and so on—comes naturally.

Most budding journalists, however, do not come by this visual sense so easily, either by birth or early training. Journalists deal by and large with ideas, both concrete and abstract, with issues, with thoughts, and with words. Those journalists wishing to enter TV news without an innate visual sense must strive even harder to familiarize themselves with the camera angles and techniques that will enable them to illustrate the words and ideas they so cherish.

It is time, then, to return to nuts and bolts. Before proceeding, we suggest you review the material in Chapter 16 regarding the types and terms of shots, camera movements, and so forth. Henceforth, we'll be using them repeatedly.

TESTING AND MAINTENANCE OF EQUIPMENT

Although TV reporters above the small-market level seldom operate cameras or ancillary equipment, they must at least be familiar with the equipment in order to know what it is capable (or not capable) of doing.

Most stations at all market levels have an engineering or technical services department charged with routine inspection and maintenance of equipment. However, certain minor adjustments may be necessary, and these can be performed by reporters or camera operators:

1. Test the camera and recorder *before* leaving the station. Is the camera battery fully charged? Is the *spare* battery fully charged? Is the tape *fresh?* (Videotape deteriorates with repeated use, resulting in streaks and sparkles that break up the picture.) Is the tape running smoothly in the recorder?

2. Test the microphone. Is the recorded sound clear and unmuffled? Or is there a "hum," an electronic buzz? If so, switch mikes. If the noise continues, switch mike *cables*. If the noise persists, the recorder needs skilled repairing.

3. Shoot 20 or 30 seconds of tape and test the picture playback on a color monitor (*not* just through the eyepiece). Is the image sharp? Are the colors true? If not, take a new white balance and try again. If the colors are still not true, skilled repairs are in order.

4. Last-minute checks: Did you pack the spare battery? Spare cassettes? Did you check the camera light? Have you got a spare bulb? Adhesive tape? A clamp? Aspirin for when you get out in the field and realize you've forgotten any of the above?

BASIC CAMERA TECHNIQUES

There are certain procedures for shooting videotape (or film, for that matter), no matter what type of camera is used:

1. **MOUNT THE CAMERA ON A TRIPOD WHENEVER POSSIBLE. IF YOU MUST HOLD THE CAMERA, HOLD IT STEADY!!!** Engrave that rule on your brain. The point is for the *subject* to move, *not* the camera. The rule is so fundamental that we shall repeat it another way: **Don't move the camera while shooting!!!** Once you frame a shot, do *not* zoom in and out. Pick a shot and hold it. Remember that "movement" is added to a piece in *editing*, not in shooting. If you want to change the shot, stop the camera, reframe the shot, then restart the camera. (True, in the heat of the moment you may have to zoom or pan with the camera rolling in order to keep the subject squarely in the frame. Fine. But never zoom or pan unnecessarily to be "artsy" or "creative." Ultimately, it's the subject of the story that counts, not the camera work.)

2. **ALWAYS SHOOT WITH SOUND.** Anchor Voice Over (AVO) stories are always run with the natural sound under the anchor's voice. This natural sound, as in radio, lends presence. It's an easy matter to kill an unwanted sound track, but if the sound is unrecorded, no one has any choice in the matter. Therefore, always make sure the mike is plugged in and that the sound is being recorded along with the picture. No exceptions.

3. **MAKE SURE THERE IS ADEQUATE LIGHT.** With modern, light-sensitive cameras, much less light is required than formerly. Most outdoor locations, and many indoor locations, have sufficient ambient light for ordinary news coverage. However, at many indoor locations—and even some outdoor ones—a camera-mounted light is a necessity. Here's why: Much indoor lighting, especially overhead lighting, casts shadows in peoples' eye sockets. These shadows are emphasized on videotape, sometimes appearing as black holes. The camera-mounted light fills in these holes. Also, avoid shooting in fluorescent lighting whenever possible; fluorescent light makes the tape look "washed out."

   A well-equipped camera crew also carries a "fill light." This is a stand-mounted light used to fill in any dark areas of a scene, such as the space *behind* an interview subject. In most modern TV news photography, fill lights are not necessary, provided that the shot is framed correctly to begin with.

4. **USE A FRESH CASSETTE AT EACH SETUP, ESPECIALLY AT EACH INTER-VIEW.** Suppose that Mayor Smith is delivering an impromptu speech on a major issue or breaking news development. And suppose that the tape runs out just as the mayor makes his or her most important remark. You can cry and you can curse—but to no avail. Nine times out of ten, however, you can avoid the mishap by making sure a fresh cassette has been inserted into the recorder ahead of time. So what if there was ten minutes' tape time left on the old cassette? Big deal. In a few days, the cassette will be degaussed (erased) for reuse anyway. Play it safe. Start with a fresh cassette, know how much shooting time is left on it, and change it *before* it runs out.

INTERVIEW SHOTS

The one-on-one interview (the much-maligned "talking head") usually accounts for most of the tape shot in connection with a news story—not necessarily for most of the edited tape used in the final piece, but the most *shot*.

It is well to remember while shooting an interview that the point of the exercise is for viewers to focus on what the subject is *saying*. Thus, any distracting camera angles or movements are to be avoided. Since most of an interview is shot in closeup, the camera should be mounted on a tripod wherever possible.

There are a number of standard shots to any interview. Here they are, *in the order in which they should be taped*.

Setup Shots

A *setup shot* should be taken at the start of every interview. A setup shot is an MS showing the interviewee face-on and the reporter facing the interviewee with his or her back to the camera, ready to ask questions. The setup shot should run for about 10 seconds and should include several seconds in which the interviewee is seen listening as the reporter asks a question. That way, a natural-looking edit can be made directly to a sound bite.

Why take setup shots? How are they used in editing? Well, you'll recall that in radio copy the lead-in to an actuality typically identifies the upcoming voice. In TV news, such identification can be made by electronic title, obviating the need to state it in copy. However, suppose you *do* want to state it in copy. Suppose you want your eventual narration to say

```
                              That's what I asked Widget
                          President Oxnard Piltdown today.
```

                                      or

```
                              Widget President Oxnard
                              Piltdown denied the charges
                              categorically.
```

In that case you need a picture to stand in *visual apposition* to your copy. Remember the basic rule about TV writing: Words and pictures must correspond. Thus, the setup shot is for the few seconds of narration that set up the sound bite. It's the visual equivalent of a lead-in.

Closeups

The interview closeup (CU) shows the subject's head and shoulders, framed in such a way that a lower-third electronic title can be inserted comfortably under the subject's chin during the telecast.

Once the setup shot is completed, the camera should tighten to the closeup. Thereafter, the shot should not—repeat, *not*—be altered during the *entire* interview proper. The camera should *not zoom* in and out. Remember that zooms can't be edited. If you want to edit a sound bite that happens to occur in the middle of a zoom, you're out of luck. So once the interview closeup is framed, stick with it.

Cutaways, Reverse Angles, and Point of View (POV)

After the interview proper, the camera operator goes on to provide the requisite editing tools. He or she will look first for a cutaway that can be shot from the position the camera is already in. While the reporter and interviewee continue to converse (perhaps they discuss the weather—although the reporter would be better advised to use this occasion to double-check the spelling of the interviewee's name and title), the camera operator perhaps shoots a closeup of the reporter's notebook as he or she scribbles notes; or perhaps a closeup of the interviewee's hands (which might be clasped).

Then, at last, the camera is ready to move. As the interviewee and reporter *remain in their positions,* the camera *moves to the opposite side* of the location to shoot from the *reverse angle.* It is from this new location that the camera will shoot *reaction cutaways* showing the reporter face-on. Here's where things can get tricky.

The camera does not see precisely what the reporter sees during the interview. The camera sees the interviewee looking directly at the reporter. But because the camera cannot occupy exactly the same space as the reporter, it will appear in the closeup that the interviewee is looking either slightly to the right or slightly to the left, depending on where the reporter is sitting (or standing). The key to finding the correct angle for reverse-angle cutaways lies in the interviewee's *eyes.* If the angle on the reporter's eyes is not the *exact opposite* of the angle on the interviewee's eyes, the cutaways will make it seem as if the two people were looking away from each other rather than at each other. Thus, if in closeup the interviewee is seen looking left, the reporter in reverse angle must be seen looking right; if the interviewee is seen looking right, the reporter must be seen looking left.

This phenomenon is called *point of view* (POV), and it can only be appreciated in the editing room. The best way of covering a jump cut caused by butting two sound bites is by inserting a reaction cutaway. But such a cutaway can not be used if the point of view (the eye direction) does not match.

Our experience is that at least half of you reading this textbook will come back with wrong-angle cutaways from your first field reporting assignment. So if it happens to *you,* don't feel badly. You'll have plenty of company. But do try to remember the formula:

Interviewee's eyes looking left = reporter's eyes looking right.

Interviewee's eyes looking right = reporter's eyes looking left.

Some of you may already have figured out one of the implications of reverse-angle photography: Because the camera can tighten to show only the reporter's face, it isn't always necessary for the interviewee to be present. In fact, some cutaways *are* shot in the interviewee's absence, because the interviewee was running late and had to leave. It's generally preferable, though, for the interviewee to be included in the shot.

(While we are on the subject of reaction cutaways, there is some dispute over what reporters should be seen *doing* in them. They should be seen listening, of course. But should they also be seen *smiling* or *nodding?* Some news executives say no, that to smile or nod indicates agreement with what the interviewee is saying, and it's clearly not a reporter's role to agree or disagree. Other news executives scoff at this, saying a smile is only human and a nod merely means "I understand," without implying partiality. If you wish to be on the safe side, however, it's probably better not to smile or nod.)

Shooting an Interview

1. WBBM-TV (Chicago) reporter Terry Savage, sound technician Bob Gadbois, and camera operator Steve Lasker set up for an interview. The reporter and interviewee are wearing clip-on microphones. Once everyone is in position and the crew has checked the operation of both sound and picture, the interview can proceed.

2. During the interview, the reporter and crew note the relative positions of the interviewee, the reporter, and the camera. Since (as shown here) the reporter is sitting slightly to the right of the camera, the interviewee will be seen looking slightly to the right. This dictates the positions for subsequent cutaways and reverse angles.

3. The interview begins with an MS (as seen here through the camera lens), also known as a "setup shot." This may prove useful in editing to "cover" the reporter's eventual lead-in copy.

4. The camera then tightens to a CU and remains there for the entire interview. The camera does *not* zoom in and out. (Note the eye direction of the interviewee. Although from her point of view she is looking to the left, TV news terminology derives from the *camera's* point of view. Thus, for our purposes, she is looking to the right.)

5. The interview proper now completed, the camera crew changes position to shoot reverse-angle editing tools, chiefly cutaways. Because they noted that the interviewee was seen looking slightly to the camera's right, the crew chooses an angle to show the reporter looking slightly to the camera's left. Ordinarily, and unless the shooting area is extremely cramped, the reporter and interviewee themselves do not have to move.

6. The reverse angle MS as seen through the camera lens. The reporter is shown listening, taking notes, and perhaps repeating a few of the questions asked in the interview proper. It is important to get the interviewee talking, however briefly; even though all we see is the back of the interviewee's head, the act of speaking causes head movement that looks natural as an editing tool.

7. The reverse angle cutaway in CU. Note that the reporter's eye direction is exactly the opposite of the interviewee's, forming a visual match that will look natural on the air. (If the interviewee cannot remain present for the cutaways, the reporter must *pretend* to be looking at someone; the eye direction must match even if no one is there.)

8. Similarly, a person who is seen during an interview to be looking to the camera's left . . .

9. . . . requires WBBM-TV reporter John Davis to be seen looking to the camera's right in the reverse angle. When doing several interviews for the same story, some interviewees should be taped looking left, others looking right. This provides a sort of "visual balance" when sound bites are edited together without intervening narration.

Reverse Questions

At the same time as the reaction cutaways are being taken, the reporter has an opportunity to repeat the questions he or she asked during the interview. The reporter looks at the interviewee and rattles off two or three questions in succession, to which the interviewee does *not* respond. Questions repeated in this fashion are called *reverse questions,* and they provide tape editors with additional tools. For example, inserting reverse questions can relieve some of the visual sameness of a long interview. However, there are very strict rules regarding how they should be shot:

1. Any question asked in reverse angle must be essentially *the same question* asked during the actual interview. Obviously, by asking a slightly different question, the reporter, already knowing the answer, could distort that answer in a crucial way. And that would be clearly unethical.
2. Because the camera can tighten to a CU of the reporter, it isn't technically necessary for the interviewee to be present during the taping of reverse questions. However, most news departments require the interviewee's presence as an *ethical* consideration. The interviewee is requested to remain present to ensure that there can be no distortion of his or her remarks. It may thus be necessary following an interview to explain to an interviewee inexperienced in television the nature and purpose of reverse questioning as an editing tool.

Frankly, some reporters use reverse questions as a means of clearing up any bobbles or poor choice of words in their original questions. Since TV is a medium where performance counts, such cosmetic use of the camera is occasionally permissible—as long as the end result is to clarify the content of a story rather than just to provide an ego trip for the reporter.

In any case, on the matter of reverse questions, as with so many ethical matters, the reporter must know his or her news department's policy.

Continuity

In TV news coverage, as in movie making, the term *continuity* refers to visual harmony. Let's say you go to see an Arnold Schwarzenegger movie. In one scene, you notice that the Terminator is wearing a jet-black T-shirt under his leather jacket. In the next scene, the T-shirt is dark blue. What happened? Did the Terminator mix up his laundry? No, the scenes were shot on different days, and someone forgot to keep track of the colors of Arnie's wardrobe.

That happens very rarely in Hollywood because people are hired for the express purpose of guarding against such visual anomalies. In TV news, though, that responsibility falls to the reporter and camera operator.

What could happen during an interview? Well, let's say you're interviewing Senator Piltdown (the Piltdowns are a large family) in his office. The good senator is doing his blustering best to explain why he has been absent from the last 6,000 roll-call votes. Amid the blustering, a member of his staff interrupts the interview to deliver a written message. The camera stops rolling during this interlude as Piltdown puts on his reading glasses to glance at the message. He chuckles, lays the message aside, and you resume the interview, followed by cutaways and reverse angles. Back at the station, playing back the tape, you decide that the best sound bite would entail a bit from the start of the interview plus a bit from the end, with one of those reaction cutaways to cover the internal jump cut. Only you find you can't edit it that way after all because, as if by magic, Piltdown is suddenly wearing eyeglasses! To viewers it would look as if he somehow managed to put them on during the 2 seconds we watched the reporter in the cutaway. (Hey, maybe the guy's got quick hands.) But if so, why? After all, he's not *reading* anything that they can see.

That is the sort of visual anomaly that can ruin continuity, and reporters and camera operators must constantly guard against it. In this example, either the reporter or the camera operator should have politely asked the senator to remove his glasses before resuming taping.

Other things to watch out for include objects in people's hands (which can seem to magically disappear or reappear out of nowhere) and smokers (whose cigarettes can seem to burn out in a trice or whose pipes can magically appear to be lit by unseen hands).

As we're about to see, there are certain "cover shots" that can be used to explain such mysteries visually, but they are a bother, and it's best to avoid having to shoot them.

Inserts

As the name implies, an *insert* is a shot, usually a CU or ECU, inserted into a sequence (series of scenes) to show in detail an object or process being described either by the reporter or by a speaker or interviewee.

Suppose that you are interviewing a home burglary victim who says,

> "What they didn't steal, they broke. They smashed everything of value. That vase over there? It's been in the family for over a hundred years."

Since this was said during an interview, the shot of the burglary victim is in CU. It doesn't show the vase. But the reporter has been listening closely and has made a note to shoot an insert of the vase following the interview. The edited sound bite can then start on the victim, and the tape editor can insert the video of the vase at the precise time we hear the victim mention it. This serves the double purpose of covering a jump cut and relieving the sameness of watching someone talk. In other words, it follows TV's mandate to *show* us details instead of merely telling us about them.

Inserts are thus extremely valuable shots, and reporters should be constantly alert for them. In particular, they should seek out:

1. *Still photographs* (preferably in color) of accident or murder victims, missing persons, and story principals who are out of town or otherwise unavailable.
2. *Documents* such as government reports, legal briefs, graphs, and diagrams.
3. *Small objects* specifically referred to by speakers or interviewees which, in the reporter's opinion, may be used either in his or her own package or as a still frame in an electronic graphic.

An insert shot as shown on WBBM-TV, Chicago. Since inserts often show documents and other textual material meant to be read by viewers, the camera must remain absolutely steady during taping—usually by mounting the document on a wall and shooting it from a tripod.

The camera lens must usually get very close to such objects in order to frame them fully. But the camera's very closeness magnifies the jarring effect of not holding it steadily. Whenever possible, therefore, objects photographed as inserts should be mounted on a wall and the camera mounted on a tripod. (A single short strip of transparent tape should be sufficient to keep a wall-mounted document in place; if that doesn't work, a document can often be set upright, leaning vertically, against the base of a lamp or other upright object on a desktop.) Professional videographers shoot small objects with a hand-held camera only if they have the arm strength to remain absolutely unwavering—or when they are in a big hurry to get to another location.

Another type of insert is the "cover shot" mentioned earlier. Let's return to the case of Senator Piltdown's eyeglasses: What's needed here (since the reporter forgot to ask the senator to remove his glasses before resuming the interview) is a shot showing the senator putting on his glasses. The shot can't be face-on because it wouldn't match the rest of what we see. So it has to be from *behind* the senator, who must be shown talking to the reporter as he puts on his glasses. The shot may then be used as a cutaway to bridge the two parts of the edited sound bite. Similarly, an interviewee may be shown lighting a pipe, dashing out a cigarette, placing an object on a desk, or picking the object up.

But to repeat: Shooting such cover shots is cumbersome and time-consuming. It is better to avoid them by being alert for visual anomalies during the main setup, and requesting that people leave their glasses either on or off, that smokers refrain from smoking during the interview process, and so forth.

"Quickie" Interviews

Many of the sound bites used on the air result not from formal, sit-down interviews, but rather from brief conversations that barely qualify for the name "interview." A so-called "quickie" interview results when either the reporter or the newsmaker is pressed for time. The interview is usually done standing up, the CU of the newsmaker hastily framed against a neutral background. The reporter uses a hand mike (instead of two lavaliere or clasp mikes), aiming it back and forth at whichever mouth is speaking.

Typically, the interview is only two or three questions long, possibly even shorter if the newsmaker comes to the point without prodding. Even so, a reaction cutaway *is* necessary as an editing tool, even if the interviewee must dash off. Here's how to shoot a reaction cutaway in the interviewee's absence.

The camera should remain stationary. However, it should swivel (pan) slightly to tighten on the reporter in CU. The reporter then pivots in the correct direction to be taped for a matching cutaway. (Remember the formula for finding the "correct" direction: eyes *left/right* or eyes *right/left*.) The reporter and camera operator share responsibility for making sure that the angles match during the editing process.

One other thing about shooting such cutaways: the position of the *microphone*. If the mike is held differently in the cutaway than it was during the interview, the result will be a visual anomaly of the type mentioned earlier. It is thus best to frame the reaction cutaway close enough on the reporter to cut the hand mike out of the picture altogether. Otherwise, the reporter must pretend to thrust it back and forth as he or she did during the interview.

Group Interviews

Very often, a reporter must interview more than one person at a time: the family of a missing child, the co-winners of a prize, the co-inventors of a new widget, and so on. Although each member of the group can be interviewed separately in the manner described earlier, the very fact of their being a group with a shared interest in the matter at hand may make it desirable to show them together in the same picture. This raises a few technical problems.

First, there won't be enough microphones to wire each participant separately. The mikes will thus have to be positioned to capture sound from more than one direction. This means the shooting location must be especially quiet.

Second, the camera may not always be focused on the specific interviewee who spontaneously pops up with a response, forcing the camera operator to adjust the shot, which may result in a jarring movement or brief loss of focus. Thus, an array of cutaways is necessary (in addition to the standard reaction shot of the reporter) to cover up the momentary loss of usable video. Separate cutaways should be shot of:

1. The reporter in CU looking *in both directions*—looking left, turning the head, and looking right. (Remember, some members of the group were looking right during the interviews, others were looking left.)
2. Each member of the group in CU, listening silently to the other members of the group. (Actually, these shots may already be available in the outtakes—the unused portions—of the interviews proper.)
3. The entire group, *taped from behind,* as the reporter listens, first turning his or her attention from left to right, holding for a moment, then turning from right to left. (The camera does not move—just the reporter's head and shoulders.)

These shots enable the tape editor to cover jarring or unfocused video from any direction.

Important: The same types of cutaways should be taken in the case of standing interviews of two or more persons where the reporter is holding a hand mike. The reporter should be seen turning not just his or her attention, but also *the microphone,* in each direction.

A Short Q/A

Questions frequently raised by beginning reporters and camera operators—and the answers:

Q: Where should the interviewee be looking — at the reporter or into the camera?

A: At the reporter. The camera is taping a conversation between two people who would normally be looking at each other, not at some piece of machinery. To look at the camera would appear unnatural.

Q: How does the reporter know when the camera is rolling?

A: The camera operator announces it, usually just by saying, "Okay, rolling." Nothing fancy.

Q: Should the reporter pause between the end of an interviewee's answer and the start of his or her next question, or should the reporter jump right in as fast as possible?

A: The reporter should pause slightly. The half-second or so of silence facilitates tape editing, reducing the likelihood of "up-cutting" either person's remarks (the same as in radio interviewing).

Q: Should the reporter really be taking notes, or should the reporter maintain unbroken eye contact with the interviewee as in a "normal" conversation?

A: Pick your own method. But if you decide not to take notes, you may forget something important later when you write your narration. For this reason, some reporters carry a small audiocassette recorder as a handy way to keep a separate record of the interview, thus relieving themselves of having to take detailed notes. The audiocassette can also be used to verify the exact wording of questions to be repeated during reverse-angle shooting.

Q: What if the interviewee gets tongue-tied or says something inaccurate through oversight rather than by design? Should the reporter intervene?

A: Yes, by stopping the interview momentarily. The reporter should say something like, "Hold on a second, please. You just said January fourth, which is next Tuesday. But I thought the vote was set for next Monday, the third." (That's a reporter who *listens!*) The interviewee, whose train of thought had caused the lapse, will be grateful. (If the interviewee wants to put his foot in his mouth about something important, fine and dandy. Don't help him in that case.) When the tape resumes rolling, the reporter should repeat the earlier question.

Q: Should a reporter ever suggest wording or substantive remarks to an interviewee?

A: No, never. That's staging.

Q: During the reaction cutaways, while the reporter is listening or pretending to listen, what should the interviewee be doing?

A: Talking, even though we see just the back of the interviewee's head and (obliquely) the lips moving. The reporter should ask a question, then listen for a few seconds while the interviewee talks. The edited video will then match the edited audio. (The reporter may have to explain to the interviewee why the camera has had to change positions).

Q: Should the interviewee actually answer the reverse questions?

A: No, because the camera is now in the "wrong" place. On occasion, though, the second hearing of the question will cause the interviewee to recall some important point he or she forgot to make during the interview. In this case, when the reporter agrees that the point is important, the camera should be set up anew in its former position. Taping can then proceed to pick up the missed point.

Q: Is one profile or eye direction better than the other?

A: No. However, when several interviews are done in connection with the same story, some interviewees should be looking right, others looking left. This provides a form of visual balance and is especially effective when conflicting views are edited together (face to face, as it were).

INTERVIEWING TECHNIQUES

Please review the radio interviewing techniques described in Chapter 12. In terms of preparation and approach, these techniques apply in television as well. The goal is to elicit comments that are both newsworthy *and* capable of being excerpted as sound bites.

However, the TV camera, with its big lens and attendant microphones and lights, can be far more intimidating to an interviewee than a mere telephone or audiocassette recorder. There is nothing subtle or casual about recording a TV interview. In major markets and at networks, three people (reporter, camera operator, and sound technician) confront a single interviewee—who thus may feel outnumbered and outgunned.

Put yourself in the interviewee's place: There's a light shining in your eyes, you're facing two or three strangers, one of whom is pointing a microphone at you and another of whom is aiming a fancy camera at you from a distance of only a few feet, and the one with the mike is trying to get you to address an issue about which you must choose your words carefully. In these conditions, you may be forgiven if you start perspiring or become tongue-tied.

Interviewing for television thus requires a special knack on the part of reporters. They should be able to put an interviewee at ease, to somehow render him or her oblivious to all the electronic paraphernalia. This is all the more difficult because reporters themselves cannot be oblivious to it. Reporters have an advantage, however: They work with cameras day in and day out, and are thus able to cope with their presence as a matter of course. Their task, then, is to project an aura of professionalism during the entire interview situation. Nothing makes an interviewee more ill at ease than a reporter who seems confused about what he or she is doing. (Would *you* be calm around a doctor who fumbles a stethoscope or a nurse who looks unsure about where to plunge the needle while taking a blood sample?) Reporters should appear to be unconcerned about the camera's presence—even though they may secretly be worried about how it's all going to turn out in the editing room.

Some people, of course, will be nervous or unresponsive (or both) no matter how professional the reporter. One of the cruel realities of television is that in practice it discriminates against some types of people, no matter how valid or valuable their opinions. TV news demands clarity of content from all concerned. But people who tremble, who ramble, whose voices crack or are extremely grating or unpleasant, or who are physically grotesque, will rarely be shown on TV—not because of some half-baked notion of protecting viewers from unpleasantness, but rather because their voice, appearance, or manner of speaking detracts attention from what they have to say and thus from the clarity of the news story itself.

On the other hand, many interviewees, especially politicians and public officials, are so accustomed to dealing with the news media that they know the requirements of television as well as any reporter. Such people are adept not only at saying what they want to say regardless of reporters' questions, but also at placing themselves in positions, relative to the camera, that display their most "flattering" angles. (Many office seekers hire "media consultants" to teach them how to do this. It can be amusing to watch such media-savvy people try to maneuver the news cameras into a position that captures their "best" profile.)

As in radio, it is well for the TV reporter to remember that he or she is the interview's manager, politely directing the interviewee where to sit or stand (but not, of course, what to say) and gently but firmly pressing for responsive answers.

DOPE SHEETS

Before proceeding, let's regroup for a moment. We've seen how reporters and camera crews hustle hither and yon, shooting tape here, interviewing people there, collecting a mass of raw visual and informational material—so much material, in fact, that it's hard to remember it all. And, indeed, memory alone is *not* sufficient. Reporters should keep an accurate record of all persons and locations of which they have tape. That record is commonly called a *dope sheet*. It usually takes the form of a sheet of paper tucked inside the videocassette carrying case.

If for no other reason, accurate dope sheets will allow reporters to recall and organize story elements in the likely event that they will have to write a narration in the field, where there will likely *not* be an opportunity to view the tape ahead of time. (That's another reason why carrying a small audiocassette recorder to tape interviews is a good idea.)

But dope sheets serve another purpose, too. Suppose that you have just shot a group interview with those famous widget experts, John Doe, Millie Moe, and Richard Roe. Nice people, you thought, especially that Richard Roe with his handlebar mustache. A courier brings the tape back to the station while you proceed to your next assignment, the county bubble-gum-blowing semifinals. There you are, notebook and camera poised to see whose face and hair become enshrouded in bubble gum, when suddenly your beeper goes off to call the station immediately. You tear yourself away from this thrilling contest to find a phone. On the other end is the writer handling the widget story. "I've spotted Moe," the writer says urgently, "but which is Doe and which is Roe?"

If you'd sent a dope sheet along with the tape, or at least scribbled a note, the writer wouldn't be bugging you or, more important, losing valuable editing and writing time because of your failure to provide basic information. Roe is the one with a mustache? Then say so on the dope sheet. If no one has a readily distinguishable characteristic, then specify their positions in the frame—right, left, or center. Or, specify who spoke first—Doe or Roe.

This sort of information is *basic* to accurate news coverage. The reporter is the member of the TV team in the best position to collect accurate identifications. He or she must make sure that the correct information gets to the other members of the team. To this end, some reporters announce the identity of all interview subjects on the tape sound track itself, spelling out names where necessary. But a written record in the form of a dope sheet to accompany the tape is the better method.

(On many shooting assignments, a reporter will receive handout material such as a news release, a text of a speech, or background material. Unless the reporter intends to use this material in writing a narration, it should be returned to the station along with the tape. Handout material can frequently be substituted for a separately written dope sheet, provided that the reporter has noted on the handout itself the identities of speakers and the order in which they appear on the tape. Sometimes the handout material will be the only source material for writers back at the station, so it's important to keep it together with the tape.)

Cassette Labeling

Labeling tape cassettes and carrying cases is the responsibility of the camera operator. The larger the news department, the more critical it is that cassettes be labeled correctly, because many more staffers will need to use them.

On each assignment, a producer or assignment editor gives the story a slug. Henceforth, as the day progresses, each story's components (videotape, narration, writer's lead-in, script, graphics order, and so on) will carry that slug, plus the date. This is to ensure that no component is "lost" or misplaced due to improper labeling.

In the field, reporters and camera operators use as many cassettes as necessary to cover a story. Each cassette should be labeled *both sequentially and cumulatively*. Here, for example, is the correct method of labeling field cassettes for a June sixteenth story slugged "Chemical Spill" which eventually required a total of four (4) cassettes:

· (cassette #1)   CHEMICAL SPILL, 6/16   1 of 4
· (cassette #2)   CHEMICAL SPILL, 6/16   2 of 4
· (cassette #3)   CHEMICAL SPILL, 6/16   3 of 4
· (cassette #4)   CHEMICAL SPILL, 6/16   4 of 4, TRACK

(Note that the reporter's narration is recorded on a separate cassette sub-labeled "track.")

WRITING AND RECORDING NARRATION (TRACK)

Writing the narration for a field report, a package, is the culmination of the reporter's craft.

Often, the writing comes at the end of a long, frustrating day of gathering various story and picture elements. Thus, the actual writing can seem somewhat anticlimactic. But it is precisely at this moment that the creative juices must be forced to flow. Only those reporters whose writing proves day in and day out that they can transcend the triteness which pervades so much small-market local TV news coverage in the United States—only *those* reporters stand a chance of moving up to larger markets and networks.

As noted elsewhere, the conditions under which TV reporters must write are often far from ideal. Time may be very short. A courier may be standing impatiently by, unable to depart for the station until the field reporter has recorded the narration for shipment along with the taped visuals. The reporter may have little physical comfort—no desk, no chair, no typewriter, and maybe no roof overhead. If he or she is lucky, the reporter may be able to sit in the news van, scrunched up, but isolated from street noise. The air will get stuffy, especially when the entire crew is in the van to record the narration.

A reporter under this kind of pressure and physical discomfort needs a capacity for a sort of self-hypnosis; he or she must shut out the outside world while concentrating on the writing. If you're the type of person who prefers to read with the radio blaring rather than in silence, you will probably have little trouble writing a narration in a battle zone. The rest of you will have to work at it—or stay away from battle zones.

Whether writing in the field or in comparative comfort back at the station, it is important to key the narration to specific elements the reporter wishes to include in the package:

1. Write descriptive copy for the visual elements to be voiced over.
2. Write lead-ins tailored to specific sound bites, and specify, either in writing or on the sound track itself, the content of the desired bites, indicating the incues whenever possible.
3. Do *not* write narration for story elements that have not been videotaped, that is, for which there are no visuals, either in the day's field tape or in file tape or graphics prepared at the station. Such narration can not be used, since it would violate the basic TV writing rule of matching sound and picture.

Countdowns

Just as in recording spots in radio, TV narrations are preceded by a "five-four-three-two-one" countdown. However, because the track is keyed to specific sound bites or NATSOT which necessarily break up the narration into several segments, *each segment should be preceded by its own countdown.* This enables the tape editor to cue up each segment speedily while assembling the package.

ON-CAMERA SEGMENTS ("STANDUPS")

Most news departments want their reporters to appear on-camera at some point during each package. Since each story is different, there can be no specific rules about when a reporter should appear or precisely what he or she should say. However, since all TV writing must respect the basic technique of correlating sound and picture, the following *general* rule is in order:

> ***Reporters should write and record voiceover narration***
> ***for all elements of which they have pictures, and they***
> ***should appear on-camera to relate or clarify something***
> ***for which they do not have pictures.***

In other words, viewers should see the actual events whenever possible. The reporter should appear to explain what can *not* be seen.

In practice this means that reporters will be periodically reassessing the possibilities as shooting progresses. We'll get back to this after examining the different kinds of on-camera segments.

Full-Length Standups

On occasion, a field report will consist entirely of an on-camera presentation. A typical occasion for this would be live minicam coverage from a location where the reporter and camera crew have just arrived and have not yet had time to shoot videotape. Such a report is called a *standup* or *standupper*—a term derived from the typical picture of the reporter at the scene, standing in front of the camera to deliver his or her text, either from memory or extemporaneously from notes. (A report in which the reporter is sitting down—say, from the bleachers at a sporting event—or even hanging upside down from a trapeze, is still called a standup.)

Full-length standuppers have become rare in TV news. Except for the aforementioned live-via-minicam example, technology has so speeded up the ability to gather and transmit pictures or create graphic representations that at least some visual elements can be found quickly for almost any TV piece.

Thus, in the normal course of everyday reporting, standups are broken into elements that form only part of the finished package. These elements are called *openers, bridges,* and *closers*.

Openers

Of all the on-camera elements, an opener (also called a *standup open*) is used the least. As the name implies, it is a shot of the reporter on-camera at the very start of a package. But producers overwhelmingly prefer a report to begin with "good pictures," that is, shots of the action rather than a shot of a reporter *talking* about the action.

Remember the newscasting context in which the reporter's package will appear: The anchor will be delivering a lead-in drawing viewers' attention to certain story details. The next thing viewers will see, whenever possible, is video highlighting those details.

Thus, on-camera openers are reserved for those rare occasions when video of the most important story element is *not* available, or when it is important to immediately establish a reporter's relationship with a story—such as an exclusive interview.

Bridges

A bridge (or *standup bridge*) comes somewhere in the middle of a package, showing a reporter delivering a text that "bridges" different story elements. It thus serves as a transition between what viewers have just seen and what they are about to see.

A bridge may involve a pan to show the reporter moving from one part of a location to another, or a zoom out to show a complete change of location (the camera opening on a static part of the new location, then widening to reveal the reporter). Thus, although bridges may be shot on the spur of the moment to capture the reporter talking to the camera during part of the action itself, they are typically *planned* shots whose precise choreography is worked out between reporter and camera operator.

Closers

An on-camera closer (or *standup close*) comes at the tail end of a package and thus includes the reporter's sign-off. Closers are the most frequently used type of standup element for the simple reason that once shooting is completed, the reporter has fitted together the pieces of the day's video jigsaw puzzle and can offer a sentence or two of perspective. For example, a closer is where a reporter can explain the ramifications of what viewers have just seen, or can tell what is expected to happen next.

Openers, bridges, and closers share certain characteristics:

1. They are short, ideally running no longer than 15 or 20 seconds.
2. Their subject matter is narrow, limited to one story element (or, in a bridge, to link two story elements).
3. They show the reporter at a specific location. The shot is framed in such a way as to show the reporter's proximity to the story.
4. The background should not be so "busy" that it competes for attention with the reporter's words.
5. The reporter is well groomed and dressed appropriately. Normally, this means a business suit for men, a suit or ensemble for women. However, it is permissible to dress more casually to suit particular stories. (No one would expect you to wear a business suit to cover a flood.)
6. The reporter's text should not—repeat, *not*—reiterate information told elsewhere in the package. Time is too valuable to permit redundancy. The text should *add* information. (In other words, we should not be seeing the reporter's face just for the sake of its beauty.)

Beginning reporters are advised to stick with closers until they gain some experience. This will permit them to organize and write their packages in a comparatively straightforward manner. Later, when they begin to awaken to the possibilities inherent in shooting different story elements at different locations, they can become more adventurous—perhaps recording a bridge or two for possible inclusion later on.

As mentioned at the start of this chapter, being a TV reporter is a little like being a movie director. Just as a movie director imposes his or her will on a production, so a TV reporter imposes his or her will on the organization of a story's presentation. With experience comes the realization that a closer need not be shot at the final shooting location. In fact, a closer may be shot at *any* location which a reporter deems suitable—as long as he or she imposes that particular organization. Ditto for bridges. All that's necessary is for the idea to be in the reporter's mind *at the time*—because thereafter, when the camera crew has already moved on to the next location, it will be too late.

Reporters are thus encouraged to shoot bridges and closers "on spec." If it turns out that they can't be used in the finished package after all, all that's lost is a little time and effort. Better to lose a little time than to lose an opportunity which will not recur.

MICROPHONE TECHNIQUE

As in recording spots in radio, recording standups and track for TV packages is not simply a matter of grabbing a microphone and talking into it. For starters, you should always try to use the *same type* of microphone for your track as you used in your interviews and standup element. Why? Because each type of microphone has its own sound quality, and the sound quality should be uniform throughout your package.

Second, it is important to eliminate as much unwanted background noise as possible. Be aware that certain closed places indoors yield poorer sound quality than does standing outdoors; small rooms with tiled surfaces—kitchens and bathrooms, for example—can make you sound as if you are standing in a fishbowl or echo chamber. For recording indoors, choose a room with carpeting or drapes, which absorb sound instead of bouncing it back into your mike.

Third, when recording outdoors in windy conditions, use a windscreen or wrap a handkerchief around the business end of the microphone. A gentle breeze blowing over a microphone can sound like a cyclone to the recording circuitry.

Don't fidget with the mike cable during recording. Moving the cable produces popping and crackling on the tape.

Don't "eat" the mike, either. Follow the same distance guidelines as for radio: mouth 6 to 18 inches away from the mike, depending on the type of mike, and taking into account the ambient noise conditions and the strength of your voice.

Take Identification and Counting Down

In television, many news departments use countdowns and take IDs before on-camera and voice-over segments alike (although this is not as widespread as in recording radio spots). A *take* is synonymous with a "try." The first try at an on-camera closer, for example, is identified aloud, facing the camera, as "Closer, Take One." If the reporter bobbles and must start over, the ID becomes, "Closer, Take Two," and so on. The reporter also counts down from five, the same as in radio. So the whole sequence goes like this:

```
                              "This is a closer, Take

              One.  Five-four-three-two-one.

              (beat)  Still unknown is whether

              the suspect..." etc.
```

Remember, if you bobble or make a factual error, you must do the *entire segment* over from the top. A bobble can't be "edited out" as in radio. The video would contain an irreparable jump cut of *you*.

A countdown should be delivered before each voice-over segment, too. And you should repeat the entire segment if you bobble. Although the tape editor could make an internal edit to cover it, it's faster just to fast-forward to your next countdown.

Because a lot of bobbles means a lot of takes and a lot of takes means a lot of lost editing time, you should indicate on the dope sheet, by number, which take is the "keeper"—the one you and the camera operator agree is the best one.

Closing Pad

You'll recall that in radio it is necessary to remain silent for a few seconds after completing an audio feed to allow time for the recording technician to close the circuitry and thus avoid unwanted noise—a sort of buffer of silence. In television, what's needed is a buffer of both sound and picture. The reporter must provide this buffer, which is usually called *pad*.

At the end of any standup element, but especially after the sign-off in a closer, the reporter remains *motionless,* eyes still directed toward the camera, mouth closed, for *at least 5 seconds*. This applies to live standup elements as well as to taped ones.

The pad is necessary in case of a delay in punching up whatever picture is to follow that of the reporter's closing on-camera words. (Reporters who forgot to remain motionless for a few seconds have inadvertently been seen scratching their noses . . . or other body parts.)

EXERCISES

(Note: You will need a camcorder, a tripod, and a hand mike with at least 15 feet of cable for the following exercises.)

1. Along with a fellow student, arrange to interview a local official, university faculty member, or student body leader on a subject of local importance or controversy. One of you will act as reporter, the other as camera operator. Conduct the interview in the manner described in this chapter, and pay special attention to the reverse-angle cutaways.

   Later, when you play back the tape, use the Still Frame function to assess each of the main shots (setup, closeup, reverse angles, inserts, and so on). In editing, will you be able to cut directly from the setup shot to a sound bite? Is there enough room in the frame under the interviewee's head to insert an identifying title? Do the eye directions of interviewee and interviewer allow their respective closeups to intercut properly?

2. Turn the above interview into a package running between 1:30 and 2:00 by writing and recording an on-camera opener and on-camera closer. Tailor the lead-in portion of your opener to a specific sound bite, then intercut a Q/A portion to cover another point or two, then summarize the ramifications of the interviewee's remarks in your closer, followed by a sign-off.

   (Memorize your on-camera segments. Rehearse them to the camera before actually rolling tape. However, if you find yourself sounding too stilted during delivery, hold a notebook containing the text in your free hand; glance down just often enough to remind yourself what to say.)

   The person who ran the camera during the interview should also write and record an on-camera opener and closer. However, his or her lead-in to a specific sound bite should be designed as a voiceover narration to the setup shot in order to identify the on-camera reporter.

3. Viewing the tape, try not to be distracted by your appearance or the quality of your voice (although we shall discuss these important considerations later on). Instead, try to assess your choice of words: Did your opener make viewers want hear what your interviewee had to say? Did your closer include new information, or did it merely repeat something viewers had already heard the interviewee say?

Reporting III:
Basic Story Coverage

20

We've been referring to reporting as "field reporting," which, although technically correct, somehow has a relaxed, almost rural connotation. In practice, broadcast news reporters are more likely to refer to themselves as "street reporters," not only urbanizing the connotation, but also showing how they perceive themselves: street-smart.

Indeed, reporters do have to be street-smart to be successful, whether in print or broadcast. But being street-smart in TV also means knowing where to go to get a desired picture and how to shoot it once on the scene. That ability comes with experience. Newcomers are likely to be overwhelmed by the technical aspects of the job, to the detriment of their substantive reporting skills. This chapter, therefore, is designed to help beginners sort out the technical and procedural matters that can at first seem daunting.*

Bear in mind that the following suggestions for specific shots and story coverage are just that—*suggestions*. No two stories, no two events, are identical. Indeed, it is a reporter's job to ferret out the details which make each event unique. However, local news does tend to fall into distinct categories: fires, road accidents, trials, parades, and so on. We offer the following guidance, category by category, to help those of you who may feel unsure of yourselves, and in the hope that many of you will quickly find that you can do well on your own.

FIRES

Fires are a staple of local news. TV broadcasters are frequently accused of devoting too much coverage to fires. Critics say TV journalists have become overly enamored of the bright, dancing pictures that fires provide for the home screen. We'll sidestep such criticism by stating one indisputable fact: No one can *predict* how much injury or damage a fire will do; a fire must first be brought under control. And since by then it may be too late to get good pictures, the assignment editor has no choice. When the

*This chapter contains specific suggestions for covering many kinds of news stories. However, some of you may prefer to test your reporting and camera skills without prior guidance. If so, we suggest you defer reading this chapter until after your first few assignments.

police or fire radio signals a fire, he or she orders a crew to the scene *immediately*. (In large cities where arson and accidental fires are virtually hourly occurrences, some newsrooms hold off until a fire reaches the two-alarm stage before dispatching crews. But everywhere else, the practice in covering a fire is *don't walk—run!*)

Upon arriving at a fire scene, the reporter and camera operator should stay well back, in order not to interfere with firefighting and rescue efforts. The camera's telephoto lens enables photography from a distance. Basic coverage from this position should include:

1. Several sustained LS and MS of the fire and firefighting activities. (Overuse of CU's makes almost every fire look alike.)
2. CU's and MS cutaways of victims, spectators, and fire equipment.

If it's a small fire, brought under control quickly without injuries (smoke inhalation is the most frequent injury in a fire), those pictures will suffice as visuals for whatever information the reporter proceeds to gather; the story, if used at all, will probably wind up as an AVO.

But if it's a big fire, causing injuries and extensive property damage, you must shoot more footage:

3. Paramedics, ambulances, and injured people being helped or carried away.
4. CU's of the burning premises' owners and residents, shot from a respectful distance. Such people, especially if related to the victims, may be emotionally distraught; their faces, photographed from a distance, should tell the story without interviewing them at this point.

Once the fire is under control, you can proceed with your interviews:

5. The ranking firefighter, framed against the smoldering scene or firefighting equipment: What caused the fire? How many injured? How? Any special firefighting problems? Special equipment used? Was it arson? (Don't forget to shoot a reaction cutaway.)
6. The victims—those willing to talk and having pulled themselves together: Where were they when the fire started? What did they do? (Remember to spell their names accurately in your notes and/or dope sheet. Remember your reaction cutaways.)

After getting clearance from the ranking firefighter, you can now move closer to the debris for:

7. CU's of fire damage. Look for the telling detail: a clock face, a child's toy, a smoldering mattress, and so forth.

Keep an eye out for an arson investigator. In many cities, an arson investigation is routine, an investigator being dispatched at first word of a fire. In other cities, the overworked Bomb and Arson Unit may not be able to send an investigator until hours or even days later. But if one does arrive, you'll want a shot or two.

Okay, you've got your information, visuals, and interviews. The next step is to call the producer of the next newscast and fill him or her in. The producer will then decide if you should do a package. (The decision will depend on how many other stories, and of what importance, are vying for air time.) If the decision is for you to go ahead, you must at least organize the package in your head *before leaving the scene*. Why? Because if you are going to do a standup element, that is the location for it. Once you leave the scene, you won't be returning. So although you may be able to write and record your narration back at the station, you must write and shoot your standup element immediately.

And remember that in writing both your standup element and narration, you should not—repeat *not*—mention the *total* number of injuries or the victims' medical conditions; leave that for the writer-written lead-in to your report. Why? Go back and reread this book's sections on the need to protect copy against developments that are apt to change before air time.

ROAD ACCIDENTS

In broadcasting, a bus is a bus, a truck is a truck, but an "auto" is a *car*—and never a "vehicle." Whenever any of the foregoing run into each other or something without wheels, the resulting road accident is another staple of local news, especially in smaller markets, where a high proportion of viewers may be personally acquainted with any victims.

As in covering fires, TV reporters and camera operators must hurry to the scene of road accidents in order to beat the tow trucks; an accident scene doesn't look like much when all that's left is an oil smudge on the pavement.

Here again, it is important not to interfere with any efforts to rescue injured or trapped victims. Keep out of the way!

Important: Car crashes and other violent events can be bloody, grisly affairs. Every news department has a policy regarding the showing of blood and gore. Reporters and camera operators must know their station's policy. Many stations broadcasting news at the dinner hour forbid "shooting bloody" or "editing bloody"—showing closeups of mangled corpses, severed limbs, or gushing wounds. There are ways of shooting such scenes to minimize the gore. How to do this is included in the following list of suggested shots:

1. An LS of the accident scene—wide enough to show not only the accident but also its immediate environment, such as interstate highway, local expressway, or residential neighborhood.
2. Several MS's of the wrecked or damaged vehicles and property, from various angles.
3. Cutaways of spectators, police, and paramedics.
4. Any scenes showing corpses, severely injured victims, or excessive blood should be *double-shot*. That is, shots showing any of the foregoing should be matched by alternative shots from angles that *obscure* most or all of the potentially offensive pictures.
5. Time permitting and story meriting, interviews of participants or witnesses. (Remember cutaways!)

Naturally, the reporter gathers factual information on the accident—names, circumstances, and so on. But the story may turn out to be more than just this one accident: Maybe one of the drivers was drunk and had a prior record of drunk driving; maybe the accident location was poorly lit or poorly marked—perhaps it was the scene of a rash of accidents; maybe state, city, or county authorities have been dragging their feet on correcting matters.

What we're getting at here is that the visuals of the story are not necessarily the *entire* story. TV newcomers tend to forget this, neglecting the basic follow-up work incumbent on reporters in *all* media.

NEWS CONFERENCES

Broadcasters generally prefer to say "news conference" rather than "press conference" to stress that all media were present, not just print. However they are called, news conferences are no longer the formal, infrequent affairs they once were. Nowadays, whenever an official or office seeker has something to say (often self-serving, to be sure) and wants to avoid giving a dozen separate interviews, he or she calls a news conference. It may take place in an office, but more likely it's in a nearby conference room or small auditorium. The point is, it's indoors, and that means you'll need a light, a tripod, and two microphones (one for the podium or conference table and one for yourself).

For TV coverage of news conferences (and most other events announced ahead of time), it is important to *arrive early*. It takes time to set up the light and podium mike, and it's a good idea to shoot a couple of cutaways *before* the newsmaker arrives (perhaps of the reporter pretending to listen and take notes). You might not get a chance to take the cutaways later, since you can never be sure what the newsmaker will say or when. If he or she happens to say something important while the camera is busy shooting cutaways, well, you're out of luck.

Frequently, news conferences provide only one element of a package—perhaps a sound bite and a few seconds of setup footage. But such limited usage must *not* be assumed. There must be enough footage to provide adequate visuals for an *entire package,* just in case the news conference alone yields major news.

So here are news conference shots to cover any eventuality:

1. Reaction cutaways of the reporter before the newsmaker arrives, plus a cutaway of other TV cameras trained on the podium
2. From the main tripod position, a sustained MS of the newsmaker walking into the room and taking his or her place behind the microphones (to serve as visuals for voiceover narration)
3. A *continuous* roll, in CU, of the newsmaker's remarks, stopping only to change cassettes if necessary
4. Time and context permitting, an ELS of the overall scene (to serve as a bridge for voiceover narration)
5. Again, time and context permitting, a hand-held shot or two from *behind* the newsmaker that shows him or her talking but does *not* show the lips
6. Additional cutaways of reporters, and the like
7. Back at the tripod position, a sustained MS of the newsmaker leaving the table or podium and exiting the room (more voiceover footage)

You now have enough visuals from enough different angles to package a report on the news conference alone. The fact that much of that effort may never be used on the air is irrelevant. The rule in TV news is: Shoot the tape and decide later how much to use.

Bear in mind that if you wish your own questions and those of other reporters to be heard on the sound track, you should carry a hand mike, not a clip-on or lavaliere mike. You will need to aim the mike at whichever reporter is speaking while the camera operator (or sound technician) temporarily boosts the volume level of the recorder.

SPEECHES

Technically, TV coverage of formal speeches or lectures is very similar to coverage of news conferences, requiring the same gear and shooting procedures. That is, enough footage must be shot to

Shooting a Speech or News Conference

After starting wide and rolling on the newsmaker arriving and striding to the podium, the camera tightens to a CU and *holds the shot.* When the reporter decides it's safe to risk missing a newsworthy remark, the camera swivels to shoot cutaways of reporters listening, taking notes, etc. The camera may also leave the tripod position momentarily in order, as shown here, to shoot from behind and to one side of the speaker *without showing the speaker's lips.*

(NBC News)

provide visuals for an entire package. However, the difference from the reporter's point of view is that he or she may be able to obtain an advance text of the speaker's remarks and thus roll only on the desired portions during the speech itself. The danger in this is that many experienced speakers sometimes depart from their prepared texts; such ad-lib comments are often more newsworthy than the prepared ones. If a speaker does depart from his or her prepared text, the reporter has no choice but to continue rolling through the unwanted parts of the text, because he or she can't be sure if or when the speaker will do it again.

A second consideration in covering formal speaking or lecture engagements is this: Controversial speakers and controversial subjects sometimes draw unruly crowds. This may take the form of demonstrators or hecklers trying to shout down the speaker. Such behavior may be rude and uncivilized, but it happens. And because it happens, journalists have an obligation to cover it.

For the TV reporter and camera operator, this means being prepared to go portable at a moment's notice. If the hecklers are hustled out of the hall, you'll want a shot of it, plus their names and organizational affiliations.

PARADES AND MARCHES

Everybody loves a parade—except perhaps TV camera operators who've lost track of how many they've covered. Bored by the proceedings as they may be, professional camera operators must remain sufficiently alert to make their parade pictures "match" on the air by providing two indispensable elements:

1. A consistent POV (point of view)
2. A master shot for sound

Each of these elements takes a bit of explaining, starting with POV. Let's say you're a spectator at a parade. You've staked out a nice spot along the parade route, right at the curb and offering an unobstructed view. Okay, here comes the parade, from your left, passing in front of you, and moving away to your right. All you have to do to follow the action is turn your head.

Now suppose you cross the street. The parade looks just as good from there, except that from your new point of view the parade is passing from your right to your left. In life this makes no difference because your senses, perceiving a vast area, allow you to reorient yourself without even thinking about it. But on television, with its narrow, boxed-in perception, the point of view makes a world of difference. If the camera crossed the street, there would appear to the tape editor (and TV viewers) to be *two different parades* going in *opposite directions,* either marching away from each other or about to trample each other.

Therefore, the first rule in covering parades, marches, or anything involving movement in a single direction is *don't cross the street.* Find an unobstructed spot and shoot everything from *that side* of the street, *including* the cutaways. Only that way will the shots look consistent, that is, *match.*

As for the second indispensable element, a master shot for sound—well, that's a bit trickier.

What's the typical sound you hear at a march or parade? A band, right? The people in the parade are not just hearing this music, they are marching or stepping *in time* to it. Thus, the videotape editor has got double trouble. First, how is he or she going to edit the music? Music has a beat, a tempo. You can't cut out part of the music and edit the remaining segments together without risking a major clash of sounds.

The VTR editor's second problem is all those marching feet. How can both the sound and the picture be made to match? After all, you don't want a bunch of feet in the air on a downbeat, do you? The marchers would look like uncoordinated clods. There is just no way to edit in mid-beat from "She Wore a Yellow Ribbon" to the "Washington Post March" and at the same time make sure the marchers don't appear to have two left feet. What to do?

Okay, puzzle fans, here's how to solve the VTR editor's problems:

1. The camera operator picks *one band* and shoots *continuously, uninterrupted,* for at least 1 minute. During that time, of course, the band will have passed the camera and no longer be

a very interesting picture. But it's the *sound* that matters most here. This shot will be the tape editor's *master sound track* over which he or she will be able to insert different video, even of different bands, without viewers being the wiser. That's because . . .

2. The camera operator also shoots other bands and marchers *without showing their feet.* Viewers will not be able to tell if the marchers are out of step, because they won't *see* any steps except for those established in the master shot. The edited parade footage will all look and sound natural.

What viewers see is thus a sort of optical illusion. Lest you think this is some type of fakery or staging, we challenge you to come up with some other way to show a one-minute version of a two-hour event. No way. The only "trick" is to make the edited version come as close as humanly possible to recapturing the flavor of the event as a whole.

Remember, on any shooting assignment where music is involved—a concert, a nightclub performance, whatever it may be—a master shot for sound is essential. It may even be necessary to do more than one, to give the tape editor a choice.

SINGING AND DANCING

To provide editing tools for coverage of a singing performance:

1. Shoot a master shot of *one entire song,* showing the performer's face.
2. Then shoot all cutaways and reverse angles of the singer from *behind* or *to the side,* so as *not* to show the singer's face, especially not the mouth. There's no way to edit lips that are singing "I Left My Heart in San Francisco" with lips that are singing "New York, New York."

Dance performances, especially ballet, are especially difficult to edit. After all, the essence of dance is coordination of feet and body with the music. Therefore, shots without feet don't work.

Hollywood solves the problem by using several cameras in different positions, rolling simultaneously. This allows the film editor to intercut at will. But a TV crew has just one camera, so the best the operator can do is to shoot *several long takes,* hoping that in at least one of them both sound and picture will be good.

PUBLICITY STUNTS

In the television age, marketing experts have grown ever more sophisticated. Public relations people, many of them former journalists, devote considerable time and effort to getting the clients or products they represent onto TV newscasts, especially at the local level. If they succeed, they get what amounts to free advertising. TV news staffers must be careful not to provide an easy forum for this kind of marketing manipulation.

Most people outside the news business do not realize the scope of the public-relations effort. In major markets, it is not unusual for a TV assignment desk to receive 1,000 "news releases" a day (yes, *a day*) by mail and by fax. In smaller markets, the number of news releases is smaller, but the volume nevertheless is equally as high when measured against population density.

The attention seekers include companies pushing goods and services, politicians seeking publicity, government agencies reporting on their activities, special interest (lobbying) groups espousing partisan points of view, and nonprofit organizations announcing fund-raising events. All of them want news coverage. Clearly, though, it is impossible to satisfy more than a handful of them. Even so, many an assignment editor, especially on a slow news day, has been lured into ordering coverage of a seemingly straightforward "event," only for the reporter and camera operator to discover on arrival that the whole thing is a publicity gimmick.

Let's say you're assigned to cover a man attempting to set a new world's record for continuous trampoline jumping. You arrive to find the man wearing a jersey emblazoned "I took the Pepsi

Challenge." A little digging (that is, asking a few questions) elicits the information that the man is being paid by Pepsico, which also bought the trampoline and hired the PR firm that contacted your station. Thus, you conclude, the "event" would not be taking place were it not for the commercial underwriting. Do you cover it anyway?

Maybe yes, maybe no. It depends on how you handle it. The "event" may turn out to be interesting, especially as a lighter item at the end of a newscast. But whatever happens, you owe it to yourself and your viewers to make clear in your copy that the "event" is being *sponsored* and is thus not the spontaneous activity of disinterested parties. Commercial sponsorship should always be labeled as such.

And there are shooting techniques to minimize the "free advertising":

1. Choose MS's that do *not* highlight overtly commercial aspects such as posters, banners, or painted vehicles.
2. Frame interviews close enough to cut out commercial messages on clothing and equipment.

In the case of our fictional trampoline jumper, this would mean shooting from a side angle that doesn't show the lettering on his jersey.

If this approach proves impossible on a publicity gimmick you are assigned to cover, remember this guideline: News is news, and ads are ads, and if ever the twain shall meet, viewers should be told.

PUBLIC HEARINGS

Public hearings, although normally orderly, are difficult to shoot because of the multiplicity of sound sources. And when they turn *dis*orderly, coverage difficulties are compounded because of the sudden multiplicity of picture sources as well.

Sometimes the organizers of public hearings arrange things so that anyone asking a question must come to a fixed location in the room, and anyone being questioned must reply from a different fixed location, such as a podium or conference table. In such cases, you know where to put your mikes and aim your camera.

Unfortunately, public hearings are seldom that well organized. Questions can come from anywhere in the room, and responders (at public hearings there are often several officials present to hear questions) can answer from anywhere they happen to be sitting. This is a nightmare for TV mikes and cameras because of the uncertainty of who's going to say what, when, and from where.

One partial solution is to use a *shotgun microphone,* so named for its ability to pick up sound from any source at which it is pointed. However, shotgun mikes are not magic. They do not pick up clear audio from distances of more than about 10 feet. But they do increase the mobility of the camera crew.

The real problem remains: How do you cover a public hearing without the camera and reporter dashing thither and yon, chasing each new mouth that opens? The solution involves not technical wizardry but rather journalistic know-how. Reporters should try to learn who will be present and what issues or complaints will be raised, by whom, and where they are sitting, *before* the public hearing gets under way. By preparing themselves and their camera operators for what is *likely* to happen, and where, reporters can often cover public hearings with a minimum of surprises and technical mishaps.

This form of "blocking out the action" ahead of time is a good idea for many types of stories. Reporters should do whatever they can to *foresee* actions and events in order to prevent the camera from being taken by surprise. It is customary for organizers of scheduled events to provide reporters with a detailed agenda of the proceedings; the agenda is *must* reading.

CRIMES

It is a fact of life in late twentieth-century America that crimes against persons and property are commonplace. In our major cities, murders, rapes, and armed robberies are so "routine" that they are often buried deep in the inside pages of newspapers and perhaps not even mentioned on radio or television. Of course, there is nothing "routine" about a murder, rape, or robbery to the victim or the victim's family. Yet the news media in large cities, like the police themselves, cannot possibly devote great attention to every crime that is committed; there just isn't enough space or time. By definition, "news" is what's uncommon and unusual. If crime, even murder, becomes commonplace, it is no longer automatically news.

But remember, we've been talking about the biggest cities, that is, broadcasting's major markets. That is *not* where most of you will begin your careers. Instead, you are likely to begin in a town where murder is extremely rare and the armed robbery of a 7-Eleven convenience store is a very big deal indeed. So you will spend a lot of time talking to police officers and learning police procedure.

In all crime coverage, reporters are heavily reliant on the police, both for accounts of the alleged circumstances and for permission to visit the crime scene while it is still fresh. This is the natural order of things, but it is not always easy for reporters to swallow. The police are naturally more interested in solving crimes than in assisting reporters; they also routinely withhold information of the sort that if made public, could in their estimation jeopardize an investigation. Reporters, for their part, while not wanting to jeopardize police work, may suspect that the police sometimes black out news coverage merely to mask their own incompetence.

Whatever the case, crime news is almost always secondhand information. But there are no such things as secondhand pictures. Thus TV reporters have an even tougher job in telling crime stories than their print and radio colleagues. TV attempts to "reconstruct" a crime, even murder, through relevant pictures. Needed are:

1. Insert shots of recent still photos of the victim(s)
2. Several angles of the crime scene itself (if allowed by police), showing police technicians going about their work
3. An interview of the ranking officer or detective at the scene or back at the precinct house
4. Interviews of witnesses and bystanders
5. Interviews of friends and relatives of the victim(s)—provided that they are not emotionally overwrought
6. In murder cases, the corpse

Grisly as it may seem, item #6—the body—is the most important shot of all. But it requires explaining. First, there's the potential blood-and-gore problem mentioned a few pages back. You should find a camera angle that does *not* show a dead face or a massive wound in closeup.

Second, you may be barred from the premises for a long time (crime scenes are off-limits until the police say otherwise). Police routine in homicide investigations is to close off the area until crime-scene technicians have combed it for evidence. A corpse is not removed until it has been examined by someone from the Medical Examiner's (Coroner's) office. However, it must thereafter be transported to a morgue or other facility for further examination and autopsy. And *that* is the shot—the draped body being carried out in a bag or on a stretcher—that producers want above all. Why? Because it is grisly without being *overtly* grisly, graphic without being *sickeningly* graphic.

So important is the "body shot" that a camera operator must be in position, ready to roll. There will seldom be advance warning. No police official will emerge to announce, "Okay, we're bringing out the body." There is often a long, attentive wait known in the news business (as in police work) as a "stakeout."

(This is one of the many, many instances when TV news reportage would suffer if reporters were required to run their own cameras. At a crime scene—as at virtually all locations where news is being gathered—reporters seek to elicit information about what is going on. They do this whether or not a camera is with them. But staking out a "body shot" immobilizes the camera. A reporter running that camera would be immobilized as well. During that indefinite period of time, he or she would not be able to continue functioning as a reporter.)

Another fact about crimes in late twentieth-century America is that most of them are never solved. In the news business, there's a pattern to crime coverage. On day 1, the day of the crime, the story is news. On day 2, if the crime was truly major, there'll be a follow-up story. On day 3—well, in

TV news there usually isn't a day 3, unless the crime that was committed 48 hours earlier was truly major. The flow of news dictates that attention be placed elsewhere.

But here's a tip: Keep in touch with whoever is heading the investigation of a crime you've covered. Call him or her every week or two. You may wind up with a minor scoop.

TRIALS

Almost all states now allow TV cameras inside courtrooms to cover trials. Specific rules are laid down by the presiding judges on a case-by-case basis. As of the early 1990s, only federal courts still barred TV cameras, and there was continuing pressure from the broadcast industry for the ban to be lifted. In the meantime, TV coverage of federal cases continued with the aid of courtroom artists hired to draw sketches of the proceedings.

From the technical and procedural point of view, TV reportage is very different depending on the type of visual coverage allowed by the judge.

With Courtroom Camera

The presence of TV cameras in courtrooms is the result both of technical innovation and of a hard-fought battle by broadcast news organizations to win for themselves what they perceive to be the same rights to cover trials as the print media. Broadcasters argue that sound and picture coverage of trial testimony, decisions by judges, and verdicts by juries is inherently the nature of broadcast news and that to forbid it amounts to discrimination in favor of print reportage.

Opponents argue that TV cameras are disruptive and thus influence the course of a trial, and may result in the declaration of a mistrial or harm the rights of the accused. Opponents also argue that television news, in its constant search for dramatic pictures, tends to favor emotional testimony over legally important testimony, and thus presents a distorted image of a trial.

The debate over TV cameras being "disruptive" has been largely settled by the invention of small cameras with light-sensitive optics (thus requiring no additional lighting) and built-in directional microphones. Such a camera is mounted in a fixed position in the courtroom, usually at spectator level, and may be operated by remote control. Thus it does not disrupt courtroom decorum in any way. Ordinary cameras and their news crews generally remain barred from courtrooms.

A courtroom camera is thus a *pool* camera. Its signal is fed to a monitor and mult-box outside the courtroom where local crews can tape the signal (or relay it live if they so choose). TV reporters may thus attend a trial while it is simultaneously being taped for them. The visuals may be edited any way they desire.

Therein lies the more important issue of *editorial judgment*. Will the reporter indeed choose the emotional sound bite over the legally important one? Since the use of such a sound bite will occupy a portion of the edited report that may be disproportionate to its importance in the day's testimony as a whole, will the result be distorted coverage? And will coverage be weighted in favor of those trial participants (attorneys and witnesses) who know how to "play" to the camera and thus provide more "appealing" tape?

You will appreciate the heavy responsibility placed on the TV reporter to ensure fairness and balance both in content and choice of pictures. We know of no other reporting situation where the reporter must give more attention to the ramifications of his or her words and pictures, for at stake are not just the reporter's ability to condense reality, but also the effects of his or her choices on both the rights of the state and the rights of the accused.

Without Courtroom Camera

Working with courtroom artists is much more difficult, both technically and procedurally, because the reporter must first coordinate with the artist what he or she wishes each sketch to show, and then must guide, in person or by phone, the shooting of the sketches on videotape.

Courtroom artists, armed with large folders of drawing paper and boxes of multicolored chalk, work for newspapers as well as for television. Although they work quickly, it is humanly impossible to draw more than just a few sketches at each courtroom session. Thus, each sketch must be representational of some major aspect of the trial. Most courtroom artists are professionals, but of necessity they pay more attention to the visual qualities of the courtroom scene than to the substance of the proceedings. So the reporter must make quick, firm decisions on what he or she wishes a sketch to show; and since it is forbidden to talk while court is in session, the decisions must be relayed by passing notes or by discreet hand signal.

Artists must remain seated once a session has begun; judges generally will not risk a disruption by permitting them to carry out their materials during testimony. Therefore, the reporter must arrange for a camera to be present outside the courtroom during a recess or meal period in order for the sketches to be shot on tape. The logistics can be nerve-wracking.

Whether their courtroom interior visuals are artists' sketches or pool-camera tape, reporters need other visuals as well to flesh out their trial stories:

1. An LS exterior of the courthouse as a possible establishing shot.
2. Shots of the plaintiffs and the defendants, as well as their attorneys, arriving and entering the courthouse. Although the principals will usually keep their lips buttoned, their lawyers may very well offer some self-serving remarks. These may be useful as sound bites (for the Early News) if they tell what the day's court session will entail—which witnesses will be called and so on.
3. Similar shots *after* the day's session, in which the lawyers may offer more self-serving remarks about how the trial has been going. Since reporters will have their own ideas about this, they can decide whether or not such sound bites should be used.
4. Shots of the *jurors* arriving and/or leaving. Jurors are instructed not to discuss a trial while it is in progress, and reporters should not attempt to goad them into remarks that could conceivably result in a mistrial. *After* a verdict has been announced, however, jurors are not only fair game, they should be actively sought out for interviews.

   In major criminal trials, juries may be sequestered, in which case the only shot of them may be in a chartered bus as they arrive or depart the courthouse. You *will* want such a shot.
5. A standup element. Visually, a report should not end with an artist's sketch or courtroom interior, which is a weak closing picture. Much stronger is a cut to a reporter's on-camera closer as he or she sums up the progress of the trial or tells what testimony or court procedure is scheduled for the next day.

As you can see, TV trial coverage demands a high degree of journalistic and technical savvy. The first time a reporter is assigned to cover a trial, he or she should take the trouble to discuss with the producer, in great detail, the visual elements the producer would like to see; with the assignment editor the precise availability of a camera and where it is to be positioned; and with the courtroom artist (that being the case) the kind of sketches the artist is good at. The aim is to reduce the logistics and the imponderables of trial coverage to a manageable minimum, to enable the reporter to concentrate on the substance of the trial.

FEATURE STORIES

After a thorough grounding in hard news, many G-A reporters find that they welcome an occasional feature assignment to break up the grind. Some reporters find that they prefer feature stories altogether, both for the challenge and for the opportunity to display their talent for originality.

As opposed to hard-news stories, which must be shot and packaged in haste to meet deadlines, feature stories are often planned and shot over a longer period of time and are "undated," that is, they may be shot and packaged, then placed on a "standby" basis for broadcast whenever time and circumstances permit. For instance, a feature story may be scheduled for broadcast on Tuesday, but if that day's news developments are especially numerous, a producer may put the cassette back "on the shelf" (defer its broadcast) until Wednesday, Thursday, or Friday. Most producers, though, strive to include at least one feature package in each newscast to counterbalance the normally heavy budget of serious, issue-oriented news.

What makes a good feature story? Words like "interesting," "off-beat," and "colorful" come to mind. But there's really no simple answer because features are almost always human-interest stories, and there is virtually no limit to the range of human activity. For our purposes, a better question might be, What makes a good feature story for *television?* Here we are on firmer ground in issuing guidelines:

1. Features must actually *show* an interesting, off-beat, or colorful activity. It is not sufficient for a reporter to describe the activity. Viewers must be able to *see* it.

2. Features thus require more planning than hard-news stories. Phone calls may not be enough. A reporter may have to visit a potential subject and location in person in order to assess their visual possibilities *before* a coverage decision is made. No producer or assignment editor wants to hear the dreaded words, "There's nothing to *see* here" after a camera crew has already arrived on the scene. That camera crew's time is extremely valuable. Producers want productivity. Wasted trips diminish productivity.

3. Features require more production time than hard-news stories. The camera operator must usually expend greater time and effort to frame the pictures more carefully. The reporter may have to interview subjects at greater length in order to elicit the most colorful sound bites. Later, in collaboration with a VTR editor, the reporter will have to spend more time keying his or her narration to specific visuals and sound bites. The finished narration must be more original, more polished than the straight-ahead, nothing-but-the-facts approach used to report hard news.

4. Almost invariably, the reporter will have to display aspects of his or her own personality. Hard-news stories require a neutral eye. Features require empathy, a personal point of view.

5. The reporter may repeatedly have to establish his or her own visual presence throughout the package, whether through an on-camera opener, an interview shot in MS instead of closeup, a second on-camera element—or all of these. These decisions must be made either in advance or at the scene itself, depending on developments during shooting. The reporter must have a keen eye for what will "play" to the audience.

6. The reporter's narration should be *protected.* It should not say "today" or name the day of the week. However, in cases where a specific time element must be named, it is the reporter's responsibility to rewrite and rerecord the narration if necessary, as a result of the package having been put on the shelf for a few days.

Of course, not all feature stories require so much advance planning, care, consideration, and production time. Many arise from the assignment desk's routine task of keeping up with local events. For example, the opening of a new children's playground or the birth of a rare animal at the local zoo are "today" events which offer opportunities for a feature approach. In these cases, producers and assignment editors are apt to look at the staff schedule and select for such assignments those reporters who have demonstrated both a knack for features and the ability to work quickly.

But to repeat something we stressed earlier: All producers and news executives prize reporters who come up with their own story ideas. This applies to features as well as to hard news.

SPORTS

Local broadcast news executives bemoan the shortage of good sports reporters, those who are able to get beyond, "Hey, coach, are ya gonna win on Saturday?" to the specific hows and whys of a team's strong points and shortcomings, and who can write clear, grammatical English. Sports news is thus a wide-open area for newcomers with solid reporting skills.

Modern TV sports reporting requires far more than a mere knowledge of the rules and the names of the players and coaches; it requires as well a knowledge of the sports industry—the economics of ownership, player contracts, local tastes and income levels—as well as the history of athletic competition and the psychological role of sports in society. Young sports reporters should not accept the view that the "average" TV sports viewer is some hairy-chested, pot-bellied lump in a T-shirt whose only exercise is the beer run to the refrigerator. In fact, interest in sports cuts across all sectors of American society, and lively conversations about football or baseball can be heard in boardrooms as well as in barrooms.

As for presentation: What is most important is showing *action*, even if such action is only a practice or training session. Sound bites of players and coaches can make for dull viewing, visually and intellectually. If during an interview a coach speaks of a particular player performing a particular action, then that player and action should be taped during practice, or the appropriate file footage taken from the station's tape library, in order to insert that video over the coach's voice. In TV sports, seeing is more important than hearing.

Whether down on the field or up in the stands, shooting should respect the same POV rules as in shooting parades: *Pick one side of the field or arena and stay there.* Do not cross to the other side. (ABC Sports, a pioneer in TV sports coverage, is careful to point out to viewers when a replay is being shown in reverse angle, to explain why, all of a sudden, the teams appear to be going in the wrong directions.)

Another thing to remember about sports reporting is that teams are composed of individual players and that an effective method in TV coverage is to zero in on just one or two of them. TV is inherently more effective in showing individuals than in showing groups. It's not enough to say, "The team played well." You should tell who, how, and why.

In short, in sports reporting the accent is on *reporting*.

ECONOMICS AND MEDICINE

We have lumped these two broad categories together not because they are related in subject matter—they aren't—but because they often lend themselves to similar treatment in TV reporting. An economic policy decided in Washington, and a medical treatment developed at, say, Johns Hopkins, may affect large numbers of people. But on television, you can't *show* large numbers of people; if you try, you find yourself uttering broad generalities which are uninteresting to hear or watch, as well as quickly forgotten.

A television report works best when it is *specific*, when it shows how a policy, issue, or event affects two or three individuals. You can't show 10 million unemployed people, but you can show how unemployment affects one family. You can't show how a new treatment affects 1,000,000 diabetics, but you can show how it affects one or two of them.

(The same is often true of natural disaster stories as well. A tornado may destroy an entire town—a shot that can be taken from the air—but what viewers are likely to remember is how it affected one or two families. The home screen is small. So should be the focus of most TV news reports.)

In an earlier chapter, we used a story about family income (see pp. 49–50) to demonstrate the pitfalls of statistics, and we said it might form the basis for a TV package. Here's how.

A reporter is handed the story and asked to "flesh it out." The reporter reads the story and pockets it as background material. He or she then proceeds to ignore the Washington dateline and begins calling local agencies—the Welfare Department, a job search counselor at the Department of Unemployment Compensation, and so on—to get *local* statistics and an overview of the *local* problem. If one or two of these officials sound well-informed and articulate, the reporter asks to interview them on camera. The reporter also asks these people for the names and telephone numbers of *local* families who might agree to be videotaped, and then calls them, one by one, to seek permission to interview them at home and to *show* how they live. If a family agrees, off go the reporter and a camera crew. If the pictures turn out to be vivid and the interviews yield a few good sound bites, that plus a sound bite from a local official will constitute the package. During the newscast, a short tell-story from the anchor, based on the Washington material, will serve as the lead-in to the local report.

In other words, a story that takes a print or radio journalist an hour or two to prepare might occupy a TV reporter and camera crew for an entire day—or longer.

"CHECKBOOK JOURNALISM"

In Chapter 16, we looked at what to do when you wish to sell exclusive camcorder video to a TV station.* Now let's look at what to do when the shoe is on the other foot, when someone with exclusive video wants to sell it to *you* (as the representative of a TV station).

The practice of paying for exclusive information (known, somewhat pejoratively, as "checkbook journalism"), especially photographs, has a long tradition in Anglo-American journalism. No doubt the very notion of "paying for the news" is abhorrent to most reporters and editors, and in the best of all possible worlds, they'd never agree to it. But the world they actually work in is fiercely competitive, and money, sometimes huge amounts of it, does change hands.

Until recent years, it was rare for TV news organizations to *initiate* an offer of payment; instead they'd wait until someone approached them with exclusive tape. However, the proliferation of consumer camcorders has resulted in a comparative bounty of available video, and many news departments no longer leave any doubt about their interest in it: As a matter of competitive advantage, they actively *solicit* consumer video, promising in advance to pay for its use.

What, specifically, should you do as a staff TV reporter, field producer, or camera operator if someone offers to sell you exclusive tape? The answer is not simple because it depends on the context of a given story. If you are unsure of the proffered tape's editorial content or technical quality, you should merely reply that you would be happy to submit the tape to your station's news executives, and a decision will be made by *them*.

Let's suppose, however, that a small aircraft crashes on landing at your local airport. You and your camera operator are the first TV news crew to arrive at the scene. You busily go about your work of shooting tape and interviewing survivors and witnesses. And one of those witnesses, it turns out, had the presence of mind to aim his or her camcorder at the plane as it came in and belly-flopped. Clearly, this is a case where you definitely want that tape. The only questions are, how much will it cost? and, will the owner sell it to your station exclusively?

Given that you probably didn't go into the news business in order to haggle over such matters, and given that you do not control the purse strings of your news department, the first thing you must do is to stall the seller until you have contacted your producer. You must act without delay; you must not allow time for a competing station to "steal" this visual material from you without a fight.

Nowadays, virtually all stations have policies for the exact procedure to follow. You should be fully aware of this procedure before going on your first field assignment. You never know when the situation will arise.

Of course, there are ways of paying for information other than money. What about taking someone to lunch, a much practiced method of "cultivating a news source"? Do you have an expense allowance to cover such contingencies? Is there a dollar limit on the amount you may spend? Must you submit a receipt in order to be reimbursed? Must you justify the expense by proving that the meal yielded useful information? Here, too, you must be familiar with your station's policy.

JUNKETS AND "FREEBIES"

Situation #1: You are assigned to cover a Rotary Club awards banquet. You arrive to find that the organizers have set a "Press Table" and they invite you to fill your plate to your stomach's content—at no charge to you or your station. Should you accept the invitation?

Situation #2: You are assigned to do a package on the rising cost of car repairs at local garages. At one of the garages you visit, the manager privately offers a free tune-up for the news van—or for your own car. Should you accept the offer?

Let's deal with Situation #2 first: The answer is a resounding "no!" You should never—repeat, *never*—accept free or discounted goods or services in connection with any story you cover, either for

*See footnote, p. 222.

yourself or for your station. To do so would constitute a clear conflict of interest, a breach of ethics for which the penalty at most news departments is instant dismissal.

On occasion, reporters are offered goods or services worth thousands of dollars, such as free travel or free house painting. In reality, such offers are not "free." They come from people and organizations who believe in *quid pro quo;* they think they can bribe you into giving them favorable news coverage, or at least into ignoring any substandard or questionable practices in which they may be engaged. Such offers must be rejected out of hand.

It must be noted, however, that many news organizations do allow certain staffers to go on press junkets. A junket is an all-expenses-paid trip aimed at winning favorable news coverage (that is, free publicity) for the organizer. Examples would be the travel industry offering free air fare and hotel lodging to travel writers, or the movie industry offering free trips to Los Angeles or New York for entertainment reporters and movie reviewers. Some large news organizations send reporters on these junkets on a *company-paid basis* in order to guarantee their editorial independence. Others, however, would not be able to attend were it not for the sponsor picking up the costs.

In the case of free travel, providers may assume that because a newspaper travel editor might accept free air fare or hotel accommodations, *all* reporters do. The assumption is false, and any reporter on the receiving end of such an offer must say so in no uncertain terms.

Situation #1 is not as easy to answer. The fact is that reporters and camera crews are routinely offered "freebies" and preferential treatment at events arranged by private organizations and enterprises. Given that TV reporters and camera crews seldom get an opportunity to eat a decent meal in the course of their workday, it is unrealistic to expect them to turn down food when their stomachs are shouting, "Feed me!"

In addition, sports anchors, reporters, and producers routinely receive free tickets to professional sporting events such as baseball, football, and basketball games. Entertainment reporters and reviewers routinely receive special screenings of movies and free theater tickets. Very few news departments ban such gratuities outright.

These may be minor matters as ethical problems go, but they *are* matters of ethics nonetheless. You may decide to accept a meal invitation or free ticket and promise yourself not to let it influence the way you cover the story. The point is, it's likely to be *your* decision, and whatever you decide will go a long way in defining what kind of journalist you eventually become.

INVESTIGATIVE REPORTING

There are several story categories—features, hostage situations, and so on—which by their very nature defy specification of editorial and camera coverage. However, there at least two areas—investigative reporting and documentaries—that deserve special attention.

Author and former NBC broadcaster Edwin Newman, in his novel *Sunday Punch,* has his protagonist, a former editorial writer, describe how he came to learn the events propelling the book's plot: "At some of the events to be described, I was present. Some I was told about. Some I was told about only after asking—this is now called investigative journalism." Newman's point is that *all* journalism is to some degree "investigative." You don't get answers to unasked questions.

In modern journalism, the term "investigative reporting" has taken on the special meaning of uncovering heretofore unreported developments, mostly of an illegal or unethical nature. Such reportage is rarer in broadcasting than in newspapers for financial rather than philosophical reasons. Only a small percentage of TV stations say they can afford to remove a reporter, producer, and camera from the daily production pool. It often takes weeks or months to investigate a story possibility, and in the end the story may not pan out either editorially or visually; in effect, the effort may go for naught. That's the risk of investigative reporting, and precious few stations are willing to run it.

Where they do exist, investigative units generally consist of a unit producer, a field producer, and one or two researchers. A reporter and camera crew usually step into the process only after the story has been firmed up through initial research and the on-camera work is ready to begin. (At a few places, reporters are assigned to the investigative unit exclusively.) As at newspapers and magazines, investigative reporting for TV involves great secrecy; therefore, as few staffers as possible are told of the proceedings, and all are sworn to keep their mouths shut at all stages of the investigation.

Preliminary Research

The first step is to learn if there is indeed a story. But even at this early stage, *two* investigations proceed simultaneously. The first seeks to learn if the story is true and can be documented; the second considers the visual possibilities: Can the story be *shown* as well as told? It isn't sufficient to learn the location of incriminating documents if the camera can't get to them for taping. If the story comes from a tipster, will the tipster agree to go on-camera? If not full-face, then in silhouette? Must his or her voice be distorted as well?

Stories which might reach fruition in print might be killed at an early stage in TV if there are no decent visual possibilities. However, with advances in electronic graphics, it is becoming possible to "create" visuals for virtually anything.*

Preliminary Execution

The next stage of TV investigative reporting roughly corresponds with the stage at which a print reporter could begin to write his or her main article: The facts are firm, and only details need to be added here and there. In TV, this is just the beginning of the production process.

A reporter and camera crew are called in, briefed, and sent into action, taping insert material, interviews, and exterior locations. To protect secrecy, this work is done swiftly, over as short a time as possible. (As we've seen, there's nothing subtle about the presence of a TV camera. People begin to wonder, "Hey, what's this all about?") Shooting continues until all the basic visuals have been videotaped.

Final Execution

The final stage occurs perhaps only hours before the broadcast breaking the investigation. Any people incriminated or accused are informed *in general terms* of what the investigating team is about to report and given a chance to tell their side. Specific allegations or findings are *not* mentioned over the phone. Instead, they are stated in person, on-camera during the interview. That's because the best shot of all may be the interviewee's initial reaction to the allegations.

This may seem unfair—springing a trap on the unwary. But remember, a subject can always decline to be interviewed. Furthermore, the surprised party can always say, "Now hold on here, give me a chance to check that out before I answer." As a general rule, an innocent party will bend over backward to cooperate. If the investigating team has done its work thoroughly, honestly, and ethically, innocent parties have nothing to fear from such tactics. And we would be less than candid if we did not say that the most dramatic footage possible is the surprised or angered face of a guilty party. The station wants it, not badly enough to be sneaky or unethical, but badly enough to set it up by the thoroughness of its investigation.

Follow-up

Even before the report is aired, the investigative team will have thought out the possible reactions and alerted the assignment desk to the potential need for reporters and camera crews to follow up the story. That's because competing stations and other news media will be doing their best to find their own angles on the story once you've broken it. And as we've seen throughout this book, the news business involves staying on top of the news every step of the way. How embarrassing it would be for a competing station to beat you on reaction to your own investigation!

There's no rule as to who gets assigned to an investigative unit. It might be long-time staffers who've proved their mettle in day-to-day general-assignment work. Or it might be specialists hired away from newspapers or magazines, because daily general-assignment reporting for TV does not

---

*Bear in mind that using graphics to tell a story visually is not the same as "re-creating" real-life events. In the late 1980s, some network news-magazine programs began using actors to "re-create" story elements. By and large, they were careful to label these re-creations as such. But the practice drew much unfavorable criticism, the critics charging that using re-creations was an intolerable mix of news and show business. By the early 1990s, the practice had dwindled considerably except at syndicated tabloid-style shows.

teach specialized investigatory skills. However, if it is your goal to be a part of a TV investigative unit, you would do well to begin to specialize *now* in research techniques and the gathering of legal evidence.

DOCUMENTARIES AND "MINISERIES"

Like investigative units, documentary units are rare birds in local television—and for the same reason: money (or, rather, lack of profitability). Station managements in general perceive news documentaries as costly frills. As proof, they point to the generally low ratings of documentaries as justification for not producing them. On the other hand, the ratings have played a role in increasing the number of quasi-documentaries known as "miniseries."

At least twice a year (but more frequently in major markets), local stations go through special ratings periods known as "sweeps." Each sweeps period lasts one full month. During that time, each local station's audience is measured meticulously: every program, every day, every 15 minutes.* The purpose of such thoroughness is to provide the sales department with accurate data to show advertisers in order to set the station's rates (prices) for selling commercial time. The ratings measured during sweeps determine the station's charges (in other words, its *income*) for the next several months—until after the *next* sweeps period. Obviously, the stakes are high. Stations pull out all the stops to attract viewers during sweeps periods, and for a local station that means boosting its local news audience. It is thus during a sweeps period that news viewers are most likely to see the audience-grabbing news features called miniseries.

As the name implies, a miniseries is a series of reports on a single subject, reported in installments on successive days. Each installment may run anywhere from 2 to 5 minutes. Thus a miniseries broadcast over five days covers roughly the same ground as a half-hour documentary, and in fact may be rescripted, reedited, and rebroadcast in that form if the subject matter and its treatment are truly excellent.

That's a big "if"—because, in truth, miniseries are frequently nothing more than frenetic, sensationalistic accounts of risqué subjects. ("Teenage Hookers Haunt Shopping Malls" and "Are Your Vegetables Being Poisoned?" are typical miniseries titles at stations desperate to boost their ratings.) For many news departments, however, sweeps periods are welcome occasions to present real reporting on important subjects.

Miniseries production usually involves far fewer staff than investigative unit production. In fact, an entire series may be the work of a single reporter and videotape editor, calling on the services, as needed, of different camera crews. Obviously, what a documentary or miniseries seeks to accomplish is to treat an important story in far greater depth than would otherwise be possible. In terms of planning and production, this means that interviews run longer to allow the reporter to probe more deeply, and the chosen sound bites may run longer, too. In a way, a miniseries simply makes greater use of the same visual elements that are gathered for a single package, going over the same ground but lingering longer at each stop along the way.

But a miniseries or documentary can also have a point of view. A reporter may reach certain conclusions, and he or she may be allowed to express those views under the heading of "analysis" or "commentary" in the final installment.

Because a miniseries is spread over several days, it can *not* be presumed that all viewers will be watching each installment. Therefore, each installment must be written and produced to stand somewhat on its own, so that viewers who missed preceding installments will not be left in the dark—arriving in the middle of the movie, so to speak. This entails a certain amount of repetition, usually accomplished by the anchor's lead-in plus opening copy along the lines of, "Last night, we saw how . . ." and so on.

*Two companies, Nielsen and Arbitron, dominate the ratings business in the United States. There is much controversy over their methods of measuring audiences and thus over the accuracy of the ratings themselves. This is a vast subject, well beyond the scope of this book. For our purposes as broadcast journalists, it is sufficient to understand that the ratings are a fact of life, and much of what transpires in broadcast news is based on them.

In news departments at all levels, reporters, writers, and producers are encouraged to propose ideas for possible miniseries. A miniseries or documentary proposal should include ideas for *visual* content as well as for editorial content.

PANEL AND MAGAZINE SHOWS

Until the explosion of local news programming in the 1970s, stations everywhere used to produce a variety of local programming: children's shows, cooking shows, and so on. Nowadays, few of such shows remain. Local programming tends to be exclusively news or news-related.

Typically, such news-related shows are broadcast weekly on Saturday or Sunday. Their formats vary widely, but two are pretty much standard: panel shows and news-magazine shows.

Panel shows are single-set interview programs in which the guests are local or visiting officials who are asked a barrage of questions by one or two of the station's own reporters or anchors plus one or two "guest" reporters from local newspapers (but never from competing stations). A staff reporter may be assigned permanently to the weekly panel or be asked to step in at the last moment. Either way, the only way the show can shed light or make news is for the panelists to have boned up on the issues, in order to ask pertinent follow-up questions instead of striking out helter-skelter.

News versus Opinion

Many TV news departments follow their newscasts with brief editorials on issues of the day. Usually, the on-camera editorialist is a high station official such as the general manager. However, as shown here, some stations allow news anchors and/or long-established reporters to offer analysis or commentary during the newscast itself. In such cases, the remarks are clearly labeled as opinion, both aurally and visually, to avoid any misunderstanding among viewers.

(WMAQ-TV, Chicago; WBBM-TV, Chicago)

"Magazine" shows get their name from their typical format, which is to treat just two or three stories per program, the way a magazine would present two or three major articles per issue. Magazine shows were introduced on many local stations following the huge success of "60 Minutes" on CBS. And the local shows often emulate the "60 Minutes" mix of hard reporting, human interest, celebrity profiles, and off-beat locations.

Such shows are considered plum assignments in both local and network television. Appointment to them is generally won only after long, successful work as a general-assignment or feature reporter. On the local level, many such shows lean squarely toward entertainment rather than important issues; thus, much emphasis may be placed on a reporter's on-camera personality rather than on his or her reporting abilities. Either way, skill in interviewing is a prime asset.

EXERCISES

(Note: You will need a camcorder, a tripod, a hand mike with 20 to 30 feet of cable, and a mike stand or clamp for at least the first of the following exercises.)

1. Cover a meeting of the local city council or of the campus student council. Package the story as hard news to run a maximum of 2:00, including an on-camera closer. Then write a 15-second anchor lead-in to the package.

2. Shoot and package a feature story, running 2:30 maximum, on an off-beat subject of local interest, such as a vegetable gardening contest, a recurring campus prank or nonacademic competition, the diet of the team mascot, an aspect of the local zoo, and so on. Include at least one on-camera bridge. Then write a 15-second anchor lead-in.

3. Cover a practice session of a local or campus athletic team and prepare a package, running a maximum of 1:30, for the sports segment of a newscast. Begin the package with an on-camera opener. Write an anchor lead-in running 10 to 15 seconds.

Performing

21

As stated twenty chapters ago, you don't have to look like Prince Charming or Snow White to be a TV anchor or reporter. However, you can't look like Freddy Krueger or the Wicked Witch of the West either. A certain modicum of appearance is required, in addition to performing ability.

No matter what TV journalists prefer to call it, a newscast is a *show,* a performance by professional broadcasters. That much is inescapable in a mass medium overwhelmingly dedicated to the proposition, as attested by the ratings, that an audience of one million and one is better than an audience of one million. Not even public television can escape the need for seasoned performers; it, too, must compete for viewers to attract a growing share of the audience willing to make tax-deductible contributions to noncommercial programming.

Only about five to ten percent of TV news personnel appear on-camera. But for this relatively small number, performing skill is a fact of life. Very few people come by it naturally. This chapter, while it can't magically change you into a prince or princess, or make you a network anchor, is designed to familiarize you with some of the cosmetic aspects of television that you are bound to encounter sooner or later.

VOICE AND POSTURE

Before continuing, please reread, if necessary, the part of Chapter 13 (Radio Newscasting) on performing in radio news. We are assuming herewith that you now have reached the level of regular practice with a tape recorder or of delivering newscasts on a campus or local radio station.

The next step is to start practicing delivering the news in front of a mirror. We're not looking yet at the way you comb your hair or wear your lipstick. We're looking just at the way you move your head: You should *not* be moving it.

In an effort to give their copy the right stress, the right intonation, the right "feel," many radio newscasters use a sort of body English. They hunch their shoulders and bob their heads up and down or from side to side. If you find yourself doing this, you must break the habit. On TV, such body movements are not only distracting, they are technical nightmares. Here's why. In closeups, both on the set and in taped standup elements, a bobbing head moves *in and out of the frame or partly disappears "behind" an upper-quadrant electronic graphic*. So it's essential to attain a delivery that relies overwhelmingly on voice inflection and facial expression while not moving the head.

If you "talk with your hands," gesticulating repeatedly and emphatically, you must suppress this habit as well. To break the habit while anchoring, hold the script in *both* hands, moving them only to change pages; while doing a standup element, rest the hand holding the microphone against your chest, and hold a notebook with the other hand, or drop your arm to the side and slightly in back of you.

Striking a Pose

However, this does not mean that you should just sit or stand there like a lump. You should strike a "dynamic" pose: shoulders erect (but not stiff), one shoulder turned slightly toward the camera. Stand in front of a mirror and try a number of poses, first left shoulder in, then right. Now run through them again, closing one eye in order to see yourself as the camera does, in two dimensions instead of three, until you find a posture that is relatively comfortable for you.

If you prefer, skip the mirror and get a friend to shoot tape of you with a camcorder. (Actually, a semi-professional video camera in a college studio is better — but we know not all of you have access to that.) That way, you'll see what you actually look like on television. Don't be surprised if you look far different than you do in real life. The TV camera doesn't show the true map of your facial features; it squashes you into a flat image. It therefore tends to make people look fleshier than they really are; the camera makes many people look like they have fat faces. So in TV, thin is in.

As you practice delivering news copy into the mirror or camera, you may feel uneasy or unnatural at first. That's because it *is* unnatural. Relax. You'll get used to it.

PERSONAL APPEARANCE

In 1983, and again in 1984, an anchor-reporter named Christine Craft sued her former employers in federal court. She charged the owners and management of a Kansas City, Missouri television station with sex discrimination and fraud. Craft claimed that contrary to the terms of her contract, she had been subjected to a "cosmetic makeover" — told how to style her hair, what clothing to wear, what type of makeup to use, and how to apply it. She further charged that the station's male anchors were not subjected to similar standards of dress or makeup. In both trials, the juries ruled in Craft's favor, awarding her $325,000 in actual and punitive damages. In 1985, however, federal appeals judges overturned both verdicts, as well as the monetary award.

Although the case of *Christine Craft* v. *Metromedia Inc.* was essentially about alleged sex discrimination and breach of contract, its subtext vividly demonstrated the importance of personal appearance in TV news. The fact is that on-camera personnel of both sexes are expected to be well groomed and "presentable" at all times. Granted, this is a subjective matter. Nevertheless, for men this means a clean-shaven face (unless a beard or mustache is the man's customary facial adornment) and a well-trimmed haircut (the so-called "blow-dry" look went out with the 1980s), neatly combed. For women this means moderate makeup and a conservative hairstyle — no pigtails, frizzes, or cutie-pie curls.

As for wardrobe, men are expected to wear a jacket and tie and women to wear simple, tasteful clothing — no trendy army fatigues, low-cut halters, or tight-fitting jerseys. Where appropriate on field assignment, reporters may wear clothing suitable to the circumstances. Both sexes should avoid loud, overbright colors as well as bold checks or stripes that "bleed," that is, that cause an electronic sparkle that plays havoc with video circuitry.

Since the lower half of the body is seldom seen on-camera, it is possible to wear blue jeans and scuffed shoes without viewers being the wiser. However, reporters are the public representatives of the news department. Daily they confront a host of people while out on assignment. Wearing scruffy or overly informal garb creates a bad impression.

A certain number of anchors (of both genders) go to extremes to "improve" their appearances, spending small fortunes on cosmetics and hair styling, and sometimes going so far as to undergo cosmetic surgery. Such people are often self-centered in the extreme and may well deserve being the butt of their colleagues' derision. And yet, the pressures on TV anchors to "look good" are enormous; those who go too far may perhaps be forgiven their excesses.

There is absolutely no reason, however, for *reporters* to go overboard in this manner.

Makeup

Thanks to today's light-sensitive cameras, it is almost never necessary for most reporters to wear special makeup in the field. On the studio set, however, where reporters appear frequently and anchors appear daily, the lighting can be harsh, giving many peoples' faces a washed-out look (regardless of race) and making the eye sockets appear sunken.

If you are among such people, you can correct the problem by applying a thin layer of pancake makeup (such as Max Factor) around the nose, mouth, chin, and especially the eyes. You will have to experiment with different colors and textures of makeup, not only because each face is different, but also because lighting conditions are different at each station. Anchors with extremely fair skin may also have to apply makeup to the backs of their hands, or to cover skin blemishes. All such makeup should be water-based rather than oil-based so that it can be washed off easily.

Major-market stations and networks often hire a staff makeup artist to apply makeup to on-set performers shortly before air time. Everywhere else, however, performers must apply their own makeup.

Understandably, men may feel sheepish at first about wearing makeup. But they eventually come to regard it as one of the occasional necessities of working in TV news.

TALKING TO THE CAMERA

Camera Position

How you look on TV depends not just on your posture in facing the camera but also on the camera's location. If the camera is positioned high, forcing you to look up as you talk into it, different aspects of your face will be emphasized than when the camera is low, forcing you to look down. Most performers prefer to look slightly upwards rather than downwards, because a low camera tends to emphasize the jowls and make faces look heavy. After a while, though, you will learn which angles and positions work best for you, and circumstances permitting, you will be able to consult with camera operators about where you'd prefer the camera to be positioned. But ask nicely—or you might get a reputation as a prima donna.

Addressing the Viewing Audience

Amid all these distractions about personal appearance and camera angles, it is sometimes hard to remember that you're talking to real live people through that impersonal camera lens. On the news set there are further distractions: camera operators wheeling equipment this way and that, a technical director (TD) giving finger countdowns on videotape roll cues, producers and production assistants dashing in with last-minute script changes, the director's voice addressing you via your earpiece, and so forth. It's hard to concentrate, much less sound relaxed. (You begin to appreciate why anchors are so highly paid.)

Eventually, though, each performer must find a personal technique that allows him or her to communicate through the camera's unblinking eye. Some reporters and anchors pretend, while delivering copy, to be addressing close friends or loved ones. Others prefer to imagine a roomful of strangers who must be forced to pay attention. Still others (the very few) take to it like ducks to water, indeed seeming to become more "alive" on-camera than in person.

Fortunately, performing on TV becomes easier the more you do it.

Teleprompters

Part of the showmanship of anchoring and reporting live on the set lies in using a Teleprompter correctly. In effect, the Teleprompter is a projector that throws the audio portion of the script on an optical screen just under the camera lens; it thus enables anchors and reporters to appear to be looking into the camera when in fact they are reading the script verbatim. Although they may be holding script pages in their hands or on the desk and glancing down from time to time, the downward glance is in reality a practiced pose. The only time they actually read from the script pages themselves is when the Teleprompter malfunctions. Otherwise, they are reading when they look up, not down.

Using a Teleprompter is not easy. It is a learned skill. In fact, newcomers might do well to rely on their actual scripts instead of the Teleprompter until they've gained enough Teleprompter practice. And during an on-camera audition, any job applicant who has never before used a Teleprompter should probably request that it be turned off in order not to be distracted; he or she should rely on a hand-held script and look up into the camera as often as possible to maintain eye contact.

(In large markets, a production staffer loads the Teleprompter with script pages and runs the machine at a rate comfortable for the anchor or reporter to follow. In small markets, however, anchors may have to load the Teleprompter themselves, as well as operate it via a remote-control device held in one hand.)

Acquiring On-Camera Skills

Without actual experience in the workplace, newcomers are at an enormous disadvantage in acquiring adequate performance skills. We have offered self-help advice, but we readily admit that this is not the same as actual experience. Knowledgeable feedback is essential. Wherever possible, therefore, newcomers should rely on a university or trade-school setting where an instructor and fellow students can offer criticism and advice. Advanced college courses in broadcast journalism often provide semi-professional studio facilities, as well as instructional guidance by former professionals. In their absence, however, students are advised to take courses in a study division outside journalism—such as Radio and TV Production, Announcing, Cinematography, Photography, and the like—where they will occasionally find themselves both in front of and behind microphones and cameras.

PERSONAL HABITS

We'd rather not have to mention this, but a fact of life in TV reporting and anchoring is that, in a modest way, on-camera personnel lead a sort of public existence. Viewers stop them on the street to

Studio technician Roz Watkins operates an electronic Teleprompter during a KCAL-TV newscast, adjusting the crawl speed of the news copy to match the reading rates of the station's anchors. Other types of Teleprompters rely on hard copies: script pages are fed sequentially and the crawl speed adjusted mechanically. In small markets, anchors may operate the Teleprompter themselves by a hand-held remote-control device. Regardless of system, reading aloud from a Teleprompter is a learned skill requiring much practice.

say hello or ask for autographs. They are often solicited by various organizations to help in fund-raising drives or to act as moderators or guest speakers. In short, apart from having their egos fed, they act as representatives of their news organizations in ways seldom demanded of print or radio journalists. For better or for worse, their personal lives and habits are more open to public scrutiny than they might like. Their employers would thus prefer them to avoid scandalous behavior—at least in public.

One other thing while we're on the subject of public perceptions: In any mass audience there will always be a certain number of cranks and a few of the outright mentally ill; they react more strongly to television news than to newspapers and radio, perhaps because TV news is delivered directly by visible, flesh-and-blood human beings. Whatever the psychological underpinnings, TV news anchors and reporters sometimes receive an alarming number of crank or perverted calls and letters. Mostly, the letters are in the nature of the following (which, typically, was handwritten and unsigned):

> Good bye Channel——. I am also writing all your advertisers.
>
> Television is a media [sic] for Education & Entertainment—not a forced doc-
> trine of Liberal Communism. Mr.——is a very fine person—compared to Joan
> Rivers & her trashy friends—Why don't you get Ed Asner, Jane Fonda & her filthy
> friends all on one program—Then all the liberals & Commies can be entertained in
> one nite—
>
> Good bye
>
> P.S. I am 84 yrs. old. Ratings on your station can only go down.

The only unusual thing about that letter is that the anonymous sender spelled most of the words right. If anything, its tone is mild. Very often, letters are obscene, racist, or both. Some contain threats of physical harm.

Unfortunately, some people don't stop at writing letters. A few deeply disturbed individuals cross the line into illegal action. There are several cases on record of men stalking or attacking women anchors or reporters who spurned their amorous advances. In one 1993 case, a former Los Angeles policewoman was jailed for stalking a local TV weathercaster when he failed to answer her love letters.

Although such overt acts may be extremely rare, they exist nonetheless, and on-camera TV news personnel, because of the semi-public nature of their work, are best advised to be wary when approached by total strangers.

AUDITION TAPES

Now and for the foreseeable future, broadcast news is and will remain a buyer's market; that is, employers can pick and choose from a large surplus of job applicants. Most news directors and their assistants are often too busy even to talk to applicants by telephone, except to tell them to "send me a tape." Audition tapes are thus the preferred medium of contact between employer and prospective employee.

In both radio and television, the most desirable material to include on audition tapes is that recorded directly off the air (called an *air check*) and edited into a tight package running no longer than 10 minutes. A radio audition tape—dubbed onto a standard audiocassette—should thus contain the equivalent of two entire five-minute newscasts or about a dozen field reports. A TV audition tape—dubbed onto a standard VHS videocassette—should contain the top ten minutes of an anchor performance or half a dozen reporting packages, if possible preceded by the anchor's lead-ins.

This raises a dilemma for many newcomers because, without a first job under their belts, they have no actual aired material at their disposal; nor do they have access to professional editing equipment to prepare and dub the tapes. This dilemma was popularized by novelist Joseph Heller as a "Catch-22" situation: You can't get a job because you lack experience, and you lack experience because you can't get a job.

Fortunately, many small-market employers recognize your predicament and are thus willing to accept nonprofessional material on audition tapes. For example, a radio news director might accept material recorded off a campus station or produced in a campus studio. A small-market TV news director might accept a VHS tape recorded and edited at a college or trade school, as long as the tape is of good quality technically and shows what the applicant can actually do. Such "amateur" tapes can lead to follow-up auditions on station premises.

Audition tapes should always be labeled with the sender's name, address, and telephone number. And they should always be accompanied by a resumé and a brief cover letter stating the applicant's perceived qualifications. (A cover letter should *not* include long-winded statements about career goals or philosophical attitudes about the role of journalism in society; an employer is interested only in an applicant's immediate qualifications for the particular job he or she may have to offer.)

Master Tapes

The proper way to make audition tapes is to first prepare a *master tape* containing the tightly edited performance material. The master tape is then used to dub the tapes which will be sent out. The master should thus be of the highest technical quality available to its preparer. A master tape itself should *never* be sent out, not even in an "emergency." There's too much risk of it getting lost, misplaced, or accidentally erased. It should remain the closely guarded personal property of the applicant.

Costs

Even if a radio-news applicant sends out between 50 and 100 audiocassettes, the expense will be comparatively small. Standard 60-minute (or 30-minute) cassettes can be bought for less than a dollar each, and postage will run less than that. By and large, applicants should not expect their tapes to be returned, although some employers will send them back if the applicant has included a self-addressed return envelope.

TV audition tapes are another matter. Although standard T-120 VHS cassettes now cost only two or three dollars each, postage will often double or triple that expense. Sending out between 50 and 100 videocassettes can thus be a costly proposition. Unfortunately, prospective employers rarely return these tapes unless applicants go to extra lengths—namely by including a self-addressed, padded return envelope (of sufficient size) and by sending a follow-up letter (after a month or so) specifically requesting that the tape be returned. Or, if expense is a real concern, an applicant might initially send just a resumé and cover letter including the statement that a tape is available on request.

PATIENCE AND PERSISTENCE

The chances are that most of you reading this book are under thirty (and probably very close to twenty) and are anxious to get on with your lives and careers. Six months may seem like a very long time to spend looking for a first job in your chosen field. To you we counsel patience. Six months is a *normal* length of time for a job search in broadcast news—normal even for people with much professional experience.

We also counsel persistence. Just because you get a "no" today doesn't mean you'll get a "no" tomorrow. Things change. Openings occur on short notice. A news director who has no openings in January may have two or three in July. You may get discouraged—that's only human. But you've got to stick with it.

Think of it this way: Is it reasonable to be any less persistent in landing that first job than in covering the news itself? If a public official says, "There's no story here," are you going to take his or her word for it, or are you going to press on? If you're a good reporter, you'll keep checking.

So if at first news directors don't acknowledge your letters or return your phone calls, write or call again. They are busy people, but sooner or later you are bound to get through.

And when you do get through—well, we shall be rooting for you.

EXERCISES

1. Write a 3-minute newscast, copy only (no tape), and anchor it on-camera. Do not memorize the script, but try to maintain eye contact with the camera as much as possible.

2. Write a 30-second set of headlines and anchor it on-camera as a promo for an upcoming newscast. Conclude with the line, "Details coming up on the Six O'clock News." Be sure that your on-camera delivery runs 30 seconds *exactly*—neither one second more nor one second less.

Index